BIRT: A Field Guide to Reporting

the eclipse series

SERIES EDITORS   Erich Gamma ▪ Lee Nackman ▪ John Wiegand

Eclipse is a universal tool platform, an open extensible integrated development environment (IDE) for anything and nothing in particular. Eclipse represents one of the most exciting initiatives hatched from the world of application development in a long time, and it has the considerable support of the leading companies and organizations in the technology sector. Eclipse is gaining widespread acceptance in both the commercial and academic arenas.

The Eclipse Series from Addison-Wesley is the definitive series of books dedicated to the Eclipse platform. Books in the series promise to bring you the key technical information you need to analyze Eclipse, high-quality insight into this powerful technology, and the practical advice you need to build tools to support this evolutionary Open Source platform. Leading experts Erich Gamma, Lee Nackman, and John Wiegand are the series editors.

Titles in the Eclipse Series

John Arthorne and Chris Laffra
Official Eclipse 3.0 FAQs
0-321-26838-5

Frank Budinsky, David Steinberg, Ed Merks, Ray Ellersick, and Timothy J. Grose
Eclipse Modeling Framework
0-131-42542-0

David Carlson
Eclipse Distilled
0-321-28815-7

Eric Clayberg and Dan Rubel
Eclipse: Building Commercial-Quality Plug-Ins, Second Edition
0-321-42672-X

Adrian Colyer, Andy Clement, George Harley, and Matthew Webster
Eclipse AspectJ: Aspect-Oriented Programming with AspectJ and the Eclipse AspectJ Development Tools
0-321-24587-3

Erich Gamma and Kent Beck
Contributing to Eclipse: Principles, Patterns, and Plug-Ins
0-321-20575-8

Jeff McAffer and Jean-Michel Lemieux
Eclipse Rich Client Platform: Designing, Coding, and Packaging Java™ Applications
0-321-33461-2

Steve Northover and Mike Wilson
SWT: The Standard Widget Toolkit, Volume 1
0-321-25663-8

Diana Peh, Alethea Hannemann, Paul Reeves, and Nola Hague
BIRT: A Field Guide to Reporting
0-321-44259-8

Jason Weathersby, Don French, Tom Bondur, Jane Tatchell, and Iana Chatalbasheva
Integrating and Extending BIRT
0-321-44385-3

For more information on books in this series visit www.awprofessional.com/series/eclipse

BIRT: A Field Guide to Reporting

Diana Peh • Alethea Hannemann • Nola Hague

♦♦Addison-Wesley

Upper Saddle River, NJ • Boston • Indianapolis • San Francisco
New York • Toronto • Montreal • London • Munich • Paris • Madrid
Capetown • Sydney • Tokyo • Singapore • Mexico City

Many of the designations used by manufacturers and sellers to distinguish their products are claimed as trademarks. Where those designations appear in this book, and the publisher was aware of a trademark claim, the designations have been printed with initial capital letters or in all capitals.

The authors and publisher have taken care in the preparation of this book, but make no expressed or implied warranty of any kind and assume no responsibility for errors or omissions. No liability is assumed for incidental or consequential damages in connection with or arising out of the use of the information or programs contained herein.

The publisher offers excellent discounts on this book when ordered in quantity for bulk purchases or special sales, which may include electronic versions and/or custom covers and content particular to your business, training goals, marketing focus, and branding interests. For more information, please contact:

    U.S. Corporate and Government Sales
    (800) 382-3419
    corpsales@pearsontechgroup.com

For sales outside the United States please contact:

    International Sales
    international@pearsoned.com

Visit us on the Web: www.awprofessional.com

 This Book Is Safari Enabled

The Safari® Enabled icon on the cover of your favorite technology book means the book is available through Safari Bookshelf. When you buy this book, you get free access to the online edition for 45 days.

Safari Bookshelf is an electronic reference library that lets you easily search thousands of technical books, find code samples, download chapters, and access technical information whenever and wherever you need it.

To gain 45-day Safari Enabled access to this book:

- Go to http://www.awprofessional.com/safarienabled
- Complete the brief registration form
- Enter the coupon code JTA9-XIRC-AR6Q-LVCH-G6AR

If you have difficulty registering on Safari Bookshelf or accessing the online edition, please e-mail customer-service@safaribooksonline.com.

Library of Congress Cataloging-in-Publication Data

BIRT, a field guide to reporting / Diana Peh ... [et al.].
    p. cm.
    Includes index.
    ISBN 0-321-44259-8 (pbk. : alk. paper)
    1. Computer software--Development. 2. Application software--Development. 3. Client/server computing. I. Peh, Diana.
    QA76.76.D47B57 2006
    005.1—dc22

    2006013999

ISBN 0-321-44259-8

Text printed in the United States on recycled paper at R.R. Donnelley in Crawfordsville, Indiana.
First printing, October 2006

Contents

Part III   Accessing and Binding Data 61

Chapter 6   Connecting to a Data Source 63

Chapter 7   Retrieving Data 81

Chapter 11   Formatting Report Content 145

Chapter 12   Sorting and Grouping Data 179

Application development tools and technology have come a long way since the late 1970s, when I took my first job out of college in Hewlett-Packard Company's IT (Information Technology) department. Of course, IT was not the term we used to refer to the discipline back then; our preferred acronym was EDP (Electronic Data Processing).

And maybe that difference between simply "processing" data and delivering "information" was reflected in our development tools. We worked on TTY terminals connected to 16-bit mini-computers over 2400 baud lines. We used simple line editors to make changes to our COBOL programs, and we kept our application data in non-relational hierarchical databases. Debugging was COBOL WRITE statements, and source code control was keeping full copies of every version on tape or in separate directories.

Reports for our applications were typically afterthoughts, and they were done by hand in the same technology we used to develop the base application, i.e., COBOL. We designed them—when we did design—by laying them out in pencil on the report design pads that IBM had developed for RPG and COBOL programmers. Because we created them without much forethought, and because junior programmers like me often got the assignment of coding them, our users often found them inadequate, and the cost of making changes to accommodate their true requirements was high.

But while today's application developer may scratch his or her head in wonder at the primitive tools and technologies we employed in building our base applications in the late 1970s, he or she may not find my description of our approach to report development so very unfamiliar.

JSP = COBOL and Banded Report Writers = Report Design Pads

The majority of Java developers still hand-code reports for their applications using JavaServer Page (JSP) technology. This is analogous to our approach of hand-coding them in COBOL and has all the same downsides: high development cost, low user satisfaction, and inflexible, high-cost maintenance.

A minority of Java developers do use tools to develop reports; however, almost all of these tools—be they commercial or open source—are what's known as "banded report writers," and they support a design metaphor that has essentially evolved from the old IBM report pads. Each section in the report writer—header, detail, footer—corresponds to a section in the report with the detail sections repeating as needed to accommodate rows from the data source.

Because they were created before the advent of the internet, banded report writers are not intuitive to web application developers, who are most comfortable with the web page-oriented design metaphor that one finds in modern graphical web development tools. In addition, web concepts—such as tables, graphical object containment and inheritance, cascading style sheets (CSS), and scripting in web-oriented languages like Java and JavaScript—are not supported.

Enter BIRT

The Eclipse Foundation's Business Intelligence and Reporting Tools (BIRT) project aims to take report development into the age of the internet. Based on industry-leading Eclipse IDE and Rich Client Platform (RCP) technology, BIRT was built from the ground up for web applications.

As Senior Vice President of Engineering for Actuate Corporation, I'm proud of the leading role my company has played in the project. We've leveraged our 10+ years of experience in the reporting and business intelligence space and put to work a significant number of full-time developers (or "committers," in Eclipse Foundation parlance) on the development of the platform. And while BIRT is a relatively young project that is only in its second major release, I think this investment is apparent in the rich and robust technology that the project provides. BIRT is an extensible, full-featured reporting platform that is ready for use in and integration with production applications.

We are seeing evidence of significant adoption already. A number of ISVs, including some very big names, have or will integrate BIRT technology into products. And BIRT is not just for Java programmers. Zend Technologies, the leader in PHP technology, is integrating BIRT technology into their Eclipse-based IDE and their Zend Platform so that PHP programmers will be able to design and run BIRT reports seamlessly in their PHP applications. Likewise, enterprise IT developers and system integrators have embraced BIRT and are already integrating it into important business applications.

All of these constituents—ISVs, IT, and SI developers—contribute to the Eclipse Foundation BIRT community, which is a vibrant one. BIRT often leads all other Eclipse projects in liveliness on the Eclipse project dashboard and is one of the most searched-for terms on the Eclipse web site. (Liveliness is a metric that measures project activity based on bug fixing, project e-mails, and newsgroup postings.) Feedback from the community has helped to drive project priorities, give direction on feature implementation, uncover defects, and once in a while, deliver some "attaboys" to the project team. Here are just a few comments posted by developers in the Eclipse BIRT newsgroup:

"I had installed BIRT the other day just to check it out and barely went through the introductory tutorial. Today I was able to drag and drop my way to replacing a

broken report (600 lines of somebody else's perl) and all I can really say is it was almost too easy."

"I gave BIRT 2.0 M3 a test run and wanted to comment on it. First of all, excellent tool, you did a wonderful job. I did a report on an existing db table and it took me almost no time to get it up and running."

"We are an ASP (application service provider) and loving the BIRT project! Great work guys!"

"Have upgraded to 2.0 M2 and must say—it rocks! . . . Thanks for all the great work."

"We love BIRT."

I hope that you will leverage the information in this book to become a successful member of the BIRT community as well. And, in the off chance that you are standing in a bookstore aisle, having picked up this book with no idea what BIRT is all about, may I suggest that you rush home—after buying the book, of course—and download the software from the Eclipse BIRT web site:

```
http://www.eclipse.org/birt
```

Take it from me—it's the best way to prevent yourself from being lumped into the same category as 1970s COBOL programmers!

Mark Coggins
Senior Vice President of Engineering, Actuate Corporation

About this book

BIRT is a powerful reporting platform that provides end-to-end reporting solutions, from creating and deploying reports to integrating report capabilities into other enterprise applications. Two companion books, *BIRT: A Field Guide to Reporting* and *Integrating and Extending BIRT*, cover the breadth and depth of BIRT's functionality.

With BIRT Report Designer's rich set of tools, report developers can create many reports, simple and sophisticated, without programming. This book teaches report developers how to create reports using the graphical tools of BIRT Report Designer. Report developers who want to go beyond the graphical tools to customize the report-generation process or incorporate complex business logic in their reports should read the second book, *Integrating and Extending BIRT*.

The first edition of this book described the functionality available in BIRT 2.0.1. To order the BIRT 2.0.1 book (ISBN 0-321-47804-5), call 1-800-811-0912 for single-copy orders, or 1-800-382-3419 for corporate purchases or bulk orders.

The current book, the second edition, describes the functionality available in BIRT 2.1. New features in BIRT 2.1 include the capability to join data sets, use named data expressions, insert page breaks before and after groups of data, use multiple master pages to design a report with different page layouts, use multiple data sets to define cascading report parameters, and create a new type of stock chart.

Who should read this book

This book is intended for people who have a basic need for reporting. You need not be an expert at creating reports nor do you need years of programming experience. Familiarity with the following subjects, however, is useful:

- HTML, for formatting report content

- SQL, for writing basic queries to extract data from a database for a report

- JavaScript, for writing basic expressions to manipulate data in the report

This book provides many examples of formatting with HTML, and writing SQL queries and JavaScript expressions, but it is not designed to teach you HTML, SQL, or JavaScript.

Contents of this book

This book is divided into several parts. The following sections describe the contents of each of the parts.

Part I, Installing BIRT

Part I introduces the currently available BIRT reporting packages, the prerequisites for installation, and the steps to install and update the packages. Part I includes the following chapters:

- *Chapter 1, Prerequisites for BIRT.* BIRT provides a number of separate packages for BIRT Report Designer as downloadable archive (.zip) files on the Eclipse web site. Two of the packages are stand-alone modules and another requires an existing Eclipse environment. This chapter describes the prerequisites for each of the available report designer packages.

- *Chapter 2, Installing a BIRT Report Designer.* BIRT provides two report designers as separate packages, which are downloadable archive (.zip) files on the Eclipse web site. This chapter describes the steps required to install each of the available report designers.

- *Chapter 3, Updating a BIRT Installation.* BIRT packages are Eclipse-based, so it is easy to update any of them from earlier releases to release 2.1 or later. This chapter describes how you can install the latest packages without interrupting your work.

Part II, Getting Started

Part II provides an overview of the report creation process and introduces the report design environment. Part II includes the following chapters:

- *Chapter 4, Learning the Basics.* This chapter presents fundamental concepts of reporting and provides a tutorial. Report developers learn that the report design process begins with a paper and pencil sketch of the proposed report layout and continues through specifying data, laying out the report, formatting, previewing, and testing. In addition, this chapter orients the reader to the software. To accomplish that objective, the chapter provides a tutorial that walks the reader through a creation of a complete report.

- *Chapter 5, Planning Your Report.* This chapter explains the planning process in greater detail. Planning is essential to creating effective and efficient reports.

A thorough understanding of user requirements and objectives makes the development process smoother and achieves better results. This chapter discusses the types of requirements and other information that a report developer should consider when determining how to set up, format, and distribute a report.

Part III, Accessing and Binding Data

Part III discusses the tasks necessary to connect to an external data source, extract, and prepare data for use in a report. Part III includes the following chapters:

- *Chapter 6, Connecting to a Data Source.* Report data comes from many different information systems. An important step in developing a report is ensuring you can connect to a system that provides data. This chapter explains how to access data in JDBC databases, text files, and XML data sources.

- *Chapter 7, Retrieving Data.* Data sources typically contain more data than is needed in an effective report. This chapter explains how to define data sets to retrieve only the data required for a report. Specifically, this chapter describes retrieving data from JDBC databases, text files, and XML sources.

- *Chapter 8, Binding Data.* The data sets you create retrieve the data you want to use in a report. Before you can use or display this data in a report, you must first create the necessary data bindings. A data binding defines an expression that specifies what data to display. This chapter explains how to create and manage data bindings.

Part IV, Designing Reports

Part IV describes the tasks that a report developer completes to design reports using BIRT Report Designer. Part IV includes the following chapters:

- *Chapter 9, Laying Out a Report.* A report developer places and arranges report data on a page to determine how report users view the information. This chapter provides an overview of the layout model and describes the report elements that BIRT Report Designer provides for organizing and displaying data. This chapter also describes techniques for creating report sections and placing report elements.

- *Chapter 10, Displaying Text.* Much of the information in any report is textual. Textual information can be static text or values derived from data set fields. Text can be as short as a single word, or span paragraphs or pages. This chapter describes the different types of textual elements that BIRT Report Designer provides, and how to use each type of element.

- *Chapter 11, Formatting Report Content.* Formatting different types of data within a report improves the clarity and visual appeal of the report. This chapter describes many formatting techniques, including how to change the display of dates, numbers, or currency values, format report elements based on conditions, and adjust the spacing between report elements.

- *Chapter 12, Sorting and Grouping Data.* Almost all reports require that a report developer structure the data that comes into the report. Grouping and sorting are two ways of structuring data to ensure that the critical relationships among various pieces of information in a report are apparent to the report user. For example, a report developer can use grouping and sorting with sales data to organize the data by region, then by office, and finally by sales representatives. This chapter also includes a tutorial.

- *Chapter 13, Aggregating Data.* One of the key features of any report is the ability to display summary, or aggregate, information. For example, a sales report can show the overall sales total, sales subtotals by product type, region, or sales representative, average sales amount, or the highest or lowest sales amounts. This chapter describes the common types of aggregate calculations, and explains how to write aggregate expressions and where to place them in a report.

- *Chapter 14, Writing Expressions.* To obtain the necessary data for a report, it is often necessary to use expressions to manipulate the raw data that comes from a data source. This chapter explains how to write JavaScript expressions and provides many examples of manipulating data, including how to convert numbers to strings, combine values from multiple data set fields, search and replace string values, get parts of a string, and calculate the time between two dates.

- *Chapter 15, Filtering Data.* Often the data from a data set includes information that is not relevant in a particular report. To exclude this extraneous information from the report, a report developer filters the data to use only the data that pertains to the report. This chapter discusses how to use BIRT Report Designer to filter data and how to enable filtering in the external data set.

- *Chapter 16, Enabling the User to Filter Data.* A report developer can use parameters to enable report users to determine which part of the data they see in the report. For example, in a report of nationwide sales figures, filtering can be used to display the data for a user-specified region. This chapter shows how to set up a report that enables a user to specify parameter values to determine what data appears in a report. This chapter also shows how to design report parameters to improve their usability and presentation.

- *Chapter 17, Building a Report That Contains Subreports.* This chapter provides examples of building and organizing subreports in a report. This chapter also includes a tutorial that provides an example of a master-detail report. This tutorial illustrates and reviews many of the topics from earlier chapters. A reader can complete the tutorial and practice applying the basic principles to build a more complex report that includes both side-by-side subreports and data set parameters.

- *Chapter 18, Using a Chart in a Report.* The graphical presentation of summary data is another way of improving the effectiveness of a report. A chart can serve as a report in itself or provide a synopsis of more complex data that appears in a report. Charts often provide an additional view of the data, highlighting or extending the information that appears in a report. This chapter introduces the types of charts that a developer can create and discusses the steps that are required to add a chart to a report. The chapter includes a tutorial that introduces a reader to the chart features.

- *Chapter 19, Displaying Data in Charts.* Setting up chart data differs somewhat from selecting typical report data and requires some specific knowledge about how to process data to produce effective charts. To modify which data appears and the arrangement of the data in the chart, you must use series, grouping, and axis settings. This chapter discusses how to define data expressions and use axis settings. Specifically, this chapter explains how to define chart series expressions, sort and group series data, and work with data on a chart axis.

- *Chapter 20, Laying Out and Formatting a Chart.* Like chart data, the steps to lay out and format a chart are distinct from the layout and formatting options for a typical report. This chapter explains how to work with the visual elements of a chart to produce the desired appearance. The tasks include positioning elements in the chart area, adding and formatting titles and labels, and changing the style of the series elements available in each chart type.

Part V, Enhancing Reports

Part V discusses features you can add to a report to improve usability and increase productivity when working with suites of reports. Part V includes the following chapters:

- *Chapter 21, Designing a Multipage Report.* Most reports display on multiple pages. Often, report developers want to specify where page breaks occur and they want to display information, such as page numbers and report titles, on every page. This chapter explains how to control pagination in a report and how to design a page layout.

- *Chapter 22, Adding Interactive Viewing Features.* To make a report more useful, you can add interactive features, such as hyperlinks or bookmarks. This chapter describes how to create and use bookmarks and tables of contents. It also describes how to add interactive features, such as highlighting, to charts.

- *Chapter 23, Building a Shared Report Development Framework.* To support a consistent appearance for a suite of reports, BIRT provides two ways to share the report development among designers. A report library contains standard report elements, such as data sources, a company logo, or a set of styles. A report template combines report elements from libraries or the BIRT palettes to provide a predefined layout and master page. Report designers who use these tools increase their productivity.

- *Chapter 24, Localizing Text.* To support international data or produce reports that can be viewed in multiple locales or languages requires planning and an understanding of the issues that are associated with working with resource files. This chapter provides an overview of the localization process and procedures for localizing text in a report.

Glossary. This section contains a glossary of terms that are useful to understanding all parts of the book.

Typographical conventions

Table P-1 describes the typographical conventions that are used in this book.

Table P-1   Typographical conventions

Item	Convention	Example
Code examples	Courier font	`StringName = "M. Barajas";`
File names	Initial capital letter, except where file names are case-sensitive	SimpleReport.rptdesign
Key combination	A + sign between keys means to press both keys at the same time	Ctrl+Shift
Menu items	Capitalized, no bold	File
Submenu items	Separated from the main menu item with a small arrow	File➤New
User input	Courier font	`2006`

Acknowledgments

John Arthorne and Chris Laffra observed, "It takes a village to write a book on Eclipse." In the case of the BIRT books, it has taken a virtual village in four countries to create these two books. Our contributors, reviewers, Addison-Wesley editorial, marketing, and production staff, printers, and proofreaders are working in Austin, Boston, Closter, Indianapolis, Inman, Los Angeles, Paris, San Francisco, San Jose, Shanghai, South San Francisco, Upper Saddle River, and Windsor.

We want to thank Greg Doench, our acquisitions editor, who asked us to write a book about BIRT and has been holding his breath ever since to see if we could possibly make the schedule that we set for ourselves. Of course, we want to acknowledge the staff at Addison-Wesley who are working to support our schedule. In particular, we would like to acknowledge John Fuller, Mary Kate Murray, Julie Nahil, Sandra Schroeder, and Beth Wickenhiser. We also want to thank Mike Milinkovich at the Eclipse Foundation and Mark Coggins at Actuate Corporation for providing the forewords for the books.

We particularly want to acknowledge the many, many managers, designers, and programmers too numerous to name who have worked diligently to produce BIRT, giving us a reason for these two books. You know who you are and know how much we value your efforts. The following technical staff members at Actuate Corporation have been of particular assistance to the authors: Linda Chan, Wenbin He, Petter Ivmark, Rima Kanguri, Nina Li, Wenfeng Li, Yu Li, Jianqiang Luo, David Michonneau, Kai Shen, Aniruddha Shevade, Pierre Tessier, Krishna Venkatraman, Mingxia Wu, Gary Xue, Jun Zhai, and Lin Zhu. In addition, we want to acknowledge the support and significant contribution that was provided by Paul Rogers.

Creating this book would not have been possible without the constant support of the members of the Developer Communications team at Actuate Corporation. Many of them and their families sacrificed long personal hours to take on additional tasks so that members of the team of authors could create this material. In particular, we wish to express our appreciation to two writers who contributed original material for these books. Mary Adler wrote the initial version of "Adding Interactive Viewing Features." Tigger Newman wrote material about accessing data sources, working with data sets, filtering data, and using parameters for release 1.0.1, which were the basis of several chapters in the first published edition. Paul Reeves revised that material for that same edition. Terry Ryan pulled together the terminology in the glossary that accompanies each of the books. In addition, Frances Buran, Chris Dufour, Bruce Gardner, Wennie Huang, Richard Kang, Melia Kenny, Cheryl Koyano, Madalina Lungulescu, Liesbeth Matthieu, Audrey Meinertzhagen, and Lois Olson all contributed to the success of the books.

I

Installing BIRT

Prerequisites for BIRT

BIRT provides a number of separate packages as downloadable archive (.zip) files on the BIRT downloads page. Some of the packages are stand-alone modules, others require an existing Eclipse environment, and still others provide additional functionality to report developers and application developers. This chapter describes the requirements for each of the available packages:

- BIRT Chart Engine
- BIRT Demo Database
- BIRT Report Designer
- BIRT Report Designer Full Eclipse Install for Linux
- BIRT Report Designer Full Eclipse Install for Windows
- BIRT Report Engine
- BIRT Rich Client Platform (RCP) Report Designer
- BIRT Samples
- BIRT SDK
- BIRT Test Suite

Requirements for the BIRT report designers

There are two designer applications that you can use to create BIRT reports:

- BIRT RCP Report Designer

BIRT Report Designer is a stand-alone module for report designers who do not have programming experience. BIRT RCP Report Designer is a stand-alone component that only requires a Java JDK. BIRT RCP Report Designer appears on the BIRT download page as RCP Report Designer.

- BIRT Report Designer

  BIRT Report Designer requires Eclipse, a Java JDK, and several other components. BIRT Report Designer is useful for report designers who may want to modify the underlying Java or JavaScript code that BIRT uses to create a report.

  You can install BIRT Report Designer in either of the following two ways:

  - Download and install an all-in-one archive file, which contains Eclipse, BIRT Report Designer, Graphics Editor Framework (GEF), and Eclipse Modeling Framework (EMF).

    The all-in-one archive file contains all the components necessary to run BIRT Report Designer except the Java SDK and itext-1.3.jar. The all-in-one archive file appears on the BIRT download page as BIRT Report Designer Full Eclipse Install.

  - Independently download and install all the components that are required to run BIRT Report Designer.

    To independently install the BIRT Report Designer component, you must first download and install Eclipse. After installing Eclipse, you must also download and install GEF and EMF. You must install itext-1.3.jar only after installing BIRT. The BIRT Report Designer archive file appears on the BIRT download page as Report Designer.

- BIRT Report Designer and SDK

  BIRT Report Designer and SDK is identical to BIRT Report Designer except that it also includes the Java source code for the plug-ins. The requirements for BIRT Report Designer and SDK are identical to the requirements for BIRT Report Designer.

This section describes the prerequisites for each designer package and lists the recommended versions for each component. Table 1-1 provides more information about supported configurations.

Table 1-1   Supported configurations

Component	Required version
Eclipse	3.2
GEF	3.2
EMF	2.2
JDK	1.4.2 or 1.5

About installing required software

Because BIRT is a Java-based platform, installing a required component typically involves only unpacking an archive. Most BIRT components are packed in archives that have an Eclipse directory at the top level. As a result, you follow the same unpacking procedure for most modules. A common installation mistake that new BIRT users make is unpacking archives in the wrong directory. Before you unpack an archive, examine its structure to confirm that you are unpacking it to the correct directory.

The BIRT web site provides the most current information about BIRT installation. To get additional tips, access the BIRT newsgroup, or see an installation demo, visit the following URL:

```
http://download.eclipse.org/birt/downloads/
```

BIRT RCP Report Designer software requirements

BIRT RCP Report Designer requires the following software:

- J2SE 1.4.2 or later

  If you do not have J2SE 1.4.2 or later already installed, choose the latest release, and install it in an appropriate location on your system. The latest JDK download is available at the following URL:

  ```
  http://java.sun.com/products/
  ```

  The JDK is available as a self-extracting executable file for Windows operating systems and as an archive file for UNIX and Linux platforms.

- iText

  iText is a library that BIRT uses to generate PDF files. Download itext-1.3.jar from the following URL:

  ```
  http://prdownloads.sourceforge.net/itext/itext-1.3.jar
  ```

  Copy itext-1.3.jar into $RCP_BIRT/plugins/com.lowagie.itext_1.3.0/lib.

BIRT Report Designer Full Eclipse Install software requirements

BIRT Report Designer Full Eclipse Install Release 2.1 requires the following software:

- Java JDK J2SE 1.4.2 or later

  If you do not have JDK 1.4.2 or later already installed, install the latest JDK release in an appropriate location on your system. The latest JDK download is available at the following URL:

  ```
  http://java.sun.com/products/
  ```

The JDK is available as a self-extracting executable file for Windows operating systems and as an archive file for UNIX and Linux platforms.

- iText

iText is a library that BIRT uses to generate PDF files. Download itext-1.3.jar from the following URL:

```
http://prdownloads.sourceforge.net/itext/itext-1.3.jar
```

You copy iText to a directory that is created upon installing BIRT. You must therefore install iText after you install BIRT. Copy itext-1.3.jar into $ECLIPSE/plugins/com.lowagie.itext_1.3.0/lib.

BIRT Report Designer software requirements

BIRT Report Designer requires the following software:

- Java J2SE 1.4.2 JDK or later

If you do not have Java already installed, choose the latest release, and install it in an appropriate location on your system. The latest JDK download is available at the following URL:

```
http://java.sun.com/products/
```

The J2SE JDK is available as a self-extracting executable file for Windows operating systems and as an archive file for UNIX and Linux platforms.

Release 2.1 requires J2SE 1.4.2 JDK or later and does not support earlier versions.

- Eclipse Platform

BIRT Report Designer Release 2.1 is only compatible with Eclipse 3.2. BIRT Report Designer does not support earlier versions of Eclipse.

You can download and install Eclipse SDK 3.2 from the following URL:

```
http://www.eclipse.org/downloads
```

The Eclipse SDK is an archive file that you must extract to your hard drive. The installation of Eclipse is complete once you extract the archive. Eclipse does not have a setup or install program.

The result of the Eclipse archive extraction is a folder named eclipse. You must specify to the archive extraction program where on your hard drive you want the eclipse folder to reside. You may extract the Eclipse archive to any location you prefer. A typical location for Eclipse is the root directory of the C drive. If you specify the root directory of the C drive, the result of installing Eclipse is the following folder:

```
c:/eclipse
```

- Graphics Editor Framework

  GEF is an Eclipse plug-in that BIRT Report Designer's user interface requires.

  Download GEF 3.2 Runtime from the following URL:

  ```
  http://download.eclipse.org/tools/gef/downloads
  ```

  GEF is available as a ZIP archive file. Extract GEF to the directory that contains Eclipse.

  Eclipse 3.2 requires GEF 3.2 and does not support earlier versions.

- Eclipse Modeling Framework

  EMF is a collection of Eclipse plug-ins that BIRT charts use. EMF download includes the required Service Data Objects (SDO) component. Download EMF and SDO 2.2 Runtime from the following URL:

  ```
  http://download.eclipse.org/tools/emf/scripts/downloads.php
  ```

  EMF is available as a ZIP archive file. Extract EMF to the directory that contains Eclipse.

  Eclipse 3.2 requires EMF 2.2 and does not support earlier versions.

- iText

  iText is a library that BIRT uses to generate PDF files. Download itext-1.3.jar from the following URL:

  ```
  http://prdownloads.sourceforge.net/itext/itext-1.3.jar
  ```

  You copy iText to a directory that is created upon installing BIRT. You must therefore install iText after you install BIRT. Copy itext-1.3.jar into $ECLIPSE/plugins/com.lowagie.itext_1.3.0/lib.

Table 1-1 lists the required configurations for developing report designs using BIRT Report Designer 2.1. You cannot use any other versions of any of the listed components.

About types of BIRT builds

The Eclipse BIRT download site makes available several types of builds for BIRT. The following list describes the types of builds that are available:

- Release build

  A release build is of production quality and passes the complete test suite for all components and features. Use the release build to develop applications.

- Milestone build

  A milestone build provides access to newly completed features. The build is stable, but it is not of production quality. Use this type of build to preview new features and develop future reporting applications that depend on those features.

- Stable build

  A stable build passes a reduced test suite. New features are in an intermediate stage of development in this type of build. Use a stable build to preview new features and provide feedback to the development team.

- Nightly build

  BIRT is built every night. As an open source project, these builds are available to anyone. These builds are part of an ongoing development process and are unlikely to be useful to report developers in general; however, if a certain feature that you require does not work, you can file a bug report. When the bug has been fixed, and the fix has been included in the build, you can download BIRT and confirm that the fix solves the problem that you reported.

2

Installing a BIRT Report Designer

BIRT provides two report designers, BIRT Report Designer and BIRT RCP Report Designer. Both designers are reporting systems that integrate with your J2EE-based web application to enable report developers to produce compelling reports in both web and PDF formats. BIRT Report Designer is for report developers who want to use programming or scripting in their report designs. BIRT RCP Report Designer does not support the use of programming or scripting in Java.

Each designer is packaged as an archive (.zip) file and can be downloaded from the Eclipse web site.

The available packages are:

- BIRT Report Designer

  If you already have installed an Eclipse environment, you can download and install BIRT Report Designer.

- BIRT RCP Report Designer

  If you have installed a Java environment, you can download and install BIRT RCP Report Designer. This designer is easier to use but does not support programming or scripting in Java.

- BIRT Report Designer Full Eclipse Install

  If you have an installed Java environment, and you want to be able to program or use JavaScript in your report design, you can download and install BIRT Report Designer Full Eclipse Install. This package contains BIRT Report Designer and all the Eclipse components that you need in one ZIP file.

Installing BIRT Report Designer

BIRT Report Designer integrates into an existing Eclipse platform on your computer by providing the report design perspective. BIRT Report Designer also includes the Software Development Kit (SDK) and the components provided in the BIRT Chart Engine, BIRT Demo Database, BIRT Report Engine, and BIRT Samples packages.

You install BIRT Report Designer by downloading an archive (.zip) file from the Eclipse web site and extracting it in your existing Eclipse environment. The following examples use BIRT Release 2.1.

Downloading and installing BIRT Report Designer

Complete the following procedure to download and install BIRT Report Designer on a Windows or UNIX system.

How to install BIRT Report Designer

1 Using your browser, navigate to the following URL:

    http://download.eclipse.org/birt/downloads/

2 From Download, choose the following build:

    Release build 2_1_0

The BIRT Release Build: 2_1_0 page appears.

3 Choose the Report Designer ZIP file:

    birt-report-framework-2_1_0.zip

The Eclipse downloads page appears. This page shows all the sites that provide this download file.

4 Choose the download site that is closest to your location.

birt-report-framework-2_1_0.zip downloads to your system.

5 Extract the archive file to the folder that contains your Eclipse directory.

Be certain to extract the archive into the directory that contains the eclipse folder and not into the eclipse folder. For example, if your eclipse folder is located at C:\eclipse, extract the archive into C:\.

6 Download and install the auxiliary file that is necessary for PDF creation, as described in the following section.

Installing the auxiliary file for BIRT Report Designer

BIRT Report Designer also requires iText, an open source Java-PDF library that BIRT uses to generate PDF versions of reports. You must install iText after you install BIRT Report Designer.

1 Download itext-1.3.jar from the following URL:

```
http://prdownloads.sourceforge.net/itext/itext-1.3.jar
```

2 Copy itext-1.3.jar to the following location in your Eclipse installation:

```
/plugins/com.lowagie.itext_1.3.0/lib
```

Testing the BIRT Report Designer installation

To test your BIRT Report Designer installation, start Eclipse, then start BIRT Report Designer. BIRT Report Designer is a perspective within Eclipse.

How to test the BIRT Report Designer installation

1 Start Eclipse.

2 From the Eclipse window menu, choose Open Perspective→Report Design. If Report Design does not appear in the Open Perspective window, choose Other. A list of perspectives appears. Choose Report Design.

Eclipse displays the BIRT Report Designer perspective.

If the test fails, see "Avoiding cache conflicts after you install a BIRT report designer," later in this chapter.

Installing BIRT Report Designer Full Eclipse Install

If you are new to Eclipse and BIRT, you can download and install this package to start developing and designing BIRT reports immediately. This package includes BIRT Report Designer, an Eclipse environment, and other required components.

In BIRT Release 2.1, the BIRT Report Designer Full Eclipse Install package contains:

- Eclipse Platform 3.2
- Graphics Editor Framework 3.2
- Eclipse Modeling Framework 2.2
- BIRT Report Designer 2.1

You install BIRT Report Designer Full Eclipse Install by downloading and extracting an archive (.zip) file. The following examples use BIRT Release 2.1.

Downloading and installing BIRT Report Designer Full Eclipse Install

Complete the following procedure to download and install BIRT Report Designer and the other necessary components on a Windows or UNIX system.

How to install BIRT Report Designer Full Eclipse Install

1 Using your browser, navigate to the following URL:

    http://download.eclipse.org/birt/downloads/

2 Select the following build:

    Release build 2_1_0

   The BIRT Release Build: 2_1_0 page appears.

3 Choose the Report Designer Full Eclipse Install ZIP file:

    birt-report-designer-all-in-one-2_1_0.zip

   The Eclipse downloads page appears. This page shows all the sites that
   provide this download file.

4 Choose the download site that is closest to your location.

   birt-report-designer-all-in-one-2_1_0.zip downloads to your system.

5 Extract the archive file.

6 Download and install the auxiliary file that is necessary for PDF creation, as
   described in the following section.

Installing the auxiliary file for BIRT Report Designer

BIRT Report Designer also requires iText, an open source Java-PDF library that
BIRT uses to generate PDF versions of reports. You must install iText after you
install BIRT Report Designer.

1 Download itext-1.3.jar from the following URL:

    http://prdownloads.sourceforge.net/itext/itext-1.3.jar

2 Copy itext-1.3.jar to the following location in your Eclipse installation:

    /plugins/com.lowagie.itext_1.3.0/lib

To test your installation, see "Testing the BIRT Report Designer installation,"
earlier in this chapter.

Installing BIRT RCP Report Designer

BIRT RCP Report Designer is a stand-alone report design application that
enables report developers to produce compelling reports in both web and PDF
formats. This application uses the Eclipse Rich Client Platform (RCP) to provide
a report design environment that is less complex than the full Eclipse platform
and SDK. If you need the project-based environment that the full Eclipse
platform provides, install BIRT Report Designer instead. BIRT RCP Report
Designer only runs on Windows.

To integrate reports that you create in BIRT RCP Report Designer into your J2EE-based web application, you also must install BIRT Report Engine. BIRT RCP Report Designer includes the components that are provided in the BIRT Demo Database package.

You install BIRT RCP Report Designer by downloading and extracting an archive (.zip) file. The following examples use Release 2.1.

Downloading and installing BIRT RCP Report Designer

Complete the following procedure to download and install BIRT RCP Report Designer on a Windows system.

How to install BIRT RCP Report Designer

1 Using your browser, navigate to the following URL:

    http://download.eclipse.org/birt/downloads/

2 Select the following build:

    Release build 2_1_0

   The BIRT Release Build: 2_1_0 page appears.

3 Choose the BIRT RCP Report Designer ZIP file:

    birt-rcp-report-designer-2_1_0.zip

   The Eclipse downloads page appears. This page shows all the sites that provide this download file.

4 Choose the download site that is closest to your location.

   birt-rcp-report-designer-2_1_0.zip downloads to your system.

5 Extract the archive to a suitable directory. You can either create a directory or choose an existing directory. The root directory of the archive is birt-rcp-report-designer-2_1_0.

6 Download and extract the auxiliary files that are necessary for report viewing and PDF creation, as described in the following section.

Installing the auxiliary file for BIRT Report Designer

BIRT Report Designer also requires iText, an open source Java-PDF library that BIRT uses to generate PDF versions of reports. You must install iText after you install BIRT Report Designer.

1 Download itext-1.3.jar from the following URL:

    http://prdownloads.sourceforge.net/itext/itext-1.3.jar

2 Copy itext-1.3.jar to the following location in your Eclipse installation:

    /plugins/com.lowagie.itext_1.3.0/lib

Testing the BIRT RCP Report Designer installation

To test the installation, start BIRT RCP Report Designer.

How to test the BIRT RCP Report Designer installation

1   Navigate to the birt-rcp-report-designer-2_1_0 subdirectory.

2   To run BIRT RCP Report Designer, double-click BIRT.exe. BIRT RCP Report Designer appears.

Troubleshooting installation problems

Installing a BIRT report designer is a straightforward task. If you extract the archive file to the appropriate location and the required supporting files are also available in the expected location, your BIRT report designer will work. Because of this fact, one of the first steps in troubleshooting an installation problem is confirming that you extracted all files to the correct location. In particular, verify that the /eclipse/plugins directory contains jar files whose names begin with org.eclipse.birt, org.eclipse.emf, and org.eclipse.gef. Beyond this step, there are a few things that you can do to resolve installation problems. The following sections describe ways of troubleshooting and resolving two common installation errors.

Avoiding cache conflicts after you install a BIRT report designer

Eclipse caches information about plug-ins for faster start-up. After you install or upgrade BIRT Report Designer, using a cached copy of some pages can lead to errors or missing functionality. BIRT RCP Report Designer can also have this problem. Symptoms of this problem include:

- The Report Design perspective does not appear in Eclipse.

- You receive the message "An error occurred" when you open a report or use the report design perspective.

- JDBC drivers that you installed do not appear in the driver manager.

The solution is to remove the cached information. The recommended practice is to start either Eclipse or BIRT from the command line with the -clean option.

To start Eclipse, use the following command:

```
eclipse -clean
```

To start BIRT RCP Report Designer, use the following command:

```
birt -clean
```

Specifying which Java Virtual Machine to use when you start a BIRT report designer

You can specify which Java Virtual Machine (JVM) to use when you start a BIRT report designer. This specification is important, particularly for users on UNIX, when path and permission problems prevent the report designer from locating an appropriate JVM to use. A quick way to overcome such problems is by specifying explicitly which JVM to use when you start the BIRT report designer.

In both Windows and UNIX systems, you can either start a BIRT report designer from the command line or create a command file or shell script that calls the appropriate executable file with the JVM path. The example in this section uses BIRT Report Designer on a Windows system.

How to specify which JVM to use when you start a BIRT report designer

On the command line, type a command similar to:

```
eclipse.exe -classpath <$JAVA_HOME>/j2sdk1.4.2_05/bin/java.exe
```

Installing a language pack

All BIRT user interface components and messages are internationalized through the use of properties files. BIRT uses English as the default language, but other languages are supported by installing a language pack that contains the necessary properties files. There are 24 BIRT language packs, four each for the following six BIRT products:

- BIRT Report Designer Full Eclipse Install

- BIRT Report Designer

- BIRT RCP Report Designer

- BIRT Report Engine

- BIRT Chart Engine

- BIRT Framework SDK

Each of the four language packs contains support for a specific set of languages. The names of the language packs are identical for each product, although the archive file names differ. The following list describes the four language packs and the languages that they support:

- NLpack1

  The NLpack1 language pack supports German, Spanish, French, Italian, Japanese, Korean, Brazilian Portuguese, traditional Chinese, and simplified Chinese.

- NLpack2

  The NLpack2 language pack supports Czech, Hungarian, Polish, and Russian.

- NLpack2a

  The NLpack2a language pack supports Danish, Dutch, Finnish, Greek, Norwegian, Portuguese, Swedish, and Turkish.

- NLpackBidi

  The NLpackBidi language pack supports Arabic and Hebrew. Hebrew is only for Eclipse runtime, GEF runtime, and EMF runtime.

The following instructions explain how to download and install a language pack.

How to download and install a language pack

To download and install a language pack, perform the following steps:

1 Point your browser to the BIRT download page at:

    http://download.eclipse.org/birt/downloads/

2 In the Download section of the BIRT download page, choose Release Build 2_1_0.

3 In the Build Documentation section of the BIRT Release Build page, choose Language Packs.

4 Download the language pack for the product and language that meets your needs.

5 Extract the language pack archive file into the directory above the Eclipse directory.

6 Start Eclipse and choose Window→Preferences→Report Design→Preview.

7 Select the language of choice from the drop-down list in Choose your locale.

8 Restart Eclipse.

If Windows is not running under the locale you need for BIRT, start Eclipse using the -nl <locale> command line option, where <locale> is a standard Java locale code, such as es_ES for Spanish as spoken in Spain. Sun Microsystems provides a list of locale codes at the following URL:

    http://java.sun.com/j2se/1.5.0/docs/guide/intl/locale.doc.html

Eclipse remembers the locale you specify on the command line. On subsequent launches of Eclipse, the locale is set to the most recent locale setting. To revert to a previous locale, launch Eclipse using the -nl command line option for the locale to which you want to revert.

3

Updating a BIRT Installation

As BIRT Report Designer is a Java-based application, updating an installation typically requires replacing the relevant files. Eclipse supports the update process for BIRT Report Designer by providing the Update Manager. BIRT RCP Report Designer is a stand-alone product, so you must replace the existing version with a newer version.

This chapter describes important considerations and the steps you should follow to update the following packages:

- BIRT Report Designer
- BIRT RCP Report Designer

Using the Eclipse Update Manager to update BIRT Report Designer installation

Use the Update Manager to find and install newer major releases of BIRT Report Designer. To install a milestone release or other prerelease version, use the manual update instructions.

How to update BIRT Report Designer installation using the Update Manager

1 In Eclipse, choose Help→Software Updates→Find and Install. Feature Updates appears.

2 Select Search for updates of currently installed features, and choose Finish. The Update Manager may display a list of update sites. Choose one to

continue. Search Results appears and displays any updates that are available.

3 Select a feature to update, then choose Next. Feature License appears.

4 To accept the license and continue installing the update, choose Next. Installation appears.

5 Choose Finish to download and install the selected updates.

Updating BIRT RCP Report Designer installation

Unlike BIRT Report Designer, BIRT RCP Report Designer is a stand-alone application. To update this application, you delete the entire application and reinstall a newer version. If you created your workspace in the birt-rcp-report-designer-<version> directory structure, you should back up your workspace or the reports that you want to keep before you delete BIRT RCP Report Designer. After you install a newer version of the application, you can copy your workspace folder back to the application's directory structure.

As a best practice, do not keep your workspace in the birt-rcp-report-designer-<version> directory structure. Keeping your workspace in a different location enables you to update your installation more easily in the future.

How to update BIRT RCP Report Designer

1 Back up the workspace directory if it is in the birt-rcp-report-designer-<version> directory structure.

2 Delete the birt-rcp-report-designer-<version> directory.

3 Download and install BIRT RCP Report Designer as described earlier in this book.

4 Restore the workspace directory, if necessary.

5 Restart BIRT RCP Report Designer with the -clean option:

```
birt -clean
```

II

Getting Started

4

Learning the Basics

This chapter provides an overview of the report design process and environment. The chapter also includes step-by-step procedures for building your first report.

About BIRT reports

A BIRT report is a structured document that displays data from an external information system, such as a database or application. Data in the report is organized and formatted so that it is meaningful and useful to the person who reads the report. A BIRT report is not a document that you type, like an essay or research paper, although you could use BIRT Report Designer to create such documents.

Using BIRT Report Designer, you can create operational reports, such as a bill of materials, a purchase order, or an invoice. You can also create reports that provide real-time information about business performance, such as the number of calls handled by your customer service organization, the number of problems handled, categorized by levels of complexity, and the number of repeat calls made by the same customer. You can use BIRT to create client-facing reports, such as account statements and transaction details. Any time that you need to gather, analyze, summarize, and present data from an information system, a report is the solution.

Overview of the report design process

Designing a report involves the following tasks. You do not have to perform all the tasks in the order in which they are presented here, but if you are new to

BIRT Report Designer or learning how to design reports, you can use this task list as a starting point.

- Plan the report.
- Start a new report design.
- Specify the data to use.
- Lay out the report.
- Format the report.
- Design a master page.
- Preview and test the report.

For those who do not have report development expertise, it is important to understand that the process of creating a report is iterative rather than linear. You typically perform each task multiple times and in different orders. You might specify the data to use, lay out data, preview the report, then modify the data set, change the layout, preview the report again, and so on, until you are satisfied with the report's contents and appearance.

Planning the report

Before you create a report, you should identify the information that you want the report to provide and decide how to present that information. It is important to think through these details, then draw a mock-up on paper, which you use to get feedback from your report users. Most people cannot visualize what a report could be without a paper and pencil sketch. Planning saves time in the long run, because you do not waste time creating a polished report that contains the wrong information or layout. More frequently, you discover in this review process that the customer wants much more and can now articulate those requirements more successfully.

Starting a new report design

If you are using BIRT Report Designer, start Eclipse, and create a new project, if you have not already done so. Eclipse requires that all files are organized in a project. No project is required if you are using BIRT Rich Client Platform (RCP) Report Designer. After you create the project, create a new report using one of the following techniques:

- Start with a report template.
- Start with a blank report.

Specifying the data to use

A report can access data from a wide variety of sources, including databases, text files, and XML documents. To set up the report to access data, complete the following tasks in this order:

- In BIRT Report Designer, choose the data source.

- Specify how to connect to the data source.
- Create a data set, or query, that identifies the data to extract from the data source.

Laying out the report

There are many ways to present information in a report. Different users have different expectations about how to visualize the data, and different types of layouts work better for different types of data. A report can display information in a tabular list, a series of paragraphs, a pie chart, a bar chart, a hierarchical list, or a series of subreports. These different layouts can be combined and customized. Laying out a report entails placing data on the page and organizing it in a way that helps the report user to grasp and analyze the information.

Formatting the report content

After you lay out data in a report, you format the report to give it a professional and polished appearance. Typical formatting tasks include highlighting certain data, applying styles to data, adjusting the spacing between rows of data, and conditionally hiding sections. You can also apply conditional formatting to data. One basic example is to display numbers in different colors depending on their values. Highlighting data makes the report more accessible to users. Key information stands out in the report, and users can absorb the information in layers.

Designing a master page

When you create a new report, BIRT Report Designer uses a default master page. The master page specifies default values for page size, orientation, and margins. It also defines a default page header and footer, where you can display page numbers or the date. You can modify the master page to design a custom page layout.

Previewing and testing the report

You should preview and test the report as you design it. The most important item to test is your data set. Verify that the data that is retrieved from the data source is what you expect before you start laying out the report. As you lay out and format the report, check the report output throughout the design process. If you add code, test and debug it as you go.

About the report design environment

BIRT Report Designer provides a flexible environment that meets the needs of both beginning report developers and experienced report developers who want the power of programming. It provides:

- Report templates that include instructions to help new report developers get started quickly

- Customizable views that enable report developers to tailor the environment to their style of working

- User-friendly tools for designing, debugging, and previewing reports

This section introduces the report design environment. If you are using BIRT Report Designer for the first time, reviewing the topics in this section can help you learn how to use BIRT Report Designer more effectively.

Procedures in this book apply to both BIRT Report Designer and BIRT RCP Report Designer unless the instructions explicitly state which platform to use. Both platforms provide the same reporting functionality. BIRT Report Designer appears within the Eclipse Workbench and therefore requires the installation of Eclipse. BIRT RCP Report Designer does not require all the Eclipse-specific tools because it is designed for report developers who want only the reporting functionality.

Starting BIRT Report Designer

The steps you take to start BIRT Report Designer depend on whether you are using BIRT Report Designer or BIRT RCP Report Designer. To start the designer, follow the instructions that are appropriate to the designer that you use.

How to start BIRT Report Designer on the Eclipse platform

1 Start Eclipse by navigating to the Eclipse directory and performing one of the following tasks:

- If you are using a Microsoft Windows system, run eclipse.exe.

- If you are using a UNIX or Linux system, run eclipse.

2 On Workspace Launcher, shown in Figure 4-1, specify a workspace in which to store your report projects:

- To create a workspace in the default location, choose OK.

- To specify a different location, choose Browse to select a different folder, then choose OK.

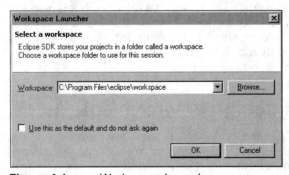

Figure 4-1 Workspace Launcher

3 From the main menu of Eclipse Workbench, choose Window→Open Perspective→Report Design to start BIRT Report Designer. The application window displays the Report Design perspective, as shown in Figure 4-2.

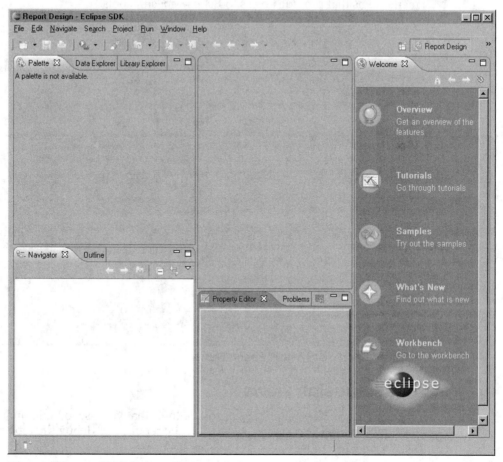

Figure 4-2 BIRT Report Designer

The Report Design perspective shows all the tools, which Eclipse calls views, for creating and managing reports. A perspective is an Eclipse mechanism for organizing the initial set and layout of views in the application window.

If you are new to the Eclipse environment, read the Eclipse online documentation at http://www.eclipse.org/documentation/main.html for information about perspectives, views, and other Eclipse user interface topics.

How to start BIRT RCP Report Designer

Start the Report Designer by navigating to the BIRT RCP Report Designer directory then running BIRT.exe.

BIRT RCP Report Designer appears, as shown in Figure 4-3. As the figure shows, this application is similar to BIRT Report Designer. BIRT RCP Report Designer, however, does not show the Navigator view and does not include menu items that provide access to Eclipse-specific tools.

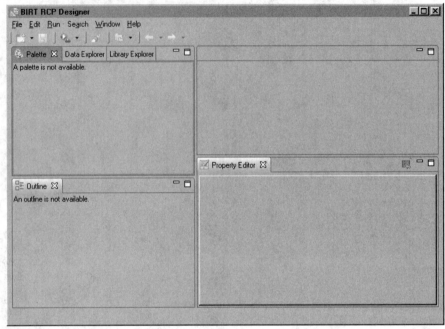

Figure 4-3   BIRT RCP Report Designer

Report design views

The BIRT Report Designer views provide tools that you use to build and customize a BIRT report design, preview the report, and debug the report. Figure 4-4 shows the BIRT Report Designer views.

Each view is a window you can close, resize, minimize, or maximize. You can also move each view to a different location, either inside or outside the application window. Change or rearrange the set of views to fit the way you work or the available screen space.

If you are using BIRT Report Designer, you can save each application window configuration as a named perspective. Then, as you work with different reports, you can choose a perspective from the list of saved perspectives. This technique is useful if the reports that you create require different sets of views or a different application window layout. For example, if some reports require access to the Library Explorer, but some do not, you can set up and save two perspectives, one with Library Explorer open, another with it closed. Similarly, if you create some reports in landscape orientation and some in portrait, you can save different perspectives with the report editor set to different sizes. Read the Eclipse online documentation for more information about working with perspectives.

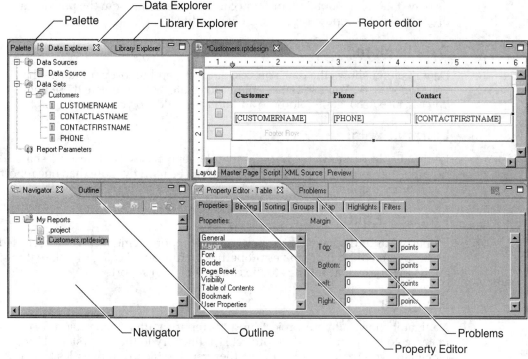

Figure 4-4   BIRT Report Designer views

Report editor

This window is where you design and preview your report. You can open multiple reports in the report editor. The report editor has five pages, which you access by choosing the tabs at the bottom of the report editor. The pages are:

- Layout editor, where you create and edit your report design. Figure 4-4 shows the layout editor.

- Master Page, which shows the master page layout.

- Script editor, where you add JavaScript code to your report. You can create many reports without programming. Typically, you write code only if you want to change the way in which BIRT generates a report.

- XML Source, which shows the XML content that BIRT Report Designer generates when you create a report.

- Previewer, which runs your report and displays the output.

Palette

The palette shows all the elements that you can use in a report to organize and display data. To lay out a report, you can drag elements from the palette and drop them in the report page in the layout editor.

Data Explorer

Data Explorer shows the data sources, data sets, and report parameters that your report uses. You use Data Explorer to create, edit, or delete these items. You can also use Data Explorer to add data set fields to your report.

Library Explorer

Library Explorer shows the libraries that the report uses. A library is a shared resource that contains report elements that can be used by more than one report. Use Library Explorer to insert report elements from a library in a report.

Property Editor

Property Editor displays the properties of the report element currently selected in the layout editor. It organizes properties by functional categories. Use it to apply style or format settings to the contents of your report.

Navigator

Navigator shows all your projects and the reports within each project. Use it to manage your report files. Each project is a directory in the file system. Using Navigator, you can open files, delete files, rename files, or move files from one project to another. If you add files to a project directory through the file system, for example, through Windows Explorer, you need to refresh the project in Navigator to update the list of reports.

BIRT RCP Report Designer does not organize report files in projects. Therefore, it does not include a Navigator view.

Outline

Outline shows the structure of your report as a tree view. It shows the hierarchy of elements in a format that is similar to the outline view of a Microsoft Word or PowerPoint document. You expand or collapse parts of the report by choosing the plus (+) or minus (−) signs. Outline also shows all the resources that are used by or defined in a report, including data sources, data sets, libraries, and styles. You can select items in Outline to edit, delete, rename, or copy them.

Problems

Problems displays messages about errors in the report designs in the current project. It describes the error, says which report file contains the error, provides the location of the file, and indicates the line numbers in which the error occurs.

Report design files

BIRT Report Designer uses a simple document model. When you create and save a report design, BIRT Report Designer creates just one file with the .rptdesign file-name extension. This file contains all the information that is necessary for generating a report.

Unlike many report design tools that generate files in proprietary formats, BIRT design files are written in XML. XML is a widely used markup language specification that was designed especially for web documents. Because BIRT uses XML to define the structure and contents of a report design, developers can leverage their knowledge of XML to get a deeper understanding of how BIRT constructs a report design. BIRT's suite of report-specific XML elements and properties is called Report Object Model (ROM).

You open a report design (.rptdesign) file with the report editor, which, by default, displays the report design in the layout editor. The layout editor provides a graphical view of the report design. If you wish, you can view the report design in the XML editor. This editor displays the XML that BIRT Report Designer generates when you create a report.

View the report design in the XML editor to see its XML code or to locate, by line number, an error that was reported in the Problems view. To understand the XML code, you can consult the ROM specification at http://www.eclipse.org/birt/phoenix/ref/.

How to open a report design

- If using BIRT Report Designer, use one of the following methods:

  - In Navigator, double-click the .rptdesign file.

  - Choose File→Open File, then select the .rptdesign file from the file system.

  If someone sends you a .rptdesign file, first save the file in a project folder, then, in Navigator, right-click the project, and choose Refresh. This action updates the project folder to include the file, which you then open using one of these two methods.

- If using BIRT RCP Report Designer, Choose File→Open File, then select the .rptdesign file from the file system.

Eclipse saves your environment settings when you exit. If you keep a file open when you exit Eclipse, this file opens automatically when you next start Eclipse.

How to view a report design in the XML editor

1 Open the report design file, using one of the procedures that is described in the previous section.

  The layout editor displays the graphical view of the report, as shown in Figure 4-5.

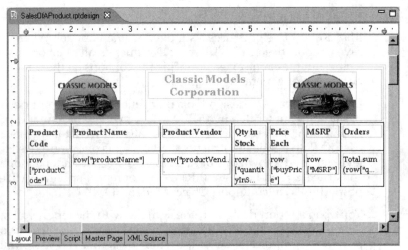

Figure 4-5 Report design in the layout editor

2 Choose the XML Source tab at the bottom of the report editor.

The XML editor displays the XML that defines the report design, as shown in Figure 4-6.

```
SalesOfAProduct.rptdesign

<?xml version="1.0" encoding="UTF-8"?>
<!-- Written by Eclipse BIRT 2.0 -->
<report xmlns="http://www.eclipse.org/birt/2005/design" version="3.2.2" id="
    <property name="createdBy">Eclipse BIRT Designer Version 2.1.0.N20060628
    <property name="units">in</property>
    <list-property name="configVars">
        <structure>
            <property name="name">ProductCode</property>
            <property name="value">S18_1749</property>
        </structure>
    </list-property>
    <parameters>
        <scalar-parameter name="ProductCode" id="4">
            <text-property name="displayName">Product Code</text-property>
            <text-property name="helpText">Please specify the product code</
            <property name="dataType">string</property>
            <property name="allowBlank">false</property>
            <property name="controlType">text-box</property>

Layout  Master Page  Script  XML Source  Preview
```

Figure 4-6 XML code for a report design

Report output formats

You can generate reports in two formats: HTML and PDF. The HTML report appears on a single page or on multiple pages, depending on how you specify pagination. The PDF report appears on multiple pages of the size that you specify and is suitable for printing.

Previewing a report

As you work on the design of a report, you typically want to see the report as it would appear to the report user. With BIRT, you can easily preview a report in HTML or PDF format. You can also view the report in the BIRT report viewer. The report viewer, shown in Figure 4-7, is an interactive viewer that provides report users with the capability to jump to specific pages or to specific sections of a report, to run a report to get the latest data, and to export report data to a comma-separated values (CSV) file.

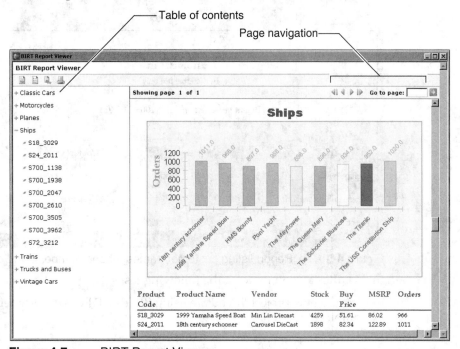

Figure 4-7   BIRT Report Viewer

The following list describes the ways to preview a report:

- To preview a report in the interactive report viewer, choose File➤View Report in Web Viewer.

- To preview a report in BIRT Report Designer, choose the Preview tab at the bottom of the layout editor. The previewer displays the report in HTML format.

- To preview a report in HTML format in a separate window, choose File➤View Report as HTML.

- To preview a report in PDF format, choose File➤View Report as PDF.

Tutorial 1: Building a simple listing report

This section provides step-by-step instructions for building a report that lists customer names, phone numbers, and contact names. The report uses data from the sample database that is supplied with BIRT Report Designer, Classic Models. Figure 4-8 shows a portion of the finished report.

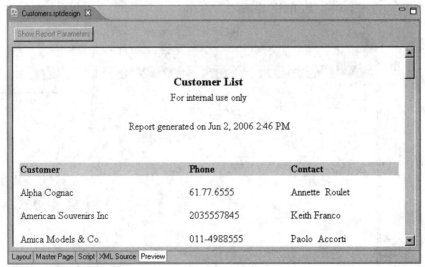

Figure 4-8　Report listing customer names, phone numbers, and contacts

In this tutorial, you perform the following tasks:

- Create a new project. If you are using BIRT RCP Report Designer, you do not complete this step.

- Create a new report.

- Build a data source.

- Build a data set.

- Lay out the report to display each row of the data set.

- Sort the data.

- Format the report to enhance its appearance.

- Create a report title.

Task 1: Create a new project

Eclipse organizes files by projects. You can create one project to organize all your reports or create multiple projects to organize your reports by categories. For each project that you create, Eclipse creates a directory in your file system.

If you are using BIRT RCP Report Designer, this task does not apply to you.

1 Choose File➤New➤Project. New Project, which appears in Figure 4-9, displays the types of projects that you can create.

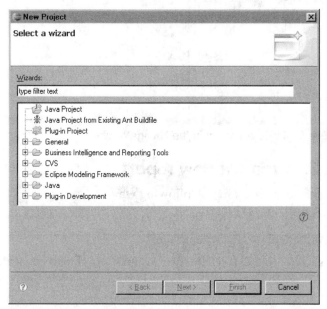

Figure 4-9 New Project

2 Expand Business Intelligence and Reporting Tools, select Report Project, then choose Next.

3 On New Report Project, in Project name, type the following text, as shown in Figure 4-10:

```
My Reports
```

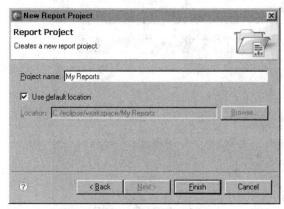

Figure 4-10 New Report Project

4 To add the project, choose Finish. You can now see the project in the Navigator view, as shown in Figure 4-11.

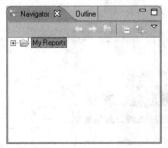

Figure 4-11   A project in the Navigator view

Task 2:   Create a new report

You can create a report in the following ways:

- Start with a blank report design.

- Use a predefined report template.

  For each template, BIRT Report Designer provides a cheat sheet, which contains step-by-step instructions, to help you create the report.

For this tutorial, you start with a blank report design.

1 Choose File→New→Report. New Report appears. Figure 4-12 shows the window that appears in BIRT Report Designer. New Report is slightly different in BIRT RCP Report Designer.

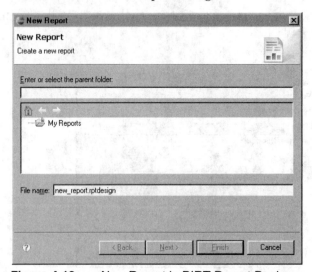

Figure 4-12   New Report in BIRT Report Designer

2 In BIRT Report Designer, under Enter or select the parent folder, select the project that you created. This step applies only to BIRT Report Designer users.

3 Type the following text as the file name:

```
Customers.rptdesign
```

4 Choose Next. New Report provides options for starting with a blank report and several report templates, as shown in Figure 4-13.

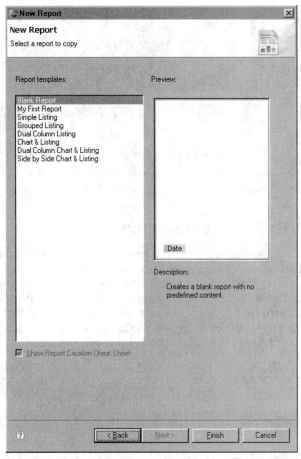

Figure 4-13   Report templates in New Report

5 Select Blank Report, then choose Finish. Your new report appears in the main window. This window displays the layout editor, as shown in Figure 4-14. The layout editor shows an empty report page.

The remainder of this tutorial provides the detailed steps for creating the customer report.

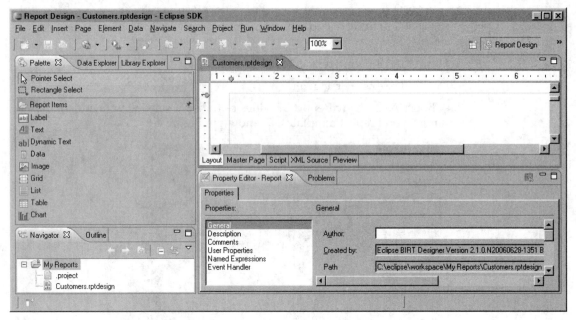

Figure 4-14   Blank report design

Task 3: Build a data source

Before you begin designing your report in the layout editor, you build a BIRT
data source to connect your report to a database or other types of data sources.
When you build a data source, you specify the driver class, data source name,
and other connection information that is specific to the type of data source. For
this tutorial, you use the sample database, Classic Models, that is already
configured for use with BIRT Report Designer. You do not need to specify the
connection information for this sample database.

1 Choose Data Explorer. If you use the default report design perspective, Data
Explorer is on the left of the layout editor, next to Palette, as shown in
Figure 4-15. If it is not open, choose Window→Show View→Data Explorer.

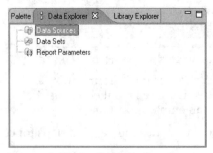

Figure 4-15   Data Explorer

2 Right-click Data Sources, then choose New Data Source from the context menu. New Data Source displays the types of data sources you can create, as shown in Figure 4-16.

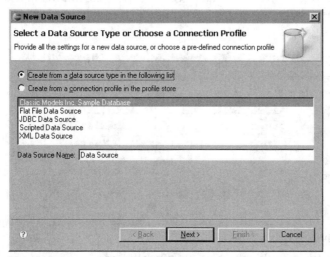

Figure 4-16   New Data Source

3 Select Classic Models Inc. Sample Database from the list of data source types. Use the default data source name, then choose Next. Connection information about the new data source appears.

4 Choose Finish. BIRT Report Designer creates a new data source that connects to the sample database. It appears within Data Sources in Data Explorer, shown in Figure 4-17.

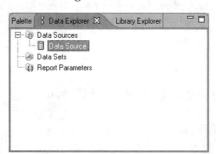

Figure 4-17   Data Sources in Data Explorer

Task 4: Build a data set

Now, you are ready to build your data set. A data set identifies the data to retrieve from the data source. If your report connects to a JDBC data source, you use a SQL SELECT statement to identify the data to retrieve.

1 In Data Explorer, right-click Data Sets, and choose New Data Set from the context menu.

2 On New Data Set, in Data Set Name, type the following text, as shown in Figure 4-18:

```
Customers
```

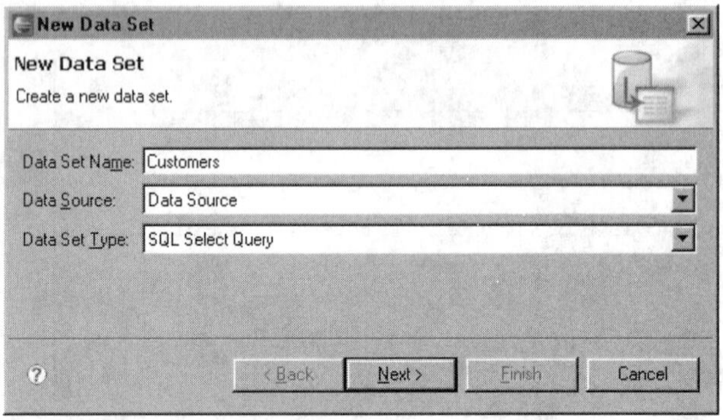

Figure 4-18 New Data Set

3 Use the default values for the other fields:

- Data Source shows the name of the data source that you created earlier.

- Data Set Type indicates that the data set uses a SQL SELECT query.

4 Choose Next.

Query displays the information to help you create a SQL query. Available Items lists all the tables in the Classic Models database. You can click the plus (+) sign next to a table to display the columns in the table. The text area on the right side of Edit Data Set shows the required keywords of a SQL SELECT statement:

```
select
from
```

5 In the text area, type the following SQL SELECT statement to specify the data to retrieve:

```
select customerName,
contactLastName,
contactFirstName,
phone
from Customers
```

Although the data set editor shows table and column names in uppercase letters, you can type these names how you prefer, because SQL is not case-sensitive. If you do not want to type the query, you can drag columns and tables from Available Items to the text area.

The SELECT statement that you created, which is shown in Figure 4-19, gets values from the CUSTOMERNAME, CONTACTLASTNAME, CONTACTFIRSTNAME, and PHONE columns in the CUSTOMERS table.

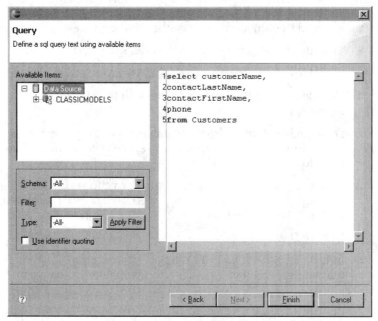

Figure 4-19   SQL SELECT statement in Edit Data Set

6 Choose Finish to save the data set. Edit Data Set displays the columns you specified in the query, and provides options for editing the data set.

7 Choose Preview Results to make sure the query is valid and that it returns the correct data. If you typed the SELECT statement correctly, you should see the results that are shown in Figure 4-20. These are the data rows that the query returns.

Figure 4-20   Data rows returned by a SQL SELECT statement

8 Choose OK.

Task 5: Lay out the report

In this procedure, you insert elements in the report page to display the data from the data set that you created previously. You start by inserting a table element, then you insert data elements in the table. It is important to understand the functionality that the table provides:

- The table iterates through all the data rows that a data set returns.

- It enables you to lay out data easily in a row and column format.

1   Choose Palette. The palette displays all the elements that you can place in a report.

2   Drag a table element from the palette, and drop it in the report in the layout editor. Insert Table prompts you to specify the number of columns and detail rows to create for the table.

3   Specify 3 columns and 1 detail row, then choose OK. A table with three columns and one detail row appears in the layout editor. Now, you are ready to insert data in the table.

4   Choose Data Explorer.

5   In Data Explorer, expand Data Sets, then expand Customers. The columns that you specified in the query appear below Customers.

6   Drag CUSTOMERNAME from Data Explorer, and drop it in the first cell in the table's detail row, as shown in Figure 4-21. The detail row displays the main data in the report. In the finished report, the detail row repeats to display all the data rows from the data set.

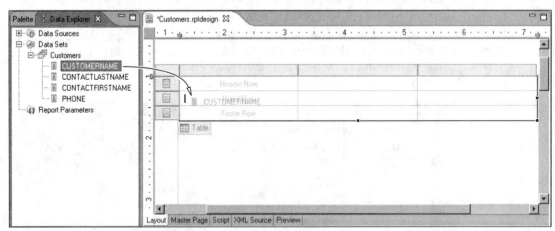

Figure 4-21   Dragging a column from Data Explorer, and dropping it in a table cell

BIRT Report Designer creates a named column, which is bound to the data set field. Select Data Binding, which is shown in Figure 4-22, displays this data binding. The data binding mechanism exists to give a name to the data set field. The report design element uses this name to access the field.

Figure 4-22   A named column that is bound to a data set field

7 Choose OK to accept the default data-binding definition.

In the layout editor, the table cell in which you dropped the CUSTOMERNAME field contains a data element that displays [CUSTOMERNAME]. Above this data element is a label element that the layout editor automatically added to the header row. This label displays the field name as static text. It serves as the column heading. Figure 4-23 shows the data and label elements.

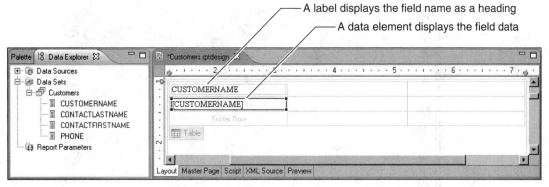

Figure 4-23   Data and label elements in a table

8 Drag PHONE from Data Explorer, and drop it in the second cell in the detail row. Choose OK to accept the default data binding.

9 Drag CONTACTFIRSTNAME, and drop it in the third cell in the detail row. Choose OK to accept the default data binding.

10 Drag CONTACTLASTNAME, and drop it in the third cell in the detail row, below CONTACTFIRSTNAME. Choose OK to accept the default data binding. The report page should look like the one shown in Figure 4-24.

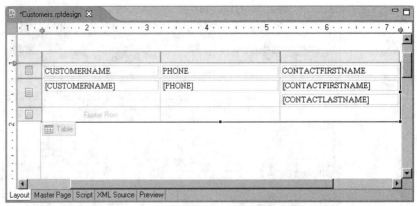

Figure 4-24   Customer and contact information added to a table

11 Choose Preview, the tab at the bottom of the layout editor. BIRT Report
Designer generates and displays the report in HTML format, as shown in
Figure 4-25. Scroll down to see the entire report. You can also preview a
report in PDF. You do so by choosing File➤View Report as PDF from the
main menu.

As Figure 4-25 shows, the data is correct, but it appears in random order. It
makes more sense to sort the data alphabetically by customer name. The
report's appearance also needs improvement.

Figure 4-25   Preview of report data

Task 6: Sort the data

When you first create and preview a report, the report displays the data rows in the order in which the query returns them. The order can vary, depending on many factors, such as how data was supplied in the data source. In most cases, you will want to change the order in which data appears in the report.

1 Choose Layout to return to the layout editor.

2 Open Property Editor, if necessary. If you use the default report design perspective, Property Editor appears below the layout editor. If it is not open, choose Window➔Show View➔Property Editor.

3 In the layout editor, select the table by selecting the Table tab in the lower left corner. This tab appears when you hover the mouse pointer over this area. Property Editor displays the properties for the table, as shown in Figure 4-26.

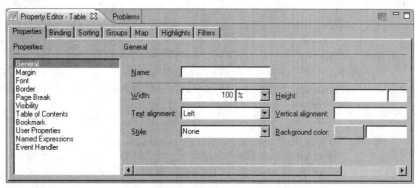

Figure 4-26   Property Editor

4 Choose the Sorting tab.

5 Choose Add to create a sort expression. A row appears under Sort Key.

6 Click in the row under Sort Key, then select the arrow button that appears, and select CUSTOMERNAME from the drop-down list.

7 Use the default Ascending value for Sort Direction, as shown in Figure 4-27.

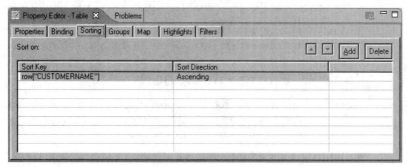

Figure 4-27   Ascending sort direction

8 Preview the report. The sorted data appears in ascending order by customer name, as shown in Figure 4-28.

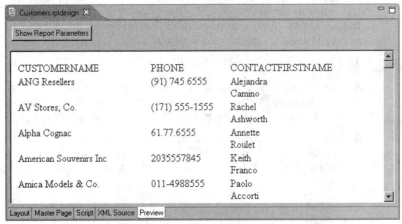

Figure 4-28 Data sorted by customer name

Notice that names with uppercase letters appear at the top of the list. BIRT sorts string data by UCS2 code point values. In ASCII-based character sets, uppercase letters have lower code point values than lowercase letters. Therefore, uppercase letters appear before lowercase letters.

9 To sort the customer names case-insensitively so that ANG Resellers appears after American Souvenirs Inc., rather than before, change the Sort Key expression in the Sorting page to the following expression:

```
row["CUSTOMERNAME"].toUpperCase( )
```

This expression uses the JavaScript toUpperCase( ) function to convert all the customer name values to uppercase before sorting. JavaScript function names are case-sensitive, so you must type toUpperCase( ) exactly as shown. References to column names are also case-sensitive. In this expression, row["CUSTOMERNAME"] is the correct name to use. If you type row["customername"], for example, BIRT Report Designer displays an error when you run the report. You can verify the capitalization of a column name by looking at the name that is displayed in Data Explorer.

10 Preview the report. The customer names appear in a different order. Names with uppercase letters do not appear at the top of the list.

Task 7: Format the report

Now that you verified that the report displays the correct data in the correct order, you can turn your attention to improving the report's appearance. You perform the following tasks in this section:

- Edit the text of the column headings.

- Format the column headings to differentiate them from the data rows.

- Display the contact first and last names on the same line.

- Increase the space between rows.

Edit the column headings

1 Choose Layout to return to the layout editor.

2 Double-click the first column heading, CUSTOMERNAME. The column heading is in the first row—the header row—of the table.

3 To replace all the highlighted text, start typing, then press Enter when you finish. To edit the text, click once to deselect the text, then position the cursor where you want to add or delete characters.

Replace CUSTOMERNAME with the following text:

```
Customer
```

4 Repeat steps 2 and 3 to change the second and third column headings to the following text:

```
Phone
Contact
```

The report design should look like the one shown in Figure 4-29.

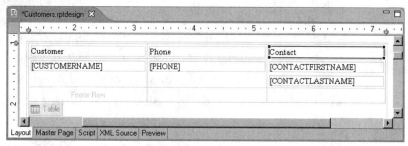

Figure 4-29   Revised column headings in a report design

Format the column headings

To format a report element, you set its properties. You can accomplish this task in two ways:

- Set an element's properties through Property Editor.

- Define a style that contains the desired properties, and apply the style to an element. Use this method to define format properties once and apply them to more than one element.

In this procedure, you use the first method to set the column headings to bold, and the second method to add color to the header row.

1 To set the column headings to bold using Property Editor:

1 Select all the column headings. To select multiple elements, press the Shift key as you click each element. Property Editor displays the properties for the selected elements, as shown in Figure 4-30.

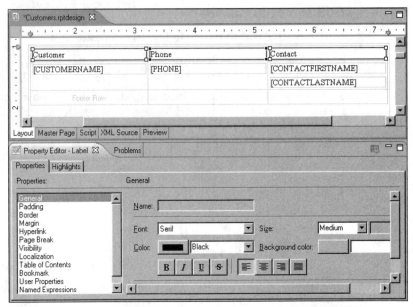

Figure 4-30   Properties for selected elements in Property Editor

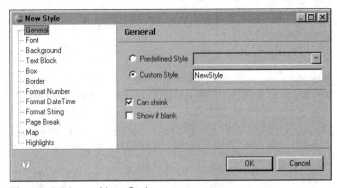

2 Choose B to format the column headings as bold text.

3 To deselect the column headings, click the white space outside the table.

2 To add a background color to the header row, using a style:

1 From the main menu, choose Element→New Style.

New Style appears, as shown in Figure 4-31. The left side displays the property categories. The right side displays the properties for the category that you select.

Figure 4-31   New Style

2 For Custom Style, specify the following name for the style:

```
table_header_row
```

3 Choose Background from the list of property categories. New Style displays the background properties that you can set.

4 Specify a color for the Background Color property, using one of the following methods:

- ❑ Select the button next to the property, then select a color from the color palette that appears.

- ❑ Select a color from the drop-down list.

Choose OK.

5 In the layout editor, select the table by selecting the Table tab in the lower left corner. This tab appears when you hover the mouse pointer over this area. Clicking the table causes guide cells to appear at the top and left side of the table, as shown in Figure 4-32.

	Customer	Phone	Contact
	[CUSTOMERNAME]	[PHONE]	[CONTACTFIRSTNAME]
			[CONTACTLASTNAME]
	Footer Row		

Guide cells

Tab

Figure 4-32 Guide cells at top and left of a table

6 Select the guide cell next to the header row. Property Editor displays the properties for the selected row.

7 Choose Properties then General to display the general properties for the row.

8 Apply the style that you just created by selecting table_header_row from the drop-down list next to Style. BIRT Report Designer applies the style to the header row and it appears in color.

3 Preview the report. The report should look like the one shown in Figure 4-33.

Figure 4-33 Report preview, showing header row style

So far, the main improvement is that the headings are clearly visible and defined.

Display first and last names on the same line

When you place multiple elements in a single cell, BIRT Report Designer creates block-level elements. If you are familiar with HTML, you know that each block element starts on a new line. To display multiple elements on the same line, you need to set them as inline elements. Alternatively, you can concatenate the first and last name values to display in a single data element, as described in this procedure.

1 Choose Layout to return to the layout editor.

2 Delete the data element that displays the contact's last name.

3 Double-click the data element that displays the contact's first name.

Select Data Binding displays all the data bindings used in the report. A check mark next to CONTACTFIRSTNAME indicates the data binding used by the data element you selected.

 4 Click in the cell that displays the dataSetRow["CONTACTFIRSTNAME"] expression, then choose the ellipsis (...) button.

Expression Builder displays the following expression in the text area at the top of the window:

```
dataSetRow["CONTACTFIRSTNAME"]
```

5 To concatenate the first and last names, type the following expression:

```
dataSetRow["CONTACTFIRSTNAME"]+" "+
    dataSetRow["CONTACTLASTNAME"]
```

Figure 4-34 shows this expression in Expression Builder. The empty quotation marks (" ") add a space between the first name and last name. You can type the expression in the text area, as shown in Figure 4-34, or double-click an item in the lower right of the window to insert it in the expression. Figure 4-35 shows a column name that you can double-click to insert into the expression.

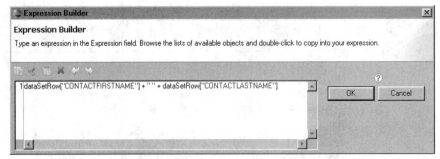

Figure 4-34   Concatenated data in Expression Builder

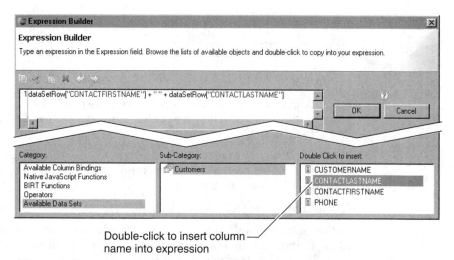

Double-click to insert column
name into expression

Figure 4-35   Concatenated data in Expression Builder

6   Choose OK to close Expression Builder, then choose OK in Select Data
    Binding to save the modified expression.

7   Preview the report. The report should look like the one shown in Figure 4-36.

Customer	Phone	Contact
Alpha Cognac	61.77.6555	Annette Roulet
American Souvenirs Inc	2035557845	Keith Franco
Amica Models & Co.	011-4988555	Paolo Accorti
ANG Resellers	(91) 745 6555	Alejandra Camino
Anna's Decorations, Ltd	02 9936 8555	Anna O'Hara
Anton Designs, Ltd.	+34 913 728555	Carmen Anton
Asian Shopping Network, Co	+612 9411 1555	Brydey Walker
Asian Treasures, Inc.	2967 555	Patricia McKenna

Layout | Master Page | Script | XML Source | Preview

Figure 4-36   Report preview, showing concatenated contact names

Increase the space between rows

The default layout adds a minimum space between table rows. Typically, you
will want to adjust the spacing between rows.

1   Choose Layout to return to the layout editor.

2   Select all the cells in the detail row, the middle row. To select multiple cells,
    use Shift-click. Be careful to select the cells, not the data elements in the cells
    or the whole row. A box appears around the selected cells, as shown in
    Figure 4-37.

Customer	**Phone**	**Contact**
[CUSTOMERNAME]	[PHONE]	[CONTACTFIRSTNAME]
Footer Row		

Figure 4-37   Selected cells in the layout editor

Property Editor displays the properties for the cells. The title that appears in Property Editor shows the type of element that you select, so you should see Property Editor - Cell.

3 Choose Padding. Property Editor displays the padding properties. These properties enable you to specify the amount of space to add to the top, bottom, left, or right of the element.

4 Set Padding—Top to 12 points.

At this point, you might wonder why you did not just select the row to adjust the row spacing instead of selecting the individual cells in the row. BIRT Report Designer does not support row padding, because some browsers do not support this feature.

5 Preview the report. The report should look like the one shown in Figure 4-38. There is more space between the rows of data.

Figure 4-38   Report preview, showing row spacing

Task 8: Create a report title

All your report needs now is a title. To display a title, you can use either a label element, a text element, or a data element:

- The label element is suitable for short, static text, such as column headings.

- The data element is suitable for displaying dynamic values from a data set field or a computed field.

- The text element is suitable for multi-line text that contains different formatting or dynamic values.

In this procedure, you use a text element and HTML tags to format the text. Note that you are not required to use HTML to create formatted text. If, however, you are well-versed in HTML or web design, you might prefer using HTML to create a block of formatted text.

1 Choose Layout to return to the layout editor.

2 Choose Palette.

3 Drag the text element from the palette, and drop it above the table.

4 On Edit Text Item, select HTML/Dynamic Text from the drop-down list that displays Plain Text.

When you select HTML or dynamic text, you can embed HTML tags or CSS properties in the text. You can type the tags or you can insert the commonly used HTML tags that the text editor provides.

5 Specify the following text in the text area, shown in Figure 4-39:

```
<CENTER><B><span style="font-size: larger">
Customer List
</B></span><BR>
<FONT size="small">For internal use only</FONT><BR><BR>
Report generated on <VALUE-OF>new Date()</VALUE-OF>
</CENTER><BR><BR>
```

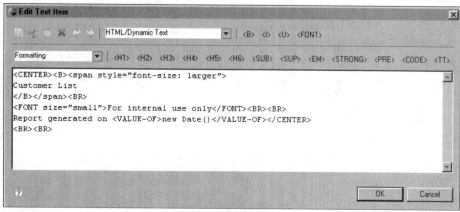

Figure 4-39 Text with HTML tags

6 Choose OK, then preview the report. The report should look like the one shown in Figure 4-40.

Figure 4-40   Report preview, showing formatted report title

As you can see, using the text element with embedded HTML enables you to

- Use different formatting for each line in a multi-line text block.
- Insert dynamic values, such as the current date.

Alternatively, you can use

- Two label elements to display the first and second lines of static text
- A data element to display the third line that contains the dynamic value

Next steps

You just built your first report and worked with some of the basic tools and features of BIRT Report Designer. There are many more tasks that you can accomplish to build more sophisticated reports. Some of these tasks, described in other chapters of this book, include:

- Connecting to your own data source
- Creating charts
- Creating report parameters for user input
- Building reports that contain subreports
- Formatting report elements based on conditions
- Hiding reports based on conditions
- Adding hyperlinks to link your report to web locations or to link one report section to another

5

Planning Your Report

The tutorial in the previous chapter demonstrates how easy it is to build reports using BIRT, so you may be puzzled when you next see a chapter recommending that you plan your report development. This chapter receives its prominent position because as you need to address more complex reporting requirements, you will find it is much more efficient to work from a plan.

You should always plan a report on paper before you begin to create the report with BIRT Report Designer. Planning helps clarify the report requirements and saves time in the long run, because you do not waste time creating and fine-tuning a report that does not meet your users' needs.

Before you start creating a report, you should have the following documents prepared:

- A specification that describes the requirements for the report project
- A prototype, or mock-up, of the report

Ideally, your documents should be reviewed and approved by your report users to determine if the proposed layout meets requirements they may not be able to predict without seeing a mock-up on paper.

In organizations with large IT departments, report developers typically receive requests for new reports that are accompanied by a specification and perhaps a mock-up of the report. Sometimes, report developers discuss report requirements with the person who requested the report, and they develop the specification and mock-up together. Either way, both documents are essential planning tools before a report developer even starts BIRT Report Designer.

If you are responsible for writing the specification, you need to identify the information that the report should provide and determine how best to present the information. This chapter provides guidelines for defining the specification and designing a mock-up of the report. If you receive a specification from somewhere else, use the guidelines to ensure that the specification covers all the information that you need.

Identifying the content of the report

This step is the most important one in the planning process. To get started, answer the following questions:

- What is the purpose of the report?

  A purpose statement helps you determine the information that you need. It also gives the report a starting point.

  The following example is a sample purpose statement:

  > The purpose of this report is to show monthly sales by region, then by sales representatives, and to flag the representatives whose sales figures fall below a certain amount.

  Make the purpose statement as specific as possible. A vague requirement, such as a monthly sales report, does not help define the precise data requirements.

- Who is going to read the report?

  A report can be viewed by different types of users. For example, sales representatives, sales managers, and the vice president of sales can all use a sales report. Each type of user is interested in different types of information and different levels of detail. Knowing the users of your report helps you plan the report data accordingly. Reviewing the list of data to be included can ensure that the data needed by each of the users is, in fact, included in the design. Having a representative from each of the groups of users available to review your proposed layout assists in ensuring that you are meeting each set of requirements.

- What information should appear in the report, and where is it coming from?

  Much of the information in a typical report is taken directly from data fields in a database, application, or text file. First, you need to know the source or sources of data for the report. Second, you need to understand how the data is structured. If, for example, the data source is a database, you need to know what tables are in it, the relationships among tables, the columns in each table, the data types, and so on. If necessary, ask your database administrator for this information.

- Does any of the data need to be calculated?

  Some report data comes directly from data fields, such as sales representative names or addresses. Some information must be calculated, such as the percentage by which sales figures exceed or fall below a certain amount.

- How will the data be calculated?

  Some data can be calculated by performing a mathematical operation on data field values, such as multiplying Item.Quantity by Item.Price to get extended prices. Some data may need to be calculated by using a JavaScript function or a user-defined function.

- Do you want to enable the report user to specify what data to display?

  You can create a report that always displays a specific set of data from the data source. You can also create a report that lets users specify what information they want to see. For example, rather than displaying sales data for all regions, you can prompt the user to specify a region for which the sales data appears in the report.

Determining how the report will be viewed

When designing a report, you need to consider and test the environment in which the report will be viewed, because the environment affects how a report appears and prints.

You should always design for the final delivery environment. This approach includes choosing the right fonts and colors, selecting the appropriate page size, fine-tuning the size of report fields and the amount of space between them, and so on.

Consider the following questions:

- Which is more important, viewing online or printing the report?

  Recognize that there are differences between online and printed reports; decide which is more important, and design for that output. For example, printed reports can vary in appearance depending upon the printer producing the output. If, for example, a report will primarily be viewed online, you can add interactive viewing features, such as hyperlinks or a dynamic table of contents.

- Will the report be viewed in HTML or as a PDF file?

  The appearance of the report differs depending on the file format. Pagination, for example, is a key difference between HTML and PDF files. A report in PDF format appears on multiple pages of a fixed size. An HTML report, on the other hand, can appear on multiple pages or in one scrollable page, depending on what you specify.

- If distributing an HTML report, what browsers are you supporting?

  Different browsers can display results differently, because they interpret HTML or CSS tags differently. If there are particular browsers that you must support, test the report in those browsers.

Considering international reporting requirements

BIRT Report Designer supports creating reports that contain international data for use in multiple locales. A locale defines a set of conventions for providing, displaying, and sorting data. Numbers, dates, and currencies appear differently in different locales. The following examples show dates in long date format when the locale is English (United States) and when the locale is German (Germany):

```
Wednesday, July 7, 2004
Mittwoch, 7. Juli 2004
```

BIRT reports automatically display date, number, and currency data according to the locale to which the report user's machine is configured. You do not have to do anything special to display these types of data in multiple locales.

When designing a report for international users, consider the following questions:

- Will the report be viewed in one locale? If yes, which locale?

  If your report will be used in a specific locale, design and test the report in that locale.

- Will the report be viewed by users in multiple countries?

  If your report will be viewed by users in multiple countries, you should consider internationalizing the report so that it appears correctly in multiple locales. For example, rather than specifying text directly in a report design, you can create text strings in an external source and provide translations of those strings. Using this technique, called localization, the report displays text in the language that is specified by the locale of the user's machine.

  Testing report output in multiple locales is an important early stage in the report design process. Develop a small sample and send that to recipients who can test the output in that locale and, in particular, can test printed output for possible glitches in fonts and layout. Even decisions such as how names are to be displayed can be challenging if the report is to be viewed by users with differing language competencies.

Deciding the layout and format of the report

After you identify the report's purpose and content, you should have a good idea how to organize and present the information. Consider these questions:

- What is the overall layout for the report data? Can all the data appear in a single section, or does the data need to be presented in multiple sections?

  A simple listing of customer names and phone numbers, for example, can be presented in a two-column table. A financial statement, on the other hand, can be a multi-sectioned report that includes a form letter, a summary of accounts and balances, and transaction details for each account.

- Do you need to organize information into groups? If yes, how?

  For example, a monthly sales report can display sales figures by region, by sales representative, or by both. To display both, you can group the information by region first, then list the sales representatives for each region.

- How do you want to sort information?

  A report can present information in the order in which it is stored in the data source, in ascending order, or in descending order. The sort order affects the readability and usability of a report.

- Do you need to summarize the data? If yes, how?

  Reports that present numerical data, such as expense reports, financial statements, and earnings reports, always contain summary sections for totals, averages, or percentages. Decide if this summary information should appear in a table, a chart, or a combination of these display options.

- Do you want to highlight information based on certain conditions?

  It is common to use formatting to emphasize certain information. For example, if a report displays a long list of customers in alphabetical order, you can display the names of the top ten customers in blue.

- Do you need to display information in page headers and footers?

  Printed reports typically display information in the page header to help users navigate multi-page reports. For example, you can display the region name in the header, so users know that sales representatives on page n are part of region x. In the page footer, you can show the page number and the report's generation date. On the other hand, online reports that present data in one continuous page do not require page headers and footers.

- Are there corporate standards that you need to follow?

  If your company produces reports for external use, such as financial statements for clients, it is likely that a report that you create needs to use corporate styles. Corporate styles typically dictate the logos, security statements, fonts, and colors that you can use.

- Are there online style sheets that you can use?

  Most organizations maintain a corporate web site and frequently use CSS to format the look and feel of web pages. You can reuse CSS styles in your reports, which enables you to create reports with the corporate look without having to recreate the styles.

- Are there report templates you can use?

  Unless your organization is just starting up, chances are report templates are available. If there are no formal templates, look at existing reports to see if you can reuse and adapt their layouts. If you are in start-up mode, examine the sample reports, and consider establishing standards for organizational reporting in common areas, such as budget variance, expenses, and vacation reporting.

Drawing a mock-up

After you make the decisions that are described in the previous sections, you are ready to create a mock-up of the report. Use any tool with which you are comfortable, such as a word processor, graphics program, or pen and paper.

A mock-up should show approximately what the finished report will look like, including the report title, page header and footer information, and all the fields in the body of the report. Using a mock-up to get feedback and approval from your primary users can save you time. With this approval, you do not waste time creating a polished report that contains the wrong information or layout.

A mock-up is especially useful when you are first learning BIRT Report Designer. With a blueprint in hand, you can focus on learning and using the tool, rather than trying to design and learn at the same time.

Considering reuse of report components

Rarely do you create just one report. Often, you create reports for different departments in your company or to meet your clients' varying reporting needs. You can approach report creation one report at a time, or you can plan and design a suite of reports. Consider these questions to evaluate which approach is more suitable:

- How many reports are you creating?
- Do the reports require common elements and styles, such as connections to the same data source, page headers and footers that display the same information, report titles in a particular font and color, or tables with a certain format?
- Do you work in a group with other report developers? If yes:
  - How similar are the report projects?
  - Do you need to collaborate on the designs?

If you create more than a couple of reports, and they contain many common elements, or if you work with other report developers on similar reports, you can streamline the report creation process by creating a collaborative and shared report development environment. With BIRT Report Designer, you can:

- Create and store common report elements in a library, which all reports can use.

- Create report templates that define a basic report structure on which new reports can be based.

With careful planning, you can create rich sets of libraries and templates that provide you and other report developers with a head start when you create a new report.

Managing report design resources

A report design typically uses external resources, such as image files, report libraries, Java files, and message files used for localization. If you work on a suite of reports that use multiple external files, you need a way to organize the files so that you can easily package and deploy them to an application server or migrate your reports to different machines.

BIRT Report Designer provides a resource folder as a way to organize all these external files for ease of deployment later. The default location of this resource folder is specified in the Preferences page, which you access by choosing Windows➤Preferences from the main menu, then choosing the Report Design Resource item. On this page, you can specify a different path for the resource folder option.

When you publish a library or create a message file in BIRT Report Designer, these files are automatically saved in the resource folder. To manage files that are created with other applications, such as image files, copy the files into the resource folder before you create the report. Then, when you insert the images in the report, select the image in the resource folder.

Deciding how the report will be deployed

Planning the report design is one phase of the planning process. You also need a plan for deploying or distributing the report. Consider these questions:

- How will the report be distributed to users?
  - Will the report be deployed from an application?
  - Will the report be sent through e-mail?
- If the report will be deployed from an application, address these questions:
  - How will the report integrate with the application?
  - Will users need a secure login to access the report?
  - Will users view a generated report, or will users generate the report to view it with real-time data?

Depending on your deployment strategy, there are a host of other questions to answer and programming tasks to perform. Deployment and integration are topics that are beyond the scope of this book and are covered in *Integrating and Extending BIRT* (Addison-Wesley, 2006).

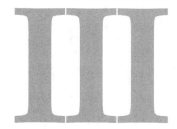

Accessing and Binding Data

6

Connecting to a Data Source

Enterprise report data is frequently stored in a variety of systems and in disparate formats. BIRT Report Designer provides wizards to set up access to the following types of data sources:

- JDBC data sources

  The most common way to access a data source is to use the JDBC protocol. BIRT reports use SQL queries and stored procedures to access these data sources.

- Text files

  BIRT reports use text files as data sources. These text files are typically created by business systems and applications that create logs.

- XML data

  BIRT reports use XML data, either as a stream or a document.

Many examples included as part of the BIRT download use the sample database, Classic Models. That database is included in the default installation as an embedded Derby database so you can work with the examples.

This chapter discusses how to use BIRT's interactive wizards to create a data source. These wizards also support creating data sources that require scripting or programming. This chapter does not discuss data sources, such as scripted data sources that use JavaScript or custom data drivers that use the Open Data Access (ODA) framework. You can find more information about using ODA on the Eclipse web site in the Data Tools project at the following URL:

```
http://www.eclipse.org/datatools/project_connectivity/
```

Working with data sources

To access data for a BIRT report, you use a BIRT data source. A BIRT data source is an object that contains connection parameters. Before you actually begin to create a data source or multiple sources for your first reports, you need to consider the issue of project and resource organization. If you plan to use only a few data sources and create only a few report designs, you might not need to consider longer term issues. BIRT Report Designer is an enterprise-class application; therefore, it provides options that you can use to manage a large number of data sources in multiple projects. If you do plan to re-use a data source in multiple report projects, you can create that data source in a library and reuse that data source from the library. The advantage of this approach is that updates to the BIRT data source in the library are subsequently available to all reports that use the library.

When you create a report design, you use the data explorer, as shown in Figure 6-1, to create and manage BIRT data sources. BIRT Report Designer supports using as many data sources as necessary for the report design. The data sources can be of different types. For example, you can use data from an RDBMS database and data from a flat file repository in the same report design.

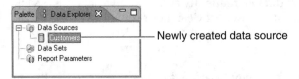

— Newly created data source

Figure 6-1   Data source in the data explorer

By default, BIRT Report Designer provides unique names for BIRT data sources, such as Data Source, Data Source1, and so on. If you prefer, you can provide a descriptive name for each of these data sources. If you do not provide a descriptive name, you may later have to open the BIRT data source and view its definition to remember what data it provides to the report.

How to create a BIRT data source

1   Open or create a report design, then choose Data Explorer.

If you are using the default application window layout, Data Explorer is on the left, next to Palette, as shown in Figure 6-2. If Data Explorer is not visible, choose Window→Show View→Data Explorer.

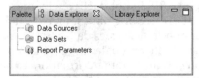

Figure 6-2   The data explorer

2 Right-click Data Sources, then choose New Data Source. New Data Source—Select a Data Source type appears, as shown in Figure 6-3.

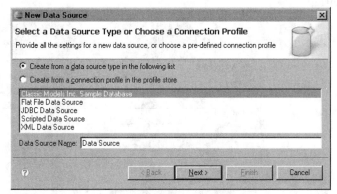

Figure 6-3   Creating a new data source

3 Specify the type and name of the data source.

Specific instructions for this step vary depending on the type of data source that you create. Subsequent sections in this chapter describe how to create the different types of BIRT data sources.

How to modify an existing BIRT data source

You can rename a BIRT data source or modify its connection properties. To rename a BIRT data source, right-click the data source in the data explorer and choose Rename from the context menu. The name that you use must be unique in the report design.

The connection properties for a JDBC data source include the driver name, URL, user name, password, and JNDI URL. To modify the connection properties of a JDBC data source, complete the following procedure:

1 Choose Data Explorer.

2 Expand Data Sources, then right-click the data source that you wish to modify. Choose Edit from the context menu, as shown in Figure 6-4.

Figure 6-4   Data source context menu

Figure 6-5 shows Edit Data Source for a JDBC data source. The options in Edit Data Source vary depending on the type of data source that you are editing.

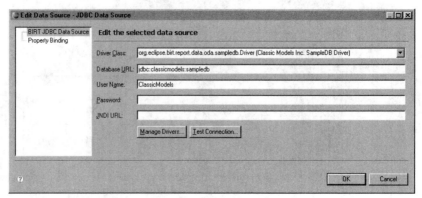

Figure 6-5   Data source connection information

3 Modify the connection information for the data source, then choose OK.

How to delete a BIRT Report Designer data source

Use the following procedure to delete any type of data source.

1 In the data explorer, right-click the data source, and choose Delete from the context menu, as shown in Figure 6-6.

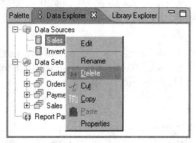

Figure 6-6   Deleting a data source

If any data sets use that data source, BIRT Report Designer displays a list of the data sets in Reference Found, as shown in Figure 6-7.

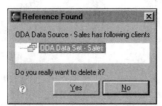

Figure 6-7   Checking dependencies that affect data sets

2 Choose Yes if you want to delete the BIRT data source.

BIRT Report Designer removes the data source from the report design. If a data set uses the deleted data source, the data explorer prepends a symbol to the name of that data set to indicate that it is unusable. In Figure 6-8, the Sales data set is marked as unusable.

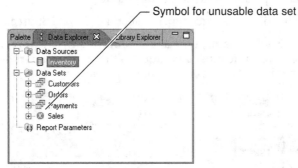

Figure 6-8   An unusable data set

Accessing data using JDBC

You can access data from any database or other data source that uses a JDBC driver. Most relational databases, such as Oracle, SQL Server, or MySQL, use JDBC drivers. To access data from a database or other JDBC data source, you perform sequentially the tasks in the following sections.

Preparing to access a database

You must ensure that the computer has access to the database or other JDBC data source. In addition, you must provide the following information:

- The driver class

  You can select from a list of detected drivers or specify a different class.

- The database URL to use to connect to the data source

- The user name, password, and JNDI URL if the data source requires this information

Creating a JDBC data source

When you create a JDBC data source, you select the driver class and provide a URL. If necessary, you provide a user name, password, and JNDI URL. If you have the appropriate driver, the driver class appears in the Driver Class drop-down list.

You can also design your report so that the report user supplies connection information when the report runs. For example, you can require report users to provide a user name and password when they run the report.

How to specify the connection information for a database or other JDBC data source

1 Create a data source.

2 Specify the type and name of the data source:

    1 In the list of data source types, select JDBC Data Source.

    2 In Data Source Name, type a name for the BIRT Report Designer data source. The name must be unique in the current report design. Figure 6-9 shows a default data source name.

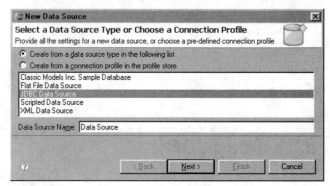

Figure 6-9   Creating a JDBC data source

3 Choose Next.

New JDBC Data Source Profile shows connection information options, as shown in Figure 6-10.

Figure 6-10   Defining JDBC connection information

3 Specify the connection information for the JDBC data source:

    1 In Driver Class, choose a driver class from the drop-down list. If you do not see the driver class that you want to use, add a driver as described later in this chapter.

    2 In Database URL, type the database URL, using the syntax that the driver requires. Typically, BIRT Report Designer displays the necessary syntax in Database URL. For a Sun JDBC/ODBC bridge, the syntax is:

```
jdbc:odbc:<data source name>
```

    where <data source name> is the name of your data source. For example, the following URL identifies the sales database:

```
jdbc:odbc:sales
```

    3 In User Name, type the user name to use when connecting to the JDBC data source. This field can be left blank if your data source does not require a user name.

    4 In Password, type the password to use when connecting to the JDBC data source. This field can be left blank if your data source does not require a password.

    5 In JNDI URL, type a JNDI URL. This field can be left blank if your data source does not require a JNDI URL.

4 To ensure that the connection information is correct, choose Test Connection.

If Test Connection returns an error, repeat the preceding steps to correct the error. Then, test the connection again.

5 Choose Finish.

The new BIRT data source appears under Data Sources in the data explorer.

Managing JDBC drivers

BIRT supports JDBC 3.0 drivers. You can get these drivers from a data source vendor or third-party web site. BIRT Report Designer includes the Apache Derby JDBC driver and the Sun JDBC-ODBC bridge driver as part of a default installation. Use the bridge driver for prototype-development purposes only. We do not recommend using the bridge driver with ODBC data sources that do not have a JDBC driver because it is not a production quality driver. Instead, we recommend using a native JDBC driver whenever possible.

To indicate which drivers are available for use, the JDBC driver manager displays symbols next to the file names in the driver list. An x indicates that a driver is no longer available in the JDBC directory. An asterisk (*) indicates that a file does not exist in the specified location. A plus sign (+) indicates that a file has been restored. For example, in Figure 6-11, the driver manager indicates that the first driver is unavailable.

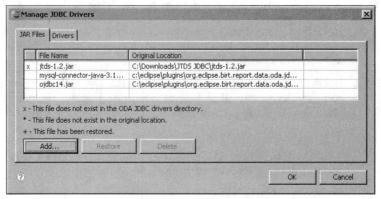

Figure 6-11   Managing JDBC drivers

Adding a JDBC driver

To install other JDBC drivers, use the JDBC driver manager. This tool supports the installation of JAR files that contain JDBC drivers. The selected JAR file is copied to the following directory:

```
eclipse\plugins
    \org.eclipse.birt.report.data.oda.jdbc_2.1.0.N20060628-1351
    \drivers
```

How to add a JDBC driver

If you have an existing JDBC data source, you can add JDBC drivers by editing the data source.

1 In BIRT Report Designer, open an existing report design.

2 Choose Data Explorer.

3 Right-click an existing JDBC data source, then choose Edit from the context menu. Edit Data Source appears, as shown in Figure 6-12.

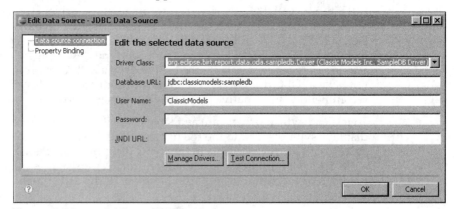

Figure 6-12   Adding a JDBC driver

4 Choose Manage Drivers. The JDBC driver manager appears, as shown in Figure 6-13.

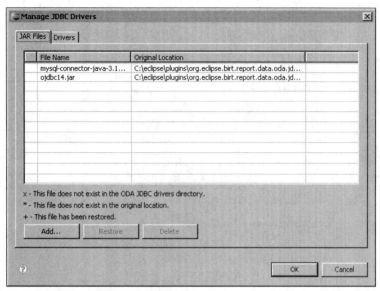

Figure 6-13   Managing JDBC drivers

5 To add the JAR files for the additional driver, choose Add, then navigate to the directory that contains the driver class file. Select the driver JAR file and choose Open.

The driver manager appears, showing the new driver class. BIRT Report Designer copies the JAR file to the Eclipse JDBC directory.

6 Choose Drivers to see the Drivers page, as shown in Figure 6-14.

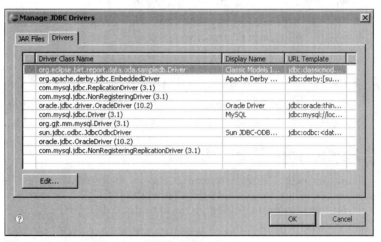

Figure 6-14   Viewing JDBC driver classes

7 Specify the properties for a driver:

    1 Select the new driver, then choose Edit. Edit JDBC Driver appears, as shown in Figure 6-15.

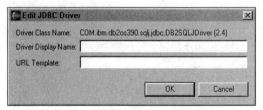

Figure 6-15   Editing a JDBC driver URL template

    2 Specify settings for the JDBC driver:

        1 In Driver Display Name, type a name that appears in the Display Name column in the driver manager.

        2 In URL Template, type the syntax suggestion that appears for this driver in Database URL on New Data Source.

    Choose OK. The driver manager displays the new display name and URL template syntax suggestion.

8 Choose OK. New Data Source—New Data Source appears.

Deleting a JDBC driver

To delete a JDBC driver use the JDBC driver manager. If the JAR file contains more than one driver, the driver manager deletes all drivers that are in the JAR file. If you unintentionally delete a driver, you can use the restore feature to restore the driver.

How to delete all JDBC drivers that are in a JAR file

1 Right-click an existing JDBC data source, then choose Edit from the context menu. Edit Data Source appears.

2 Choose Manage Drivers to open the driver manager.

3 Select the JAR file that contains the driver, then choose Delete.

BIRT Report Designer removes the JAR file and any drivers that it contains. BIRT Report Designer does not delete the JAR file from the operating system.

Restoring JDBC drivers

You can use the JDBC driver manager to restore a driver that was accidentally deleted. When you restore the driver, the JDBC driver manager copies the driver file from a specified location to the JDBC driver folder in your Eclipse installation.

How to restore a JDBC driver

1 In the data explorer, right-click a JDBC data source, then choose Edit from the context menu. Edit Data Source appears.

2 In Edit Data Source, choose Manage Drivers to open the driver manager.

3 Select the driver to restore, then choose Restore. BIRT Report Designer restores the driver from the original location to the Eclipse JDBC driver directory and replaces the asterisk (*) next to the file name with a plus sign (+), as shown in Figure 6-16.

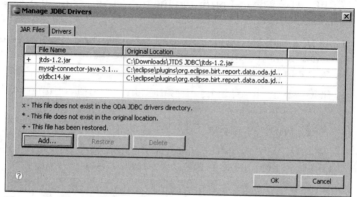

Figure 6-16   JDBC driver restored

Accessing data in text files

BIRT provides a driver that can access data from a text file that contains comma-separated column names and values. To access data from a text file, you perform the tasks in the following sections.

Preparing to access your text file

To use a text file, you must

- Know the file name and location
- Know what character set the file uses
- Confirm that the computer that created the report design has access to the text file

Text file rules

A text file that you use for report data must follow these rules:

- The first line of the text file must contain the names of the columns, separated by commas.

Optionally, you can use the second line of the file to specify the data types of the columns. See Table 6-1 for a list of supported data types. The remaining lines in the file must contain values for the columns, separated by commas. If you use the second line to specify data types, list the data types in the same order as the columns, and separate them with commas.

- Each line must contain the same number of fields.

- The file cannot include empty lines between records.

- Each record must occupy a separate line, delimited by a line break, such as CRLF or LF. The last record in the file can either include or omit an ending line break.

- Data in a field can be surrounded by more than one set of quotation marks. Quotation marks are required only if the data contains one or more commas within a field.

- A field can enclose single quotation marks and commas with double quotation marks, such as:

```
"He said, 'Yes, I do.'"
```

- If a field without content has zero or more spaces, the field is treated as NULL and evaluated as NULL in comparison operations.

- The file name and extension can be any name that is valid for your operating system. You do not have to use TXT or CSV as the file extension.

The following example shows a valid sample text file. The text file has two lines of metadata and three lines of data:

```
FamilyName,GivenName,AccountID,AccountType,Created
STRING,STRING,INT,STRING,TIME
"Smith","Mark",254378,"Monthly",01/31/2003 09:59:59 AM
"Johnson","Carol",255879,"Monthly",09/30/2004 03:59:59 PM
"Pitt","Joseph",255932,,10/01/2005 10:32:04 AM
```

Text file data types

Table 6-1 lists and provides information about the abbreviations that you use for the data types.

Table 6-1   Supported data types in flat files

Abbreviation	Data type	Examples
BIGDECIMAL	java.sql.Types.NUMERIC	
DATE	java.sql.Types.DATE	YYYY-MM-DD or MM/DD/YYYY
		Examples:
		2003-01-31
		01/31/2003

Table 6-1   Supported data types in flat files *(continued)*

Abbreviation	Data type	Examples
DOUBLE	java.sql.Types.DOUBLE	
INT	java.sql.Types.INTEGER	
STRING	java.sql.Types.VARCHAR	
TIME	java.sql.Types.TIME	hh:mm:ss and all DATE format strings such as "YYYY-MM-DD" Examples: 2003-12-31 12:59:59 A 01/31/2003 12:59:59 pm
TIMESTAMP	java.sql.Types.TIMESTAMP	YYYY-MM-DD hh:mm:ss.nnnnnn

Creating a flat file data source

To access a text file, you create a flat file data source and specify its property values, such as the file location and the character set that the file uses. When you create a flat file data source, you select a directory that contains the text file to use. After you create the data source, you can change the file location by editing the data source.

How to specify the connection information for accessing a text file

1   Create a data source.

2   Specify the type and name of the data source:

    1   In Data sources, select Flat File Data Source.

    2   In Data Source Name, type a name for the data source. This name must be unique in the current report design.

    3   Choose Next. New Flat File Data Source Profile—Select Folder appears, as shown in Figure 6-17.

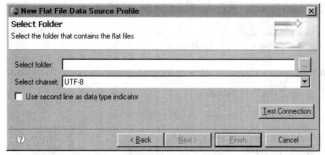

Figure 6-17   Selecting flat file directory and character set

3 Specify the connection information for the text file:

    1 In Select folder, type the location of the folder, or choose the ellipsis (...) button to navigate to and select the folder.

    2 In Select charset, select the character set that the text files in this folder use.

    3 If the second line of the text file specifies the column data types, select Use second line as data type indicator. This setting applies to all data sets that use this data source. Create separate data sources for files that do and do not use the second line to specify the column data type.

4 Choose Finish to display the new data source in the data explorer.

Accessing XML data

BIRT provides a driver to access data structured as XML. To access data from an XML data source, you perform the tasks in the following sections.

Preparing to access XML data

The XML data that a report accesses must well-formed. To be well-formed, it must conform to the XML 1.0, third edition specification. You can find more information about this specification at the following URL:

```
http://www.w3.org/TR/REC-xml/
```

The XML data can be a file, a URL, or a java.io.InputStream. An input stream only works in an embedded application, and you must pass the stream as an AppContext to the Engine API.

You must know the name and location of the XML data. Ensure that your computer has access to the data and that the report developer and report user have the appropriate permissions. BIRT supports good XML usage practices by allowing you to use an XML schema to validate your XML files. A schema is not required unless you want to view the file schema while you design reports.

Creating an XML data source

To access XML data, you create an XML data source and specify its property values, such as the XML file location.

How to specify the connection information for accessing an XML file

1 Create a data source.

2 On New Data Source, in Data sources, select XML Data Source.

3 In Data Source Name, type a name for the data source. The name must be unique in the current report design.

4 Choose Next to display the XML Data Source page, as shown in Figure 6-18.

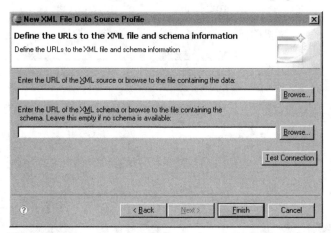

Figure 6-18   Defining XML source and schema information

5 To specify the location of the XML data, type the location of the file in Enter the URL of the XML source, or choose the browse button to navigate to and select the file.

6 If you have an XML schema file, provide the URL. Type the location of the schema file, or choose the browse button to navigate to and select the file. A schema is not required.

7 Choose Finish. The new data source appears under Data Sources in the data explorer.

Setting connection properties when a report runs

When you create a report design, you can use static information to create a BIRT data source and data set. For example, you can provide a user name and password that the report uses to access a database. The database uses whatever roles and privileges are assigned to the hard-coded report user.

If you want to change the report user when the report runs, you must configure your report to enable run-time definition of data source properties. A typical example is allowing a report user to provide his credentials when the report runs. When a user provides a user name and password, the database authentication system determines the correct objects to use to generate the report. To enable this functionality, you create report parameters for the user name and password, then you associate the user name and password data source properties with the report parameters.

How to enable users to provide connection information when a report runs

1 Open or create a report design.

2 In the data explorer, right-click Report Parameters, then choose New Parameter. New Parameter appears, as shown in Figure 6-19.

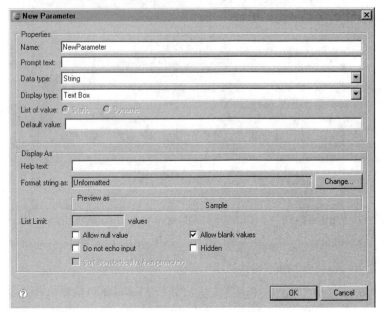

Figure 6-19 Creating parameters for run-time connection

3 Specify the following basic attributes:

   1 In Name, type a name for the report parameter. For example, the following text specifies a user name parameter:

```
username_param
```

   2 In Prompt text, specify a word or sentence to prompt the report user to provide a parameter value.

   3 In Data type, choose a type.

   4 Choose OK. The parameter appears under Report Parameters in the data explorer.

4 Repeat steps 2 and 3 to create an additional report parameter, such as:

```
password_param
```

5 In the data explorer, right-click an existing data source, and choose Edit.

6 In Edit Data Source, choose Property Binding. In Property Binding, the data source properties appear.

7 Specify the report parameters that a report user must provide to access the data source:

   1 To specify a User Name, choose the ellipsis (...) button at the right.

2   In Expression Builder, associate a report parameter with a connection property:

   1   Under Category, choose Report parameters. All appears under Sub-Category.

   2   Choose All. Under Double Click to insert, BIRT Report Designer displays the report parameters that you created.

   3   Double-click the report parameter that you want to bind to the data source property. The report parameter appears in the expression builder's work area. For example, Figure 6-20 shows a parameter, username_param, in the expression builder's work area.

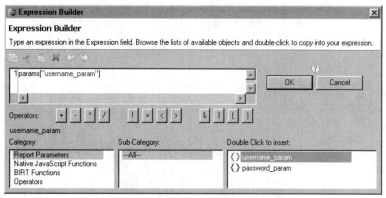

Figure 6-20   Viewing report parameters

   4   Choose OK. The expression builder closes. The report parameter appears in the User Name field.

3   To specify an additional report parameter, repeat steps 1 and 2, for example to bind the report parameter, password_param.

8   In Edit Data Source, choose OK. Preview your report to confirm that the user is prompted for a user name and password.

Troubleshooting data source problems

BIRT Report Designer displays information about data source connection problems in several different places. Error reports can appear in the previewer, the problems view, the error log view, and as pop-up messages. Generally, BIRT Report Designer displays JDBC connection-related problems in pop-up error messages. If the connection information is syntactically correct, but the data source is not available, you see a pop-up message and entries in the error log view.

If a problem is an improperly defined data set, errors appear in the problem view. You cannot manually delete items from the problem view. They display until you resolve the problem or delete the object that is creating the problem.

If you have problems connecting to a data source from BIRT Report Designer, try connecting using a data source manufacturer or third-party tool to confirm that the connection string works as expected. This troubleshooting exercise can help you determine whether to focus your troubleshooting on a driver or on the parameters that you have provided.

If you make changes to your connection parameters and BIRT Report Designer behaves as though it is still using the original values for the parameters, you must restart Eclipse using the -clean option. What has happened is that Eclipse is using cached information that contains the previous values. To clear the cache, the only option is to exit Eclipse and restart using the -clean option.

Retrieving Data

After you create a BIRT data source, you create a data set to specify what data to retrieve from the data source. This chapter discusses the different types of data sets that you create using the graphical tools in BIRT Report Designer: SQL SELECT Query, SQL Stored Procedure Query, Flat File, and XML. Though specific tasks for defining a data set vary depending on the data source type that you are using, the general steps are:

- Defining the name and type of the data set.

- Describing what data to retrieve:

  - For JDBC data sources that use a SQL SELECT query or stored procedure, you define the query or procedure.

  - For data sources that use files or URLs, such as XML or flat file data sources, you provide a URL or file location and map the data into a relational structure of tables and columns.

- Defining any computed fields that you want to use in the data set.

- Defining filters to limit the data that the data set returns to the report.

- Defining parameters to specify, at run time, the data to retrieve from the data source.

Creating a BIRT data set

To create a data set, you must have an existing data source. This section uses a SQL SELECT query to illustrate how to create a data set using a JDBC data source. Specific instructions for creating the various types of data sets appear later in this chapter. Basic data set creation, modification, and deletion operations are the same. For example, you rename or delete a data set in the same way, regardless of the data set type.

How to create a data set

This procedure uses a JDBC data source as an example.

1 Choose Data Explorer.

2 Create a data source, or choose an existing data source.

3 Right-click Data Sets, and choose New Data Set from the context menu.

4 On New Data Set, specify the properties of the data set:

   1 In Data Set Name, specify a name for the data set. The data set name must be unique in the report design.

   2 In Data Source, use the drop-down list to choose a data source to use for this data set.

   3 In Data Set Type, select a data set type. Figure 7-1 shows an example of the definition of a SQL Select Query data set.

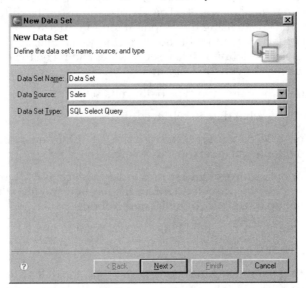

Figure 7-1   Defining a data set

5 Choose Next.

6 On Query, specify the data to retrieve from the data source. Depending on the type of data set that you create—SQL Select Query, or SQL Stored Procedure Query—BIRT Report Designer displays different query syntax in the text area. Figure 7-2 shows the syntax that you see when you select the SQL Select Query data set type.

Figure 7-2   Query options for a SQL Select Query data set

7 When you finish defining the query, choose Finish to save the data set. Edit
Data Set, shown in Figure 7-3, displays the columns you specified in the
query, and provides options for editing the data set.

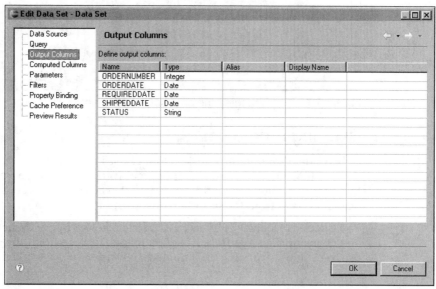

Figure 7-3   The data set editor

Changing the data source for a data set

You typically change the data source a data set uses when you want to change the data source from a test system to a production system. You can change the data source only if the original and new data sources are of the same type. For example, you cannot change from a JDBC data source to an XML data source.

While BIRT Report Designer lets you change to any data source of the same type, it makes sense to change only to a data source that contains the same types of data organized in the same structure, because the data set contains instructions to retrieve a particular set of data that is stored in a particular structure.

How to change the data source for a data set

In Data Explorer, right-click the data set, and choose Edit. On Edit Data Set, choose Data Source, and choose a different data source from the drop-down list, as shown in Figure 7-4, then choose OK.

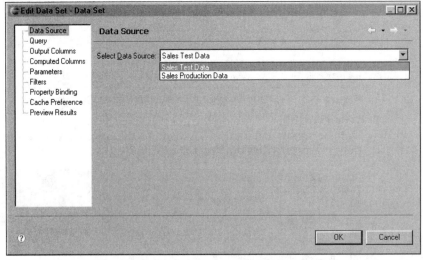

Figure 7-4   Changing the data source for a data set

Deleting a data set

Delete a data set if your report no longer uses the data set. If you try to delete a data set that a report uses, a warning message appears. If you delete a data set that provides data to a report element that is being displayed, and you do not delete the data from the report layout, errors appear in the report preview.

You can delete a data set by using the Delete key or by right-clicking the data set and choosing Delete from the context menu. You can undo the deletion if you use the Undo feature (Ctrl+Z) immediately after you delete the data set.

Selecting data

BIRT uses data based on a relational model. A relational model organizes data in a two-dimensional table consisting of rows and columns. A JDBC data source provides data in exactly this way. For other data sources, such as XML and flat files, you define a mapping so the data can be used in a relational structure of tables, rows, and columns. This section explains how to obtain data from JDBC, flat file, and XML data sources.

Using a SQL query to retrieve data

Typically, a JDBC data set accesses data using a SQL query. A SQL query is a SQL SELECT statement that specifies what data to retrieve from a database or other JDBC data source. Because there are many books about SQL, this section does no more than to discuss how to write a basic SQL SELECT statement and how to combine data from multiple tables.

Creating a SQL query using SELECT

SQL is a query language you use to retrieve data from a database. It describes the data that you want to retrieve, but it does not specify how to retrieve the data. You do not have to know how the data is saved or stored. You simply need to know the names of the tables and columns that are used and understand the relationships among the tables.

A SQL query consists of one or more statements. The first statement of a SQL query is the SELECT statement that specifies which columns you want to retrieve from the database. The SELECT statement contains two required clauses: SELECT and FROM. The SELECT clause lists the columns that you want to retrieve. The FROM clause specifies the table from which you want to get the selected columns of data. Here is an example of a SQL statement that selects the firstname and lastname columns from a table called customers:

```
SELECT customers.firstname, customers.lastname
   FROM customers
```

A SQL SELECT query can also include other statements that limit what data a query returns. You use the WHERE clause to specify criteria that results must meet and use ORDER BY to sort results. Here is an example of the same SQL statement, using the WHERE and ORDER BY clauses:

```
SELECT customers.firstname, customers.lastname
   FROM customers
   WHERE customers.lastname = 'CHANG'
   ORDER BY customers.lastname, customers.firstname
```

Combining data from multiple tables

Typically, you have to select data from two or more tables to get complete data for your report. This operation is called a join. You join tables in a database through a common column called a key. For example, suppose you want to get the orders for every customer. The database, however, stores customer information in a Customers table, and order information in an Orders table, as shown in Figure 7-5. Both tables contain a column called CustomerID. You can join the customers and the orders table using the CustomerID column.

Customers

CustomerID	CustomerName
01	Mark Smith
02	Maria Hernandez
03	Soo-Kim Young
04	Patrick Mason

Orders

OrderID	Amount	CustomerID
110	251.49	02
115	145.75	03
120	176.55	01

Figure 7-5   Database stores customer and order information in two tables

To get order information for every customer, you can use the following SELECT statement:

```
SELECT Customers.CustomerName, Orders.Amount
FROM Customers, Orders
WHERE Customers.CustomerID = Orders.CustomerID
```

The WHERE clause in this example specifies that the query returns rows where the CustomerID in both tables match. Figure 7-6 shows the results that the SELECT statement returns.

Result

CustomerName	Amount
Mark Smith	176.55
Maria Hernandez	251.49
Soo-Kim Young	145.75

Figure 7-6   Results returned by SELECT statement

Alternatively, you can use the JOIN keyword to select data from the two tables. The rest of this section describes the different types of joins you can use, and the results that each join returns. The following SELECT statement uses INNER JOIN and returns the same results shown in Figure 7-6:

```
SELECT Customers.CustomerName, Orders.Amount
FROM Customers
INNER JOIN Orders
ON Customers.CustomerID = Orders.CustomerID
```

The INNER JOIN clause returns all rows from both tables where there is a match. If there are rows in the Customers table that do not match rows in the

Orders table, those rows are not listed. In the example, Patrick Mason is not listed in the result set because this customer does not have a matching order.

To obtain all the customer names, whether or not a customer has an order, use the LEFT JOIN clause:

```
SELECT Customers.CustomerName, Orders.Amount
FROM Customers
LEFT JOIN Orders
ON Customers.CustomerID = Orders.CustomerID
```

LEFT JOIN returns all rows from the first (left) table, even if there are no matches in the second (right) table. Figure 7-7 shows the results of the SELECT statement with the LEFT JOIN clause. Here, Patrick Mason is listed in the result set even though he does not have an order, because the record is in the first table.

Result

CustomerName	Amount
Mark Smith	176.55
Maria Hernandez	251.49
Soo-Kim Young	145.75
Patrick Mason	

Figure 7-7   Results of a left join

Conversely, if you want to get all rows from the second table (the Orders table in our example), even if there are no matches in the first table (the Customers table), use RIGHT JOIN. In our example, all the rows in the second table match rows in the first table, so the result is the same as in Figure 7-7. If, however, the Orders table had contained rows that did not have matches in the Customers table, those rows would also have been returned.

Note that in all the examples, the SELECT statements specify the columns being joined: Customers.CustomerID and Orders.CustomerID. You must specify the columns to join. If you do not, the result is what is commonly referred to as a cartesian join. In a cartesian join, all rows in the first table are joined with all rows in the second table. If the first table has 1000 rows and the second table has 10,000 rows, the cartesian join returns 10,000,000 rows, a result you rarely want.

The inner, left, and right joins are the most common types of joins. For more information about these joins and others that your database supports, see the database manufacturer's documentation.

How to create a SQL query for a JDBC data set

1   In Edit Data Set, choose Query. By default, Available Items displays all schemas in the data source. You can use the filter options to specify schemas or objects to display.

2   To see the tables in a schema, expand the schema, as shown in Figure 7-8.

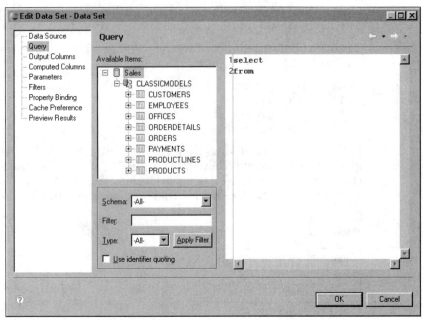

Figure 7-8   Viewing a schema

- If you want to see only views in the JDBC data source, in Type, select View, and choose Apply Filter. If you want to see all tables, views, and stored procedures, select All, and choose Apply Filter.

- If the data source has a large number of objects, you can limit the number of object names that are retrieved by typing one or more letters in the Filter field and choosing Apply Filter. Available Items displays the objects that have names that begin with the same letter or letters that you typed. You also can use SQL filter characters for the database that you are using. For example, on some databases, an underscore (_) matches any single character, and the percent sign (%) matches any sequence of characters.

- If the database supports schemas, a Schema drop-down list is available. Select a schema to display only objects from that schema.

3 To display the columns in a table or view, click the plus sign (+) beside a table or view name. Click the plus sign next to a stored procedure to see its input and output parameters.

4 In the text area, type a SQL statement that indicates what data to retrieve from the JDBC data source. You can also drag tables, views, and columns from Available Items to the text area to insert their names in the SQL statement at the insertion point, as shown in Figure 7-9.

For some databases, if a table or column name contains spaces or SQL reserved words, you must enclose the name in quotation marks (" "). If you drag and drop tables and columns, and those items need to be enclosed in double quotation marks, select the Use identifier quoting option. When this option is selected, the data set editor inserts the quotation marks around a table or column name when you drop it in the text area.

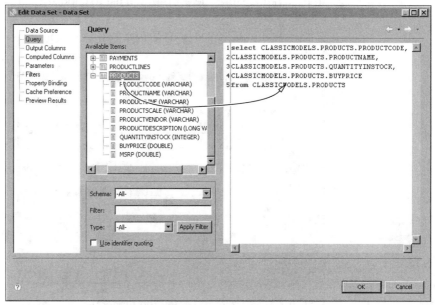

Figure 7-9   Adding a table to a SQL query

5 Choose OK to save the data set.

Using a stored procedure to retrieve data

BIRT Report Designer also supports using a stored procedure to create a data set. Support for stored procedures, however, is limited in important ways. BIRT uses only one result set that is returned by a stored procedure. If your stored procedure returns multiple result sets, only the first result set that it returns is accessible to the BIRT report.

BIRT relies on the capabilities of the underlying JDBC driver in its support for stored procedures. For more robust support, a JDBC driver must fully implement the JDBC interfaces that are related to stored procedures, including those that provide its metadata. The jTDS project on SourceForge.net, for example, provides a pure Java (type 4) JDBC 3.0 driver for Microsoft SQL Server that does support stored procedures.

Unlike SQL queries, stored procedures can have output parameters, so BIRT Report Designer supports previewing output parameters that a stored procedure generates to confirm that the procedure is working as expected.

How to specify a stored procedure for a JDBC data set

1 Create a new data set on a data source that contains a stored procedure.

Specify the properties of the data set:

1 In Data Set Name, specify a name for the data set.

2 In Data Source, use the drop-down list to choose a data source to use for this data set.

3 In Data Set Type, select SQL Stored Procedure Query, as shown in Figure 7-10.

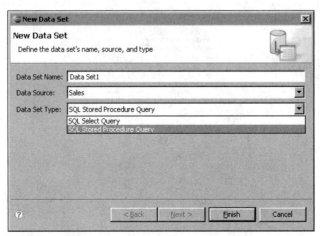

Figure 7-10   Creating a stored procedure

Choose Next. Query displays a template stored procedure, as shown in Figure 7-11.

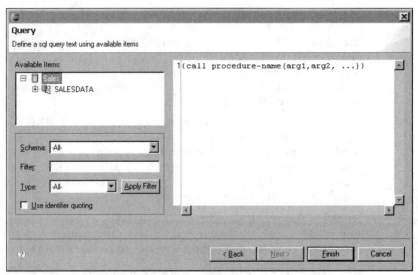

Figure 7-11   Displaying stored procedures in a database

2 In Available Items, navigate to the stored procedure. Select the stored procedure, and drag it to the text area. The stored procedure name appears at the insertion point. In the text area, type the required information to execute the stored procedure. For example, you should include any arguments that are passed to the stored procedure.

To type the stored procedure, enclose the call statement in left and right braces, for example:

```
{call getTable('ClassicModels.Customers')}
{call getClientOrders('103')}
```

If you type the stored procedure without the braces, BIRT treats the statement as a regular RDBMS call, so execution is dependent on the RDBMS of your data source.

3 Choose Finish to save the data set. Edit Data Set displays the columns returned by the stored procedure, and provides options for editing the data set.

Specifying what data to retrieve from a text file

After you create a flat file data source, you create a flat file data set that uses the data source. You cannot use SQL to define what data to select from the file. Rather, you indicate which fields in the file act as columns. In this way, you define a relational structure, the table, rows, and columns, that BIRT can use.

How to create a data set to access data from a text file

1 Create a flat file data set on a flat file data source. Specify the following properties in New Data Set:

   1 In Data Set Name, specify a unique name for the data set.

   2 In Data Source, use the drop-down list to choose the flat file data source to use for this data set, then choose Next.

2 On Select Columns, in File filter, select the file-name extension that the text file uses.

3 In Select file, select a text file from the drop-down list. The left pane displays the columns that are available in the selected file.

4 In the left pane, below Select file, select the columns to retrieve for the data set, and move them to the right pane. You can select columns in a few ways:

   ▪ Select a column, then choose Select.

   ▪ Press Shift while you click to select multiple columns, then choose Select.

   ▪ Choose Select All to include all columns. Figure 7-12 illustrates a text file in which all columns are selected.

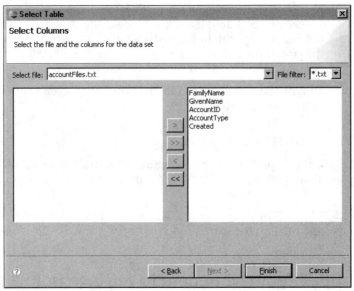

Figure 7-12　　Selecting columns from a text file

5 Choose Finish to save the data set. Edit Data Set displays the columns you
selected, and provides options for editing the data set.

Specifying what data to retrieve from an XML data source

After you create an XML data source, you can create an XML data set that uses
the data source. BIRT uses XPath expressions to define paths to XML elements
and attributes that act as tables and columns. In this way, you can map a
relational structure that BIRT can use to retrieve the data. A single XML data
source can be used to make any number of data sets, but a single XML data set
can include only one table definition, and can return only one result set.

BIRT uses an XPath implementation that uses Document Object Model (DOM),
which means that the available memory of your system limits the size of the
XML document that you can use. You should test your XML documents to
ensure that they will work as needed. To use large XML documents, you must
implement an XPath implementation that uses Simple API for XML (SAX).

To define a table and columns in an XML document, you use a wizard to select
XML elements and attributes, and BIRT creates the corresponding XPath
expressions. You can also manually write or edit XPath expressions. This section
defines the most common ways to write an XPath expression to use an element
or attribute as a table or column in an XML data set. This section is not a
substitute for formal XPath user documentation. Examples in this section refer
to sample XML data that appear at the end of the section.

The most important syntax rules to consider when you create XPath expressions to define tables and columns are:

- Any path that starts with a forward slash (/) is an absolute path.

- The XPath expression that defines the table mapping must be an absolute path, for example:

  ```
  /library/book
  ```

- A path is considered relative to the table level that is defined when the XML data set was created, unless it begins with a forward slash.

- You can only use XPath expressions that locate elements along parent-child axes. For example, the following path is not acceptable:

  ```
  book/library
  ```

  The following path is acceptable:

  ```
  /library/book
  ```

- For attribute paths you can use a single forward slash or left and right brackets. For example, the following paths are equivalent:

  ```
  title/@lang
  title[@lang]
  ```

- To define an element's attribute as a column, use either of the following syntax forms:

  ```
  author/@name
  author[@name]
  ```

- To define a table-level attribute as a column, use either of the following syntax forms:

  ```
  /@category
  [@category]
  ```

- To filter data rows, you can use either of the following predicate expression syntaxes:

  - Single-position predicates in the abbreviated form. The following example selects the first author listed:

    ```
    author[1]
    ```

  - Single-equality conditions based on an attribute value. For example, you can select an element by using the value of an attribute of the element. In this example, only books that are in English are selected:

    ```
    title[@lang='eng']
    ```

- XPath functions are not supported.

The examples in the instructions in this section use the following XML data:

```xml
<?xml version="1.0"?>
<library>
  <book category="COOKING">
    <title lang="es">The Spanish Cook Book</title>
    <author name="Miguel Ortiz" country="es"/>
    <year>2005</year>
  </book>
  <book category="CHILDREN">
    <title lang="en">Everyone is Super Special</title>
    <author name="Sally Bush" country="us"/>
    <year>2005</year>
  </book>
  <audio format="CD" category="MUSIC">
    <title lang="en">We All Sing Perty</title>
    <artist name="Mary Rogers" country="us"/>
    <year>2005</year>
  </audio>
  <audio format="CD" category="MUSIC">
    <title lang="en">The Bluest Blues</title>
    <artist name="Barry Sadley" country="us"/>
    <year>2005</year>
  </audio>
</library>
```

How to create a data set to access data from an XML file

1 Create an XML data set on an XML data source. Specify the following properties in New Data Set:

   1 In Data Set Name, specify a unique name for the data set.

   2 In Data Source, use the drop-down list to select an XML data source to use for this data set, then choose Next.

2 On XML Data Set, specify the XML source in one of the following ways:

- In the text box, type the path to the XML data, or choose Browse to navigate to and select an XML file.

- To use the file specified in the data source definition, select Use the XML file defined in data source.

When you finish, choose Next.

3 Define the table mapping:

   1 In XML Structure, navigate to the element in the XML data that represents the table level of your data, and select the element. Choose the right arrow. The XPath expression appears.

2   Select the XPath expression that defines the path to the record-level element in your XML data, as shown in Figure 7-13, then choose OK.

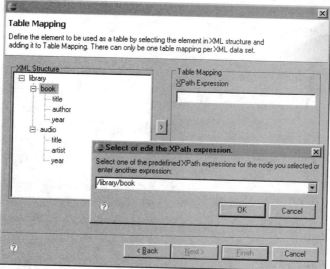

Figure 7-13   Creating an XML data set

3   Choose Next.

4   Define the column mapping:

1   In XML structure, navigate to and select the element or attribute in the XML data that represents a column, then choose the right arrow. Column Mapping displays the default column mapping properties for the element or attribute you selected. Figure 7-14 shows an example of the default column mapping for an attribute named category.

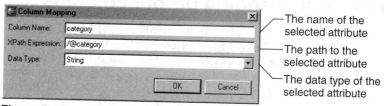

Figure 7-14   Column mapping properties

2   On Column Mapping, you can edit the column mapping properties. Choose OK. The column is displayed and can be edited.

□   To directly edit a path, select the XPath field, and edit the path.

□   To remove a column, select the column, and choose the red x to delete the mapping.

□   In Table Preview, choose the Preview button to see a sample of your data. See Figure 7-15 for an example.

5 Repeat the preceding steps for every column that you want to add. Figure 7-15 shows an example of column mappings in an XML data set.

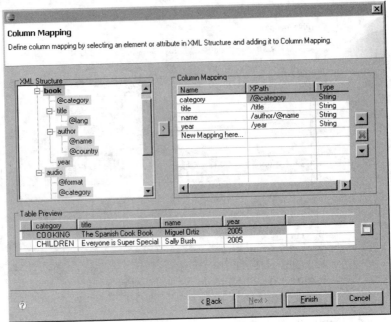

Figure 7-15   Mapping columns for an XML data set

6 Choose Finish to save the XML data set. Edit Data Set displays the columns you mapped, and provides options for editing the data set.

Viewing and changing output columns

In Output Columns, you optionally can add an alias or display name for each column. BIRT Report Designer uses the display name in Data Explorer and for the column headings in a table. For example, you can give a column that is named $$CN01 a display name of Customer Name to make the column easier to identify in Data Explorer and more user-friendly in the column heading of a table.

Use an alias if you want to use a shorter or more recognizable name when you refer to the column in code. For example, you can give a column named $$CN01 an alias of custName so that you can write row["custName"] instead of row["$$CN01"]. If you do not specify a display name for the column, BIRT Report Designer displays the alias in Data Explorer and for the column headings in a table.

How to view and change output columns

1 To verify the list of columns selected for retrieval, choose Output Columns from the left pane of Edit Data Set. Output Columns displays the names of the columns, as shown in Figure 7-16.

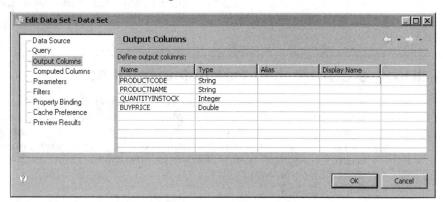

Figure 7-16   Viewing the output columns for a data set

2 In Display Name, for a column that you want to change, type the name of the column to be displayed as the default column heading in the report, then choose OK.

Previewing a data set

You can use Preview Results to verify that the data set returns the expected data. Figure 7-17 shows an example of a result set returned by a JDBC data set. Preview Results shows up to 500 data rows that are returned by the query or data definition in the data set. If you expect to preview data frequently, or if you are working with large or complex data sets, you can configure the data set cache, so you can work more efficiently.

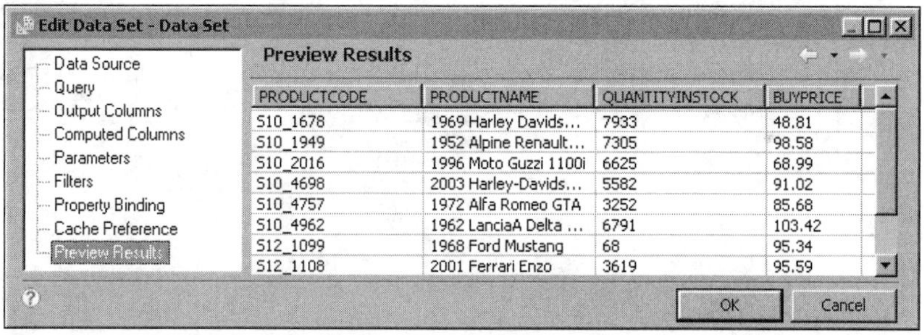

Figure 7-17   Previewing the results of a data set

How to change the number of rows that appear in Preview Results

1 Choose Window➤Preferences.

2 On Preferences, click the plus sign (+) beside Report Design to expand the item.

3 Choose Data Set Editor.

4 On Preferences—Data Set Editor, in Maximum number of rows to display, type the number of rows to display, then choose OK.

Adding a computed field to a data set

A data set can contain computed data as well as data that is returned from a data source. Computed data displays the result of an expression, typically involving one or more columns from a data source. For example, if each row that is returned from the data source contains a price and a quantity, you can create a computed field that calculates the total amount paid, using the following expression:

```
row["pricequote"] * row["quantity"]
```

You also can concatenate values from multiple fields, using the + operator, or calculate values using JavaScript functions. The expression builder provides a list of operators and functions that you can use to build expressions.

You can also define a computed field in the report layout. Defining computed fields in the data set is, however, the preferred approach. Defining the computed field in the data set separates business logic from the presentation of the data. Defining the computed field in the data set also enables you to verify the results of the calculation in the Preview Results page of Edit Data Set. You can determine whether the expression for the computed field is correct before you work on the report layout and how to display the computed field. Figure 7-18 shows an example computed field, Total_cost.

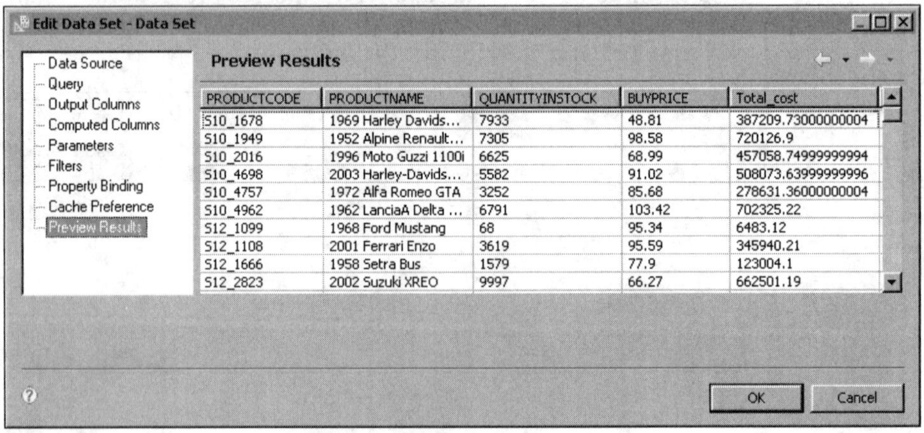

Figure 7-18   An example computed field, Total_cost

How to add a computed field to a data set

1 In Edit Data Set, choose Computed Columns, then specify a computed field:

   1 In Column Name, select the first empty row, and type the name of the computed field.

   2 In Data Type, select a data type for the computed column.

   3 In Expression, specify the expression to calculate the desired value. You can either type the expression or use the expression builder to construct the expression. To use the expression builder, complete the following steps:

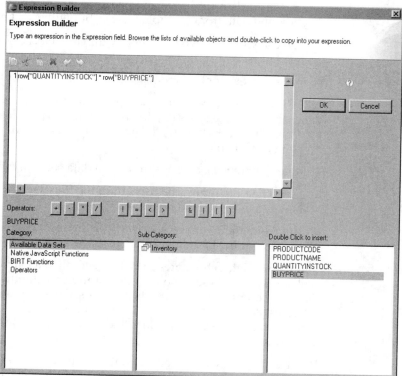

   1 Choose the ellipsis (...) button to open the expression builder. In Category, select Available Data sets, then select your data set.

   In the top pane, type an expression. You can also double-click an item to add it to the expression at the insertion point. Figure 7-19 shows how to create an expression for a computed column.

Figure 7-19   Creating an expression for a computed column

2 Choose OK. Computed Columns displays the computed field and expression that you created.

2 To see all the columns that are specified in the data set, choose Output Columns.

3 Choose Preview Results to confirm that the computed field returns the correct data.

4 Choose OK. BIRT Report Designer saves the data set.

Joining data sets

The capability to join data sets is a useful and easy way to combine data from two data sources. You can, for example, combine data from two XML files, or combine data from a text file with data from a database table. Before you can join data sets, you must, of course, create the individual data sets. For example, to combine data from an XML file with data from a text file, you must first create the XML data set and the text file data set.

Joining data sets is similar to joining tables in a database, described earlier in "Combining data from multiple tables," but with two limitations:

■ You can join only two data sets. Within a database, you can join more than two tables.

■ You can create only three types of joins: inner, left outer, and right outer.

Like the database joins, you must specify a column on which to join the two data sets. The three types of joins you can use to join data sets yield the same results as the similarly-named database joins. The following list summarizes the function of each join type:

■ Inner join returns all rows from both data sets if there is a match.

■ Left outer join returns all rows from the first data set, even if there are no matches in the second data set.

■ Right outer join returns all rows from the second data set, even if there are no matches in the first data set.

Joining two data sets creates a BIRT object called a joint data set. Just as you can with a regular data set, you can add computed columns and filters to a joint data set, and preview the results it returns. Once you understand well the concepts of joining data sets, you can be creative about combining data from more than two sources, assuming the data from the various sources relate in some way.

While each joint data set can join only two data sets, you can use a joint data set as one or both of those data sets. For example, you can create joint data set A and joint data set B, then join both of them. Doing so, in effect, combines data from four data sets. Figure 7-20 illustrates this concept.

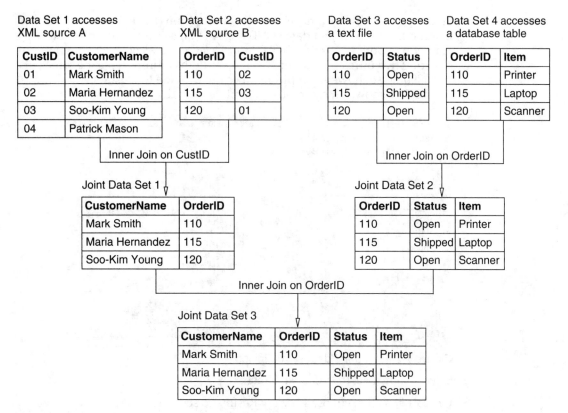

Figure 7-20 Combining data from four data sets

As Figure 7-20 shows, each data set can return data from different types of sources. You could also use joint data sets to join multiple tables in a single database. For performance reasons, however, this technique is not recommended. Where possible, you should always join multiple tables through the SELECT statement, as described earlier in this chapter. You should create joint data sets only to:

- Combine data from disparate data sources.

- Combine data from non-relational data sources, such as XML files or text files.

How to join data sets

1　In Data Explorer, right-click Data Sets, and choose New Joint Data Set.

2　On the left of New Data Set, click the arrow button, and from the drop-down list, choose the first data set for the joint data set. The columns of the first data set appear.

3　On the right of New Data Set, choose the second data set for the joint data set. The columns of the second data set appear.

4 Select the columns to join. Select one column from the first data set, and one column from the second data set. Typically, you select the columns that are common to both data sets. BIRT Report Designer does not prevent you from selecting two unrelated columns as long as both columns have the same data type. Doing so, however, typically does not provide the results you want. Figure 7-21 shows an example of a joint data set definition.

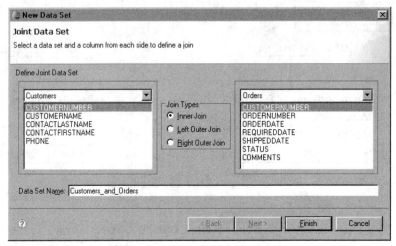

Figure 7-21   Joint data set definition

5 Select a join type, then choose Finish.

6 On Edit Data Set, choose Preview Results to see the rows returned by the joint data set.

Using additional data set options

Depending on the type of the data source, you may have additional options that you can set when you define the data set. Specifically, you can create a dynamic query that accepts input from a user when the report runs. You can also set a query time-out setting and define data set cache preferences to improve the efficiency of your work as you develop a report.

Creating a dynamic query

Even if you do not know how to program in Java or JavaScript, you can define a dynamic query that accepts input from a user when the report runs.

How to define a dynamic query

1 On the Query page of a data set, define a SQL query, such as:

```
SELECT CUSTOMERNAME FROM CUSTOMERS
```

2 Create a table in the report layout that uses this data set.

3 Create a report parameter, such as a String parameter called "passName".

4 In Edit Data Set, choose Property Binding, and define the query text to use the report parameter that you created:

```
"SELECT CustomerName From CUSTOMERS WHERE CustomerName LIKE '"
    + params["passName"] + "'"
```

5 Choose OK.

Setting data set cache preferences

While you create a report, you frequently preview results to confirm that the report is working as expected. If you are working with a large or complex data source, you can spend a considerable amount of time waiting for data to appear. You can use the BIRT Report Designer cache to store some or all of a data set to reduce the time to display the data preview. BIRT Report Designer uses the system's temporary directory to store the cache.

BIRT Report Designer invalidates the data set cache whenever you change the data set name, query definition, data set definition, or data source. BIRT Report Designer refreshes the cache the first time that you preview the report after you make any of these changes.

BIRT Report Designer uses data set cache preferences when you design a report. These preferences are not used when a report runs after it is deployed.

How to set cache preferences

1 In Edit Data Set, choose Cache Preference. Cache Preference displays the data set caching options.

2 Choose Cache data set data for report preview. BIRT Report Designer enables the cache options.

3 Specify the size limit of the data set cache. Figure 7-22 shows a sample configuration.

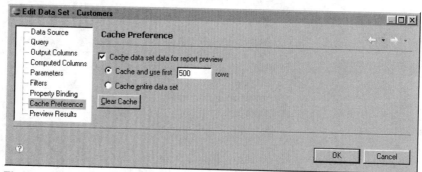

Figure 7-22   Setting data set cache preferences

- To cache a portion of the data set, select Cache and use first, then type the number of rows to cache in the rows box.

- To cache the entire result set, select Cache entire data set.

- To clear the cache, choose Clear Cache. After you choose Clear Cache, BIRT Report Designer displays a message that states that the cache has been cleared.

4 Choose OK.

8

Binding Data

The data set or data sets you create return the data you want to use in a report. Before you can use or display data set data in a report, you must first create the necessary data bindings. As the first tutorial demonstrated, to display the data in a report, you simply drag data set fields from Data Explorer to a table in the layout editor.

You might also remember in that same tutorial that when you dragged a data set field to the layout editor, BIRT Report Designer first displayed a dialog called Select Data Binding. This dialog, shown in Figure 8-1, shows the data binding that BIRT Report Designer creates each time you insert a data set field. This data binding, called a column binding, defines an expression that specifies what data to display. The column binding also defines a name that report elements use to access data.

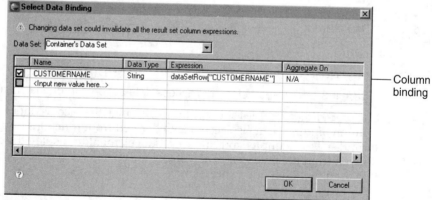

Figure 8-1   Select Data Binding showing a column binding

Understanding column bindings

For each piece of data to display in a report, there must be a column binding. For this discussion, note that data refers to dynamic data, and not static text that you type for a label. Dynamic data is data from a data set, or data that is calculated from a function or a formula. The data is dynamic, because the values are not fixed at design time.

The default column binding, which BIRT Report Designer creates for a data set field, uses the data set field name as the name of the column binding. You can change the name of the column binding, and you might want to do so if the data set field name is not descriptive. In Figure 8-1, the expression defined for the column binding is dataSetRow["CUSTOMERNAME"]. This expression indicates that the column binding accesses data from the data set field, CUSTOMERNAME. In the layout editor, the column-binding name appears within square brackets ([ ]) in the report, as shown in Figure 8-2.

Default label ─────── CUSTOMERNAME

Column-binding ─── [CUSTOMERNAME]
name
　　　　　　　　　　　Footer Row

　　　　⊞ Table

Figure 8-2　　　Data element displaying the column-binding name

Column bindings form an intermediate layer between data set data and report elements—such as chart, data, dynamic text, and image elements—that display data. Figure 8-3 illustrates this concept. Report elements can access data only through column bindings.

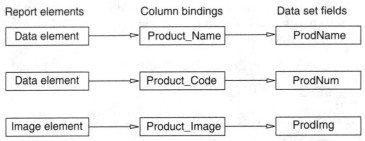

Figure 8-3　　　Report elements access data set data through column bindings

The preceding examples show column bindings that access data set data. Column bindings can also access data derived from functions or user-defined formulas. For example, you can use a data element to display the current date derived from the JavaScript Date object. You would create a column binding that used the following expression:

```
new Date()
```

Figure 8-4 shows this column binding defined in Select Data Binding.

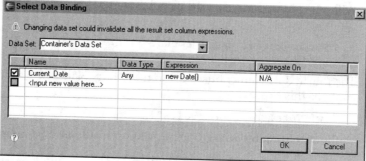

Figure 8-4   User-defined column binding

Descriptive names

One of the benefits of using column bindings is that you control the names used in the report. Instead of displaying data set field names, which are often not descriptive enough, or formulas, which can be long, you can specify short and descriptive names. If you share report designs with other report developers, descriptive names make that design much easier to understand. Modifying and maintaining a report design that has user-friendly names is easier. When deciding what names to use, consider that, in the layout editor, elements display up to 20 characters.

Dynamic updates of calculated data

Another advantage of column bindings becomes apparent when you work with calculated data. When a report needs to display a series of related calculated data, column bindings enable you to create and update calculations easily. For example, assume a report contains the following four data elements:

- The first data element uses column binding, Total_National_Sales, which defines the following expression to calculate the sum of all order amounts:

```
Total.sum(row["Order_Amount"])
```

- The second data element uses column binding, Total_State_Sales, which defines the following expression to calculate the sum of order amounts in each state:

```
Total.sum(row["Order_Amount"])
```

This expression is the same as the previous expression, but both return different results, because they perform the aggregate calculation over different sets of rows.

- The third data element uses column binding, Percent_State_Sales, which uses the previous column bindings to calculate a state's total sales as a percentage of the overall sales. The expression is:

```
row["Total_State_Sales"]/row["Total_National_Sales"] * 100
```

Without column bindings, the calculation would have to be more complicated:

```
Total.sum(row["Order_Amount"], null, "state")/
    Total.sum(row["Order_Amount"], null, "overall") * 100
```

■ The fourth data element uses column binding, National_Profit, which contains this expression:

```
row["Total_National_Sales"] - row["Total_Costs"]
```

Without column bindings, this calculation would also be more complicated:

```
Total.sum(row["Order_Amount"], null, "overall") -
    Total.sum(row["Item_Cost"])
```

You have already seen how column bindings make expressions shorter and more readable. Now, consider the case where you need to update one calculation that is used by other calculations. Suppose you need to change how the total national sales is calculated, from

```
Total.sum(row["Order_Amount"])
```

to

```
Total.sum(row["Order_Amount"]) -
    Total.sum(row["Order_Amount"]) * 0.08
```

Because the third and fourth data elements use the total national sales calculation in their calculations, without column bindings, you would have to manually edit those calculations as well. Without column bindings, you would have to revise the expression for the fourth element as follows:

```
(Total.sum(row["Order_Amount"]) -
    Total.sum(row["Order_Amount"]) * 0.08) -
    Total.sum(row["Item_Cost"])
```

By using column bindings, any change to the first calculation automatically applies to the third and fourth calculations. Instead of modifying three expressions, you modify only one. Your work is faster and less error-prone.

Creating column bindings

As discussed previously, when you drag a data set field from Data Explorer to a table in the layout editor, BIRT Report Designer creates the column binding. The table that contains the data set fields displays the list of column bindings when you select the table and choose the Binding tab on Property Editor. Figure 8-5 shows an example of a table's binding information.

In Figure 8-5, the CUSTOMERNAME, PHONE, and COUNTRY column bindings were generated by BIRT Report Designer when the data set fields, CUSTOMERNAME, PHONE, and COUNTRY were inserted in the table.

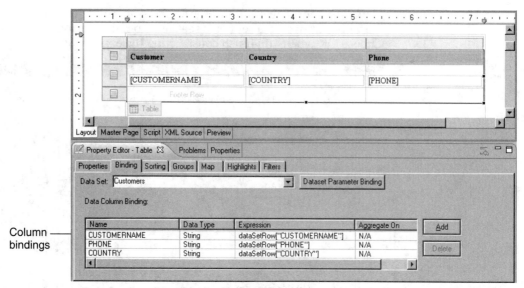

Figure 8-5   Binding information for a selected table

Column bindings

When you insert a dynamic text, text, image, or data element from the palette, you must manually create the column binding if you want the element to display dynamic data. If the information to display is static—for example, a specific image stored in a file system, or literal text—then column binding is not applicable.

How to create a column binding

This procedure shows an example of creating a column binding for a data element that was added to the report shown in Figure 8-5.

1 Drag a data element from the palette and drop it in the table. Select Data Binding displays all the column bindings defined previously for elements in the table.

2 Create a new column binding:

   1 Select the first empty row and, in Name, specify a unique name for the column binding.

   2 In Data Type, select a data type appropriate for the data returned by the expression you specify next. If you are not sure what the data type is, use the default type, Any.

   3 In Expression, specify the expression that indicates the data to return, using one of the following methods:

      ❏ Type the expression directly in the Expression field.

      ❏ If you need help constructing the expression, click in the empty field, then choose the ellipsis button to launch Expression Builder.

Figure 8-6 shows an expression in Expression Builder that combines the values of two data set fields selected from the Customers data set. Choose OK when you finish constructing the expression.

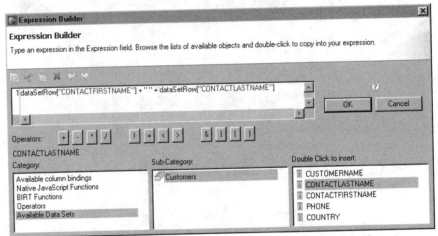

Figure 8-6   Expression Builder showing a column-binding expression

4   In Aggregate On, use the default value, N/A. The Aggregate On option applies only to aggregate expressions that perform calculations over a specified set of data rows.

Figure 8-7 shows an example of a completed column binding.

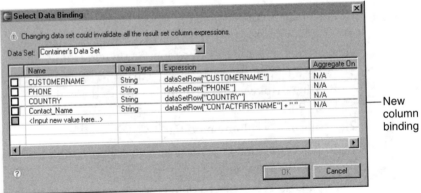

Figure 8-7   Example of a user-defined column binding

3   Select the column binding you created by clicking the check box next to the column-binding name, then choose OK. The data element uses the selected column binding. When you preview the report, the data element displays the data defined in the column binding.

Editing and deleting column bindings

Be careful when editing or deleting column bindings. More than one element can use a column binding, and a column binding can refer to other column bindings. Renaming or deleting a column binding that is used by multiple elements often results in errors in the report design. Consider the following scenario:

BIRT Report Designer creates a column binding named CUSTOMER_COUNTRY at the table level that refers to the data set field, CUSTOMER_COUNTRY, when you drop the field in a table. You create a sort condition to display rows alphabetically by country names. The sort expression uses the CUSTOMER_COUNTRY column binding. Later, you select the data element that uses CUSTOMER_COUNTRY, and you change the column-binding name to COUNTRY. When you run the report, you get an error message, because the sort expression still refers to the CUSTOMER_COUNTRY column binding, which no longer exists. Similarly, if you delete the CUSTOMER_COUNTRY column binding, the same error occurs, because the sort expression now refers to a non-existent column binding.

If you edit the name of a column binding, you need to manually update all other elements that refer to the column binding. In the previous example, you would need to edit the table's Sort Key value to use the renamed column binding. Do not confuse this type of change with changes to a column binding's defined expression. Earlier in this chapter, you saw examples of how a change to a calculated-data expression cascaded to other expressions that used the higher level expression. Remember these guidelines:

- A change to a column binding's expression applies to other column bindings that refer to that column binding.

- A change to a column binding's name does not change other references to that column binding. Column-binding names are case sensitive. COUNTRY and Country are two different names.

More about column-binding expressions

When you write an expression for a column binding, the expression can refer to data set fields, other column bindings, functions, and operators. Until you become familiar with writing expressions, you should use Expression Builder to construct expressions. Expression Builder displays the items—data set fields, column bindings, functions, and so on—that you can use in a column-binding expression.

The items available in Expression Builder change depending on where you define the column binding. For example, if you insert a data element in a table that contains other column bindings, the data element can access those column bindings. If you insert a data element directly on the report page, the data element cannot access column bindings defined for the table or any other report element.

When you select an item in Expression Builder, Expression Builder adds the item to the expression with the proper syntax. When a column-binding expression refers to a data set field, the syntax is:

```
dataSetRow["datasetField"]
```

When a column-binding expression refers to another column binding, the syntax is:

```
row["columnBinding"]
```

If you use Expression Builder to construct column-binding expressions, you do not need to remember what syntax to use. You will find it helpful, though, to understand what each syntax means, because the expression examples that appear throughout the book use both syntaxes.

IV

Designing Reports

9

Laying Out a Report

You can present information in a report in many ways. You can display information in a tabular list, a nested list, a chart, a series of text blocks, or a series of subreports. More complex report layouts can use a variety of these different presentations in a single report. Laying out a report entails placing data on the page and organizing the information in a way that helps a user to read and understand the information in the report.

Because there are infinite ways to lay out a report, it helps to work from a paper design. If you try to design and create the report layout at the same time, you can lose track of the data that you want to place in the report, or you can finish laying out one part of the report before you realize that you can better present the data using another layout.

Before you begin to lay out your report, verify in Data Explorer that your data set or data sets return the data that you want to use in your report. In many cases, the layout of a report is driven by the data.

Understanding the layout model

Like most documents, reports tend to be very structured. A report typically consists of distinct sections or a series of content blocks, as shown in Figure 9-1. BIRT Report Designer provides an intuitive way to lay out a report. A visual layout editor displays a page to which you add content, such as data fields, charts, pictures, or text blocks, in each section of the report.

A section can consist of one or multiple elements. The first section of a report, for example, is typically the report title. This section might contain just one text element. Another section, which displays a list of customer records, might

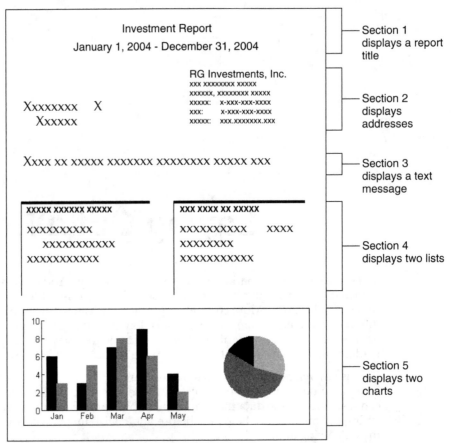

Figure 9-1   Report sections

contain four data fields and four column headings. More complex sections can contain multiple subsections to display items such as multiple lists that appear side by side or a combination of lists, charts, and text blocks. A key concept to understand about sections is that each section is a horizontal block of content.

You lay out the contents of each section of a report in the same way that you read a report—you start from the top of the report and go from left to right until the end of the report. By dividing a report into sections, you can manipulate each section independently. For example:

- Use a different set of data for each section.

- Size and format each section independently.

- Specify page breaks before or after each section.

- Conditionally show or hide each section.

About the report layout elements

BIRT Report Designer provides a variety of elements for building a report. To lay out a report, you drag report elements from the palette and drop them on the page in the layout editor. Report elements fall into two general categories:

- Elements that display information
- Elements that organize multiple elements in a section

Table 9-1 provides a summary of the report elements that you can use to lay out your report. Details about using these report elements appear later in this chapter or elsewhere in this book.

Table 9-1   Report layout elements

Report element	Description
Label	Displays a piece of static text.
Text	Displays text that can contain HTML formatting and dynamic values.
Dynamic text	Displays memo or CLOB (Character Large Object) data from a data set field. The data typically consists of large amounts of text.
Data	Displays a computed value or a value from a data set field.
Image	Displays any image that a web browser supports.
Chart	Displays data from a data set in a variety of chart types, including pie charts, bar charts, and line charts.
Grid	Organizes multiple report elements in a static table.
Table	Organizes data from a data set in a dynamic table.
List	Organizes data from a data set in a variety of layouts. By contrast, a table element organizes elements in a row-and-column format only.

Overview of the layout process

To lay out a report, follow these general steps:

- Identify the sections in your report.
- For each section, insert either:
  - A single report element, such as a text element
  - A container element to organize multiple report elements in a section
- For sections that contain multiple elements, insert report elements in each container. You can insert containers within a container to create nested sections.

- Preview each section as you complete it. If you wait until you finish laying out the report before you verify the output, and there are errors, it can be difficult to determine which part of the report causes the problems.

Creating the sections of a report

Most sections in a report contain multiple elements. BIRT Report Designer provides three types of containers for organizing elements in a section:

- Grid
- Table
- List

The following sections describe each container element.

Organizing elements in a grid

Use a grid to arrange static elements, such as text and pictures, in a section. The grid is similar to the HTML table in a web page. It is ideal for creating report title sections and page headers and footers, as shown in Figure 9-2 and Figure 9-3.

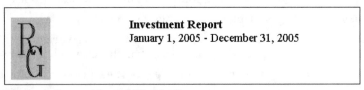

Figure 9-2   Report title section

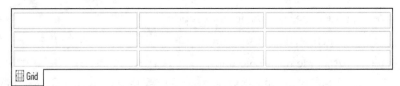

Figure 9-3   Report footer section

When you place a grid on the page, the layout editor displays a row-and-column structure, such as the one shown in Figure 9-4. By default, all the columns have the same width. All the rows have the same height.

Figure 9-4   Row-and-column structure of a grid

The grid layout automates the task of aligning blocks of content. When you place report elements in the cells, the report elements are automatically aligned horizontally and vertically. If you have used other reporting tools that provide a free-form layout editor that lack this capability, you will appreciate the automatic alignment feature that the grid provides. Placing report elements and then aligning them manually is time-consuming.

Using BIRT Report Designer, you can add, delete, and resize rows and columns in the grid, as needed. Figure 9-5 shows a report title section that consists of a picture and two text elements, arranged in a grid with one row and two columns of different sizes.

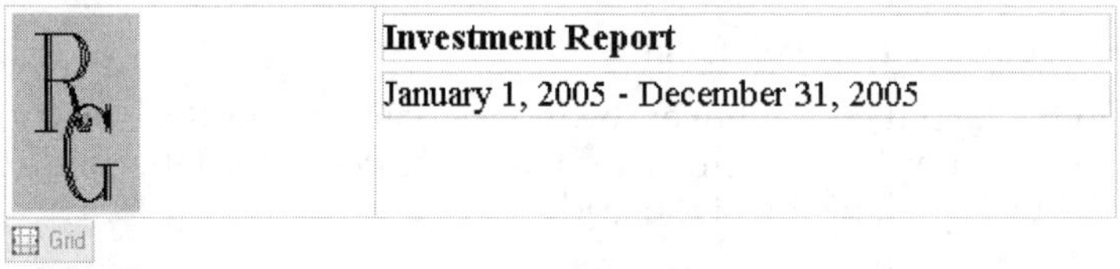

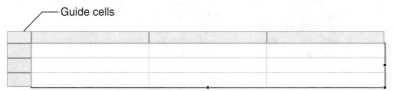

Figure 9-5   Grid with rows and columns resized

You can also format individual rows, columns, and cells to customize their size, color, borders, and text alignment. Chapter 11, "Formatting Report Content," describes these tasks.

Adding rows and columns

When you insert a grid, you specify the number of rows and columns that you want to start with. Depending on the number of report elements that you place in the grid, you might need to add rows or columns later.

How to add a row or column

1   In the layout editor, hover the mouse pointer over the bottom left corner of the grid until you see the Grid tab, then choose the tab. Guide cells appear at the top and left side of the grid, as shown in Figure 9-6.

Guide cells

Figure 9-6   Guide cells support adding rows and columns

2   Right-click the guide cell next to where you want to add a row or column.

3   Choose one of the following items from the context menu to add a row or column in the desired location:

- Insert➤Row➤Above

- Insert➤Row➤Below

- Insert→Column to the Right
- Insert→Column to the Left

Deleting rows and columns

When you insert a grid, you specify the number of rows and columns that you want. If you do not place report elements in all the rows or columns, you can delete the empty rows and columns, so the grid takes less space in the layout editor. By default, empty rows and columns do not appear as blank space in the generated report. If you want an empty row or column to appear as blank space, set the row or column to a specific size.

How to delete a row or column

1 In the layout editor, hover the mouse pointer over the bottom left corner of the grid until you see the Grid tab, then choose the tab. Guide cells appear at the top and left side of the grid.

2 Right-click the guide cell of the row or column that you want to delete. If the row or column contains elements, the elements are also deleted.

3 Choose Delete from the context menu.

Organizing elements in a table

Use a table to display dynamic data in a row-and-column format. Dynamic data is data from a data source, such as a database or XML document. The data is dynamic, because the values are not fixed in the report design. Instead, when the report runs, the report connects to the data source, retrieves the specified data, and displays the current data. Figure 9-7 shows an example table that displays customer names and phone numbers from a data source.

Customer	Phone
Advanced Design Corp.	(914) 555-6707
CompuEngineering	(518) 555-3942
CompuSolutions Co.	(201) 555-9867
Computer MicroSystems Corp.	(508) 555-7307
Computer Systems Corp.	(201) 555-8624
Design Boards	(717) 555-5704
Design Boards Co.	(914) 555-7468

Figure 9-7 Table data in a generated report

When you place a table on the page, the layout editor displays a row-and-column structure, such as the one shown in Figure 9-8.

Like the grid, the table layout automates the task of aligning report elements. Unlike the grid, the table iterates through all the data rows that a data set returns to display the dynamic list of data.

Figure 9-8   Row-and-column structure of a table

Note that a table can display data from one data set only. When you create a data set, ensure that it returns all the data that you want to display in a table. If the data that you need is stored in two database tables, write a query that joins the two tables. Alternatively, you can create two data sets and use two tables, one table for each data set.

Deciding where to place elements in a table

The table contains three types of rows in which you place report elements. Table 9-2 describes the types of information that you typically place in each row.

Table 9-2   Table row descriptions

Table row	Description
Header	Elements that you place in the header row appear at the beginning of the section. If the data in the table appears on multiple pages, the contents of the header display at the top of every page. You can display the header contents only once, at the beginning of the section, by turning off the table's Repeat Header option. Place elements in the header to: ■ Display a title. ■ Display column headings, such as Customer Name, Address, and Phone, above the data in a customer list. ■ Display summary information, such as the number of customers in the list.
Detail	Elements that you place in the detail row represent the dynamic data in the section. The detail row displays each row from the data set. For example, display the main data, such as customer names, addresses, and phone numbers, in a customer list.
Footer	Elements that you place in the footer row appear once, at the end of the section. For example, display summary information, such as totals.

Figure 9-9 shows a table layout for displaying a list of customer names and their phone numbers. The finished report displays the list that appears in Figure 9-7.

Figure 9-9   Table layout for customer names and phone numbers

Binding a table to a data set

When you place a data set field in a table, BIRT Report Designer:

- Binds, or associates, the data set with the table. By binding these items, the table has the information that it needs to iterate through the data rows that the data set returns.

- Creates a column binding, which binds the data set field with a named column.

- Creates a data element that uses the column binding to display data from the data set field.

You can view this binding information on the table's binding properties page. To do so, select the table, then choose the Binding tab at the bottom of Property Editor. Figure 9-10 shows the binding properties page.

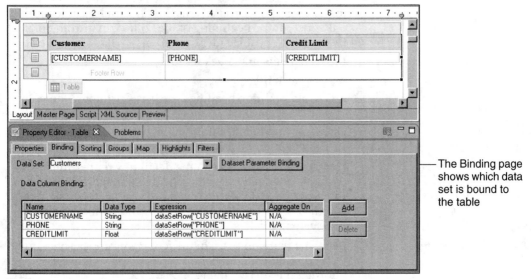

Figure 9-10   Property Editor's Binding page for a selected table

You can also manually bind a table to a data set through this page. The easiest approach, however, is to place a data set field in the table and let BIRT Report Designer do the binding. If you are not placing data set fields in the table, but are inserting other types of elements, such as dynamic text elements or image elements that need to access data set data, then you need to manually bind the data set with the table before you insert those elements in the table.

A table can be bound to only one data set. BIRT Report Designer prevents you from inserting a field from a different data set. If you manually change the data set that is bound to a table after you place fields in the list, you need to delete the fields, because the table no longer has information about them.

If, however, you do not change the data set binding, and you delete all the fields from a table, the table maintains its binding to the data set. To insert fields from a different data set into a table, you need to change the table's data set binding first. Deleting all the fields from the previous data set does not remove the original binding.

How to bind a data set to a table

1 In the layout editor, hover the mouse pointer over the bottom left corner until you see the Table tab, then choose the tab.

2 Choose the Binding tab at the top of Property Editor. The Data Set field shows either the name of the data set that is currently bound to the table or None if no data set is bound to the table.

3 From the Data Set drop-down list, select a data set. BIRT Report Designer binds the data set to the table. It also creates a column binding for each data set field. Now elements placed in the table can access all the fields in the data set.

Adjusting table rows and columns

You can add, delete, and resize rows and columns in the table, as necessary. You add and delete table rows and columns in the same way that you add and delete grid rows and columns. These tasks are described earlier in this chapter.

A table can contain any number of header, detail, and footer rows. For example, you can add two header rows, one to display summary information and the other to display column headings.

Organizing elements in a list

Use a list element to display dynamic data in any format other than a table. For example, use the list element to create form letters, one for each customer in a data set. Figure 9-11 shows an example PDF report that displays a series of form letters. Each letter is the same except for the recipient's name, which is dynamically derived from a customer name field.

Figure 9-11   The list element supports the creation of form letters with dynamic data

When you place a list on the page, the layout editor displays the structure that appears in Figure 9-12.

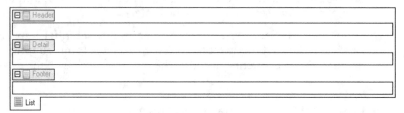

Figure 9-12   List structure

Deciding where to place elements in a list

Like the table, the list iterates through all the data rows that a data set returns to display data. Table 9-3 describes the three areas in a list.

Table 9-3   List area descriptions

List area	Description
Header	Elements that you place in Header appear once, at the beginning of the section. For example, display introductory information, such as a description of the report.
Detail	Elements that you place in Detail display dynamic data. The amount of data that appears is determined by the number of data rows that your data set returns. For example, print a letter for each customer in the data set.
Footer	Elements that you place in Footer appear once, at the end of the section. For example, display summary information, such as the number of records in the report.

Figure 9-13 shows a list layout that displays a form letter for each customer. The form letter is created using a text element that contains HTML formatting. The generated report displays the form letters that appear in Figure 9-11.

Figure 9-13 shows the most basic use of the list element. Typically, you use the list element to present data in more complex layouts. For example, you need a report that consists of many subreports. Each subreport goes to a single customer and consists of a cover letter, a summary account statement, and a detailed statement. To create this type of report, you define data sets that return each customer and the required account information, use grids and tables to create each section of the subreport, and place all the sections in a list element. For an example that shows the use of a list to organize subreports, see Chapter 17, "Building a Report That Contains Subreports."

Figure 9-13   List element with a text element in the detail area

Binding a list to a data set

Like the table, a list must be bound to a data set if the elements within the list need to access data set data. The binding principles and procedures for the table are the same for the list.

Placing report elements

You can place report elements in a page using one of the following techniques:

- Drag an element from the palette and drop it in the page.

- Use the Insert menu to place an element after a selected element. If none of the elements on the page are selected, the new element is added at the end.

- Drag a data set field from Data Explorer and drop it in a table, grid, or list.

When you drag an element from the palette, two cursors appear in the layout editor. The arrow cursor tracks your mouse movement. The straight cursor, shown in Figure 9-14, moves to the left or bottom of an existing report element when you move the mouse pointer around on the page. Watch the straight cursor. It shows you where the element will be placed when you release the mouse button.

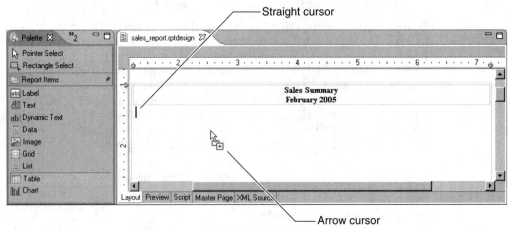

Figure 9-14 Straight cursor and arrow cursor indicate placement of an element

If you drop the element when the straight cursor is below an element, the new element appears on the next line, after the existing report element. Figure 9-15 shows the new element in the design.

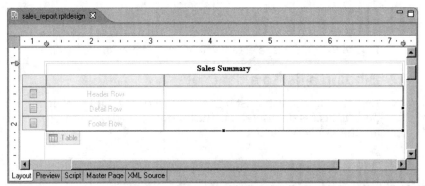

Figure 9-15 Inserted element, placed beneath existing text element

Placing report elements side by side

The layout editor does not allow you to place report elements side by side directly on the page. For example, you cannot place two text elements, two tables, or a picture and a text element next to one another. The layout editor inserts the second element below the first one. To place multiple elements horizontally across the page, place them in a container element, such as a grid or table.

Inserting data set fields

Most of the information in a report is derived from data set fields. The report displays this data as it is stored in the data source. For example, in a customer orders report, you place customer name, order number, item, quantity, and price fields in the report.

To insert all the fields in a data set, choose Data Explorer, expand Data Sets, then drag the data set, and drop it in the page. BIRT Report Designer creates a table and the required column bindings, and places all the fields in the detail row of the table. The fields appear in the order in which they appear in the data set.

Often, however, you do not want to insert all the fields, or you want to insert them in a particular order. To place individual data fields, first insert a container element, typically a table, in which to place the fields. Although you can place data fields in a grid or directly on the page, you typically place fields in the detail row of a table or a list. If you place a field in a grid or in the page, only one value appears in the generated report. Unlike a table or list, the grid and page do not go through all the data rows in a data set.

To access and insert data set fields, choose Data Explorer, expand Data Sets, then select the data set. You can then drag data set fields from Data Explorer and drop them in the container, as shown in Figure 9-16.

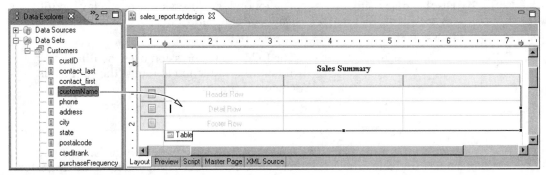

Figure 9-16   Use Data Explorer to insert data set fields in the report

Inserting computed fields

A computed field displays the result of an expression rather than stored data. For example, a database stores the prices of order items and the quantities that were ordered. To display the extended prices, you specify the following expression to calculate the values:

```
row["pricequote"] * row["quantity"]
```

Table 9-4 lists other examples of when to use computed fields and the types of expressions that you can specify.

Table 9-4   Examples of expressions in computed fields

Uses for computed fields	Examples of expressions

Display data that concatenates values from multiple fields	The following expression displays a customer's first and last names, which the data source stores in two fields:
	
	```\nrow["firstname"] + " " +\n row["lastname"]\n```
	
	The following expression displays a full address by concatenating values from four fields in the data source:
	
	```\nrow["address"] +", " + row["city"] +\n ", " + row["state"] + " " +\n row["postalcode"]\n```

Display data that is calculated from multiple fields	The following expression calculates a customer's available credit: ```\nrow["creditlimit"] - row["balance"]\n```

Display data using a JavaScript or BIRT function	The following expression uses the JavaScript Date object to return the current date:
	
	```\nnew Date( )\n```
	
	The following expression uses the BIRT Total.Sum( ) function to return the sum of all extended prices:
	
	```\nTotal.sum(row["pricequote"] *\n row["quantity"])\n```

JavaScript is a case-sensitive language. You must type keywords, function names, and any other identifiers with the correct capitalization. You must, for example, type the Date( ) function as Date( ), not date( ) or DATE( ). If you need help constructing expressions with the correct syntax, choose objects, functions, and operators from the lower part of Expression Builder.For more information about writing expressions or using Expression Builder, see Chapter 14, "Writing Expressions."

You can create a computed field using either of the following techniques:

- Define the computed field in the data set.

- Define the computed field in the report layout.

The first technique is preferable, because:

- You can test the results of the calculation by choosing Preview Results in the data set editor.

- The computed field is available to any table, list, or chart that uses the data set. It appears in the list of fields for that data set.

- BIRT Report Designer processes the computed values once, rather than multiple times, if the same computed field is used in multiple places in the report.

To create a computed field in the report layout, drag a data element from the palette, and drop it in the desired location, then in Select Data Binding create a column binding that defines the expression that returns the computed values. If you insert the data element directly on the page or in a grid, and you want to write an expression that refers to a data set field, you must first bind the data element to the appropriate data set. On the hand, if you insert the data element in a table or a list, the data element has access to the data set bound to the table or list.

Inserting images

Images add visual appeal to reports. You can add a company logo and pictures of merchandise, and you can use icons instead of text labels. These images can originate from a file system, a web server, or a data source. Images are often used as decoration, but you can also use them as data. A product database, for example, might contain images of each item. If you create a report with product information, you can add product images to the report.

BIRT supports the following types of image files: BMP, JPG, JPEG, JPE, JFIF, GIF, PNG, TIF, TIFF, and ICO. To display an image, insert the image element in your report. You have four choices when you insert an image. You can:

- Link the image from any location to the report.

- Link the image from the BIRT resource folder to the report. The resource folder is a central location for external files used by reports. Rather than link in images from various locations, you may find it more convenient to store all image files in the resource folder, because packaging files for deployment will be much easier.

- Embed the image in the report.

- Refer to the data set field that contains the images.

Use one of the first three methods to display a specific, or static, image. Typically, you display a static image once, so you insert the image directly on the report page, in a grid cell, or in the header row of a table. Use the fourth method to display a set of images returned by a data set. In this case, you typically want to display all the images in the data set field, so you insert the image element in the detail row of a table.

When displaying a static image, you need to decide whether to link or embed the image. Visually, there is no difference between a linked image and an embedded image. The difference is how changes to the image file affect what your report displays. If you link the image, any change you make to the original image file is reflected in the report. If you embed the image, changes to the original image file have no effect on the image that appears in the report. Use the guidelines in Table 9-5 to determine whether to link or embed an image in a report.

Table 9-5 Guidelines for linking and embedding images

When to link	When to embed
You expect to modify the original image, and you want the report to reflect future changes.	You expect to modify the original image, but you do not want the report to reflect future changes.
You do not expect to move or delete the original image file. Moving or deleting the image file breaks the link.	The original image file might be moved or deleted without your knowledge.

How to insert a linked image

1 Drag the image element from the palette, and drop it in the desired location on the page. New Image Item appears, as shown in Figure 9-17.

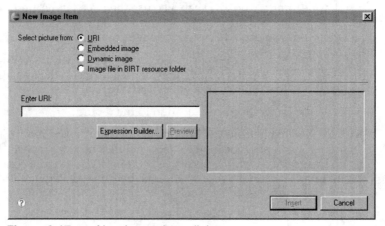

Figure 9-17 New Image Item dialog

2 To link to an image stored in the resource folder:

   1 In Select picture from, choose Image file in BIRT resource folder.

   2 Choose Browse to find the image file in the designated resource folder.

   3 Select the image file, and choose OK.

   4 Choose Insert to insert the image in the report. If you want to view the image before inserting it, choose Preview.

3 To link to an image stored in any other location:

   1 In Select picture from, select URI.

2   Under Enter URI, specify the location of the image file. Enclose the URI in double quotation marks (" ").

The following expression is an example of a URL for a file in a remote location:

```
"http://mysite.com/images/companylogo.jpg"
```

The following expression is an example of a URI for a file that is on the local file system:

```
"file:///c:/myprojects/images/companylogo.jpg"
```

You would specify a local file system location only for testing in the early stages of report development. A deployed report cannot access resources on a local machine.

3   Choose Insert to insert the image in the report. If you want to view the image before inserting it, choose Preview.

How to insert an embedded image

1   Drag the image element from the palette, and drop it in the desired location on the page.

2   On New Image Item, in Select picture from, select Embedded image. If you previously inserted images, New Image Item displays the names of those images, as shown in Figure 9-18.

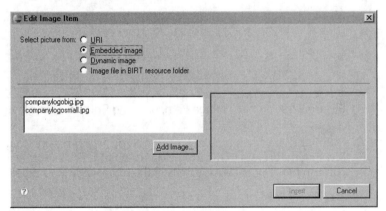

Figure 9-18   New Image Item, showing embedded image names

3   To embed a new image, choose Add Image.

4   On Open Image File, find and select the image to embed, then choose Open. New Image Item displays the image.

5   Choose Insert. The image appears on the page.

How to insert images that are stored in a data source

1   In Data Explorer, create a data set that includes the image field.

2 In the layout editor, insert a table element on the page.

3 Bind the table to the data set:

   1 Select the table and, in Property Editor, choose Binding.

   2 On the Binding page, in Data Set, choose the data set that contains the image field. BIRT creates a column binding for each field in the data set.

   3 Take note of the name of the column binding that refers to the image data set field.

4 Drag the image element from the palette, and drop it in the detail row of the table.

5 On New Image Item, select Dynamic image. New Image Item displays Enter dynamic image expression and buttons to help you create the required expression to associate the image element with the images in the data set, as shown in Figure 9-19.

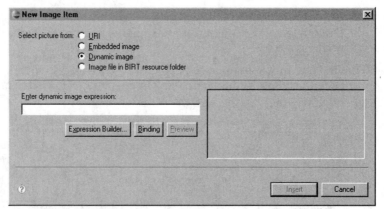

Figure 9-19 New Image Item, showing Enter dynamic image expression field

6 In Enter dynamic image expression, type an expression to use the column binding that refers to the image data set field. For example, if the name of the column binding is IMAGE, this is the expression you type:

```
row["IMAGE"]
```

You can also use Expression Builder to construct the expression if you are not sure what syntax to use. In Expression Builder, choose Available Column Bindings, then choose the appropriate column binding.

7 Choose Insert. The image element appears on the page in the layout editor. It shows an X. The actual images appear only when you preview the report.

10

Displaying Text

A report typically presents most of its information in textual format. In fact, we can safely assume that all reports contain text. Even if a report consists primarily of charts or pictures, it still uses text to label charts, display titles, describe the charts or pictures, and so on.

Textual information can be

- Static text, which is text that you type in the report. You use static text in a report title, column headings, or to write a summary about the report.

- String, number, or date values that are derived from data set fields. The majority of information in a report typically comes from data set fields.

- String, number, or date values that are derived from JavaScript expressions. Reports often contain information that is calculated, such as the report-generation date, or the number of records in a report table.

Textual information can be as short as a single word, or span multiple paragraphs, even pages. BIRT Report Designer handles all lengths of text elegantly. When you insert a textual element, you do not need to worry about specifying an element size that is large enough to display all the text. BIRT Report Designer automatically adjusts the size of elements to accommodate their contents.

Types of textual elements

To support the wide variety of text that a report can display, BIRT Report Designer provides a rich set of textual elements. Table 10-1 describes these elements, and Figure 10-1 shows a report that displays the different types of textual information.

Table 10-1   Descriptions of BIRT textual elements

Textual element	Use to
Data	Display dynamic values that are derived from data set fields, computed fields, or JavaScript expressions. You can add literal, or static, text to the dynamic data. Doing so, however, changes the entire expression to a string, and, if the dynamic value is a number or a date, you can no longer format it as a number or a date.
Dynamic text	Display memo or Character Large Object (CLOB) data from a data set field. This type of data typically consists of large amounts of text.
Label	Display a small amount of static text, such as a report title or column heading.
Text	Display the following types of user-specified text: ■ Multiline text ■ HTML text that contains multiple style formats, for example, text with paragraph styles, such as bulleted lists and numbered lists, or text formats, such as bold or italics ■ Text that combines static text with dynamic values, such as a form letter that includes customer names and addresses that are stored in a data source ■ Interactive content driven by code, which you specify using the <script> tag

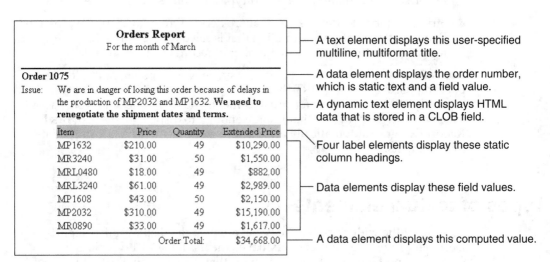

Figure 10-1   Textual elements in a report

Figure 10-2 shows how the report in the previous illustration appears in the layout editor.

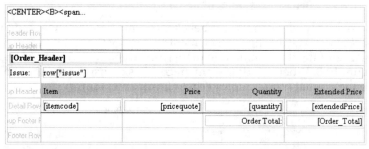

Figure 10-2　　Textual elements in the report design

Deciding which textual element to use

In many cases, you can use several textual elements to accomplish the same task. For example, you can use a label element, a text element, or a data element to display a static report title like the one in the following example:

```
Sales Report for Quarter One, 2005
```

When you start applying complex formats or combining static text with dynamic data, you need to use the appropriate textual element to achieve the best results. This section provides guidelines and examples for determining the best textual element to use for different purposes. When you understand the differences among the textual elements, read the rest of this chapter for details about using each element.

Formatting words differently in a static string

The previous example showed how you can use a label, text, or data element to display a static title. If, however, you want to format words in the title differently, as shown in the following example, you can accomplish this task only by using the text element. With the label and data elements, formats apply to the entire string.

```
Sales Report for Quarter One, 2005
```

Combining static text with dynamic data

To display the following text, where Order Total: is static text, and the number is a dynamic, or calculated, value, you can use a text element or a data element:

```
Order Total: 74050
```

If, however, you want to format the dynamic value so that it appears as a currency value with comma separators and decimal places, as shown in the following example, use the text element. The text element enables you to format different parts of text differently.

```
Order Total: $74,050.00
```

Alternatively, you can use a label element and a data element to display the preceding text. Use the label element to display the static text portion, Order Total:, and the data element to display the dynamic portion, as shown in Figure 10-3. When the data element consists of just the number value, you can use the Format Number property to format the number.

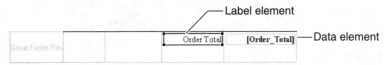

Figure 10-3   Label and data elements in the layout editor

Figure 10-4 shows the output of the preceding report design.

Order Total:	$59,664.00

Figure 10-4   Label and data elements in a report

The difference between using the label and data elements and using the text element is how you control the space between the static text and the dynamic value. Using the text element, you can easily specify one character space between the two. If you use the label and data elements, the spacing is determined by various factors, such as text alignment and column widths. In the previous example, the label element and data element are both right-aligned.

Displaying dynamic data that contains HTML tags

Many data sources store large amounts of text that contain internal formatting, as shown in the following example. Data like this is typically stored in CLOB fields.

```
<html><b>Customer log 04/12/05 13:45:00</b><br>Customer called
to enquire about order. He says order 2673-9890 was supposed
to arrive on 04/10/05. Records show that the order is on
backorder. Customer says he received no notification about the
status of his order. He wants to cancel the order if it is not
shipped by 04/15/05.<br><i>Action Items:</i><ul><li>Call
distributor about delivery status. <li>Send email to customer
about delivery status.</ul></html>
```

To display the text with the specified HTML formats, you can use the text element or the dynamic text element. If, however, you want to combine static text with dynamic text, use the text element. If you add static text to the dynamic text element, for example, "Customer Issue " + row["Issue"], the dynamic data appears in the report exactly as it appears in the field, including the HTML tags.

Figure 10-5 shows how the text element displays the static text, Customer Issue:, with the dynamic text. The text element converts the HTML tags to formatting and layout attributes. For example, text within the <b> and </b> tags appears in bold.

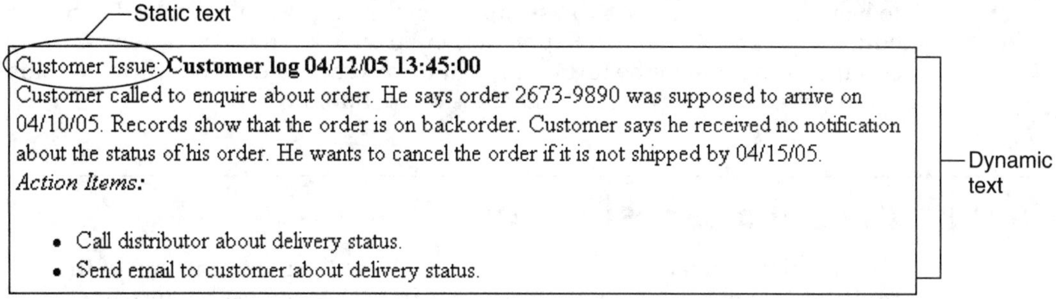

Static text

Customer Issue: **Customer log 04/12/05 13:45:00**
Customer called to enquire about order. He says order 2673-9890 was supposed to arrive on 04/10/05. Records show that the order is on backorder. Customer says he received no notification about the status of his order. He wants to cancel the order if it is not shipped by 04/15/05.
Action Items:

- Call distributor about delivery status.
- Send email to customer about delivery status.

Dynamic text

Figure 10-5   Static and dynamic text in a text element

Figure 10-6 shows how the dynamic text element displays the text when you add static text to the dynamic text. The HTML tags appear because the content is converted to string type.

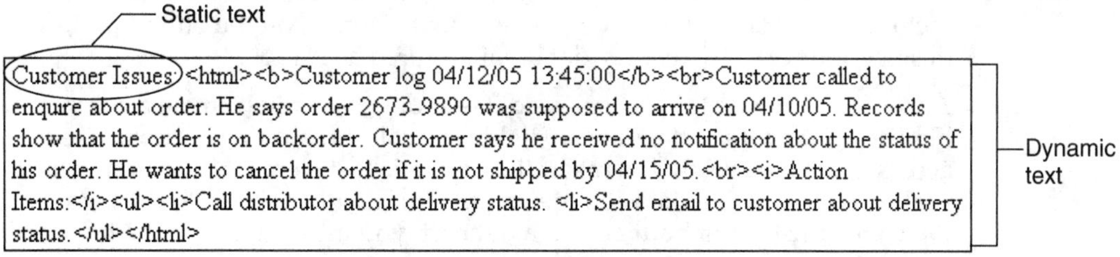

Static text

Customer Issues: <html><b>Customer log 04/12/05 13:45:00</b>
Customer called to enquire about order. He says order 2673-9890 was supposed to arrive on 04/10/05. Records show that the order is on backorder. Customer says he received no notification about the status of his order. He wants to cancel the order if it is not shipped by 04/15/05.
<i>Action Items:</i><ul><li>Call distributor about delivery status. <li>Send email to customer about delivery status. </ul></html>

Dynamic text

Figure 10-6   Static and dynamic text in a dynamic text element

Displaying dynamic data that a JavaScript expression returns

An expression is any valid combination of literals, variables, functions, or operators that evaluates to a single value. Both the text element and the data element can display the results of any valid JavaScript expression, including multiline expressions, such as the one in the following example:

```
if (row["creditScore"] > 700){
   displayString = "Your loan application has been approved."
   }
else{
   displayString = "Your loan application has been denied."
   }
```

The main difference is that it is easier to edit JavaScript expressions in a data element. When you double-click a data element, its value expression appears in

Expression Builder, which uses color for keywords and provides easy access to JavaScript functions and operators.

When you use a text element, its contents appear in the text editor. The first time that you specify a dynamic value in the text editor, Expression Builder appears to help you construct the expression. When the expression is inserted in the text editor, you cannot relaunch Expression Builder to edit the expression. You can edit the expression in the text editor, but the text editor does not provide color coding or access to JavaScript functions or operators.

Using a dynamic text element

You can place a dynamic text element directly on the page or in any of the container elements. Typically, you place it in a table or a list because the dynamic text element displays CLOB data from a data set field, and only the table and list elements iterate through the rows in a data set.

Unlike most data set fields, you do not simply drag a CLOB field from Data Explorer and drop it in the table or list. You can, but if the CLOB data is HTML text, the data element displays the contents of the field exactly as it appears, including the HTML tags. The dynamic text element, on the other hand, is designed to correctly display data that is stored as HTML.

As with any element that displays data set data, you must create a column binding that refers to the data set field. The column binding, in turn, needs access to the data set. If you insert the dynamic text element in a table or list that is already bound to a data set, the column binding has access to the data set. If the table or list is not bound with a data set, you must first bind the table or list with the data set.

How to use a dynamic text element

1   Make sure the table or list in which you want to insert a dynamic text element is bound to the data set that contains the CLOB data. To verify or create the data set binding:

    1   Select the table or list.

    2   Choose Binding on Property Editor.

    3   On the Binding page, in Data Set, select the data set.

2   Create a column binding that refers to the data set field that contains the CLOB data:

    1   On the table's Binding page, choose Add.

    2   On Expression Builder, choose Available Data Sets, choose the data set, then double-click the CLOB field. Choose OK to save the expression. The new column binding appears in Data Binding with the column name highlighted.

3   Replace the name New Binding with a name of your choice, then choose OK.

3   Drag the dynamic text element from the palette, and drop it in the table or list.

4   On Expression Builder, choose Available Column Bindings, choose the table under Sub-Category, then double-click the column binding you created. Choose OK to save the expression.

5   In the layout editor, select the dynamic text element. Property Editor displays the properties of the dynamic text element.

6   Choose General properties, then choose one of the following values for Content type:

- Auto

    Choose this value if you do not know the format of the field contents. If the content contains HTML tags, BIRT Report Designer interprets it as HTML and displays the content correctly. If the content is plain text, BIRT Report Designer displays it correctly also.

- HTML

    Choose this value if you know that all the field contents are HTML.

- Plain

    Choose this value to display the field contents exactly as they appear in the data source. If the content contains HTML tags, BIRT Report Designer displays the HTML tags.

7   Preview the report to verify that the report displays the text from the specified data set field.

Using a label element

You can place a label directly on the page or in any of the container elements. When you insert a label, the layout editor displays an empty label with a cursor in it, as shown in Figure 10-7.

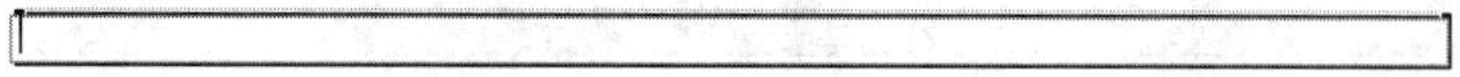

Figure 10-7   Empty label in the layout editor

Start typing the text that you want to display, then press Enter when you finish.

Figure 10-8 shows the result.

Sales Report

Figure 10-8   Label text in the layout editor

You can edit the text in the label by double-clicking the label or by selecting the label and pressing F2, then typing the new text.

You can change the format of the text by selecting the label, then setting the desired style properties in the property editor. You can, for example, specify a different font, text alignment, size, or color. These properties apply to the entire text string. You cannot, for example, set one word to bold and another to italic. If variable formats are a requirement, use a text element instead.

Using a text element

You can place a text element directly on the page or in any of the container elements. When you insert a text element, the layout editor displays the text editor, as shown in Figure 10-9.

First, decide what type of text you want to create. You have two choices:

- Plain text
- HTML or dynamic text

HTML or dynamic text enables you to create highly formatted text using HTML tags or CSS properties. The text can contain placeholders for data set field values and expressions, which enable you to mix static text with dynamically generated values. Plain text, on the other hand, cannot contain internal formatting or dynamic values. A text element that is set to plain text functions like a label element.

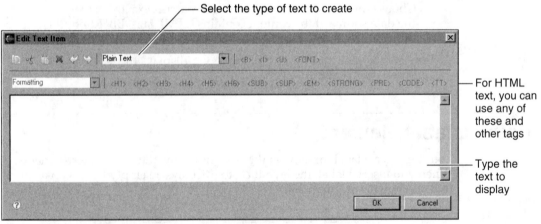

Figure 10-9   Edit Text Item

After you select the text type, type the text that you want to display in the report. If you selected HTML/Dynamic text, you can use HTML tags or CSS properties in the text. You can type the tags manually, or you can insert the commonly used HTML tags that the text editor provides.

The following sections provide a few examples of text you can create using a text element of HTML/Dynamic type.

Applying multiple style formats in a text element

Using HTML, you can format individual words and lines in a text element. The following example shows two lines with different font sizes and styles.

Text that you supply:

```
<CENTER><B><span style="font-size: larger">
Shipped Orders Report
</B></span><BR>
<FONT size="small">For the month of March</FONT></CENTER>
```

Output:

Shipped Orders Report
For the month of March

Combining a JavaScript expression with static text in a text element

BIRT Report Designer provides a useful tag, VALUE-OF, which you can use to insert a dynamic value in a text element. Using the VALUE-OF tag, you can insert any JavaScript expression.

The following example shows static text combined with a value that a JavaScript function returns.

Text that you supply:

```
Report generated on <VALUE-OF>new Date()</VALUE-OF>
```

Output:

```
Report generated on Jan 19, 2006 12:30 PM
```

The following example shows static text combined with a conditional expression and a field value expression.

Text that you supply:

```
Dear <VALUE-OF>row["Sex"] == "M" ? "Mr." : "Ms."</VALUE-OF>
    <VALUE-OF>row["Name"]</VALUE-OF>,
```

Output:

```
Dear Mr. Scott Johnson,
Dear Ms. Ella Fitzgerald,
```

As the example shows, a conditional expression can have one of two values based on a condition. The syntax for this conditional expression is

```
condition ? value1 : value2
```

If the condition is true, the expression has the value of value1; otherwise, it has the value of value2.

Alternatively, you can use an if...else statement within the VALUE-OF tag. The following text displays the same results as the preceding conditional expression:

```
Dear <VALUE-OF>if(row["Sex"] == "M"){
Title = "Mr."
}
else{
Title = "Ms."
}</VALUE-OF>
<VALUE-OF>row["Name"]</VALUE-OF>,
```

Combining a value from a data set field with static text in a text element

The following example shows how to use the VALUE-OF tag to insert dynamic values that data set fields return.

Text that you supply:

```
Dear <VALUE-OF>row["contact_firstname"]</VALUE-OF>,
<p>
Thank you for your recent order. Order <VALUE-OF>
    row["orderID"]</VALUE-OF> will be shipped by <VALUE-OF>
    row["shipByDate"]</VALUE-OF>.
```

Output:

```
Dear Bob,

Thank you for your recent order. Order 1115 will be shipped by
Apr 17, 2005 12:00AM.
```

You can display field values in a text element only if the following two requirements are met:

- The text element has access to the data set that contains the fields.

  - If you place the text element directly on the page, you must bind the text element to the data set that contains the field value. To do so, select the text element, choose the Binding tab in the property editor, then select the data set to which to bind. Placing the text element directly on the page, however, displays only one occurrence.

  - If you place the text element in the detail row of a table or a list to display all values of a data set field, bind the table or list to the data set.

- A column binding is created for each data set field. The column binding refers to the data set field. The VALUE-OF tag, in turn, refers to the column binding.

Formatting dynamic values in a text element

The previous examples show how to use the VALUE-OF tag to insert dynamic values that a JavaScript function or a field returns. Sometimes the returned values are not in the format that you want. You can reformat the values using the format attribute, as shown in the following example.

Text that you supply:

```
<VALUE-OF format="MM-dd-yy">new Date()</VALUE-OF><br>
<VALUE-OF format="$#,###.00">row["orderTotal"]</VALUE-OF><br>
<VALUE-OF format="(@@@) @@@-@@@@">row["phone"]</VALUE-OF>
```

Output:

```
04-17-05
$321,000.00
(415) 123-5555
```

The format pattern must be enclosed in quotation marks. You can use any format pattern that the Format Number, Format DateTime, and Format String properties support. Information about these properties is in Chapter 11, "Formatting Report Content."

Displaying data set field values that are stored as HTML text

Sometimes values in a data set field contain HTML text. If you insert such a field in a report, BIRT Report Designer displays the content of the field exactly as it appears in the data source, including the HTML tags.

To display the text with its intended formatting, use a text element or a dynamic text element instead of a data element. As described earlier in this chapter, the text element enables you to add static text to the dynamic text, whereas the dynamic text element displays all the HTML tags if you add static text.

To use the text element, select HTML/Dynamic text as the text type, then use the VALUE-OF tag to insert the value of the field, and set the format attribute to HTML, as shown in the following example.

Text that you supply:

```
Notes: <VALUE-OF format="html">row["CustomerNotes"]</VALUE-OF>
```

Formatting Report Content

Formatting is what you do to make a report visually appealing and effective. You format a report, for example, to highlight certain data, change the display of dates, numbers, or currency values, adjust the spacing between report elements, or display data based on a specified condition.

BIRT Report Designer provides many options for customizing the appearance of report elements that you place in a report. Using various formatting properties, you can change the alignment, color, font, size, and other properties of these report elements. You also can add background colors, draw borders around elements, and so on.

If you are familiar with CSS, you can apply your knowledge of CSS properties, because BIRT follows the CSS specification as closely as possible. Many of the formatting properties that you see in BIRT Report Designer are the same as CSS formatting properties.

The formatting options are available through the following views:

- Property Editor. This view organizes commonly used properties by functional categories. The properties that appear vary depending on which report element you are formatting. Figure 11-1 shows some of the categories of properties that are available through the property editor.

- Properties. This view shows a list of the properties that you can set for an element, as shown in Figure 11-2. This view also shows more complex properties that are not available in the property editor. The default application window layout does not display the Properties view. To display it, choose Window➤Show View➤Properties.

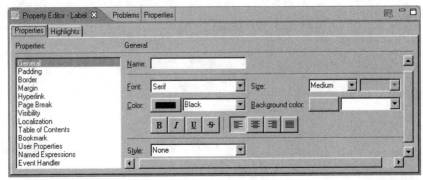

Figure 11-1   Property Editor, showing categories of properties for a label
element

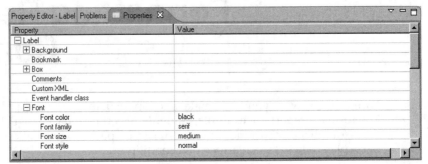

Figure 11-2   Properties view, showing the properties for a label element

Formatting data

You format the data in a report element by selecting the element then setting
property values using the property editor or the Properties view. If you apply a
format using the property editor, your format choices appear in the Properties
view. Similarly, if you update a format using the Properties view, the change is
reflected in the property editor.

You can customize how data appears by modifying the following settings:

- Formats of numbers, text, dates, and times

   BIRT Report Designer provides common format styles in which to display
   numbers, currency, or date values. If you do not choose a format, BIRT
   Report Designer displays the data as it appears in the data source. If you
   want to use some combination of formatting that these styles do not provide,
   you can create a custom format.

- Font typeface, point size, and color

   When choosing fonts, remember that for the report user to view the report
   with the fonts that you choose, the fonts must be installed on the user's

system. If your report will be distributed widely, select default fonts that are installed on all systems. You specify font attributes by setting the font properties in the General category of the property editor.

- Text style as bold, italic, underline, or strike through

  These settings are available under the General category of the property editor.

- Text justification as left, center, right, or justified

  These settings are available under the General category of the property editor.

Formatting numeric data

You can apply number formats only to decimal-, float-, or integer-type data. You can, for example, display integer-type numbers with decimal values, in scientific notation, or with a currency symbol.

Number formats have no effect on numbers that are string type. For example, a Customer_ID field can be defined as string type and display number values, such as 325. Number formats have no effect on these values.

You can display numeric data using either a text element or a data element, depending on what you want to accomplish. When you drag a data set field from Data Explorer and drop it on the report page in the layout editor, BIRT Report Designer automatically creates a data element to display the values of the data set field. The procedure for formatting data differs for a text element and a data element, as described in the following sections.

Formatting numeric data in a data element

You specify the format of numeric data in a data element by setting the data element's Format Number property, as shown in Figure 11-3.

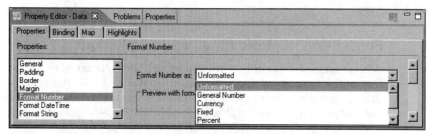

Figure 11-3   Format Number property values

Table 11-1 lists the types of number formats that you can choose and provides examples of how the formatted data appears.

Table 11-1   Examples of number formats

Format type	Example of data display
General Number	3000.00
Currency	$3,000.00
Fixed	3000.00
Percent	300000.00%
Scientific	3.00E+03

You can also define your own formats. You can, for example, specify the number of digits after the decimal or add literal characters to the numbers. To define a custom format, you use special symbols to construct a format pattern. BIRT Report Designer supports the Java numeric formatting that is defined by the DecimalFormat class. For details about the supported formatting symbols, see the Javadoc for DecimalFormat.

Table 11-2 shows examples of custom format patterns and their effects on numeric data.

Table 11-2   Results of custom number format patterns

Format pattern	Data in the data set	Results of formatting
0000.00	12.5	0012.50
	124.5	0124.50
	1240.553	1240.55
#.000	100	100.000
	100.25	100.250
	100.2567	100.257
$#,###	2000.00	$2,000
	20000.00	$20,000
ID #	15	ID 15

Formatting numeric data in a text element

When you insert dynamic data in a text element, you use the VALUE-OF tag. To format the dynamic data, include, within the VALUE-OF tag, a format attribute that specifies which format you want, as shown in the following examples. You must enclose the format value in double quotation marks (" ").

```
<VALUE-OF format="$#,###.00">row["orderTotal"]</VALUE-OF>
<VALUE-OF format="#.000">row["unitTotal"]</VALUE-OF>
```

You can use any format pattern that the Format Number property supports, as described in the preceding section.

Formatting date-and-time data

You can display date-and-time data in different formats. You can display dates and times in short, medium, or long formats. If the report runs on a machine that supports a different locale, the date data appears in the locale-appropriate format.

You can display date-and-time data using either a text element or a data element, depending on what you want to accomplish. When you drag a data set field from Data Explorer and drop it on the report page in the layout editor, BIRT Report Designer automatically creates a data element to display the values of the data set field. The procedure for formatting data differs for a text element and a data element, and is described in the following sections.

Formatting date-and-time data in a data element

You specify the format for date-and-time data in a data element by setting the element's Format DateTime property. As Figure 11-4 shows, BIRT Report Designer provides many common date-and-time formats from which to choose.

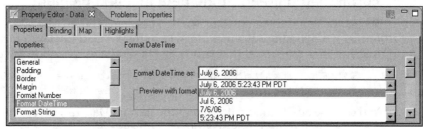

Figure 11-4   Format DateTime property values

You can also define your own date-and-time formats. You can, for example, specify two-digit months, use two digits for the year, or add the day of the week. To define a custom format, you use special symbols to construct a format pattern. BIRT Report Designer supports the Java formatting that is defined by the SimpleDateFormat class. For details about the supported formatting symbols, see the Javadoc for SimpleDateFormat.

Table 11-3 shows examples of custom format patterns and their effects on a date that is stored as 4/15/2005 in the data source.

Table 11-3   Results of custom date formats

Format pattern	Results of formatting
MM-dd-yy	04-15-05
E, M/d/yyyy	Fri, 4/15/2005
EEEE, M/dd/yy	Friday, 4/15/05
MMM d	Apr 15

(continues)

Table 11-3   Results of custom date formats *(continued)*

Format pattern	Results of formatting
MMMM	April
yyyy	2005
W	3 (the week in the month)
w	14 (the week in the year)
D	105 (the day in the year)

Specify custom formats if your report will be viewed in only one locale, because custom formats always display date or time data in the specified format. For example, if you use the format MM-dd-yy, the date January 10, 2006, always appears as 01-10-06, regardless of the locale in which the report is viewed. For locales in which dates are displayed in date-month-year format, a 01-10-06 date is interpreted as October 1, 2006.

Formatting date-and-time data in a text element

When you insert dynamic data in a text element, you use the VALUE-OF tag. To format the dynamic data, include, within the VALUE-OF tag, a format attribute that specifies the format that you want, as shown in the following examples:

```
<VALUE-OF format="MM-dd-yyyy">row["orderDate"]</VALUE-OF>
<VALUE-OF format="M/d/yy hh:mm:ss">new Date()</VALUE-OF>
```

You can use any format pattern that the Format DateTime property supports, as described in the preceding section.

Formatting string data

Typically, you format string data to fix inconsistent or poorly formatted data that is retrieved from the data source. The data source, for example, can store names with inconsistent capitalization or phone numbers in 1234567890 format. To fix these problems, specify the desired string format.

You can display string data using either a text element or a data element, depending on what you want to accomplish. When you drag a data set field from Data Explorer and drop it on the report page in the layout editor, BIRT Report Designer automatically creates a data element to display the values of the data set field. The procedure for formatting data differs for a text element and a data element, and is described in the following sections.

Formatting text in a data element

You specify a text format by setting the data element's Format String property, as shown in Figure 11-5.

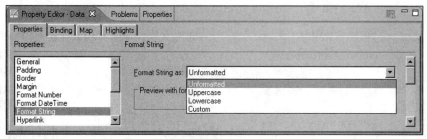

Figure 11-5   Format String property values

Table 11-4 lists the types of string formats that you can choose and provides examples of how the formatted data appears.

Table 11-4   Examples of string formats

Format type	Description	Example of data display
Lowercase	Converts the string to lowercase	smith
Uppercase	Converts the string to uppercase	SMITH

You can also define custom string formats using special symbols. Table 11-5 describes these symbols.

Table 11-5   Symbols for defining custom string formats

Symbol	Description
@	Character placeholder. Each @ character displays a character in the string. If the string has fewer characters than the number of @ symbols that appear in the format pattern, spaces appear. Placeholders are filled from right to left, unless you specify an exclamation point (!) at the beginning of the format pattern. See Table 11-6 for examples.
&	Same as @, except that if the string has fewer characters, spaces do not appear. See Table 11-6 for examples.
!	Specifies that placeholders are to be filled from left to right. See Table 11-6 for examples.
>	Converts string characters to uppercase.
<	Converts string characters to lowercase.

Table 11-6 shows examples of custom format patterns and their effects on text data.

Table 11-6   Results of custom string format patterns

Format pattern	Data in the data source	Results of formatting
(@@@) @@@-@@@@	6175551007 5551007	(617) 555-1007 ( ) 555-1007
(&&&) &&&-&&&&	6175551007 5551007	(617) 555-1007 () 555-1007
!(@@@) @@@-@@@@	6175551007 5551007	(617) 555-1007 (555) 100-7
!(&&&) &&&-&&&&	6175551007 5551007	(617) 555-1007 (555) 100-7
!(@@@) @@@-@@@@ + ext 9	5551007	(555) 100-7 + ext 9
!(&&&) &&&-&&&& + ext 9	5551007	(555) 100-7 + ext 9
>&&&-&&&&&-&&	D1234567xy	D12-34567-XY
<&&&-&&&&&-&&	D1234567xy	d12-34567-xy

Formatting text data in a text element

When you insert dynamic data in a text element, you use the VALUE-OF tag. To format the dynamic data, include, within the VALUE-OF tag, a format attribute that specifies the format that you want, as shown in the following examples:

```
<VALUE-OF format="(@@@) @@@-@@@@">row["phone"]</VALUE-OF>
<VALUE-OF format=">">row["custName"]</VALUE-OF>
```

You can use any format pattern that the Format String property supports, as described in the preceding section.

Formatting with styles

You can customize the appearance of each report element by setting its visual properties using the property editor. Depending on the number of elements that you want to format, this task can take a while, especially if you often change the appearance of elements. BIRT Report Designer solves this problem by providing a style mechanism that is similar to HTML CSS and Microsoft Word styles.

A style is a named set of formatting characteristics that you can apply to a report element to quickly change its appearance. When you apply a style, you apply an entire group of formats—font size, color, alignment, borders, and so on—in one step. For example, you want to format all the column headings in your report as Arial, small, blue, and center-aligned. Instead of formatting the column heading in four separate steps, you can achieve the same result in one step by applying a style.

Using styles, you can

- Create a consistent appearance for similar report elements.

- Update the appearance of a set of report elements by changing a single style.

When you first create a report, it does not contain any styles. The report displays elements with default formatting values. To use styles to format report elements, you must first create them. If you have designed web pages and you use a CSS file that defines styles, you can import those styles into your report design.

Creating styles

BIRT Report Designer styles are a hybrid of CSS and Microsoft Word styles. You can

- Create a named style, and apply it to a report element. For example, you can create a style called ColumnHeading, then apply the style to all column headings in your report. This approach is like Microsoft styles in that you create a Body Text style then apply this style to selected paragraphs.

- Apply style properties to predefined style names, or selectors. These predefined style names correspond to the different types of report elements. For example, you can apply style properties to a style called table-header, and all table headers in your report will be formatted accordingly. This technique is like CSS in that you associate styles with HTML elements, such as <H1> or <P>.

You will find it useful to create styles using both techniques. The first technique is useful for creating specialized styles for different types of text content, such as important notes, offer notices, or copyrights. The second technique provides a powerful way to define style properties once for a container element and have those properties cascade to the container's contents. For example, if you want to apply a default format, such as the Arial typeface, to all elements in a report, you can apply the format to the predefined style name, report. After doing so, all text in the report appears in Arial.

Table 11-7 lists the predefined style names for which you can set style properties.

Table 11-7   Predefined style names

Predefined style name	Applies style properties to...
chart	Charts
grid	Grids, including elements within them. For example, if you specify a background color, the entire grid displays the specified color. If you specify a font style, all textual elements in the grid display in the specified font style.

(continues)

Table 11-7   Predefined style names *(continued)*

Predefined style name	Applies style properties to...
label	Label elements
list	Lists, including elements in them
list-detail	Detail area of lists, including elements in that area
list-footer	Footer area of lists, including elements in that area
list-header	Header area of lists, including elements in that area
report	All elements in the report
table	Tables, including elements in them
table-detail	Detail rows of tables, including elements in the rows
table-footer	Footer rows of tables, including elements in the rows
table-header	Header rows of tables, including elements in the rows
text	Text elements

If you create styles using the cascading model, it is best to design a set of styles from the top-level container down. At the top level, define style properties that you want to apply to all elements, then add style properties at each successive level. For example, you can:

- Use the report style to specify a default font family and font size for the entire report.

- Use the table style to specify a default font size and text alignment for all data in the table.

- Use the table-header style to specify bold font and a background color for table headers.

Any element that you insert in a table header inherits the style properties from the report, table, and table-header styles. Any element that you insert in a table detail inherits style properties from the report and table styles. Figure 11-6 shows the results of applying the cascading concept to styles.

Not all style properties cascade. For example, the background color, margins, borders, and padding properties do not cascade from a container to the elements within it. In these cases, cascading the style does not make good design sense. For example, it does not make sense to cascade border values, because designs typically use different border values for different elements. A design might use a border around a table without using borders around rows, columns, cells, or elements in cells.

Text element uses the font, serif, and size, medium, as specified by the report style.

Customer Report

Name	Address
Advanced Design Corp.	613 Furth Circle, New Rochelle, NY 12066
Advanced Design Inc.	5905 Pompton St., NYC, NY 10022
Advanced Engineering Inc.	7123 Baden Av., Allentown, PA 70267
Advanced MicroSystems	2440 Pompton St., Glendale, CT 97561
Advanced MicroSystems Co.	3675 Furth Circle, Newark, NJ 94019
Advanced Solutions	1507 Moss Rd., Cambridge, MA 51247
Advanced Solutions Inc.	2732 Spinnaker Dr., Albany, NY 16381
Advanced Specialists Corp.	2304 Long Airport Avenue, Nashua, NH 62005
Brittan Design Inc.	5594 Pompton St., Boston, MA 51003
CompuBoards	18731 Douglas Av., Allentown, PA 70267
CompuDesign Co.	7044 Furth Circle, Brickhaven, MA 58339
CompuEngineering	1352 Baden Av., Albany, NY 16381
CompuMicroSystems Corp.	8281 Industrial Way, Sneadon's Landing, NY 21739

Data in the table header uses the font, serif, as specified by the report style and the size, small, from the table style. The table-header style specifies the bold font and grey background color.

Data in the table detail uses the font, serif, as specified by the report style and the font size, small, from the table style.

Figure 11-6   Report that shows the use of cascading styles

For details about each property, including the cascading rule, see the ROM Style specification document, which is available at the following URL:

```
http://www.eclipse.org/birt/
```

How to create a style

1   In the layout editor, select the report element to which you want to apply a style. If you want to create a style but not apply it to any elements, click in an empty area on the report page.

2   Choose Element→New Style. New Style appears, as shown in Figure 11-7. The left side displays the property categories. The right side displays the properties for the category that you select.

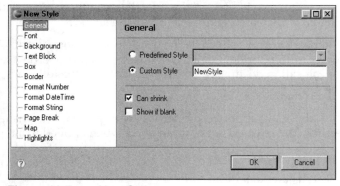

Figure 11-7   New Style

3   Specify one of the following settings:

- To apply style properties to a specific type of report element, select Predefined Style, and select a style from the drop-down list.

- To create a user-named style, specify a unique descriptive name for Custom Style. Ensure that the name is not the same as any of the predefined style names. If you specify a name that is the same as a predefined style, your custom style takes precedence, and you will no longer be able to use the predefined style to apply cascading styles.

4 Set the desired style properties by selecting a property category on the left and specifying property values.

5 When you finish setting style properties, choose OK to save the style. If you selected an element before you created the style, BIRT Report Designer applies the style to that element.

Importing styles

Most organizations maintain web sites, and most of the web pages on these sites use CSS to define their look and feel. As a report designer, you can reuse the styles from the CSS file by importing them into your reports. The benefits of doing so are obvious—you save time by not having to reinvent the styles, and your reports reflect the standard style.

You can import any number of styles from a CSS file. If you import a style whose name matches the name of an existing style in the report, BIRT Report Designer appends a number to the name of the imported style. For example, if your report contains a style named TopLevelHeading, and you import a style with the same name, the imported style's name changes to TopLevelHeading1.

When you import styles, BIRT Report Designer copies them to your report. It does not link the CSS file to the report. Therefore, any changes that you make to the styles in the CSS file do not affect the styles in the report.

Imported styles appear in the list of available styles with all the styles that were created with BIRT Report Designer. You apply an imported style to a report element, edit the style's properties, or delete it in the same way that you do with a style that was created with BIRT Report Designer.

BIRT Report Designer supports the CSS2 specification. Not all CSS2 properties, however, are supported. For a list of unsupported properties, see the Style and CSS specification document, which is available at the following URL:

```
http://www.eclipse.org/birt/
```

Styles that use unsupported properties are imported. The unsupported properties, however, do not have an effect when applied to a report element.

How to import styles

1 Select the layout editor.

2 Choose Element➤Import CSS Styles.

3 On Import CSS Styles, in File Name, specify the name of the CSS file whose styles you want to import. You can choose Browse to find the file. Import CSS Styles displays all the styles that are defined in the CSS file. Figure 11-8 shows an example of the styles in a CSS file named base.css.

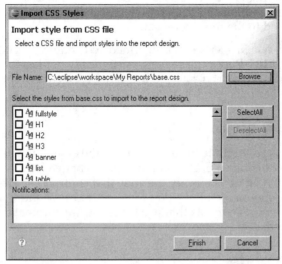

Figure 11-8   Examples of styles defined in a CSS file

4 Select the styles that you want to import. To import all the styles, choose Select All.

5 When you finish making your selections, choose Finish. BIRT Report Designer copies the styles to the report. Figure 11-9 shows an example of a list of styles in the Outline view.

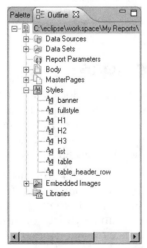

Figure 11-9   Style list in Outline view

Applying a style

After you create or import styles for your report, you can apply them to specific report elements by right-clicking the report element, choosing Style➤Apply Style, then selecting one of the styles in the list. The list displays all the styles that you created and imported. Choose None to remove the style that is currently applied to the report element.

If you applied style properties to predefined style names, such as table-header or table-footer, BIRT Report Designer automatically applies the style properties to all those types of report elements. You cannot selectively apply predefined styles to only some elements of that type.

Modifying a style

One of the most powerful features of styles is the ease with which you can change the look of your report. If you decide to change fonts or font sizes in the entire report, all you do is modify the style that controls the font properties. To modify a style, choose Element➤Edit Style, then choose the style that you want to modify. All report elements that use that style are automatically updated to use the new formatting.

Deleting a style

You can delete any style at any time. You should, however, delete only styles that you no longer need. If you delete a style that is applied to a report element or elements, the affected elements lose the formats that the style applied. Before you delete a style that is in use, BIRT Report Designer displays the names of the elements that are affected and prompts you to cancel or confirm the deletion.

To delete a style, choose the Outline view. Under Styles, right-click the style that you want to delete, then choose Delete.

Formatting data based on conditions

When you format a report element, the format applies to all instances of the element in the generated report. For example, if you specify that an item price appears in the Arial typeface and blue, all item prices in the generated report appear in Arial and blue. This type of formatting is called absolute formatting. The appearance of the element is set when you design the report.

You can, however, change the format of an element according to its value or the value of another element. For example, you can specify that item prices appear in green if the value exceeds $1,000.00 and in a default color if the value is equal to or less than $1,000.00. This type of formatting is called conditional formatting. With conditional formatting, the appearance of the element is set when the report runs.

The following examples are some common uses of conditional formatting:

- Show numbers in a different color if they are negative.
- Highlight delinquent accounts by using a different typeface or font style.
- Highlight the top ten customers by displaying their names in a colored box.

Creating a formatting rule

BIRT Report Designer provides an easy way to apply conditional formatting to report elements. You use the Highlights page of the property editor, where you create a formatting rule that defines when and how to change the appearance of an element. When you create a formatting rule, you specify the following information:

- The condition to meet in order to apply a format, for example, row["OrderTotal"] Greater than 50000
- The format to apply, for example, font color = blue

Figure 11-10 shows an example of a formatting rule.

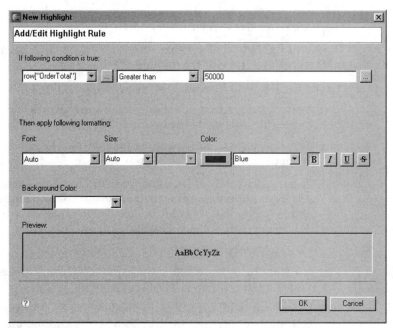

Figure 11-10   The New Highlight dialog, showing a formatting rule

How to create a formatting rule

1 In the layout editor, select the report element that you want to conditionally format.

2 Choose the Highlights tab in the property editor. The Highlights page appears, as shown in Figure 11-11. It is empty if you have not yet specified any formatting rules for the selected element.

Figure 11-11   Highlights page

3 Choose Add to add a new formatting rule.

4 On New Highlight, create the rule for applying a particular format to the report element by completing the following steps:

1 Think of the rule in plain English first. For example:

   ```
   If the order total is greater than $50,000.00, then set
   the font color to blue and the font style to bold.
   ```

   There are two parts to the rule: If and Then.

   The New Highlight dialog helps you specify the If and Then parts of the rule by breaking them down to more specific parts.

2 Specify the If part of the rule by completing the following steps:

   1 In the first field, specify the first part of the If expression. Using the example rule, this part is order total:

      ❑ If the order total values come directly from the selected element, from the drop-down list, choose Value of this data item.

      ❑ If the order total values come from another data element, specify the expression that refers to the relevant column binding, which refers to the data set value or calculated value you want. The following expression is an example:

         ```
         row["OrderTotal"]
         ```

       If you want help constructing the expression, use Expression Builder by choosing the ellipsis (...) button.

   2 In the second field, specify the second part of the If expression by selecting an option from the list. Using our example rule, this part is Greater than.

   3 In the third field, specify the third part of the If expression. Using our example rule, this part is a value of 50000, as shown in Figure 11-12.

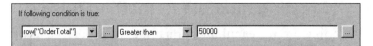

Figure 11-12 Elements of the If expression in New Highlight

You have now completed the If part of the rule, which specifies:

```
If row["OrderTotal"] is greater than 50000
```

3 Specify the Then part of your rule, which is "then set the font color to blue and the font style to bold," by completing the following steps:

❑ Choose Color, then select a color from the color picker.

❑ Choose B to select the Bold format, as shown in Figure 11-13.

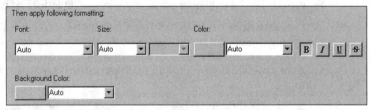

Figure 11-13 Elements of the Then expression in New Highlight

Choose OK.

The formatting rule that you created appears in Highlight List, as shown in Figure 11-14. The rule takes effect the next time that you run the report.

Figure 11-14 Highlight List

5 Preview the report to test your formatting rule.

Modifying a formatting rule

To modify a formatting rule, you use the same highlight tool that you use to create the rule. Select the element for which you want to modify the formatting rule, choose the Highlights tab in the property editor, then double-click the rule to modify. You can change any part of the rule, such as the condition that triggers the formatting or the format properties to apply. The modified rule takes effect the next time that you run the report.

Creating multiple formatting rules

You can create multiple formatting rules for an element. You can, for example, create three rules to set the values of an order total data element to one of three colors, depending on the dollar amount. Figure 11-15 shows an example.

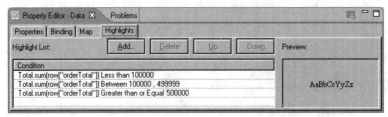

Figure 11-15   Highlights page, showing multiple format rules for an element

You can create any number of rules, and you can base conditions on the value of the selected element or on the value of other elements. Using the previous example, you can also change the color of the order total value based on the value of another data element, such as order ID. Figure 11-16 shows this example.

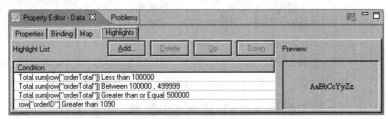

Figure 11-16   Conditional format for orderTotal based on the value of orderID

For each row of data, BIRT Report Designer evaluates the rules in the order in which they appear in the list of rules. As it evaluates each rule, BIRT Report Designer applies the specified format properties if the condition is met. If multiple rules with different conditions use the same format property, the later rule can override the format that the earlier rules specify.

Consider this example:

- The first rule sets order total values to red if they are less than 100000.

- The fourth rule sets order total values to blue if the order ID is larger than 1090.

If an order total value is 50000 and the order ID is 2000 (the conditions in both rules are true), the order total value appears in blue, not red, because the fourth rule supersedes all rules before it. If, however, the fourth rule sets order total values to italics rather than to blue, the value appears in red and italics.

When you create multiple rules for an element, plan the rules carefully. Consider the effect of individual rules and how the order of the rules changes the results. Test thoroughly to verify that the report displays the results that you expect. If necessary, you can change the order of the rules by selecting a rule and moving it up or down the list using the up or down arrow buttons on the Highlights page.

Deleting a formatting rule

All formatting rules that you create for an element take effect when you run the report. If you do not want a formatting rule to apply to an element, you must delete the rule from the Highlights page of the selected element.

Alternating row colors in a table

If a table displays many rows, it can be hard to read the data. A common solution is to set the rows to alternating colors, as shown in Figure 11-17.

Customer	Address	Phone
Atelier graphique	54, rue Royale, Nantes, 44000, France	40.32.2555
Signal Gift Stores	8489 Strong St., Las Vegas, NV 83030, USA	7025551838
Australian Collectors, Co.	636 St Kilda Road, Level 3, Melbourne, Victoria 3004, Australia	03 9520 4555
La Rochelle Gifts	67, rue des Cinquante Otages, Nantes, 44000, France	40.67.8555
Baane Mini Imports	Erling Skakkes gate 78, Stavern, 4110, Norway	07-98 9555
Mini Gifts Distributors Ltd.	5677 Strong St., San Rafael, CA 97562, USA	4155551450
Havel & Zbyszek Co	ul. Filtrowa 68, Warszawa, 01-012, Poland	(26) 642-7555

Figure 11-17   Conditional formatting that displays rows in alternating colors

To create this effect, use the conditional formatting feature, as described in the preceding section. The general condition that you specify is this: If the row number is even, set it to color A. If the row number is odd, set it to color B.

How to alternate row colors

1   Select the detail row in the table, as shown in Figure 11-18.

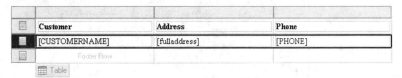

Figure 11-18   Detail row, selected

2   In General properties in the property editor, choose a color for Background Color. This color is the default color for the detail rows.

3   Choose the Highlights tab in the property editor to create a formatting rule to apply a different color to alternate rows. The property editor displays the Highlights page.

4   Choose Add to create a formatting rule.

5 On New Highlight, in the first field, type the following expression:

```
Total.runningCount() % 2
```

Total.runningCount( ) returns the current row number. The modulus (%) operator returns the remainder of a division. 2 specifies the number by which to divide. With this expression, even-numbered rows return 0, and odd-numbered rows return a non-zero value.

6 In the second field, choose either Equal or Not Equal.

- Choose Equal to apply the formatting rule to even-numbered rows.
- Choose Not Equal to apply the formatting rule to odd-numbered rows.

7 In the third field, type 0.

0 specifies the value to compare to the result of the expression, Total.runningCount( ) % 2.

You just completed the If part of the formatting rule:

```
If Total.runningCount() % 2 Equal (or Not Equal) 0
```

8 Specify the color to assign to the even- or odd-numbered rows by choosing a color for Background Color. Figure 11-19 shows an example of a completed format rule. The rule sets the background color of even-numbered rows to silver.

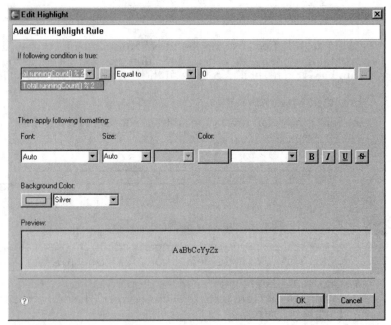

Figure 11-19   Edit Highlight dialog, showing a complete format rule

Choose OK.

9 Preview the report. The detail rows should appear in alternating colors.

You can use Total.runningCount( ) and the % operator with different values to alternate colors for a different number of rows. For example, the following highlight expressions change the row color for every three and every five rows, respectively:

```
Total.runningCount() % 6 Larger than or Equal 3
Total.runningCount() % 10 Larger than or Equal 5
```

Specifying alignment of content in a table or grid

Content in a table or grid aligns horizontally and vertically. When you place elements in the cells of a table or grid, BIRT Report Designer, by default, aligns content as follows:

- Aligns text horizontally to the left
- Aligns content vertically to the cell's baseline

Aligning text horizontally

You can change the horizontal alignment of text by setting the text-alignment property to one of the following values: left, right, center, or justify. This property is equivalent to the CSS text-align property.

You can align content by applying the text-alignment property to individual data elements, to cells, to an entire row, or to the entire table or grid. To align all text in a table in the same way, set the text-alignment property at the table level. To align all text in a particular row, set the property at the row level.

Figure 11-20 shows the results of using the different property values.

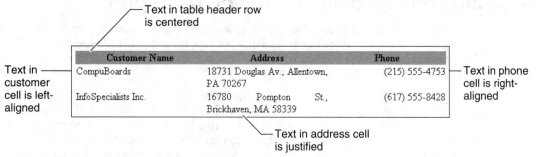

Figure 11-20   Text-alignment properties

Aligning content vertically

You can change the vertical alignment of content by setting the vertical-alignment property to one of the following values: baseline, subscript, superscript, top, text top, middle, bottom, or text bottom. This property is equivalent to the CSS vertical-align property.

You can align content vertically by applying the vertical-alignment property to a content element or individual cells. Some of the property values make sense only if applied to inline elements, some only if applied at the cell level. For example:

- The vertical-alignment property of each table or grid cell determines its vertical position within the row, and only the baseline, top, middle, and bottom values make sense. Figure 11-21 shows the results of using a different vertical-alignment value for each grid cell.

Figure 11-21   Vertical-alignment property settings for cells

- The vertical-alignment property of inline report elements determines the vertical position of an inline element, relative to its container or to the element's line. An inline element is one that has no line break before or after it. Two inline elements in a cell or section appear side by side on a single line. You typically use the superscript, subscript, top, and bottom values to adjust the alignment of two elements. Figure 11-22 shows the results of using a different vertical alignment value for the second element in each cell.

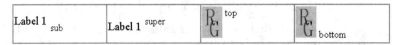

Figure 11-22   Vertical-alignment property settings for inline elements

Adjusting the spacing of content in a report

The default layout adds a minimum amount of space between elements in a report. After you lay out elements in your report, preview the report in HTML or PDF to see if you need to adjust the spacing between contents. Reports render differently in HTML and PDF.

For an HTML report, the contents adjust automatically to the size of the window unless you specify a specific value for the table width. In PDF, the contents of table cells appear on one or multiple lines, depending on the sizes of the columns. The entire table occupies as much space horizontally as is available unless you specify a specific value for the table width. The available, or printable, area is determined by the page size and margin sizes of the master page.

Figure 11-23 shows the default spacing for report elements in a report design. As the figure shows, a table contains columns of equal width unless you specify explicit column widths.

Customer List		
Customer	**Address**	**Phone**
[customName]	[fulladdress]	[phone]
	Footer	

Figure 11-23 Default spacing in a report design

Figure 11-24 shows the report output in HTML. The default layout displays rows of content with very little space between them. You can resize a row to increase the space between rows and resize a column to adjust its width.

Customer List

Customer	Address	Phone
Signal Engineering	149 Spinnaker Dr., New Haven, CT 97823	(203)555-7845
Technical Specialists Co.	567 North Pendale Street, New Haven, CT 97823	(203)555-9545
SigniSpecialists Corp.	5290 North Pendale Street, NYC, NY 10022	(212)555-1957
Technical MicroSystems Inc.	4092 Furth Circle, NYC, NY 10022	(212)555-7413
InfoEngineering	2678 Kingston Rd., NYC, NY 10022	(212)555-1500
Advanced Design Inc.	5905 Pompton St., NYC, NY 10022	(212)555-8493
Technical Design Inc.	897 Long Airport Avenue, NYC, NY 10022	(212)555-7818

Figure 11-24 Default spacing in an HTML report

When the size of the browser window decreases, text in the table cells wraps, as shown in Figure 11-25. You can specify a fixed width for the table if you do not want the contents in the table to adjust to the browser window.

http://127.0.0.1:50443/viewer/run?__report=C:/eclipse/workspace/DocSamples/c... _ □ ×

Customer List

Customer	Address	Phone
Signal Engineering	149 Spinnaker Dr., New Haven, CT 97823	(203) 555-7845
Technical Specialists Co.	567 North Pendale Street, New Haven, CT 97823	(203) 555-9545
SigniSpecialists Corp.	5290 North Pendale Street, NYC, NY 10022	(212) 555-1957
Technical MicroSystems Inc.	4092 Furth Circle, NYC, NY 10022	(212) 555-7413
InfoEngineering	2678 Kingston Rd., NYC, NY 10022	(212) 555-1500
Advanced Design Inc.	5905 Pompton St., NYC, NY 10022	(212) 555-8493

Figure 11-25 Report output in HTML when browser window size is reduced

Figure 11-26 shows the same report in PDF format. The data fits in three columns of equal size, which results in white space on the right. There is also very little space between the rows and columns.

Customer List

Customer	Address	Phone
Signal Engineering	149 Spinnaker Dr., New Haven, CT 97823	(203) 555-7845
Technical Specialists Co.	567 North Pendale Street, New Haven, CT 97823	(203) 555-9545
SigniSpecialists Corp.	5290 North Pendale Street, NYC, NY 10022	(212) 555-1957
Technical MicroSystems Inc.	4092 Furth Circle, NYC, NY 10022	(212) 555-7413
InfoEngineering	2678 Kingston Rd., NYC, NY 10022	(212) 555-1500
Advanced Design Inc.	5905 Pompton St., NYC, NY 10022	(212) 555-8493
Technical Design Inc.	897 Long Airport Avenue, NYC, NY 10022	(212) 555-7818
Design Solutions Corp.	7824 Baden Av., NYC, NY 10022	(212) 555-3675
TekniSystems	7476 Moss Rd., Newark, NJ 94019	(201) 555-9350
InfoDesign	3449 Long Airport Avenue, Newark, NJ 94019	(201) 555-2343
Computer Systems Corp.	4030 Long Airport Avenue, Newark, NJ 94019	(201) 555-8624

Figure 11-26   Default spacing in a PDF report

To adjust the spacing of content in a report, use one of the following techniques:

- Resize the rows or columns of a table or grid to adjust spacing of content in a table or grid.

- Insert an empty row or column in a table or grid, and specify a specific size for the row or column.

- Resize the margins, borders, and padding of elements.

The first two techniques provide more predictable results. The padding and margin properties can yield varying results in different web browsers, depending on how the browser interprets these properties.

Resizing rows and columns

The quickest way to change the size of a row or column is to drag the row or column boundary to the desired height or width. You can also resize a row or column by setting a specific row height or column width. You will find that setting a specific row height or column width is often preferable to dragging a row or column boundary, because what you see in the layout editor is not what you get in the output. In the layout editor, the sizes of data, text, and label elements adjust to fit up to 20 characters of their content or expression.

The row height that you specify is the row's minimum height. It is not a fixed height. If it were, long content would be truncated. The column width that you specify, on the other hand, is a fixed width. Long blocks of content wrap to multiple lines.

By default, table and grid rows and columns do not appear in the output if they are empty. For example, if a grid has three rows, but only one row contains content, the output does not display blank space. If, however, you specify a size for the empty rows, the rows appear.

How to resize a column or row by dragging its boundary

1 Select the tab at the bottom left corner of the grid or table. Guide cells appear at the top and left sides of the grid or table.

2 In the guide cell area, select a row or column boundary, and drag it until the row or column is the size that you want, as shown in Figure 11-27.

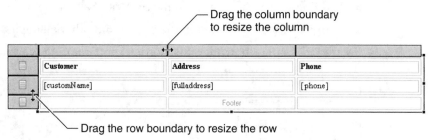

Figure 11-27 Resize rows or columns by dragging boundaries

How to specify a row height

1 Select the tab at the bottom left corner of the grid or table. Guide cells appear at the top and left sides of the grid or table.

2 Select the guide cell of the row that you want to resize. The property editor displays the row properties, as shown in Figure 11-28.

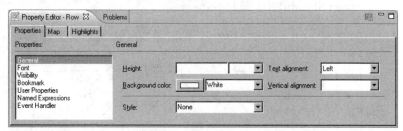

Figure 11-28 Property Editor, showing row properties

3 In the General category, specify a value for Height. This value sets the minimum height for the row. You can specify different units of measurements, including inches, centimeters, millimeters, and points.

How to specify a column width

1 Select the tab on the bottom left corner of the grid or table. Guide cells appear at the top and left sides of the grid or table.

2 Select the guide cell of the column that you want to resize. The property editor displays the column properties that you can set.

3 In the General category, specify a value for Width. This value sets a fixed width for the column. You can specify different units of measurements, including inches, centimeters, millimeters, and a percentage of the total grid width.

Resizing margins, borders, and padding of elements

As in CSS, BIRT Report Designer provides three properties to define the horizontal and vertical space between elements:

- Border is a visible or invisible line around the element.
- Padding is the space between the content of an element and the border.
- Margin is the space between the border and other elements.

Figure 11-29 shows how margins, borders, and padding work together.

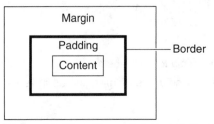

Figure 11-29   Properties that define the space between elements

You can use the padding and margin properties of an element to adjust the horizontal and vertical spacing of content in a report. Figure 11-30 shows how to set a label element's Padding Bottom property to increase the space between the report title and the table below it.

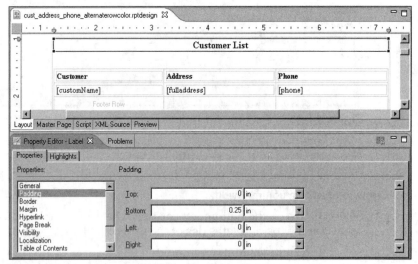

Figure 11-30   Use the Padding Bottom property to set the space below an element

Figure 11-31 shows the report output. You can get the same result by increasing the table's Margin Top property.

Customer List

Customer	Address	Phone
Signal Engineering	149 Spinnaker Dr., New Haven, CT 97823	(203) 555-7845
Technical Specialists Co.	567 North Pendale Street, New Haven, CT 97823	(203) 555-9545
SigniSpecialists Corp.	5290 North Pendale Street, NYC, NY 10022	(212) 555-1957
Technical MicroSystems Inc.	4092 Furth Circle, NYC, NY 10022	(212) 555-7413
InfoEngineering	2678 Kingston Rd., NYC, NY 10022	(212) 555-1500

Figure 11-31   Report output, showing the result of the Padding Bottom setting

Displaying content across multiple columns

Grid and table columns enable you to align report elements easily and neatly. Often, however, you need to display text or data across multiple columns to enhance the report's appearance. For example, compare the layout of the reports in Figure 11-32.

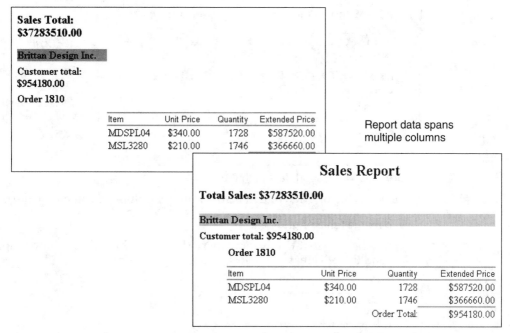

Report data displayed within five columns

Report data spans multiple columns

Figure 11-32   Two reports, one without column spanning, one with column spanning

In the first report, data appears in a five-column table. The first column of the table contains the sales total, customer name, customer total, and order number. The order details occupy the rest of the columns. To fit five columns, each column is fairly narrow. Some of the content in the first column wraps onto two lines. If you increase the width of the first column, the second column moves too far to the right. Figure 11-33 shows the design for the first report.

In the second report, the sales total, customer name, and customer total spans multiple columns, so that the text appears on one line. The second column starts farther to the left, eliminating extra space on the left of the detailed content.

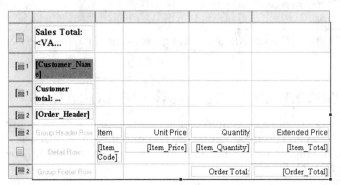

Figure 11-33   Report design without column spanning

Figure 11-34 shows the design for the second report.

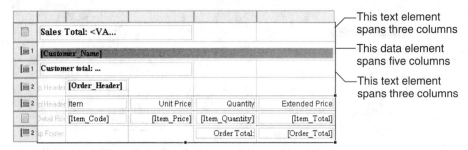

Figure 11-34   Report design that uses column spanning

To display table or grid content across multiple columns, you merge the cells.

How to merge table or grid cells

1   Select the cells that you want to merge by using Shift-click. A border appears around the cells that you select, as shown in Figure 11-35.

Sales Total: <VA...				

Figure 11-35   Cells selected for merging

2   Right-click within the border, then choose Merge from the context menu. The cells merge into one, as shown in Figure 11-36.

Figure 11-36 Merged cells

Specifying alternate values for display

Data in a data source can sometimes be cryptic or appear in abbreviated form. For example, gender values may be M or F rather than male or female. Credit rankings may be 1 to 5 rather than excellent, good, average, fair, or poor.

BIRT Report Designer enables you to specify alternate values to display if you do not want to use the original values in your report. You use a data element's map property to create rules for mapping data values. You create one map rule for each data value that you want to replace. For example, to map M and F to Male and Female, respectively, you create two map rules.

How to map data values to different display values

1 Select the data element for which you want to replace values. The property editor displays the properties for the data element.

2 Choose the Map tab at the bottom of the property editor. Map List appears, as shown in Figure 11-37.

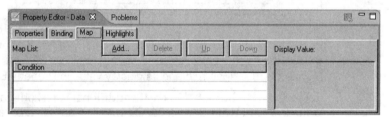

Figure 11-37 Map List

3 Choose Add to create a map rule.

4 On New Map Rule, in the first field, specify the expression that refers to the data set field for which you want to replace values. If you need help specifying the expression, choose the ellipsis (...) button to use Expression Builder. The following is an example of an expression:

```
row["creditrank"]
```

1 In the second field, select an operator from the list. For example:

```
Equal
```

2 In the third field, specify the value to replace. For example:

```
"A"
```

You must enclose string values in quotation marks (" ").

3   In the last field, specify the value that you want to display. For example:

    `Excellent`

    Figure 11-38 shows an example of a completed map rule.

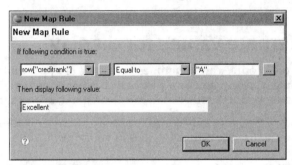

Figure 11-38   Map rule

4   Choose OK. The rule that you created appears in Map List. When you select the rule, the display value appears in the box at the right, as shown in Figure 11-39.

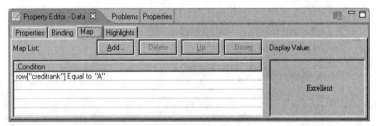

Figure 11-39   Map rule and its display value in Property Editor

5   Repeat steps 3 through 4 to create additional rules, one for each data value that you want to replace. Figure 11-40 shows an example of three map rules that were created for the selected data element.

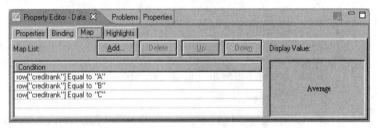

Figure 11-40   Three map rules for an element

5   Preview the report to check the results of your map rules.

Hiding elements based on conditions

In most cases, you add an element to a report because you want to display the contents of the element. There are many good reasons, however, for hiding report elements conditionally. With creative use of an element's visibility property, you can customize the data that your report displays, depending on conditions that you specify. You specify a condition by writing a Boolean expression that evaluates to either true or false. The following are some examples of conditionally hiding an element, and the corresponding Boolean expressions to apply to the visibility property:

- Display a text message only for certain records. You want your report to display a message when an account balance falls below a certain amount, such as $1,000.00. First, create a text element that displays something like "Your account balance is below the minimum balance required to waive the service fee." Then, you conditionally hide the text element by setting its visibility property to the following expression:

```
row["accountbalance"] > 1000
```

When the expression returns true, the text element is hidden. Notice that you have to think the opposite when specifying the expression. You have to think about when you do not want the text to appear, rather than when you do. In this example, you want to display a message when the balance is less than $1,000.00. Therefore, you hide the text element when the balance is greater than $1,000.00.

- Display a text message if a report returns no data. If your report uses parameters to prompt users to specify the data that they want to view, and it is possible for the report to return nothing, you can display a message, such as "No records found." To accomplish this task, you create a text or label element that displays the message, then you conditionally hide the element by setting its visibility property to the following expression:

```
Total.count( ) != 0
```

Total.count( ) returns the number of data rows in a table. When Total.count( ) returns zero, the message appears. Because this function is an aggregate function that processes all data rows in a table, you must place the text or label element in the header or footer row of the table.

- Display different pictures, depending on the values of a field. To add visual interest to your report, you want to display two stars next to an order total that equals or exceeds $10,000.00, one star for totals between $5,000.00 and $10,000.00, and nothing for totals less than $5,000.00. Create two pictures—one with two stars and the other with one star—and insert them next to the element that displays the order number. Conditionally hide the two-star picture with the following expression:

```
row["ordertotal"] <= 10000
```

This expression hides the two-star picture when the order total is less than $10,000.00.

Conditionally hide the one-star picture with the following expression:

```
row["ordertotal"] < 5000 || row["ordertotal"] > 10000
```

This expression hides the one-star picture if the order total is less than $5,000.00 or more than $10,000.00.

■ Display different report sections, depending on the values of a field. For example, you want to display W2 information for full-time employees and 1099 information for contractors. Create two report sections, one with W2 information and another with 1099 information. Conditionally hide the report with W2 information using the following expression:

```
row["classification"] == "contractor"
```

This expression hides the full-time employee W2 information when the employee is classified as a contractor. Conditionally hide the report with 1099 information using the following expression:

```
row["classification"] == "fulltime"
```

This expression hides the contractor 1099 information when the employee is classified as full-time.

The visibility property also provides you with the option of:

■ Hiding an element, depending on the output format. For example, you can hide an element for HTML output and display it for PDF output.

■ Specifying different visibility conditions for PDF and HTML output. For example, you can hide an element in HTML if its value is x and hide an element in PDF if its value is y.

How to conditionally hide an element

1 Select the element to hide conditionally.

2 In Property Editor, choose Visibility. The Hide Element option appears, as shown in Figure 11-41.

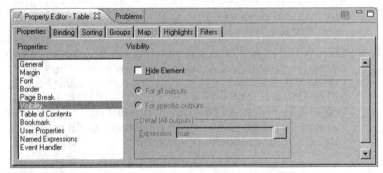

Figure 11-41   Hide Element option in Property Editor

3 Select Hide Element to specify that this element be hidden. If you want the element to always be hidden, this is all you need to do. If you want to conditionally hide the element, specify the condition.

4 Select the report format to which you want to apply the hide condition:

- To apply the hide condition for all report formats, select For all outputs.

- To apply the hide condition for certain report formats, select For specific outputs. Also select this option if you want to apply different conditions, depending on the report format.

5 Specify the hide condition:

 1 Choose Expression Builder.

 2 On Expression Builder, create an expression that specifies the hide condition. Remember, you have to think about when you want to hide the element, not when you want it to appear.

 For example, to display the text message, Jumbo, when a loan amount exceeds $363,000.00, conditionally hide the text element using the following expression:

```
row["ordertotal"] < 363000
```

 This expression hides the text message when loan amounts are less than $363,000.00.

 3 Choose OK.

6 Preview your report to test the conditional visibility.

Sorting and Grouping Data

When you first create a report and preview the data, the report displays the data in the order in which your data source returns it. The order varies, based on how data was entered in the data source and how you joined tables in the query.

In most cases, you will want to change the order in which data appears in the report. A customer phone list, for example, is easier to use if it is in alphabetical order. A sales report is more useful if it presents sales figures from highest to lowest, or the reverse, if you want to see low to top performers.

Compare the reports in Figure 12-1.

Report displays data in natural order

Customer	Phone
Signal Engineering	(203) 555-7845
Technical Specialists Co.	(203) 555-9545
SigniSpecialists Corp.	(212) 555-1957
Technical MicroSystems Inc.	(212) 555-7413
InfoEngineering	(212) 555-1500
Advanced Design Inc.	(212) 555-8493
Technical Design Inc.	(212) 555-7818
Design Solutions Corp.	(212) 555-3675
TekniSystems	(201) 555-9350
InfoDesign	(201) 555-2343
Computer Systems Corp.	(201) 555-8624
SigniDesign	(201) 555-5888
Advanced MicroSystems Co.	(201) 555-3722
TeleMicroSystems	(201) 555-5171

Report sorts data by customer name

Customer	Phone
Advanced Design Corp.	(914) 555-6707
Advanced Design Inc.	(212) 555-8493
Advanced Engineering Inc.	(215) 555-3197
Advanced MicroSystems	(203) 555-4407
Advanced MicroSystems Co.	(201) 555-3722
Advanced Solutions	(617) 555-3842
Advanced Solutions Inc.	(518) 555-9644
Advanced Specialists Corp.	(603) 555-8647
Brittan Design Inc.	(617) 555-2480
CompuBoards	(215) 555-4753
CompuDesign Co.	(617) 555-2663
CompuEngineering	(518) 555-3942
CompuMicroSystems Corp.	(914) 555-9081
CompuSolutions Co.	(201) 555-9867

Figure 12-1   Reports showing unsorted and sorted data

The report on the left displays customer names in the order the data set returns them, which is also called natural order. The report on the right displays customer names in alphabetical order. This report presents the data sorted by customer name.

Now, compare the reports in Figure 12-2. The report on the left sorts the data alphabetically by customer name. The report on the right also sorts the data alphabetically by customer name, but adds an additional sort criterion, by state. This report first groups the data by state. Within each state, the report sorts data by customer name.

Report sorts data by customer name

Customer	Phone
Advanced Design Corp.	(914) 555-6707
Advanced Design Inc.	(212) 555-8493
Advanced Engineering Inc.	(215) 555-3197
Advanced MicroSystems	(203) 555-4407
Advanced MicroSystems Co.	(201) 555-3722
Advanced Solutions	(617) 555-3842
Advanced Solutions Inc.	(518) 555-9644
Advanced Specialists Corp.	(603) 555-8647
Brittan Design Inc.	(617) 555-2480
CompuBoards	(215) 555-4753
CompuDesign Co.	(617) 555-2663
CompuEngineering	(518) 555-3942
CompuMicroSystems Corp.	(914) 555-9081
CompuSolutions Co.	(201) 555-9867

Report groups customers by state

Customer	Phone
CT	
Advanced MicroSystems	(203) 555-4407
Design Design	(203) 555-1450
Signal Engineering	(203) 555-7845
SigniSpecialists	(203) 555-2570
Technical Boards	(203) 555-2373
Technical Specialists Co.	(203) 555-9545
MA	
Advanced Solutions	(617) 555-3842
Brittan Design Inc.	(617) 555-2480
CompuDesign Co.	(617) 555-2663
Computer MicroSystems Corp.	(508) 555-7307
Design Engineering Corp.	(617) 555-6274

Figure 12-2   Reports showing two different sorting techniques

As you can see from the examples, sorting and grouping are two essential ways to organize data for more effective viewing and analysis.

Sorting data

As the previous section describes, you sort data to display report data in a more meaningful order. Without sorting, a report can be much less usable. For example, it often displays data in seemingly random order, because that was the way the data was entered into the data source.

You can sort data in ascending or descending order, and you can sort by as many fields as you like. For example, you can sort a list of customers by credit rank, then by customer name.

Figure 12-3 shows the first six data rows in three lists. The first list is unsorted, the second sorts data by credit rank, and the third sorts data first by credit rank, then by customer name.

Data is unsorted | Data is sorted by credit rank | Data is sorted by credit rank, then by customer name

Credit	Customer
B	Signal Engineering
A	Technical Specialists Co.
C	SigniSpecialists Corp.
A	Technical MicroSystems Inc.
A	InfoEngineering
A	Advanced Design Inc.

Credit	Customer
A	Technical Specialists Co.
A	Technical MicroSystems Inc.
A	InfoEngineering
A	Advanced Design Inc.
A	Technical Design Inc.
A	Design Solutions Corp.

Credit	Customer
A	Advanced Design Inc.
A	Advanced MicroSystems
A	Advanced MicroSystems Co.
A	Advanced Solutions
A	Advanced Solutions Inc.
A	Advanced Specialists Corp.

Figure 12-3   Three examples of sorting list data

Ways to sort data

You sort data in one of two ways:

- Specify sorting in the data set query so that the database processes the data before sending the results to BIRT. Specify sorting in the query whenever possible. Databases are efficient at sorting data, especially if they have indexes to optimize sorts.

- Sort data in BIRT. Use this method if your data source, such as a text file, does not support sorting. If you group data, BIRT handles all sorting automatically.

How to sort data through the query

1 In Data Explorer, create a new data set, or edit an existing one.

2 In the query text area, write an ORDER BY clause in the SELECT statement. For example, the following statement returns customer information and sorts rows by credit rank, then by customer name.

```
SELECT Customers.customerName,
Customers.phone,
Customers.creditRank
FROM Customers
ORDER BY Customers.creditRank, Customers.customerName
```

3 Choose Preview Results to verify the data that the query returns. The rows should be sorted by the fields in the ORDER BY clause.

4 Choose OK.

How to sort data in BIRT

The instructions in this section assume that you already inserted data in a report.

1 In the layout editor, select the table element or list element that contains the data that you want to sort. Property Editor displays the properties for the table or list.

Figure 12-4 shows an example of a selected table and the table's properties.

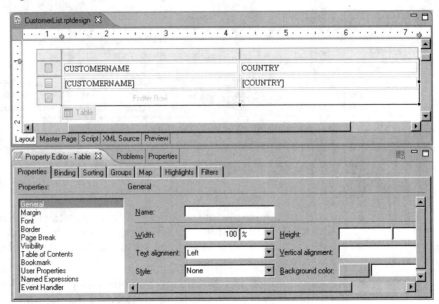

Figure 12-4   Properties for a selected table

2 Choose the Sorting tab in Property Editor.

3 On the sorting page, choose Add to specify the field to sort. The first line displays Key for Sort Key and Ascending for Sort Direction.

4 Select the cell under Sort Key. Two buttons appear on the right, as shown in Figure 12-5. The arrow button displays a list of fields by which you can sort. The ellipsis (...) button launches Expression Builder.

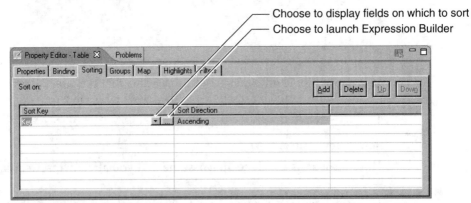

Figure 12-5   Tools for sorting on a field or launching Expression Builder

5 Complete one of the following steps:

- To specify a field to sort by, select the arrow button, and choose a field.

- To specify an expression by which to sort the data, choose the ellipsis button, then provide an expression in Expression Builder.

6 Specify the sort order by selecting Ascending or Descending under Sort Direction.

7 Preview the report. The data in the details section appears in a different order.

Sorting string data case-insensitively

BIRT and some databases sort string data according to UCS2 code point values, so uppercase letters precede lowercase letters. For example, "Z" appears before "a." The following list of values is an example of how BIRT sorts string data:

```
ANG Resellers
AV Stores, Co.
Alpha Cognac
American Souvenirs Inc
Anna's Decorations, Ltd
abc Shops
```

Most of the time, report users prefer to view a list of names in simple alphabetical order, without regard to capitalization. To display string values in case-insensitive alphabetical order, use JavaScript's toUpperCase( ) or toLowerCase( ) function to convert the values to all uppercase or all lowercase before sorting.

The following expression is an example of a sort key expression that you specify on the sorting page of Property Editor:

```
row["CUSTOMERNAME"].toUpperCase()
```

Using this expression, the previous list of values appears alphabetically as:

```
abc Shops
Alpha Cognac
American Souvenirs Inc
ANG Resellers
Anna's Decorations, Ltd
AV Stores, Co.
```

Grouping data

It is common for reports to present data that is organized into meaningful groups. For example, rather than displaying a basic list of orders, an orders report can group orders by customers, then group customers by state. In addition to providing a more effective way to view data, grouped reports have other advantages over reports that are not grouped.

When you group data, you can:

- Add titles or other text at the beginning of each group.

- Add subtotals, counts, averages, or other summary information at the beginning or end of each group.

- Insert a page break before or after each group.

- Automatically generate a table of contents that displays the values of every group. The table of contents supports navigating to specific locations in the report.

- Remove duplicate field values.

Compare the reports in Figure 12-6 and Figure 12-7. The report in Figure 12-6 displays customer order information in a simple list. The data rows are sorted by customer name, then by order number. Notice the repeated customer name and order ID information.

Customer	Order ID	Item	SKU Price	Quantity	Total Price
Brittan Design Inc.	1810	MSL3280	$210.00	1746	$366,660.00
Brittan Design Inc.	1810	MDSPL04	$340.00	1728	$587,520.00
CompuBoards	1075	MP2032	$310.00	49	$15,190.00
CompuBoards	1075	MP1632	$210.00	49	$10,290.00
CompuBoards	1900	MP2032	$310.00	13	$4,030.00
CompuBoards	1900	MP1632x	$221.00	13	$2,873.00
CompuBoards	1900	MSL3290	$300.00	13	$3,900.00
CompuBoards	1900	MDSPL04	$340.00	13	$4,420.00
CompuBoards	1900	MPL1632	$303.00	13	$3,939.00
CompuBoards	1900	MVL1664	$320.00	13	$4,160.00
CompuBoards	1900	MPL2032	$650.00	13	$8,450.00
CompuDesign Co.	1615	MSL3290	$300.00	386	$115,800.00
CompuDesign Co.	1615	MPL1632	$610.00	384	$234,240.00
CompuDesign Co.	1660	MP1632s	$290.00	306	$88,740.00

Figure 12-6 Report showing data in a simple list

The report in Figure 12-7 shows data from the same data set. Unlike the first report, it groups the data rows by customers and order numbers, removing the repeated customer names and order numbers. The customer name and order totals appear at the beginning of each customer group. The order number appears at the beginning of each order group, and a subtotal appears at the end of each order. When the report is displayed in the BIRT report viewer, a table of contents appears to the left of the report.

To create the report in Figure 12-7, you use the customer and order ID fields to create two groups. The customer group is the outer, or top, group. The orders group is within the customer group. You can create as many groups as you want. In the example report, you could, for example, create a third group to organize customers by state. You could also add a fourth group to organize states by region. Practically, however, a report that contains too many groups can make the report difficult to read.

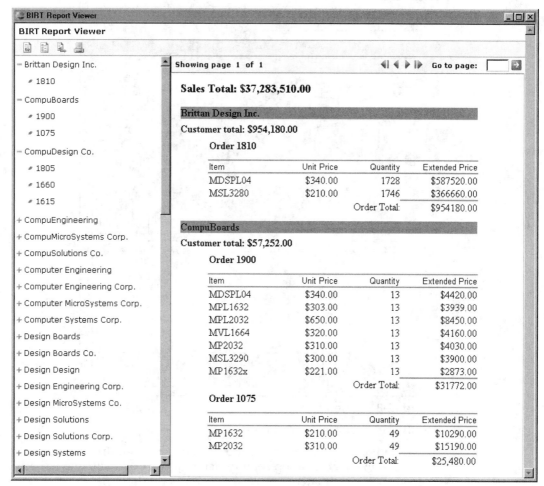

Figure 12-7   Report showing data in groups

How to group data

The instructions in this section assume that you already inserted data in your report.

1 In the layout editor, select the table element or list element that contains the data that you want to group.

2 Choose Element→Add Group. New Group, shown in Figure 12-8, displays the properties you can set for the group.

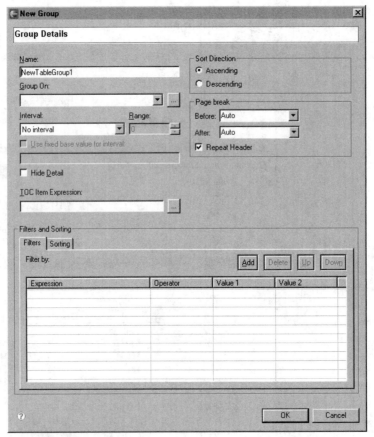

Figure 12-8   New Group

3 Specify the properties of the group:

- For Name, type a name for the group. The name identifies the group and appears in the Edit Group context menu, so you can easily find a specific group for editing later.

- For Group On, select the field on which you want to group. The drop-down list displays all the fields associated with the table. You can group on a field in the table or a field that you have not used in the table. To group on a field that you have not used in the table, you must first create the column binding. Column binding is described in Chapter 8, "Binding Data."

- For Interval, you can select a grouping interval, then specify a range. You can also specify the initial value to use for calculating numeric intervals. For information about grouping by intervals, see "Grouping data by intervals," later in this section.

- For Hide Detail, specify whether or not to display the detail rows. Select this option to display only summary data in the group's header or footer rows.

- For TOC Item Expression, specify the expression that returns the values to display in the auto-generated table of contents. By default, the group values appear in the report's table of contents.

- For Sort Direction:
  - Select Ascending to sort the group values in ascending order.
  - Select Descending to sort the group values in descending order.

- For Page Break, you can control where page breaks occur. If you want to display each group of data on its own page, you can insert a page break before or after each group. For more information about setting page breaks, see Chapter 21, "Designing a Multipage Report."

- For Filters, you can specify a filter condition to select group values that meet a certain criteria. For information about filtering group values, see Chapter 15, "Filtering Data."

- For Sorting, you can specify that the group values be sorted by a field other than the field on which the data is grouped. For information about sorting group values, see "Sorting data at the group level," later in this chapter.

Choose OK to save the group.

The table shows two new rows, group header and group footer. Figure 12-9 shows the new rows. BIRT Report Designer places a data element in the group header automatically. This data element displays the values of the field (PRODUCTCODE, in this example) on which the group is based.

Product	Price	Quantity	Total
[PRODUCTCODE]			
[PRODUCTCODE]	[PRICEEACH]	[QUANTITYORDERED]	[EXTENDEDPRICE]
Group Footer Row			
Footer Row			

Figure 12-9   Group header and group footer rows in a table

4 Preview the report. The data is organized in groups.

5 To create additional groups, repeat all the previous steps.

Grouping data by intervals

When you create a group, BIRT's default behavior is to group data by a single value, such as a customer name, an order ID, or a date. In the detailed orders report shown earlier in this chapter, each customer name starts a new group, and each order ID starts a new group within the customer group.

Sometimes, it is more useful to group data by a specific interval. A sales report, for example, can present sales by quarters, rather than by dates. Similarly, you can group data in a shipping report by weeks or months, rather than by dates.

Compare the reports in Figure 12-10 and Figure 12-11. The report in Figure 12-10 groups shipping information by dates.

Shipping Schedule

Ship by	Order ID	Customer name
01/02/2006	1440	Advanced Engineering
01/02/2006	1445	Technical Design Corp.
01/03/2006	1355	Signal MicroSystems
01/04/2006	1400	InfoSpecialists Inc.
01/05/2006	1320	CompuDesign Co.
01/09/2006	1410	Brittan Design Inc.
01/10/2006	1420	Exosoft Corp
01/11/2006	1250	Technical Solutions Inc.
01/11/2006	1325	SigniMicro Systems
01/12/2006	1500	CompuBoards

Figure 12-10   Dates grouped by single date values

The report in Figure 12-11 groups the same shipping information by weeks.

Weekly Shipping Schedule

Week of 01/02/2006

Ship by	Order ID	Customer name
01/02/2006	1440	Advanced Engineering
01/02/2006	1445	Technical Design Corp.
01/03/2006	1355	Signal MicroSystems
01/04/2006	1400	InfoSpecialists Inc.
01/05/2006	1320	CompuDesign Co.

Week of 01/09/2006

Ship by	Order ID	Customer name
01/09/2006	1410	Brittan Design Inc.
01/10/2006	1420	Exosoft Corp
01/11/2006	1250	Technical Solutions Inc.
01/11/2006	1325	SigniMicro Systems
01/12/2006	1500	CompuBoards

Figure 12-11   Dates grouped into weekly intervals

As the reports show, grouping by interval provides the following benefits:

- Organizes a long report into shorter, more readable pieces

- Summarizes data further for more effective analysis

The following sections describe in more detail how to group string, numeric, and date-and-time data by intervals.

Grouping string data by intervals

When you group string data by interval, the interval that you specify is a prefix of a particular length. For example, if a customer group sorts customers by name, you can group customers by the first letter of their names, or the first two letters, or the first three letters, and so on.

You typically group by the first letter to group names by letters of the alphabet. In a customer list, for example, you might want to group all customers whose names begin with A under the heading A, all customers whose names begin with B under the heading B, and so on.

You can group by multiple letters to group items whose names contain special prefixes for classification or categorization. A computer parts vendor, for example, might use the prefix ME for all memory chips, CP for CPU boards, MO for monitors, and so on. In this case, creating a computer parts list that groups names by the first two letters lends itself to logical groupings by part type.

Figure 12-12 shows the results of grouping names by the first letter, the first two letters, and the first three letters. Lines separate the groups.

Grouping by first letter	Grouping by two letters	Grouping by three letters
Customers	**Customers**	**Customers**
Accere	Accere	Accere
Accor	Accor	Accor
Acer	Accuview	Accuview
Acme	Acer	Acer
Adamark	Acme	Acme
Advair	Adamark	Adamark
Aegis	Advair	Advair
Altria	Aegis	Aegis
BayView	Altria	Altria
	BayView	BayView

Figure 12-12   Results of grouping string data by intervals

How to group string data by intervals

1   Create a group using the instructions in "How to group data," earlier in this chapter.

2   Set the Interval field in the group editor to Prefix.

3   Set Range to the number of characters by which to group.

Grouping numeric data by intervals

When you group numeric data by intervals, you group by a range of numbers. For example, if an order group sorts orders by numeric ID, you can group the orders by intervals of 10, 50, 100, 1000, and so on.

The interval that is best for any set of numeric data depends on the range of numeric values. If the numbers range from 100 to 200, it makes sense to group in intervals of 10s. If the numbers range from 100 to 1000, you might want to group in intervals of 100.

Figure 12-13 shows the results of grouping numbers by intervals of 10, 100, and 1000. Lines separate the groups.

Grouping by 10s   Grouping by 100s   Grouping by 1000s

Order ID	Order ID	Order ID
1070	1070	1070
1080	1080	1080
1085	1085	1085
1095	1095	1095
1340	1340	1340
1345	1345	1345
1405	1405	1405
2005	2005	2005
2030	2030	2030
3015	3015	3015
3020	3020	3020
3025	3025	3025

Figure 12-13   Results of grouping numeric data by intervals

Groups are calculated from the first value in the data set. If the first number is 1070, and you use an interval of 10, the first group contains values from 1070 to 1079, the second group contains values from 1080 to 1089, and so on. In the example report that shows a grouping interval of 1000, the numbers 2005 and 2030 are not in a separate group, which is what you might expect, because the first group contains numbers from 1070 to 2069. The second group contains numbers from 2070 to 3069.

Rather than using the first data set value as the starting, or base, value for determining the grouping of numbers, you can specify a different base value to group numbers in more predictable ranges. Compare the two reports in Figure 12-14.

Grouping by 1000s
No base value specified

Grouping by 1000s
Base value of 1000

Order ID
1070
1080
1085
1095
1340
1345
1405
2005
2030
3015
3020
3025

Order ID
1070
1080
1085
1095
1340
1345
1405
2005
2030
3015
3020
3025

Figure 12-14   Results of grouping with no base value and a base value of 1000

A base value of 1000 provides better results than a base value of 1070 when grouping by intervals of 1000. Rather than grouping numbers in groups of 1070–2069 and 2070–3069, the second report uses more logical groups of 1000–1999 and 2000–2999.

How to group numeric data by intervals

1 Create a group using the instructions in "How to group data," earlier in this chapter.

2 Set the Interval field in the group editor to Interval.

3 Set Range to the desired grouping interval.

4 If you want to specify a starting value to use for calculating groups, select Use fixed base value for interval, and specify a number.

Grouping date-and-time data by intervals

When you group date-and-time data by intervals, you group data by time periods, such as hours, days, weeks, months, and so on. Grouping by time periods is useful for reports that display information that has a time or schedule focus, such as weekly shipping schedules or quarterly sales figures.

The reports in Figure 12-15 show the results of grouping dates by weeks, months, and quarters. The lines separate the groups. Weekly groups start on Mondays, monthly groups start on the first date of the month, and quarterly groups are January 1–March 31, April 1–June 30, July 1–September 30, and October 1–December 31. If you group by year, the groups start on January 1 and end on December 31.

Grouping by weeks	Grouping by months	Grouping by quarters

Ship Dates	Ship Dates	Ship Dates
January 9, 2006	January 9, 2006	January 9, 2006
January 15, 2006	January 15, 2006	January 15, 2006
	January 30, 2006	January 30, 2006
January 30, 2006		February 5, 2006
February 5, 2006	February 5, 2006	March 7, 2006
March 7, 2006	March 7, 2006	
		April 5, 2006
April 5, 2006	April 5, 2006	April 12, 2006
	April 12, 2006	June 18, 2006
April 12, 2006		June 30, 2006
	June 18, 2006	
June 18, 2006	June 30, 2006	July 7, 2006
June 30, 2006	July 7, 2006	October 1, 2006
July 7, 2006		
	October 1, 2006	
October 1, 2006		

Figure 12-15   Results of grouping date-and-time data by intervals

If you do not want to use the default start value for date-and-time groups, you can specify a different base value to group dates in different ranges. For example, if an organization's fiscal year is October 1 to September 30, and you want to group ten years worth of data into yearly groups by fiscal year rather than by calendar year, you can specify a base value such as 10/01/1995. The report will display the data in the following groups: October 1, 1995–September 30, 1996; October 1, 1996–September 30, 1997; October 1, 1997–September 30, 1998; and so on.

How to group date-and-time data by intervals

1   Create a group using the instructions in "How to group data," earlier in this chapter.

2   Set the Interval field in the group editor to one of the time period values, such as Year, Month, Week, Day, or Hour.

3   Set Range to the number of units to include in each group. For example, if you selected Week as the interval, specify 2 as the range to group data in two-week periods.

4   If you want to specify a different starting value to use for calculating groups, select Use fixed base value for interval, then specify a date.

Sorting data at the group level

When you create a group, the default setting specifies sorting the group values by the grouping field in ascending order. For example, if you create an order ID group, the default setting is to sort order ID values in ascending order. You can, however, sort the group values by a different field. For example, rather than sort group values by order ID, you can sort by order total.

Sorting at the group level is different from sorting at the detail row level. When you sort at the detail row level, you specify the sorting criteria on the Sorting page in Property Editor. When you sort at the group level, you specify the sorting criteria through the Groups page.

The report in Figure 12-16 groups sales data by product code. The group header, highlighted with a grey background, displays the product code and the sales total. The product code group uses the default sorting, which sorts by product code in ascending order, such as S10_1678, S10_1949, S10_2016, and so on.

S10_1678			$6,702.15
Order Number	Quantity Sold	Price Per Unit	Order Total
10211	41	$90.92	$3,727.72
10223	37	$80.39	$2,974.43
S10_1949			$16,769.28
Order Number	Quantity Sold	Price Per Unit	Order Total
10206	47	$203.59	$9,568.73
10215	35	$205.73	$7,200.55
S10_2016			$7,996.11
Order Number	Quantity Sold	Price Per Unit	Order Total
10201	24	$116.56	$2,797.44
10223	47	$110.61	$5,198.67

Figure 12-16   Results of sorting group values in ascending order

The report in Figure 12-17 contains the same data as the report in Figure 12-16, but rather than sorting by product code, it sorts by the product sales total in ascending order.

S10_1678			$6,702.15
Order Number	Quantity Sold	Price Per Unit	Order Total
10211	41	$90.92	$3,727.72
10223	37	$80.39	$2,974.43
S10_2016			$7,996.11
Order Number	Quantity Sold	Price Per Unit	Order Total
10201	24	$116.56	$2,797.44
10223	47	$110.61	$5,198.67
S10_1949			$16,769.28
Order Number	Quantity Sold	Price Per Unit	Order Total
10206	47	$203.59	$9,568.73
10215	35	$205.73	$7,200.55

Figure 12-17   Results of changing the sort order of groups

By changing the field on which groups are sorted, you can choose the information to emphasize. As Figure 12-17 shows, the report can group sales data by product code but list them in order of sales total, which is often a more useful way to present sales information.

How to sort data at the group level

1 Create a group using the instructions in "How to group data," earlier in this chapter. Figure 12-18 shows the group editor. You can specify sorting in two ways. The first way is to specify sorting by the grouping field. The second way enables you to specify a different field by which to sort and also enables you to specify a sort expression.

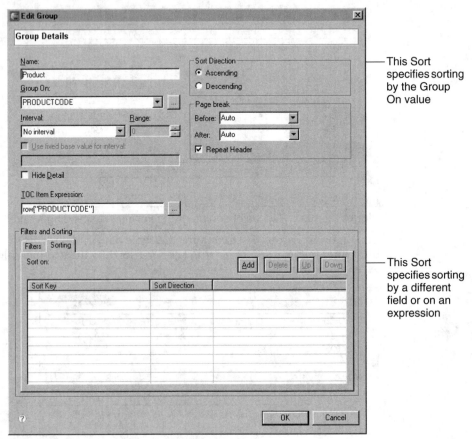

This Sort specifies sorting by the Group On value

This Sort specifies sorting by a different field or on an expression

Figure 12-18 Sorting options in Edit Group

2 In Filters and Sorting, choose Sorting.

3 Choose Add to specify the field on which to sort the group values. Placeholder values appear on the first line.

4 Select the line under Sort Key. Two buttons appear on the right. The arrow button displays a list of fields by which you can sort. The ellipsis button (...) launches Expression Builder.

5 Specify the sort expression.

6 Specify the sort order by selecting Ascending or Descending under Sort Direction. Choose OK. Figure 12-19 shows an expression that sorts the group values by sales totals in ascending order.

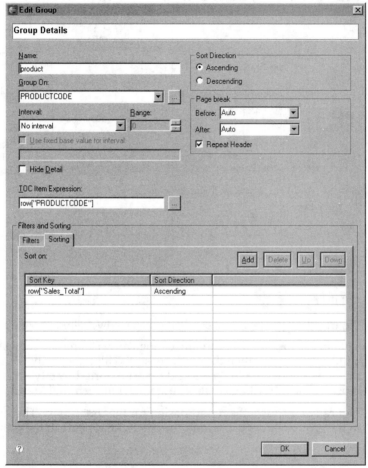

Figure 12-19 Sorting expression in Edit Group

7 Preview the report.

Creating multiple groups

When you create multiple groups, the order in which you create them determines how the report groups data. Before you create groups, think about their order. For example, if you want to group data by state, then by city, create the groups in that order. In other words, state is the table or list's first, or top-level, group, and city is the second, or inner, group.

The reports in Figure 12-20 show the results of creating the state and city groups in different orders. The first report shows the output when the state group is the top-level group. The second report shows the output when the city group is the top-level group.

Report groups data by state, then by city

Report groups data by city, then by state

CT			NY		
	Bridgewater			Albany	
		Design Design			CompuEngineering
		SigniSpecialists			Signal MicroSystems
	Glendale				Technical Systems Corp.
		Advanced MicroSystems			Advanced Solutions Inc.
		Technical Boards	PA		
MA				Allentown	
	Boston				InfoBoards
		Technical Systems Inc.			Technical Design Corp.
		Design Systems			CompuBoards
		Brittan Design Inc.			Advanced Engineering Inc.
		TeleBoards Co.			TekniMicroSystems Co.
		Design Engineering Corp.	MA		
	Brickhaven			Boston	
		Signal Design Corp.			Technical Systems Inc.
		InfoEngineering			Design Systems
		InfoSpecialists Inc.			Brittan Design Inc.
		SigniEngineering Co.			TeleBoards Co.
					Design Engineering Corp.
			MA		
				Brickhaven	

Figure 12-20   Results of creating groups in two different orders

Data in the first report is organized logically. The report shows each state in alphabetical order, then the cities are sorted alphabetically within each state. On the other hand, data in the second report is sorted by city first, resulting in repeated state headings that are organized in seemingly random order.

Figure 12-21 shows the report design for the first report. The state field appears in the group header 1 row, and the city field appears in the group header 2 row.

Figure 12-21   Report design grouping data by state, then by city

You can create groups using any of the following procedures. The procedure you use depends on your preference and whether you are creating all the groups for the first time or adding groups to an existing group structure.

- To create groups that follow the order in which you create them, use one of the following procedures:

  - Select the table or list, then choose Element➤Add Group from the main menu to create each group. For example, if you create a state group first and a city group second, the state group is the top-level group, and the city is the inner group.

  - Select the table or list, then choose the Groups tab on Property Editor. Like the previous technique, the order in which you create the groups determines the order in which data is grouped.

- To add a group at the top level, select the table or list, then choose Insert Group➤Above from the context menu. For example, if you already created a city group, use Insert Group➤Above to add a state group as the top-level group.

- To add a group at the lowest level, right-click the table or list, then choose Insert Group➤Below from the table or list's context menu. For example, if you already created a state group, choose Insert Group➤Below to add a city group as the inner group.

- To add a group between two existing groups, use one of the following procedures:

  - Right-click the group row above which to create the new group, then choose Insert Group➤Above.

  - Right-click the group row below which to create the new group, then choose Insert Group➤Below.

All the techniques display the Edit Group dialog box, where you define the properties of a group. If you inadvertently create groups in the wrong order, you can easily change the order of the groups. You do not have to delete and recreate the groups.

Changing the order of groups

The Groups page in Property Editor shows all the groups that you create for a particular table or list. You must use this page, shown in Figure 12-24, to change the order of groups. You can also add, edit, and delete groups using this page.

You cannot change the order of groups by moving data elements in the layout editor. This action affects only the display position of the data values. Compare the report designs in Figure 12-22. The state and city data elements are transposed by dragging and dropping in the layout editor.

State data element placed in group header 1
City data element placed in group header 2

State data element moved to group header 2
City data element moved to group header 1

Figure 12-22 Report designs with transposed state and city elements

Now, compare the corresponding report output, shown in Figure 12-23. The first report shows data sorted by state, then by city. The second report displays the city values above the state values. The report data, however, is still sorted by state first, then by city.

CT	Bridgewater
	CT
Bridgewater	
Design Design	Design Design
SigniSpecialists	SigniSpecialists
Glendale	CT
Advanced MicroSystems	Advanced MicroSystems
Technical Boards	Technical Boards
MA	Boston
Boston	MA
Technical Systems Inc.	Brittan Design Inc.
Design Systems	Design Engineering Corp.
Brittan Design Inc.	Design Systems
TeleBoards Co.	Technical Systems Inc.
Design Engineering Corp.	TeleBoards Co.
Brickhaven	MA
Signal Design Corp.	CompuDesign Co.
InfoEngineering	InfoEngineering
InfoSpecialists Inc.	InfoSpecialists Inc.
SigniEngineering Co.	Signal Design Corp.

Figure 12-23 Reports showing the effects of transposing state and city elements

How to change the order of groups

1 Select the table or list whose groups you want to re-order.

In Property Editor, choose the Groups tab. The Groups page displays the groups defined in the table or list, as shown in Figure 12-24.

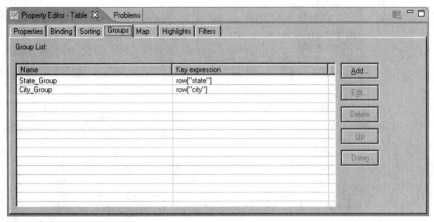

Figure 12-24 Groups page

This page displays the group names in the order in which the report currently groups the data.

2 Select a group from the list, then use the Up or Down button to move the selected group up or down the list. In the layout editor, the data elements change positions to reflect the new grouping order.

3 Repeat the previous step until you finish changing the order of groups.

Adding group headings

If your report contains groups, you typically add a descriptive heading that appears at the beginning of each group to identify the data within the group. When you create a group, BIRT Report Designer automatically inserts a data element in the group header row to serve as the group heading. This data element displays the values of the field on which the group is based. For example, if you group data by state, the data element displays a state name for each group.

Unlike column headings, which are static, group headings change based on the content of the group. If a report groups data by customers, for example, you can display the customer name at the beginning of each group. For a customer list that groups names by the first letter, the titles for the groups are A, B, C, and so on. For a shipping schedule that groups data by weeks, the titles for the groups could be Week of 01/02/06, Week of 01/09/06, and so on.

The reports in Figure 12-25 show examples of headings that change with each group. Bold text highlights the group headings. If you do not use group headings, it is unclear where one group ends and another begins. Remove the A and B headings from the Customers report, for example, and the report looks like a list sorted alphabetically. You can add a line or space between groups to indicate a change in group, but a descriptive heading makes it easier for users to find information in the report.

Customer Orders		
Advanced Design		
Order 1010		
Item	Quantity	Price
M12	2	$60.00
M15	1	$55.00
Order 1015		
Item	Quantity	Price
R50	1	$20.00
...		
Advantix Inc		
Order 1050		
...		

Customers
A
Accere
Accor
Acer
Acme
Adamark
Advair
B
BayView
Beaucoup
...

Weekly Shipping Schedule	
Week of 01/02/06	
Ship date	Order ID
01/02/06	1015
01/03/06	1025
01/03/06	1026
01/04/06	1020
01/05/06	1022
01/06/06	1030
Week of 01/09/06	
Ship date	Order ID
01/09/06	1029

Figure 12-25   Examples of group headings that change

Displaying group headings in the detail row

Headings that are in a group header row appear above the detail rows. Sometimes, a report looks better if the headings appear in the first detail row of each group. Compare the examples in Figure 12-26. The example on the left shows the group headings, which are order numbers, in a row above the detail rows. The example on the right shows the group headings in the detail row.

Group headings (order numbers) appear above the detail rows

Group headings (order numbers) appear in the first detail row

Order 10200		
	S24_1785	$3,285.81
	S32_1374	$2,831.85
	S32_4289	$1,764.45
		$7,882.11
Order 10202		
	S32_2206	$901.53
	S32_4485	$2,530.84
		$3,432.37

Order 10200	S24_1785	$3,285.81
	S32_1374	$2,831.85
	S32_4289	$1,764.45
		$7,882.11
Order 10202	S32_2206	$901.53
	S32_4485	$2,530.84
		$3,432.37

Figure 12-26   Two ways to display group headings

To display group headings on the same line as the first detail row, you drop the cell that contains the heading, using the Drop property. You cannot just move the group heading to the detail row, because it would be repeated for every row. To drop a cell, you must observe the following rules:

- There must be an empty cell below the cell that contains the group heading. Otherwise, the cell content overwrites the content in the cell below it.

- If a table contains multiple group header rows, you can drop only cells in the group header row directly above the detail row.

- You can only drop cells in a group header row. You cannot drop cells in a detail or group footer row.

You can drop a group header cell so that it spans the detail rows, or all the rows in the group, including the group footer row. You see a difference only if the group header cell has a border or background color. Compare the examples in Figure 12-27. The example on the left drops the group header cell to the detail rows. The example on the right drops the group header cell to all the rows in the group.

Notice that the cell color in the example on the left extends to the last detail row, whereas the cell color in the example on the right extends to the group footer row. If the cell did not have a background color, the output would look the same whether you set the cell's Drop property to Detail or All. The order numbers always appear in the first detail row of each group.

Group header cell (shown in color) dropped to the detail rows

Order 10200	S24_1785	$3,285.81
	S32_1374	$2,831.85
	S32_4289	$1,764.45
		$7,882.11
Order 10202	S32_2206	$901.53
	S32_4485	$2,530.84
		$3,432.37

Group header cell dropped to all rows in the group

Order 10200	S24_1785	$3,285.81
	S32_1374	$2,831.85
	S32_4289	$1,764.45
		$7,882.11
Order 10202	S32_2206	$901.53
	S32_4485	$2,530.84
		$3,432.37

Figure 12-27   Reports showing different settings for the Drop property

Figure 12-28 shows the portion of the report design that generates the previous example output.

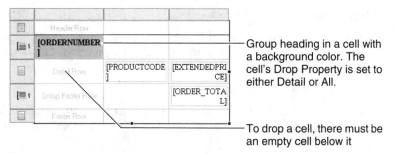

Group heading in a cell with a background color. The cell's Drop Property is set to either Detail or All.

To drop a cell, there must be an empty cell below it

Figure 12-28   Report design that generates a dropped cell

How to drop a group heading to the detail row

1   Select the cell that contains the group heading you want to drop. The cell directly below it must be empty.

2   On Property Editor, choose General from the list of properties.

3   For Drop, select one of the following values:

   ▪   Detail—Select this value to drop the group heading so that it spans only the detail rows.

- All—Select this value to drop the group heading so that it spans all the rows in the group, including the group footer row.

These values display a difference in the generated report only if the cell has borders or background color.

4 Preview the report. The group heading appears in the first detail row of each group.

Specifying expressions for group headings

Unlike column headings, which you create using static text, you specify expressions for group headings because the heading values are dynamic. In other words, the value changes based on the group's content. You can use a data set field, a computed field, or a text element with dynamic values, depending on the value that you want to display.

Typically, you use a computed field to combine a field value and static text. Sometimes, you use a JavaScript function to display the values you need. The following list shows some examples of expressions that you can use for group headings:

- To display the customer name as the group heading, use the customer name field as the expression:

```
row["customerName"]
```

- To display a group heading that combines static text with a field, insert a data element, and use an expression like the following example:

```
"Order " + row["orderID"]
```

- To create headings (A, B, and so on) for a customer list that is grouped by the first letter, insert a data element, and use the JavaScript charAt( ) function to get the first letter of the name in each group:

```
row["customerName"].charAt(0)
```

- To create headings that display the names of months (January, February, and so on) for each group of dates, insert an HTML text element, and use the following expression:

```
<VALUE-OF format="MMMM">row["shipByDate"]</VALUE-OF>
```

Tutorial 2: Grouping report data

This tutorial provides instructions for grouping customer data by credit limit. It uses the report that you built in Tutorial 1: "Building a simple listing report," in Chapter 4, "Learning the Basics." In the first tutorial, you built a simple report that listed customers in alphabetical order. In this report, you organize customers into credit limit groups of $50,000.00, such as 0–49999, 50000–99999, 100000–149999, and so on.

Before you begin this tutorial, you must complete the first tutorial. In this tutorial, you perform the following tasks:

- Open the report design.
- Save the report as a new file.
- Add the credit limit field to the data set.
- Add credit limit data to the report.
- Group customer data by credit limit.
- Display credit limit ranges in the group header.
- Display aggregate information.
- Format the report.
- Preview the report in the BIRT report viewer.
- Display credit limit ranges in the table of contents.

Task 1: Open the report design

In the first tutorial, you created Customers.rptdesign in a project folder named My Reports. Open Customers.rptdesign using one of the following procedures:

- If you are using BIRT Report Designer, open the file through Navigator:
    1 Open Navigator by choosing Window→Show View→Navigator. Navigator shows all the project folders and report files you create.
    2 Navigate to the My Reports folder, then double-click Customers.rptdesign.
- If you are using BIRT RCP Report Designer, use the main menu to open the file:
    1 Choose File→Open File.
    2 Navigate to and select Customers.rptdesign, then choose Open.

The file opens in the layout editor, as shown in Figure 12-29.

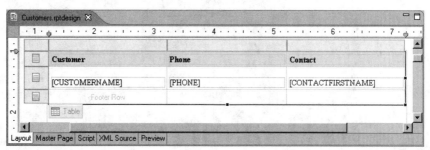

Figure 12-29   Customer report design in the layout editor

Task 2: Save the report as a new file

Rather than editing directly the report that you created in the first tutorial, save Customers.rptdesign as a new file.

1 Choose File→Save As. Save As displays the file's current name and location.

2 For File name, change Customers.rptdesign to Customers_grouped.rptdesign, then choose Finish. BIRT Report Designer makes a copy of Customers.rptdesign. The new file appears in the layout editor.

Task 3: Add the credit limit field to the data set

In order for the report to display credit limit data, you must add the CREDITLIMIT field to the data set.

1 Choose Data Explorer, expand Data Sets, then double-click Customers. Edit Data Set displays the SQL query for the Customers data set.

2 In the query, add a comma (,) after phone.

3 On the next line, add the following text:

```
creditLimit
```

The modified query should look like the one shown in Figure 12-30.

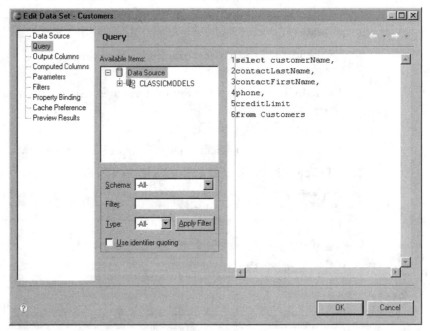

Figure 12-30 Query with creditLimit field added

4 Choose Preview Results to verify that the query returns rows with credit limit information.

5 Choose OK to save the data set.

Task 4: Add credit limit data to the report

In this procedure, you insert the credit limit field in the existing table.

1 In the layout editor, select the table. Guide cells appear at the top and left side of the table.

2 Right-click the guide cell above the first column, then choose Insert→Column to the Left, as shown in Figure 12-31.

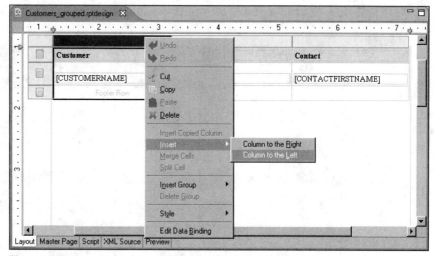

Figure 12-31 Inserting a column to the left of an existing column

A new column appears.

3 In Data Explorer, expand Data Sets, then expand Customers. The Customers data set displays the fields specified in the query.

4 Drag the CREDITLIMIT field from Data Explorer, and drop it in the detail row cell next to [CUSTOMERNAME]. BIRT Report Designer creates a named column, which is bound to the data set field. Select Data Binding displays this column binding.

5 Choose OK to accept the default column binding.

In the layout editor, the table displays the field that you added. The table also shows the label element that the layout editor automatically added to the header row. This label serves as the column heading and displays the field name as static text. The report should look like the one shown in Figure 12-32.

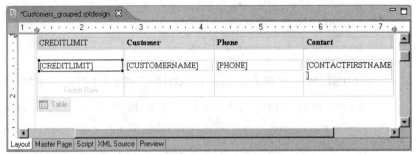

Figure 12-32 Result of adding the credit limit field in the layout editor

6 Edit the CREDITLIMIT label so that it appears as **Credit Limit**.

7 Preview the report. The report should look like the one shown in Figure 12-33.

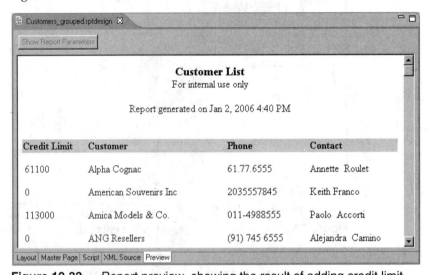

Figure 12-33 Report preview, showing the result of adding credit limit

Some of the customers have a credit limit of 0. These are new customers who have not yet been approved for a line of credit.

Task 5: Group customer data by credit limit

The report is currently sorted alphabetically by customer name. Recall that in the first tutorial, you specified that the rows in the table be sorted by customer name. In this procedure, you group the data by credit limit in intervals of 50,000. When you group data, BIRT sorts the rows into groups first, then it sorts the rows within each group, assuming that you also specify a sort condition at the table level. As you will see when you complete this task, the data rows within each credit limit group will be sorted by customer name.

1 Choose Layout to return to the layout editor.

2 Right-click the table, and choose Insert Group➤Above. New Group, shown in Figure 12-34, displays the group properties you can set.

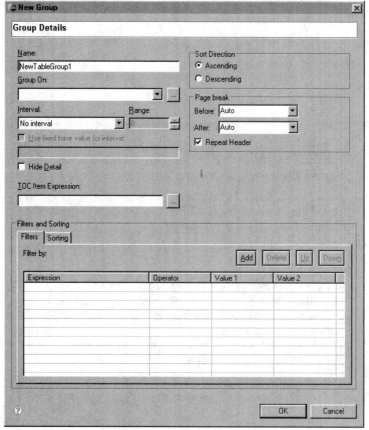

Figure 12-34 New Group

3 Follow these steps to specify grouping by credit limit in intervals of 50000:

   1 For Name, type the following text as the group name:

```
credit_group
```

   2 For Group On, select CREDITLIMIT from the drop-down list.

   3 For Interval, select Interval from the drop-down list.

   4 For Range, type 50000.

   5 Use the default values for the other options. Choose OK.

The table in the report design displays a group header and a group footer row, as shown in Figure 12-35. The table also shows the data element that the layout editor automatically added to the group header row. This data element serves as the group heading and, in the generated report, displays the first credit limit value of each group.

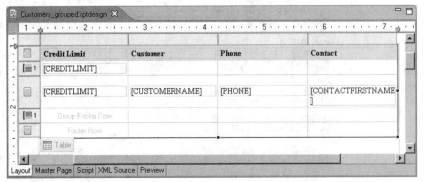

Figure 12-35   Group header and group footer rows in a report design

4   Select the [CREDITLIMIT] data element that appears in the group header row. Do not select the [CREDITLIMIT] data element that appears in the detail row.

5   In Property Editor, choose General, then choose B to format the group heading as bold text.

6   Preview the report. Scroll down the report to view all the data. The report organizes data into four credit limit groups. At the beginning of each group, you see the following numbers in bold: 0, 61100, 113000, 227600. These numbers match the first credit limit value of each group. Within each group, customer names are sorted in alphabetical order. Figure 12-36 shows one of the four credit limit groups.

The group header displays the first value in each group

Figure 12-36   Report preview, showing one of the four credit limit groups

Task 6: Display credit limit ranges in the group header

Rather than display the first value of each group in the group header, the report is easier to navigate if it displays the credit limit range for each group, as follows:

```
0 - 49999
50000 - 99999
100000 - 149999
```

This procedure shows how to write a JavaScript expression to display these credit limit ranges. The procedure also shows how to create a column binding with which to associate the JavaScript expression.

1 Choose Layout to return to the layout editor.

2 Select the table, and choose Binding on Property Editor.

3 Create a new column binding:

   1 Choose Add.

   2 In Expression Builder, type the following expression:

```
for(i=50000; i<300000; i+=50000){
    if( row["CREDITLIMIT"] < i ){
        rangeStart = i-50000;
        rangeEnd = i-1;
        break;
    }
}
displayString=rangeStart + " - " + rangeEnd;
```

     Choose OK. The new column binding appears on the binding page of Property Editor with the column name highlighted.

   3 Replace the name New Binding with the following name:

     CREDIT_GROUP_HEADER

4 Update the CREDITLIMIT data element in the group header to use the new column binding. Double-click the data element and select CREDIT_GROUP_HEADER, then choose OK.

5 Preview the report. The group headers display the credit limit ranges. Figure 12-37 shows the 50000 - 99999 group header.

Figure 12-37 Report preview, showing credit limit ranges

Task 7: Display aggregate information

One of the benefits of grouping data is that you can add summary, or aggregate, information at the beginning or end of each group. In this procedure, you display the number of customers in each group and the number of all customers that are listed in the report.

1 Choose Layout to return to the layout editor.

2 Display the number of customers in each group:

    1 Drag a data element from the palette, and drop it in the first cell in the group footer row. Elements that are in the group footer appear at the end of every group.

    2 On Select Data Binding, create a new column binding:

        1 On a new row, in Name, type the following text:

```
GROUP_CUSTOMER_COUNT
```

        2 Use the default data type, Any.

        3 In Expression, type the following aggregate expression:

```
"Customers: " + Total.count()
```

        Total.count( ) returns the number of rows.

        4 Use the default Aggregate On value, credit_group. This value indicates that the Total.count( ) function returns the number of rows in each credit limit group.

        5 Select the column binding you just created, and choose OK. The data element uses the selected column binding.

3 Preview the report. The report displays the number of customers at the end of each group, as shown in Figure 12-38.

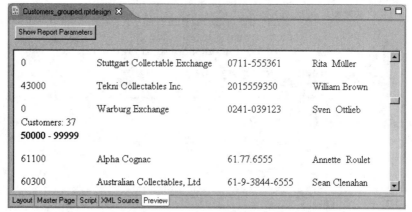

Figure 12-38 Report preview, showing a count for each group

3 Choose Layout to return to the layout editor.

4 Display the number of all customers:

1 Select the table. Guide cells appear at the top and left side of the table.

2 Right-click the guide cell on the left of the first row, Table - Header, then choose Insert➤Row➤Above.

A new table header row appears above the row that displays the column headings. It appears in color, because it inherited the properties of the row that follows it.

3 Select the new row, and, in Property Editor, change its background color to white.

4 Drag a data element from the palette, and drop it in the first cell in the new table header row. Elements that are in the table header appear at the beginning of the section.

5 On Select Data Binding, create a new column binding:

1 On a new row, in Name, type the following text:

```
TOTAL_CUSTOMER_COUNT
```

2 Use the default data type, Any.

3 In Expression, type the following expression, which combines static text with an aggregate calculation:

```
"Number of customers: " + Total.count()
```

4 Use the default Aggregate On value, ALL. This value indicates that the Total.count( ) function returns the number of rows in the entire table.

5 Select the column binding you just created, and choose OK. The data element uses the selected column binding. The report design should look like the one shown in Figure 12-39.

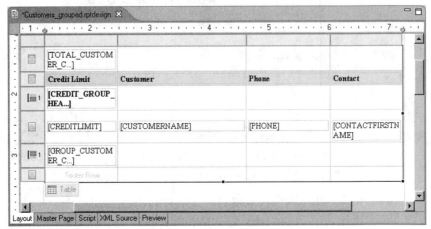

Figure 12-39 Report design, showing a total count for customers

5 Preview the report. The report displays the number of customers at the beginning of the table, as shown in Figure 12-40.

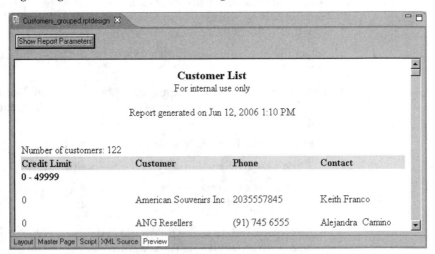

Figure 12-40 Report preview, showing a total number of customers

Task 8: Format the report

Now that the report displays the correct data, you can focus on improving the report's appearance. You perform the following tasks in this section:

- Remove credit limit data from the detail rows.
- Display group headings on the first row of each group.
- Separate each group with a line.

Remove credit limit data from the detail rows

To verify that data appears in the correct credit limit groups, it is useful to display each customer's credit limit. Now that we have verified the data, we can delete the individual credit limit information from the report.

1 Choose Layout to return to the layout editor.

2 Delete the [CREDITLIMIT] data element from the detail row.

3 Preview the report. It should look like the one shown in Figure 12-41.

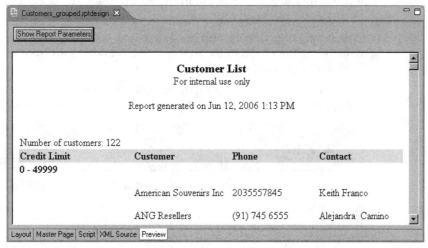

Figure 12-41   Report preview, without credit limit data for each row

Display group headings on the first row of each group

The credit limit group headings appear in their own rows, above the detail rows of each group. In this procedure, you drop the group headings so that they appear in the first detail row.

1 Choose Layout to return to the layout editor.

2 Select the cell that contains the group heading, as shown in Figure 12-42. Be sure to select the cell and not the data element in the cell.

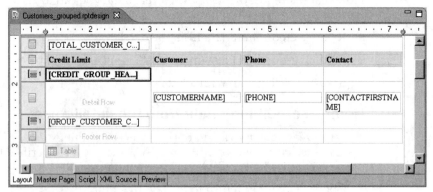

Figure 12-42 Group heading cell selected

3 In the General properties of Property Editor, set Drop to Detail. In the report design, the group heading still appears above the detail row because technically the element is still in the group header row.

4 In the Padding properties of Property Editor, set Padding—Top to 12 points. This setting aligns the group headings more precisely with the detail rows' data. Remember that, in the first tutorial, we added a 12-point padding to the top of the detail row cells.

5 Preview the report. The group headings appear in the first row of each group, as shown in Figure 12-43.

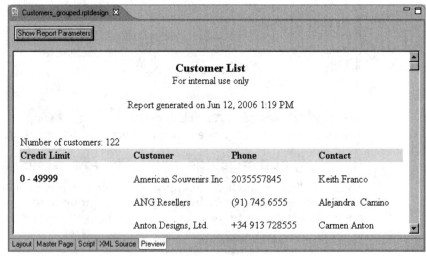

Figure 12-43 Report preview, showing dropped group headings

Separate each group with a line

Drawing a line to separate each group makes it easier to see the groups of data.

1 Choose Layout to return to the layout editor.

2 Select all the cells in the group footer row. To select multiple cells, use Shift-click.

3 Choose Border in Property Editor, then set the border properties:

- Set Style to a solid line.
- Choose the button that shows the bottom border.

4 Add more space between the line and text above it. While the cells are still selected, choose the Padding properties in Property Editor, and set Bottom to 6.0 points.

5 Preview the report. A line appears at the end of each group, as shown in Figure 12-44.

Figure 12-44   Report preview, showing a line between groups

Task 9:   Preview the report in the BIRT report viewer

So far, you have been checking the report output in the BIRT Report Designer previewer. This time, you will use the report viewer to see what the report looks like when it is deployed. The report viewer provides additional functionality, including the capability of navigating to specific sections of a report using a table of contents. When you create groups in a report, BIRT automatically generates a table of contents, using the group values to show the hierarchy of the report.

1 Choose File➞View Report in Web Viewer. The report appears in the report viewer.

2 Choose the table of contents button, the left button at the top of the window, to display the table of contents. The table of contents displays the first value in each of the four credit limit groups. When you select a value, the report displays the corresponding section of the report. If you select 61100, for example, the report shows the customer rows in the 50000 - 99999 credit limit range, as shown in Figure 12-45.

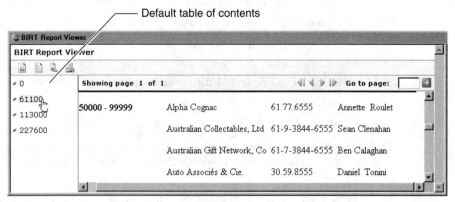

Figure 12-45 Select a value in the table of contents to view the corresponding data

Task 10: Display credit limit ranges in the table of contents

Rather than display the first value of each credit limit group, the table of contents makes more sense if it displays the same credit limit range values as the report. You accomplish this task by using the same JavaScript expression that you used previously to display credit limit ranges (0 - 49999, 50000 - 99999, and so on) in the group header.

1 Return to BIRT Report Designer.

2 In the layout editor, select the table, then choose the Groups tab in Property Editor.

3 Double-click credit_group in the list of groups. Edit Group displays the properties of the group. TOC Item Expression is set, by default, to the grouping field, row["CREDITLIMIT"].

4 Choose the ellipsis (...) button, and in Expression Builder, replace the row["CREDITLIMIT"] expression with the following expression. This is the same column-binding expression that is used by the data element in the group header. Rather than typing the expression again, you can copy it from the data element and paste it here.

```
for(i=50000; i<300000; i+=50000){
   if( row["CREDITLIMIT"] < i ){
      rangeStart = i-50000;
      rangeEnd = i-1;
      break;
   }
}
displayString=rangeStart + " - " + rangeEnd;
```

5 Choose OK.

6 Preview the report in the report viewer to verify the change in the table of contents. The table of contents displays the credit limit ranges, as shown in Figure 12-46.

Updated table of contents

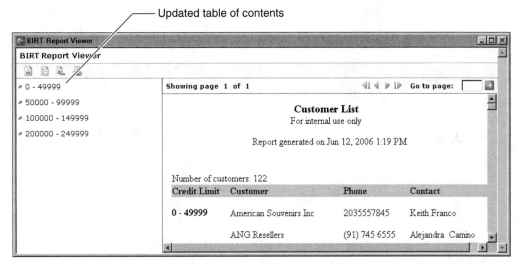

Figure 12-46 Updated table of contents, displaying credit limit ranges

13

Aggregating Data

One of the key features of any report is the ability to display summary, or aggregate, information. For example, a sales report can show the overall sales total; sales subtotals by product type, region, or sales representatives; average sales figures; or the highest and lowest sales figures.

Aggregating data involves performing a calculation over a set of data rows. For a simple listing report, the aggregate calculations are performed over all the data rows in the report. The listing report in Figure 13-1 displays aggregate data at the end of the report.

Customer	Payment Date	Check Number	Amount
Saveley & Henriot, Co.	16 January 2004	FU793410	$49,614.72
Men 'R' US Retailers, Ltd.	18 January 2004	DG700707	$21,053.69
Osaka Souveniers Co.	19 January 2004	CI381435	$47,177.59
Auto Canal+ Petit	28 January 2004	HJ217687	$49,165.16
Euro+ Shopping Channel	30 January 2004	HJ32686	$59,830.55
Double Decker Gift Stores, Ltd	31 January 2004	PO860906	$7,310.42
Corrida Auto Replicas, Ltd	06 February 2004	NA377824	$22,162.61
Auto Associés & Cie.	10 February 2004	EP227123	$5,759.42
West Coast Collectables Co.	13 February 2004	PB951268	$36,070.47
Frau da Collezione	17 February 2004	LL427009	$7,612.06
Handji Gifts& Co	28 February 2004	LA318629	$22,474.17
Signal Collectibles Ltd.	29 February 2004	PT550181	$12,573.28
Clover Collections, Co.	01 March 2004	NM916675	$32,538.74

Summary Information
Number of records: 13
Average payment: $28,718.68   Aggregate
Largest payment: $59,830.55   data
Smallest payment: $5,759.42

Figure 13-1   A simple listing report that displays detail and aggregate data

In the example, BIRT calculates the average payment in the report by adding the payment amounts in every row, then dividing the total by the number of rows. Similarly, BIRT returns the largest and smallest payment amounts by comparing the payment amount in every row in the report.

For a report that groups data, as shown in Figure 13-2, you can display aggregates for each group of data rows, and for all the data rows in the report.

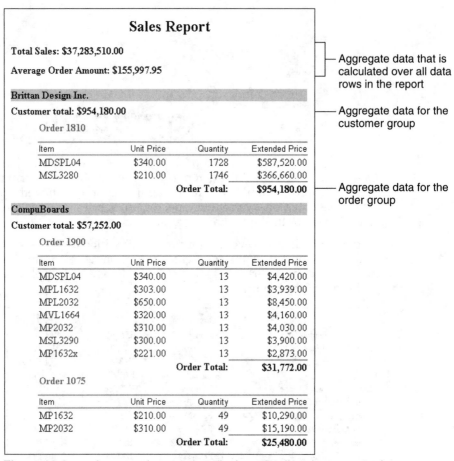

Figure 13-2   A grouped report that displays detail and aggregate data

Types of aggregate calculations

BIRT provides a wide range of functions in the Total class that support aggregate calculations over sets of data rows. These functions are custom JavaScript functions that BIRT defines. As with native JavaScript functions, you must use the correct capitalization when you type the function name, as shown in Table 13-1. For detailed information about each aggregate function, see Scripting Reference in BIRT's online help.

Table 13-1   Aggregate functions

Aggregate function	Description
Total.ave( )	Returns the average value of a specified numeric field over all data rows.
Total.count( )	Counts the number of data rows in the set.
Total.countDistinct( )	Counts the number of unique values for a specified field.
Total.first( )	Returns the value of a specified field in the first data row.
Total.isBottomN( )	Returns a boolean value that indicates if the value of a specified numeric field is one of the bottom n values.
Total.isBottomNPercent( )	Returns a boolean value that indicates if the value of a specified numeric field is one of the bottom n percent values.
Total.isTopN( )	Returns a boolean value that indicates if the value of a specified numeric field is one of the top n values.
Total.isTopNPercent( )	Returns a boolean value that indicates if the value of a specified numeric field is one of the top n percent values.
Total.last( )	Returns the value of a specified field in the last data row.
Total.max( )	Returns the highest value of a specified field in the set of data rows.
Total.median( )	Returns the median, or mid-point, value for a set of values in a specified numeric field.
Total.min( )	Returns the lowest value of a specified field in the set of data rows.
Total.mode( )	Returns the mode, which is the value that occurs most often for a specified field.
Total.movingAve( )	Returns the moving average of a specified numeric field over a specified number of values. This type of calculation is typically used for analyzing trends of stock prices.
Total.percentile( )	Returns the percentile value for a set of values in a specified numeric field, given a specified percent rank.

(continues)

Table 13-1   Aggregate functions *(continued)*

Aggregate function	Description
Total.percentRank( )	Returns the rank of a number, string, or date-time value of a specified field as a percentage of the data set. The return value ranges from 0 to 1.
Total.percentSum( )	Returns the percentage of a total of a specified numeric field.
Total.quartile( )	Returns the quartile value for a set of values in a specified numeric field.
Total.rank( )	Returns the rank of a number, string, or date-time value of a specified field.
Total.runningCount( )	Returns the row number, up to a given point, in the report.
Total.runningSum( )	Returns the total, up to a given point, in the report.
Total.stdDev( )	Returns the standard deviation of a specified numeric field over a set of data rows. Standard deviation is a statistic that shows how closely values are clustered around the mean of a set of data.
Total.sum( )	Sums the values of a specified numeric field in the set of data rows.
Total.variance( )	Returns the variance of a specified numeric field over a set of data rows. Variance is a statistical measure of the spread of data.
Total.weightedAve( )	Returns the weighted average of a specified numeric field over a set of data rows. In a weighted average, some numbers carry more importance (weight) than others.

Placing aggregate data

Where you place aggregate data is essential to getting the correct results. For aggregate calculations, such as Total.sum( ), Total.ave( ), Total.max( ), and Total.mode( ), which process a set of data rows and return one value, you typically insert the aggregate data in the following places in a table:

- At the beginning of a group, in the group header row
- At the beginning of a table, in the header row
- At the end of a group, in the group footer row
- At the end of the table, in the footer row

You can place this type of aggregate data in a table's detail row, but the data would not make much sense, because the same aggregate value would appear repeatedly for every row in the group. On the other hand, you typically insert aggregate calculations, such as Total.runningSum( ), Total.movingAve( ), Total.percentRank( ), and Total.Rank( ), in the detail row of a table. These functions process a set of data rows and return a different value for each row.

The report in Figure 13-3 groups data rows by customer, then by order ID. It displays totals for each order, totals for each customer, and a grand total of all sales. At the detail level, the report displays the running total for each line item.

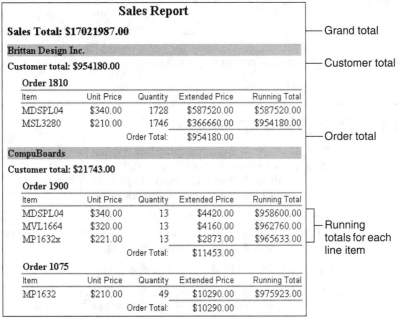

Sales Report

Sales Total: $17021987.00 ——— Grand total

Brittan Design Inc. ——— Customer total
Customer total: $954180.00

Order 1810

Item	Unit Price	Quantity	Extended Price	Running Total
MDSPL04	$340.00	1728	$587520.00	$587520.00
MSL3280	$210.00	1746	$366660.00	$954180.00
		Order Total:	$954180.00	

——— Order total

CompuBoards
Customer total: $21743.00

Order 1900

Item	Unit Price	Quantity	Extended Price	Running Total
MDSPL04	$340.00	13	$4420.00	$958600.00
MVL1664	$320.00	13	$4160.00	$962760.00
MP1632x	$221.00	13	$2873.00	$965633.00
		Order Total:	$11453.00	

—— Running totals for each line item

Order 1075

Item	Unit Price	Quantity	Extended Price	Running Total
MP1632	$210.00	49	$10290.00	$975923.00
		Order Total:	$10290.00	

Figure 13-3   Report showing totals for groups and running totals for detail row

To display the aggregate data as shown in the preceding report example, complete the following steps:

- To display the grand total at the beginning of the report, place the aggregate data in the table's header row.

- To display the customer total at the beginning of each customer group, place the aggregate data in the customer group's header row.

- To display the order total at the end of each order group, place the aggregate data in the order group's footer row.

- To display the running totals, place the aggregate data in the table's detail row.

Figure 13-4 shows the report design.

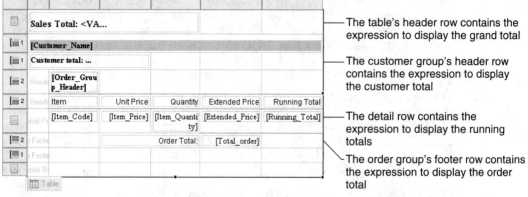

Figure 13-4   Aggregate calculations in a report design

Writing aggregate expressions

This section describes the expressions that you use to calculate the subtotals and totals that appear in the report example in the preceding section. As with all dynamic data, you define the aggregate expressions in a column binding. Then you insert a report element that uses the column binding.

- To display the grand total in the table's header, you can use either an HTML text element or a data element. Both elements enable you to use a combination of static text and dynamic data.

  - Text to use in an HTML text element:

    ```
    Sales Total: <VALUE-OF format="$#.00">
    Total.sum(row["Extended_Price"])</VALUE-OF>
    ```

  - Expression to use for a data element:

    ```
    "Sales Total: $" + Total.sum(row["Extended_Price"]) +
       ".00"
    ```

- Similarly, to display the customer total in the customer group's header, you can use an HTML text element or a data element.

  - Text to use in an HTML text element:

    ```
    Customer total: <VALUE-OF format="$#.00">
       Total.sum(row["Extended_Price"])</VALUE-OF>
    ```

  - Expression to use in a data element:

    ```
    "Customer Total: $" + Total.sum(row["Extended_Price"]) +
       ".00"
    ```

- To calculate and display the order total in the order group's footer, use a data element. In this report example, a data element is more convenient, because only the dynamic value is necessary.

```
Total.sum(row["Extended_Price"])
```

- To calculate and display the running totals in the detail row, use a data element and this expression:

```
Total.runningSum(row["Extended_Price"])
```

Notice that the group subtotals and report total are calculated with the same basic aggregate expression, Total.sum(row["Extended_Price"]). When you create multiple groups and place aggregate expressions in the headers or footers of various group levels, BIRT automatically calculates totals for the corresponding groups.

Figure 13-5 shows the column bindings defined for the table that contains all the report data. The Aggregate On values indicate the level at which aggregate calculations apply. The ALL value indicates that the aggregate calculation is applied to all rows in the table. The Orders value indicates that the aggregate calculation is applied to rows in the Orders group. The N/A value indicates that aggregation is not applicable, because the expression is not an aggregate expression.

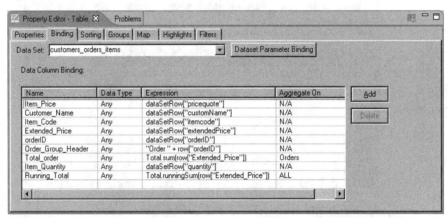

Figure 13-5   Column bindings

Typically, you supply only a data set field (or a column binding that refers to a data set field) as an argument to an aggregate function, as shown in the following examples:

```
//Return the highest payment amount
Total.max(row["paymentAmount"])

//Return the lowest score
Total.min(row["score"])
```

```
//Return the average price
Total.ave(row["price"])

//Return the number of unique order IDs
Total.countDistinct(row["orderID"])

//Return the first date in the data set
Total.first(row["paymentDate"])

//Return the last name in the data set
Total.last(row["customerName"])
```

The exception is Total.count( ), which does not take a data set field as an argument. Total.count( ) returns the number of rows in a group or in the entire report, depending on where you place it.

Accessing aggregate functions in the expression builder

If you use the expression builder to access the aggregate functions, these functions are listed under BIRT Functions—Total, as shown in Figure 13-6.

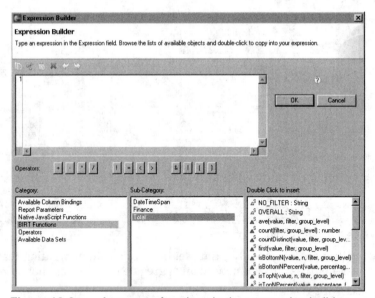

Figure 13-6   Aggregate functions in the expression builder

How to construct an aggregate expression in the expression builder

1   In Expression Builder, under Category, select BIRT Functions. Sub-Category displays the classes of functions that BIRT defines.

2   Select Total to display the aggregate functions.

3 Double-click the aggregate function that you want to use. The function appears in the expression area of Expression Builder.

4 Within the parentheses, ( ), of the function, specify the data set field, or column binding that refers to the data set field, whose values you want to aggregate:

  1 Under Category, choose Available Data Sets or Available Column Bindings.

  2 Under Sub-Category, choose the data set that contains the field, or the element that contains the column bindings.

  3 Double-click the data set field or column binding to insert it between the parentheses of the aggregate function.

5 Choose OK to save the expression.

Filtering aggregate data

When you calculate aggregate data, you can specify a filter condition to use to determine which rows are factored in the calculation. For example, you can exclude rows with missing or null credit limit values when you calculate an average credit limit or include only deposit transactions when you calculate the sum of transactions.

To specify a filter condition when you aggregate data, specify a filter expression that evaluates to true or false. Include the filter expression as an argument to the aggregate function. You specify the filter expression either as the second or third argument, depending on the function. The exception is Total.count( ), where the filter expression is the first argument, because this function does not reference a data set field.

The following expressions are examples of aggregate expressions that include a filter condition:

■ This expression returns the sum of extended prices for item MSL3280 only:

```
Total.sum(row["extendedPrice"], row["itemCode"]=="MSL3280")
```

■ This expression returns the average order amount for closed orders only:

```
Total.ave(row["orderAmount"], row["orderStatus"]=="Closed")
```

■ This expression returns the number of rows in a group or a table (depending on where you place the expression) and counts only rows where the order amount exceeds $10:

```
Total.count(row["orderAmount"] > 10)
```

Excluding null values from an aggregate calculation

When you calculate the sum of a numeric field, it does not matter if some of the rows contain null values for the specified numeric field. The results are the same, regardless of whether the calculation is 100 + 75 + 200 or 100 + 75 + 0 (null) + 200. In both cases, the result is 375. Note that null is not the same as zero (0). Zero is an actual value, whereas null means there is no value.

Some aggregate calculations return different results when null values are included or excluded from the calculation. The average value returned by the calculation without the null value in the previous example is 125 ((100 + 75 + 200)/3). The average value of the calculation with the null value, however, is 93.75 ((100 + 75 + 0 + 200)/4). Similarly, Total.count( ) returns a different number of total rows, depending on whether you include or exclude rows with null values for a specified field.

By default, aggregate functions include all rows in their calculations. To exclude null values, you must specify a filter condition. The following expressions are examples of aggregate expressions that filter out rows that contain null values in specified fields:

- This expression returns the average transaction amount. The calculation includes only rows in which the transaction amount is not null.

    ```
    Total.ave(row["transactionAmount"],
        row["transactionAmount"] != null)
    ```

- This expression returns the total number of rows in a group or a table, excluding rows in which the creditLimit field has no value. Here, the filter expression is the first argument, because Total.count( ), unlike the other aggregate functions, does not reference a data set field.

    ```
    Total.count(row["creditLimit"] != null)
    ```

Counting rows that contain unique values

When you use Total.count( ) to return the number of rows in a group or table, BIRT counts all rows. Sometimes, you want to get the count of distinct values. For example, a table displays a list of customers and their countries, as shown in Figure 13-7. The table lists 12 customers from 4 different countries.

If you insert a data element that uses the expression Total.count( ) in the header or footer row of the table, Total.count( ) returns 12, the number of rows in the table. If, however, you want to get the number of countries, use Total.countDistinct( ), as shown in the following expression:

```
Total.countDistinct(row["country"])
```

In the example report, Total.countDistinct( ) returns 5, not 4 as you might expect, because like the other aggregate functions, Total.countDistinct( ) counts rows with null values. The third row in the table contains a null value for country. To get the real count of countries that are listed in the table, add a filter condition to the aggregate expression, as follows:

```
Total.countDistinct(row["country"], row["country"] != null)
```

This expression counts only rows in which the country value is unique and not null.

```
Customers with orders over 10K

Customer                      Country
───────────────────────────────────────
American Souvenirs            USA
Land of Toys Inc.             USA
Porto Imports
La Rochelle Gifts             France
Gift Depot                    USA
Dragon Souvenirs              Singapore
Saveley & Henriot, Co.        France
Technics Stores Inc.          USA
Osaka Souvenirts Co           Japan
Diecast Classics Inc          USA
Collectable Mini Designs      USA
Mini Wheels Co                USA
```

Figure 13-7   A table that lists customers and their countries

Getting an aggregate value from another group

As the example report in "Placing aggregate data," earlier in this chapter shows, you typically insert an aggregate expression in the header or footer of a group to calculate and show aggregate information for that particular group. For example, to calculate the sum of orders for each customer, you insert an expression, such as Total.sum(row["extendedPrice"]), in the header of the customer group to display the information at the beginning of each customer group or in the footer to display the information at the end of each customer group.

Sometimes, however, you might want to display an aggregate value from a different group. The report shown in Figure 13-8 displays the grand total (the sum of all customer orders) in each customer group.

The Total.sum(row["extendedPrice"]) expression in the customer group calculates the sum of extended prices over all data rows in the customer group only. The overall total, however, is calculated over all the data rows in the report's data set.

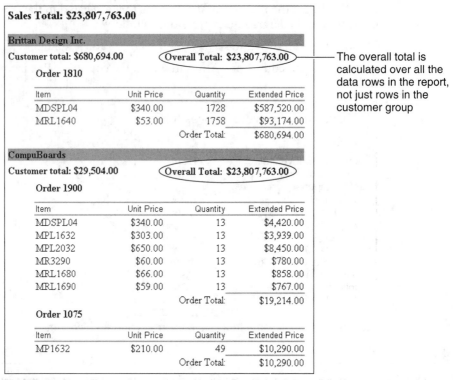

Sales Total: $23,807,763.00

Brittan Design Inc.

Customer total: $680,694.00   Overall Total: $23,807,763.00 — The overall total is calculated over all the data rows in the report, not just rows in the customer group

Order 1810

Item	Unit Price	Quantity	Extended Price
MDSPL04	$340.00	1728	$587,520.00
MRL1640	$53.00	1758	$93,174.00
		Order Total:	$680,694.00

CompuBoards

Customer total: $29,504.00   Overall Total: $23,807,763.00

Order 1900

Item	Unit Price	Quantity	Extended Price
MDSPL04	$340.00	13	$4,420.00
MPL1632	$303.00	13	$3,939.00
MPL2032	$650.00	13	$8,450.00
MR3290	$60.00	13	$780.00
MRL1680	$66.00	13	$858.00
MRL1690	$59.00	13	$767.00
		Order Total:	$19,214.00

Order 1075

Item	Unit Price	Quantity	Extended Price
MP1632	$210.00	49	$10,290.00
		Order Total:	$10,290.00

Figure 13-8   Report displaying a grand total for each customer

To display the overall total in the customer group header, you must specify the group for which you want an aggregate value. You accomplish this task in either of the following ways:

- In the column-binding definition, specify the following expression, and set Aggregate On to ALL:

```
Total.sum(row["extendedPrice"])
```

- In the column-binding definition, specify the following expression:

```
Total.sum(row["extendedPrice"], null, "overall")
```

The key piece of this expression is the value that you supply as the third argument to the Total.sum( ) function. The value "overall" refers to the overall total for all the rows in the data set. This value overrides the value set for Aggregate On. Note that, because you need to supply a value for the third argument, you need to also specify a value for the second argument, which takes a filter condition. The example uses the null value, because a filter is not required. Filtering aggregate data is described earlier in this chapter.

Similarly, if you want to display the customer total in the order ID group, you can accomplish the task using either of the following ways:

- Specify the following expression, and set Aggregate On to Customers:

```
Total.sum(row["extendedPrice"])
```

- Specify the following expression:

```
Total.sum(row["extendedPrice"], null, "Customers")
```

If you use the second method, you can supply different types of values for the third argument. For example, you can specify the group index instead of the group name. In our example, the Customers group is the first group, so its index is 1. An index value of 0 gets the overall total. For example, the following expressions return the same results:

```
Total.sum(row["extendedPrice"], null, "Customers")
Total.sum(row["extendedPrice"], null, 1)
```

The following expressions also return the same results:

```
Total.sum(row["extendedPrice"], null, "overall")
Total.sum(row["extendedPrice"], null, 0)
```

The ability to access the aggregate value from any group of data in the report is useful. Not only can you display the values, you can use them in calculations that require aggregate values from multiple groups. Percentage calculations, for example, require a subtotal and an overall total. Information about calculating percentages is in the following section.

Calculating percentages

Some percentage calculations require aggregate values from two different groups of data. For example, a report displays each regional sales total as a percentage of the total national sales. To calculate this aggregate data for each region, two totals are required:

- The total of all sales in each region.

- The overall total of sales across all regions.

Figure 13-9 shows an example of a report that displays sales data that is grouped by state, then by product. The report shows two percentage calculations:

- A state's total sales as a percentage of the overall sales.

- A product's total sales as a percentage of the state's total sales.

Figure 13-10 shows the report design.

Sales By State and Product

Total Sales: $342,592.81

California — 40.67%

Product Code	Total Units	Amount	% of Total Amount
S10_1678	152	$12,652.59	9.08%
S10_1949	214	$42,223.67	30.31%
S10_2016	125	$13,044.24	9.36%
S10_4698	146	$25,475.89	18.29%
S10_4757	186	$24,579.28	17.64%
S10_4962	156	$21,345.86	15.32%
Totals:		$139,321.53	

This aggregate value displays a state's total sales as a percentage of the overall sales

These aggregate values display a product's total sales as a percentage of the state's total sales

Connecticut — 7.59%

Product Code	Total Units	Amount	% of Total Amount
S10_1678	34	$3,026.00	11.63%
S10_1949	34	$6,630.34	25.49%
S10_2016	40	$4,282.00	16.46%
S10_4698	41	$7,940.06	30.52%
S10_4962	28	$4,136.72	15.90%
Totals:		$26,015.12	

Massachusetts — 18.74%

Product Code	Total Units	Amount	% of Total Amount
S10_1678	78	$6,821.58	10.63%
S10_1949	70	$14,210.11	22.14%
S10_2016	97	$11,145.67	17.36%
S10_4698	48	$7,790.91	12.14%
S10_4757	122	$15,392.48	23.98%
S10_4962	69	$8,833.36	13.76%
Totals:		$64,194.11	

Figure 13-9   Percentage calculations in a grouped report

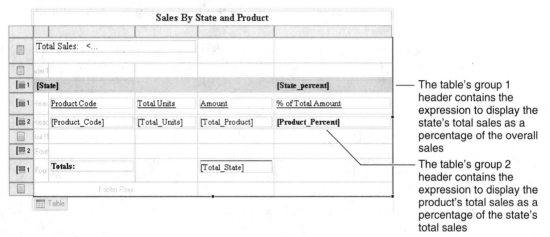

The table's group 1 header contains the expression to display the state's total sales as a percentage of the overall sales

The table's group 2 header contains the expression to display the product's total sales as a percentage of the state's total sales

Figure 13-10 Percentage calculations in a report design

Calculating the product's total sales as a percentage of a state's total sales

To calculate this percentage for the report design shown in Figure 13-10, specify the following expression for a column binding whose Aggregate On value is set to Product:

```
Total.sum(row["extendedPrice"])/
    Total.sum(row["extendedPrice"], null, "State")
```

As the previous section describes, you obtain the aggregate value of another group by specifying the name of the group. In this example, the value "State" identifies the group whose total you want. The second argument is null, which means that there is no filter.

Alternatively, you can create three column bindings, one for each discrete piece of the calculation. The first column binding defines the expression to calculate the product total:

```
Total_Product: Total.sum(row["extendedPrice"])
Aggregate On Product
```

The second column binding defines the expression to calculate the state total:

```
Total_State: Total.sum(row["extendedPrice"])
Aggregate On State
```

The third column binding defines the expression to calculate the percentage. This expression refers to the previous column bindings, Total_Product and Total_State.

```
Product_Percent: row["Total_Product"]/row["Total_State"]
Aggregate On N/A
```

Calculating the state's total sales as a percentage of the overall sales

To calculate this percentage for the report design shown in Figure 13-10, specify the following expression for a column binding whose Aggregate Value is set to State:

```
Total.sum(row["extendedPrice"])/
   Total.sum(row["extendedPrice"], null, "overall")
```

The value "overall" specifies the overall total for the entire data set.

Alternatively, you can create three column bindings, one for each discrete piece of the calculation. The first column binding defines the expression to calculate the state total:

```
Total_State: Total.sum(row["extendedPrice"])
Aggregate On State
```

The second column binding defines the expression to calculate the overall total:

```
Total_All: Total.sum(row["extendedPrice"])
Aggregate On ALL
```

The third column binding defines the expression to calculate the percentage:

```
State_Percent: row["Total_State"]/row["Total_All"]
Aggregate On N/A
```

Displaying the percentage values in the correct format

The values returned by the previous calculations range from 0 to 1. To display a value, such as 0.8, as 80%:

1 Select the data element that displays the percentage value.

2 In Property Editor, choose Format Number, then choose the Percent format.

3 Choose the settings that you want, including the number of decimal places and the placement of the percent symbol.

Creating a summary report

Reports typically display both detail and aggregate data. A summary report is a report that shows only aggregate data. Summary reports, such as the top ten products or sales totals by state, provide key information at a glance and are easy to create.

When you create a report that contains data in detail rows and aggregate data in header or footer rows, you can change such a report to a summary report by hiding the contents in the detail rows. To hide these contents, you can use any of the following techniques:

- Choose the group whose detail rows you want to hide, and in the group editor, select the Hide Detail option.

- Select the detail row, and use the visibility property to hide the contents of the row.

- Delete the contents from the detail row. A report does not need to display the values of the data rows to perform aggregate calculations on the data rows.

The first and second techniques provide the flexibility of maintaining two versions of a report. The third technique, on the other hand, results in a summary report only. To change the report to display details, you would have to add the data back to the detail row.

Take a closer look at the report design in Figure 13-10. The report contains data only in the header and footer rows, and almost all the data elements display totals. Rather than display individual sales records in the detail rows, the report shows only the sales total for each product.

To create a top n or bottom n summary report, insert the aggregate data in the header or footer row. Then create a filter for the group that contains the data, and use a filter condition, as shown in the following examples:

```
//Show only the top ten orders
Total.sum(row["extendedPrice"]) Top n 10

//Show only orders in the top ten percent
Total.sum(row["extendedPrice"]) Top Percent 10

//Show only the lowest five orders
Total.sum(row["extendedPrice"]) Bottom n 5

//Show only orders in the bottom one percent
Total.sum(row["extendedPrice"]) Bottom Percent 1
```

Figure 13-11 shows a top ten report. Figure 13-12 shows the report design.

Top 10 Sales Representatives	
Gerard Hernandez	$1,258,577.81
Leslie Jennings	$1,081,530.54
Pamela Castillo	$868,220.55
Larry Bott	$732,096.79
Barry Jones	$704,853.91
George Vanauf	$669,377.05
Peter Marsh	$584,593.76
Loui Bondur	$569,485.75
Andy Fixter	$562,582.59
Steve Patterson	$505,875.42

Figure 13-11   Top ten report

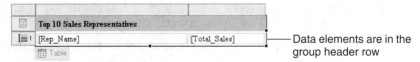

Data elements are in the
group header row

Figure 13-12   Top ten report design

The data elements that display the sales representative names and their sales
totals are in a group header row. This report groups sales data rows (not shown
in the report) by sales representatives. To display only the top ten sales
representatives, a filter is in the group definition, as shown in Figure 13-13.

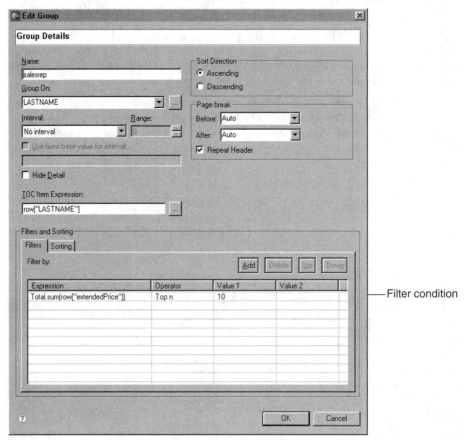

Filter condition

Figure 13-13   Top ten filter, defined in the group

14

Writing Expressions

You can create many reports using data that comes directly from a data source simply by dragging the data set fields from Data Explorer to the report. Sometimes, however, you want to display information that is not in the data source, or you want to display data differently than it appears in the data source. You might also want to sort data using a formula, rather than sorting on an existing field. For these cases, and many others, you write expressions using JavaScript.

An expression is a statement that produces a value. An expression can be a literal value, such as

```
3.14
"It is easy to create reports with BIRT"
```

When you drag a field into the report, BIRT Report Designer creates the expression for you. The expression specifies the name of the field whose values the report displays. For example, the following expressions get values from the customerName field and the phone field, respectively:

```
dataSetRow["customerName"]
dataSetRow["phone"]
```

An expression can contain any combination of literal values, fields, operators, variables, and functions, as long as it evaluates to a single value. In the following examples, the first expression combines static text with a field, the second expression uses a JavaScript function, and the third expression multiplies the values of two fields:

```
"Order Total: " + row["orderTotal"]
row["orderDate"].getYear()
row["itemQuantity"] * row["itemPrice"]
```

This chapter describes some common uses and examples of expressions in reports. It does not describe all the functions, objects, or operators that you can use in expressions. If you are new to JavaScript, you will find it useful to read a book about JavaScript.

Basic concepts

This section describes some of the basic concepts that you need to understand and remember when writing JavaScript expressions. Understanding these concepts helps you avoid some common mistakes.

Data types

One of the fundamental concepts to understand is data types. Data types are the types of values—numbers, strings, and Booleans, for example—that can be represented and manipulated in any programming language. Every database field has a certain data type, every piece of report data has a certain data type, and every expression that you create returns a value of a particular data type.

This concept is important, because, if the expression that you write does not handle data types properly, you get errors or the results are not what you want. For example, you cannot perform mathematical calculations on numbers if they are of string type, and you cannot convert a date field to uppercase characters.

If you write an expression to manipulate a data set field, verify its type, particularly if the field values are numbers. Numbers can be of string or numeric type. For example, databases typically store zip codes and telephone numbers as strings. Item quantities or prices are always of numeric type so that the data can be manipulated mathematically. IDs, such as customer IDs or order IDs are usually of numeric type so that the data can be sorted in numeric order, such as 1, 2, 3, 10, 11, rather than in alphanumeric order, such as 1, 10, 11, 2, 3.

To see the data type of a field, open the data set in Data Explorer, and choose Output Columns. Output Columns displays the fields in the data set and their types, as shown in Figure 14-1.

Case sensitivity

JavaScript is a case-sensitive language. This feature means that a keyword, a function name, a variable name, or any other identifier must always be typed with the correct capitalization. You must, for example, type the getDate( ) function as getDate( ), not as GetDate( ) or getdate( ). Similarly, myVar, MyVar, MYVAR, and myvar are four different variable names.

Data set field names are case sensitive. If you refer to a data set field in an expression, specify the field name with the same capitalization that the data source driver uses to identify the field. As mentioned previously, Output Columns in the data set editor shows the fields. If you use Expression Builder to write an expression, selecting a field to insert in the expression ensures that the correct field name is used.

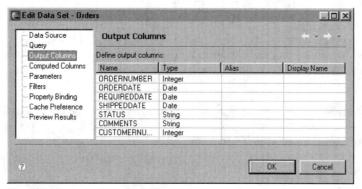

Figure 14-1   Output Columns

Multiline expressions

You can write an expression that contains multiple lines, as shown in the following example:

```
firstInitial = row["customerFirstname"].charAt(0);
firstInitial + ". " + row["customerLastname"];
```

The expression looks like lines of program code, because it is. Expressions can be small pieces of code that do something. The expression in the previous example does the following tasks:

- It extracts the first character of a string value in a customerFirstname field and assigns the value to a variable named firstInitial.

- Then, it combines the firstInitial value, a period, a space, and the value in a customerLastname field.

An expression can contain as many lines as you need. Just remember that an expression returns a single value. If an expression contains several lines, it returns the results of the last line. The previous expression returns a value, such as T. Rae.

The lines are called statements, and they are separated from each other by semicolons. If you place each statement on a separate line, as shown in the example, JavaScript allows you to leave out the semicolons. It is, however, good practice to use semicolons to separate statements.

Using Expression Builder

Expression Builder is a tool that you use to create, modify, and view expressions. It provides a list of the objects, functions, and operators that you can include in expressions. Expression Builder is particularly useful when you are learning how to write expressions in JavaScript and discovering which BIRT and JavaScript functions you can use.

Expression Builder is available when you need to specify an expression, such as when you create a computed column in Data Explorer, when you filter data, when you insert a data element, when you specify a data series for a chart, or when you want to display dynamic data in a text element. Figure 14-2 shows Expression Builder.

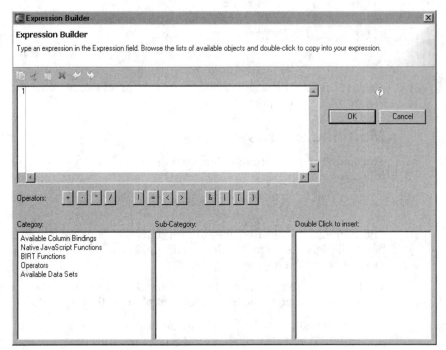

Figure 14-2   Expression Builder

You open Expression Builder by choosing one of the buttons that appear in Figure 14-3.

Figure 14-3   Expression Builder access buttons

Expression Builder consists of two parts:

- The top part of Expression Builder is where you create or edit an expression. When you choose objects from the bottom part, they appear in this area. You can also type an expression directly here.

- The bottom part provides a hierarchical view of the column bindings, report parameters, JavaScript functions, BIRT functions, operators, and data set fields that you can select to build an expression. The items that appear under

Category vary, depending on the context of the expression. When you select an item in Category, its contents appear in Sub-Category. When you select an item in Sub-Category, its contents—which you insert in an expression—appear in the box that is the farthest to the right. Figure 14-4 shows an example.

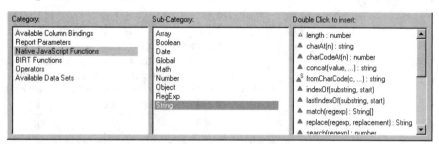

Figure 14-4 Functions for String class

Table 14-1 provides detailed descriptions of the items in Expression Builder's Category column.

Table 14-1 Categories in Expression Builder

Item	Description
Available Column Bindings	Displays the column bindings—references to data set fields—that are available to the current report element. An element can access column bindings that are defined on the element itself and on the element's container.
Report Parameters	Displays the report parameters that you created using Data Explorer. Report parameters are typically used to get input from users when they run the report.
Native JavaScript Functions	Displays native JavaScript functions by objects, such as String, Date, Math, and so on. Use these functions to manipulate or calculate data. For summary information about a function, hover the mouse over the item to display a ToolTip. For detailed information, see a JavaScript book.
BIRT Functions	Displays the JavaScript functions that are defined by BIRT. The functions are categorized in these objects: DateTimeSpan, Finance, and Total. Use these functions to calculate data. For summary information about a function, hover the mouse over the item to display a ToolTip. For detailed information, see "Scripting Reference" in BIRT's online help.

(continues)

Table 14-1   Categories in Expression Builder *(continued)*

Item	Description
Operators	Displays types of JavaScript operators, such as Assignment, Comparison, Computational, and Logical.
Available Data Sets	Displays the data set or data sets that are available to the current report element. Expand the data sets to select fields to use in an expression. You can access data set fields only when you create a column-binding expression or when you create a computed field in the data set editor.

Manipulating numeric data

Numeric data is probably the most commonly manipulated type of data. Expressions can perform a basic operation, such as multiplying a price field by a quantity field to calculate an extended price, or more complex calculations, such as a financial calculation that returns the depreciation value of an asset. You can use functions to calculate aggregate information, such as totals, averages, medians, modes, and so on, as discussed in Chapter 13, "Aggregating Data."

Both JavaScript and BIRT provide a wide range of functions for manipulating numeric data. In Expression Builder, look under Native JavaScript Functions—Number and Math and under BIRT Functions—Total and Finance. The following sections describe common number-manipulation tasks and provide examples of expressions.

Computing values from multiple numeric fields

If your report primarily displays values from numeric fields, it most likely contains computed values as well. An invoice, for example, typically shows the following computed values:

- Extended prices that display the result of unit price * quantity for each line item

- Sales tax total that displays the sum of extended prices * tax rate

- Invoice total that displays the sum of extended prices + shipping + sales tax

Order of precedence

When a calculation involves more than two numbers and different operators, remember the order of precedence, which is the order in which operators are evaluated. Consider the following math expression:

```
55 + 50 + 45 * 2
```

If you did each operation from left to right in these steps:

```
55 + 50 = 105
105 + 45 = 150
150 * 2 = 300
```

Your answer would be 300.

If you specify the math expression in a data element, BIRT Report Designer returns 195, which is the correct answer. The difference in answers lies in the order of precedence. This concept is one that you might remember from math class. Multiplication and division are evaluated first from left to right across the expression. Then, addition and subtraction are evaluated from left to right across the expression. Using the previous example, the expression is evaluated as follows:

```
45 * 2 = 90
55 + 50 = 105
105 + 90 = 195
```

If you want the addition performed first, instead of the multiplication, enclose the addition part within parentheses, as follows:

```
(55 + 50 + 45) * 2
```

The following list describes examples of expressions that compute values from multiple numeric fields.

- The following expression calculates a total price after deducting a discount and adding an 8% tax that applies to the discounted price:

```
(row["extendedPrice"] - row["discount"]) +
    (row["extendedPrice"] - row["discount"]) * 0.08
```

- The following expression calculates an invoice total, which includes the total of all extended prices, an 8% sales tax, and a 10% shipping and handling charge:

```
Total.sum(row["extendedPrice"]) +
    (Total.sum(row["extendedPrice"]) * 0.08) +
    (Total.sum(row["extendedPrice"]) * 0.10)
```

- The following expression calculates a gain or loss in percent:

```
(row["salePrice"] - row["unitPrice"])/row["unitPrice"] * 100
```

Division by zero

If you divide the value of one numeric field by another and the denominator value is 0, the result is infinity (∞).

For example, if the following expression:

```
row["total"]/row["quantity"]
```

evaluates to:

```
150/0
```

the data element that contains the expression displays ∞.

The return value is infinity, because dividing a number by zero is an operation that has no answer. Mathematicians consider this operation undefined, illegal, or indeterminate.

If you do not want the infinity symbol to appear in the report, you can replace it with a string value, such as Undefined, or replace it with an empty string ("") to display nothing. The infinity symbol is a numeric value, therefore, you must convert it to a string before replacing it with a different string.

The following expression replaces ∞ with Undefined:

```
// Convert number to a string
x = row["total"]/row["quantity"] + ""
// Replace ∞ with the word Undefined
x.replace("Infinity", "Undefined")
```

Converting a number to a string

You can convert a number to a string using one of the following techniques:

- Use the JavaScript toString( ) function

- Add an empty string ("") to the number

The following expressions yield the same result. If the value of orderID is 1000, both expressions return 10005.

```
row["orderID"].toString( ) + 5
row["orderID"] + "" + 5
```

Any time that you combine a literal string with a number, JavaScript converts the number to a string. Be aware of this fact, especially if you want to also manipulate the number mathematically. For example, the following expression changes orderID to a string:

```
"Order ID: " + row["orderID"]
```

If you want to perform a calculation and also add a literal string, do them in separate steps. Perform the calculation first, then append the string, as shown in the following example:

```
orderIDvar = row["orderID"] + 10;
"Order ID: " + orderIDvar;
```

If the value of orderID is 1000, the expression returns:

```
Order ID: 1010
```

Manipulating string data

Often, a data source contains string or text data that is not in the right form for your reporting needs. For example, you want to sort a report by last name, but the data source contains last names only as part of a full name field. Or, conversely, you want to display full names, but the data source stores first names and last names in separate fields.

JavaScript provides a wide range of functions for manipulating strings. In Expression Builder, look under Native JavaScript Functions—String. The following sections describe some of the common string-manipulation tasks and provide examples of expressions.

Substituting string values

Sometimes, you need to substitute one string value for another. Perhaps data was added to the data source inconsistently. For example, some addresses contain "Street," and some contain "St." You can replace entire string values or just parts of a string by using the replace( ) function in JavaScript.

The replace( ) function searches for a specified string and replaces it with another string. It takes two arguments: the string to replace, and the new string. The following expression searches for "St." in an address field and replaces it with "Street."

```
row["address"].replace("St.", "Street")
```

What if you need to search for and replace multiple strings in a single field? Add as many replace( ) functions as you need to the expression, as shown in the following example:

```
row["address"].replace("St.", "Street").replace("Ave.",
    "Avenue").replace("Blvd", "Boulevard")
```

As with any global search-and-replace operation, be aware of unintended string replacements. For example, the row["address"].replace("St.", "Street") expression replaces St. Mary Road with Street Mary Road. In this case, rather than just searching for "St.", you need to search for "St." at the end of a line. To specify this type of search, you need to specify a string pattern to search, rather than a literal string. For more information about searching for patterns, see "Matching string patterns," later in this chapter.

If you need to replace entire strings, rather than just a part of the string, you can use the mapping feature instead. The mapping feature is ideal for replacing known sets of values. For example, a gender field contains two values, M or F. You can map the M value to Male, and F to Female. For more information about mapping values, see "Specifying alternate values for display" in Chapter 11, "Formatting Report Content."

Combining values from multiple fields

Each field in a database often represents a single piece of information. A customer table, for example, might contain these fields: customerFirstname, customerLastname, addressLine_1, addressLine_2, city, state, zip, and country.

You can create a customer report that uses data from all these fields by dragging each field to a table cell. The generated report, however, does not look professional, because the space between each piece of data is uneven, as shown in Figure 14-5. The spacing is uneven because the size of each table column adjusts to fit the longest string.

Name		Address					
Jean	King	8489 Strong St.		Las Vegas	NV	83030	USA
Susan	Nelson	5677 Strong St.		San Rafael	CA	97562	USA
Julie	Murphy	5557 North Pendale Street		San Francisco	CA	94217	USA
Kwai	Lee	897 Long Airport Avenue		NYC	NY	10022	USA
Jeff	Young	4092 Furth Circle	Suite 400	NYC	NY	10022	USA

Figure 14-5   Report with separate field values

The solution is to combine, or concatenate, the first and last names and place the concatenated name in a single table cell. Similarly, concatenate all the address-related fields and place the full address in a single table cell. In JavaScript, you concatenate string values using the + operator.

For the name, add a literal space (" ") between the name fields so that the first and last name values do not run together. For the address, add a comma and space between all the fields, except between state and zip. For these fields, add only a space between them.

For this example, you would use the following expressions:

```
row["customerFirstname"] + " " + row["customerLastname"]

row["addressLine1"] + ", " + row["addressLine2"] + ", " +
    row["city"] + ", " + row["state"] + " " + row["zip"] + ", "
    + row["country"]
```

The report now looks like the one shown in Figure 14-6.

Name	Address
Jean King	8489 Strong St., null, Las Vegas, NV 83030, USA
Susan Nelson	5677 Strong St., null, San Rafael, CA 97562, USA
Julie Murphy	5557 North Pendale Street, null, San Francisco, CA 94217, USA
Kwai Lee	897 Long Airport Avenue, null, NYC, NY 10022, USA
Jeff Young	4092 Furth Circle, Suite 400, NYC, NY 10022, USA

Figure 14-6   Report with combined field values

Several addresses display the word null, because the addressLine2 field contains no data. In a database, a null value means no value was supplied. In cases where you concatenate fields that might contain no data, you need to remove the word null from the returned string value. This task is described in the next section.

Removing null values from combined fields

When you concatenate string values, JavaScript converts null values to the word null. The example report in the previous section displayed addresses with the word null when the addressLine2 field did not contain a value, for example:

```
8490 Strong St., null, Las Vegas, NV 83030, USA
```

You can remove the word null by using the replace( ) function. In this example, use replace( ) in the expression to search for "null, " and replace it with an empty string. You should also search for the comma and space after null to remove the extra comma and space that is added after the addressLine2 field. If you search only for "null" you get the following results:

```
8490 Strong St.,  , Las Vegas, NV 83030, USA
```

You use the following expression to remove null values from a concatenated address:

```
(row["addressLine1"] + ", " + row["addressLine2"] + ", " +
   row["city"] + ", " + row["state"] + " " + row["zip"] + ", "
   + row["country"]).replace("null, ","")
```

Searching for and replacing "null, " does not, however, take into account missing values in the state and country fields. The state value does not have a comma after it, so you need to search for "null ". The country value does not have a comma or space after it, so you need to search for "null".

To replace null values in the state and country fields, add two more replace( ) functions to the expression:

```
(row["addressLine1"] + ", " + row["addressLine2"] + ", " +
   row["city"] + ", " + row["state"] + " " + row["zip"] + ", "
   + row["country"]).replace("null, ","").replace("null ","")
   .replace("null","")
```

Getting parts of a string

Sometimes, you want to display only a portion of a string. For example:

- An address field stores a full address, but you want to display only the zip code or the state.

- A name field stores a full name, and you want only the first or last name.

- An e-mail field stores e-mail addresses, and you want only the user name that precedes the @ symbol.

Depending on the content of the string and which part of a string you need—the first part, the last part, or a part after or before a particular character—the expression that you specify varies. The JavaScript functions that you are likely to use in the expression include the functions shown in Table 14-2.

Table 14-2   Getting information about a string

JavaScript	Use to
charAt( )	Get the character at the specified position of a string. Note that in JavaScript, the first character starts at 0, not 1.
indexOf( )	Find the first occurrence of a specified character and return its position in the original string.
lastIndexOf( )	Find the last occurrence of a specified character and return its position in the original string.
length	Get the length of a string. Note that length is a property of a string, not a function, so you do not use parentheses, ( ), after the keyword, length.
substr( )	Return a substring of a specified length, starting from a particular position in the original string.

The following examples show how to get different parts of a string. Assume a customerName stores names in first name and last name format, such as Robert Allen.

- To get the first name:

  - Use indexOf( ) to get the position of the space character that separates the first name from the last name.

  - Use substr( ) to get the first name, starting from the first character and for a specified length. The first character for JavaScript starts at 0, not 1. The length that you need to specify is equal to the position of the space character, and not the position of the space character minus 1, as you might think. Consider the name Robert Allen. Logically, the space between the first and last names is the seventh character, but JavaScript counts its position as six. To return the first name, Robert, excluding the space, you want substr( ) to return six characters.

  The following expression returns the first name:

  ```
  spaceCharPosition = row["customerName"].indexOf(" ");
  newStringtoDisplay =
      row["customerName"].substr(0, spaceCharPosition);
  ```

- To get the last name, you use indexOf( ) and substr( ) again. The difference is the arguments that you specify for substr( ). To get the last name, you want to start from the character after the space, and the number of characters that you want is the length of the entire string minus the length up to the space.

The following expression returns the last name:

```
spaceCharPosition = row["customerName"].indexOf(" ");
newStringtoDisplay =
    row["customerName"].substr(spaceCharPosition + 1,
    row["customerName"].length - spaceCharPosition);
```

- To get the first name initial and the last name to display, for example, R. Allen:

  - Use the expression in the previous example to get the last name.

  - Add a statement that gets the first letter in the customerName field. You can use substr(0,1) to get only the first character. You can also use charAt(0), which returns a character in a specified position of a string.

  - Add a statement to combine the first name initial, a period, a space, and the last name.

  The following expression returns the first name initial and last name:

```
firstNameInitial = row["customerName"].charAt(0);
spaceCharPosition = row["customerName"].indexOf(" ");
lastName = row["customerName"].substr(spaceCharPosition + 1,
    row["customerName"].length - spaceCharPosition);
newStringtoDisplay = firstNameInitial + ". " + lastName;
```

Matching string patterns

The previous section described some techniques for getting parts of a string for display. Sometimes you need to match patterns, rather than literal substrings, in string values. You can, for example, use pattern-matching to

- Filter rows to display only customers whose last names start with a particular string pattern.

- Search for string patterns, using wildcard characters, and replace with a different string.

To perform pattern-matching, you use regular expressions. A regular expression, also known as regexp, is an expression that searches for a pattern within a string. Many programming languages support regular expressions for complex string manipulation. JavaScript regular expressions are based on the regular expression features of the Perl programming language with a few differences.

In JavaScript, a regular expression is represented by the RegExp object, which you create by using a special literal syntax. Just as you specify a string literal as characters within quotation marks, you specify a regular expression as characters within a pair of forward slash (/) characters, as shown in the following example.

```
var pattern = /smith/;
```

This expression creates a RegExp object and assigns it to the variable pattern. The RegExp object finds the string "smith" within strings, such as smith, blacksmith, smithers, or mark smith. It would not match Smith or Mark Smith, because the search is case sensitive.

You can perform complex pattern-matching by using any number of special characters along with the literal string to search for, as shown in Table 14-3.

Table 14-3   Examples of regular expressions

Regular expression	Description
/y$/	Matches any string that contains the letter "y" as its last character. The $ flag specifies that the character to search is at the end of a string.
	Matches: Carey, tommy, johnny, Fahey.
	Does not match: young, gayle, faye.
/^smith/i	Matches any string that starts with "smith". The ^ flag specifies that the string to search is at the beginning of a string. The i flag makes the search case insensitive.
	Matches: Smith, smithers, Smithsonian.
	Does not match: blacksmith, John Smith
/go*d/	Matches any string that contains this pattern. The asterisk (*) matches zero or any number of the character previous to it, which is "o" in this example.
	Matches: gd, god, good, goood, goodies, for goodness sake.
	Does not match: ged, gored.
/go?d/	Matches any string that contains this pattern. The question mark (?) matches zero or one occurrence of the character previous to it, which is "o" in this example.
	Matches: gd, god, godiva, for god and country.
	Does not match: ged, gored, good, for goodness sake.
/go.*/	Matches any string that contains "go" followed by any number of characters. The period (.) matches any character, except the newline character.
	Matches: go, good, gory, allegory
/Ac[eio]r/	Matches any string that contains "Ac" followed by either e, i, or o, and r.
	Matches: Acer, Acir, Acor, Acerre, National Acer Inc.
	Does not match: Aceir, Acior, Aceior.

There are many more special characters you can use in a regular expression, too many to summarize in this section. In addition, the RegExp object provides several functions for manipulating regular expressions. If you are familiar with regular expressions in other languages, note that some of the syntax of JavaScript regular expressions differs from the syntax of Java or Perl regular expressions. Most notably, JavaScript uses forward slashes (/ /) to delimit a regular expression, and Java and Perl use double quotation marks (" ").

Using pattern-matching in filter conditions

In BIRT Report Designer, regular expressions are particularly useful when creating filter conditions. For example, a filter condition can contain a regular expression that tests whether the value of a string field matches a specified string pattern. Only data rows that meet the filter condition are displayed. You can, for example, create a filter to display only rows where a memo field contains the words "Account overdrawn", where a customer e-mail address ends with ".org", or where a product code starts with "S10".

When you use the filter tool in BIRT Report Designer to specify this type of filter condition, use the Match operator, and specify the regular expression, or string pattern, to match. Figure 14-7 shows an example of specifying a filter condition that uses a regular expression.

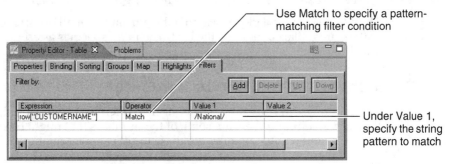

Figure 14-7   Example of regular expression

In this example, the filter condition is applied to a table in the report design. In the generated report, the table displays only customers whose names contain the word National.

Using pattern-matching to search for and replace string values

So far, this chapter has described some of the syntax that is used to create regular expressions. This section discusses how regular expressions can be used in JavaScript code to search for and replace string values. Recall that in "Substituting string values," earlier in this chapter, we used replace( ) to search for a specified string and replace it with another.

Sometimes, you need the flexibility of searching for a string pattern rather than a specific string. Consider the example that was discussed in that earlier section.

The row["address"].replace("St.", "Street") expression replaces St. Mary Road with Street Mary Road. To avoid these types of erroneous search-and-replace actions, use the following expression to search for "St." at the end of a line. The $ flag specifies a match at the end of a string.

```
row["address"].replace (/St.$/, "Street")
```

Consider another example: In your report, you display the contents of a memo field. You notice that in the content, the word JavaScript appears as javascript, Javascript, and JavaScript. You want JavaScript to appear consistently in the report. To do so, you can write the following expression to search for various versions of the word and replace them with JavaScript:

```
row["memoField"].replace("javascript",
    "JavaScript").replace("Javascript", "JavaScript")
```

This expression searches for the specified strings only. It would miss, for example, JAVASCRIPT or javaScript. You can, of course, add as many versions of the word you can think of, but this technique is not efficient.

An efficient and flexible solution is to use a regular expression to search for any and all versions of JavaScript. The following expression replaces all versions of JavaScript with the correct capitalization, no matter how the word is capitalized:

```
row["memoField"].replace(/javascript/gi, "JavaScript")
```

The g flag specifies a global search, which means that all occurrences of the pattern are replaced, not just the first. The i flag specifies a case-insensitive search.

Converting a string to a number

A data source can store numbers as strings. Telephone numbers, zip codes, user IDs, and invoice numbers are some of the numbers that might be stored as strings. If you want to manipulate these numbers mathematically, you need to convert them to numeric type using the parseInt( ) or parseFloat( ) JavaScript function. The following example converts an invoice ID to an integer and adds 10 to it:

```
parseInt(row["invoiceID"]) + 10
```

If the invoiceID is 1225, this expression returns 1235. If you did not convert invoiceID to a real number, the result of adding 10 to invoiceID is 122510.

Manipulating date-and-time data

Both JavaScript and BIRT provide a wide range of functions for manipulating dates. In Expression Builder, look under Native JavaScript Functions—Date, and under BIRT Functions—DateTimeSpan. The following sections describe some of the common date-manipulation tasks and provide examples of expressions.

Displaying the current date

Reports typically display the date on which it is generated, so that users can tell if the data in the report is up-to-date. To display the current date, use the following expression in a data element:

```
new Date( )
```

When the report is run, the current date appears in the format that is determined by the locale setting on the user's system. If, for example, the locale is English (United States), the date appears as follows:

```
6/18/05 12:30 PM
```

If you want to display the date in a different format, such as June 18, 2005, use Property Editor to set the data element's Format DateTime property to the desired format.

Getting parts of a date or time as a number

You can use the JavaScript date functions, such as getDay( ), getMonth( ), and getYear( ), to get the day, month, or year of a specified date field. Similarly, with the getHours( ), getMinutes( ), and getSeconds( ) functions, you can get the hour, minute, or second of a specified time field. All these functions return values as numbers. For example, getDay(row["orderDate"]) returns 1 for a date that falls on Monday. Except for getDate( ), which returns the day of the month, the range of return values for the other functions start at 0. The return values for getMonth( ), for example, are between 0, for January, and 11, for December. Similarly, getDay( ) returns 0 for Sunday and 6 for Saturday.

If you want to display parts of a date in a different format, for example, display the month as a word such as January, February, and so on, use Property Editor to set the data element's Format DateTime property to the desired format.

Calculating the time between two dates

It is often useful to calculate and display the number of days, months, or years between two dates. For example, a data source might store two dates for each order record—the date on which the order was placed and the date on which the order was shipped. To provide information about order fulfillment trends, you can use BIRT's DateTimeSpan functions to calculate and display the number of days between the order date and the ship date:

```
DateTimeSpan.days(row["orderDate"], row["shippedDate"])
```

You can also display the number of hours between the two dates, using the following expression:

```
DateTimeSpan.hours(row["orderDate"], row["shippedDate"])
```

Use a different DateTimeSpan function, depending on the range of time between two dates. For example, you would not use DateTimeSpan.month( ) to calculate the amount of time between order dates and ship dates, because, if orders are usually shipped within two weeks, DateTimeSpan.month( ) will often return 0.

Calculating a date

You can add or subtract a specified amount of time to or from a date to calculate a new date. For example, the following information is stored for each order record: the date on which the order was placed and the shipment time in days. You want to calculate the date that customers can expect to receive their orders. Given those two fields, you can calculate the new date by adding the number of shipping days to the date on which the order was placed. You use BIRT's DateTimeSpan.addDate( ) function to calculate the new date. addDate( ) takes four arguments: the starting date, the number of years, the number of months, and the number of days.

The following expression shows how to calculate the expected delivery date:

```
DateTimeSpan.addDate(row["orderDate"], 0, 0, row["shipTime"])
```

Another function that you can use to calculate a new date is DateTimeSpan.subDate( ). Use this function to subtract days, months, or years to arrive at a new date. It takes the same four arguments as addDate( ).

Using Boolean expressions

A Boolean expression returns one of two values: true or false. The following expressions are basic Boolean expressions:

```
row["sales"] > 5000
row["state"] == "CA"
row["orderDate"] >= "03/01/2006"
```

In the first expression, the sales value is tested to be greater than 5000. If the value is greater than 5000, the expression returns true. If it is not, the expression returns false.

In the second expression, the state value is tested for CA. If the value is CA, the expression returns true; if not, the expression returns false. For Boolean expressions, you must use comparison operators. As the second expression shows, you use ==, not the assignment operator, =. The expression row["state"] = "CA" returns CA. It does not return a true or false value.

In the third expression, the order date is tested to be greater or equal to 03/01/2006. The date value that you enter depends on your machine's locale. You must enclose the date value in double quotation marks ("").

A Boolean expression can be as complex as you need. It can contain a combination of And (&&) and Or (| |) operators, along with the comparison operators. The following expressions are examples of complex, or compound, Boolean expressions:

- The following expression returns true if an order total is greater than or equal to 5000 and an order ID is greater than 2000. Both conditions must be true.

```
row["orderTotal"] >= 5000 && row["orderID"] > 2000
```

- The following expression returns true if the state is CA or WA. Only one condition needs to be true.

```
row["state"] == "CA" || row["state"] == "WA"
```

- The following expression returns true if three conditions are true:

  - The state is CA or WA.

  - The order total is greater than 5000.

  - The order ID is greater than 2000.

```
(row["state"] == "CA" || row["state"] == "WA") &&
   (row["orderTotal"] > 5000 && row["orderID"] > 2000)
```

You use a Boolean expression to:

- Conditionally display a report element.

- Specify conditions with which to filter data.

- Specify conditions with which to perform particular tasks. You can, for example, use a Boolean expression in an if statement to do something when the expression is true and to do something else when the expression is false.

```
if (row["creditScore"] > 700) {
   displayString = "Your loan application has been
   approved."
   }
else{
   displayString = "Your loan application has been denied."
   }
```

You seldom use a Boolean expression on its own unless you want to display true or false in the report.

15

Filtering Data

Data sources typically contain large amounts of data. Reports usually only need a specific subset of data that meets certain criteria. You can select specific records to use in a report by using filters. For example, rather than get information about all customers, you can create filters to select customers in a certain region or customers with a certain credit rank. You can also design filters that provide the report user with the opportunity to specify the filter criteria when the report runs. This chapter discusses creating filters for which you specify the criteria.

Filtering opportunities

Generally, one goal in developing reports with acceptable performance is to limit the amount of data you use to just the data that meets your needs. You can limit, or filter, data in different ways depending on the type of data source you are using and the type of report you are creating.

The first opportunity you have for filtering is by using any filtering techniques provided by your data source. For example, JDBC-compliant databases allow users to run SQL queries that use restrictive WHERE clauses. In fact, best practices recommend designing databases with filtering in mind. You can achieve optimal report performance by filtering data while it is still in the database.

After BIRT retrieves the data from the data source, there are several more opportunities for filtering. The decision on where and when to filter is largely dependent on efficiency. Instead of creating two different data sets that are very similar, for example, you can create one data set that contains information to be used by both a table and a list.

You can use a combination of filtering techniques. For example, if you are accessing data from a database, you can write a query that filters some rows and use other techniques to filter additional rows. Figure 15-1 shows the effects of using various filtering techniques at different points in processing data.

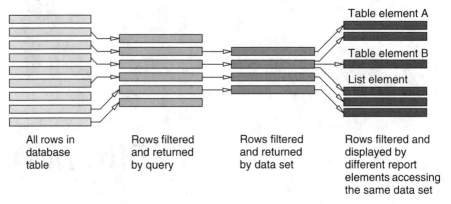

| All rows in database table | Rows filtered and returned by query | Rows filtered and returned by data set | Rows filtered and displayed by different report elements accessing the same data set |

Figure 15-1   Filtering opportunities

Specifying conditions on row retrieval

If your report accesses data from a database or an XML data source, you can specify filter conditions to retrieve a certain set of data from the data source. This section covers some typical ways to filter data in a database or XML data source.

Filtering database data

When you create a JDBC data set, you use a SQL SELECT statement to specify which rows to retrieve from the database. To select only rows that meet certain criteria, add a WHERE clause to the SELECT statement. The WHERE clause consists of the keyword WHERE, followed by a search condition that specifies which rows to retrieve.

For example, the following statement returns only customers from the USA:

```
SELECT *
FROM Customer
WHERE country = 'USA'
```

As another example, the following statement returns only customers from USA and whose credit limit exceeds $10,000.00:

```
SELECT customerName
FROM Customer
WHERE country = 'USA'
AND creditLimit > 10000
```

In the following example, the statement returns all customers from USA or Canada:

```
SELECT customerName
FROM Customer
WHERE country = 'USA'
OR country = 'Canada'
```

How to filter the rows to retrieve from a JDBC data source

This procedure assumes that you have already created a JDBC data set using a SQL query or stored procedure.

1 In Data Explorer, double-click the data set to which to add a filter condition.

2 On Edit Data Set, add a WHERE clause to the SELECT statement to specify a filter condition. For examples and information about the types of filter conditions that you can specify, see the next section.

3 Choose Preview Results to verify that the query returns only the rows that meet the filter condition.

Types of SQL filter conditions

Table 15-1 describes the types of filter conditions and provides examples of filter conditions that are used in WHERE clauses.

Table 15-1   Examples of filter conditions in the WHERE clause

Type of filter condition	Description	Examples of WHERE...

Comparison	Compares the value of one expression to the value of another expression	`quantity = 10`
		`custName = 'Acme Inc.'`
		`custName > 'P'`
		`custState <> 'CA'`
		`orderDate > {d '2005-06-30'}`

Range	Tests whether the value of an expression falls within a range of values. The test includes the endpoints of the range.	`price BETWEEN 1000 AND 2000`
		`custName BETWEEN 'E' AND 'K'`
		`orderDate BETWEEN`
		`    {d '2005-01-01'}`
		`    AND {d '2005-06-30'}`

(continues)

Table 15-1   Examples of filter conditions in the WHERE clause *(continued)*

Type of filter condition	Description	Examples of WHERE...

Membership	Tests whether the value of an expression matches one value in a set of values	`officeCode IN (101,103,104)`
		
		`itemType IN ('sofa', 'loveseat', 'endtable', 'clubchair')`
		
		`orderDate IN ({d '2005-10-10'}, {d '2005-10-17'})`

Pattern-matching	Tests whether the value of a string field matches a specified pattern	`custName LIKE 'Smith%'` (% matches zero or more characters) `custName LIKE 'Smiths_n'` (_ matches one character) `custState NOT LIKE 'CA%'`

Null value	Tests whether a field has a null, or missing, value	`manager IS NULL`
		
		`shipDate IS NULL`
		
		`shipDate IS NOT NULL`

SQL provides many other operators and options that you can use to create more complex search conditions. For more information about the WHERE clause, see the SQL documentation for your JDBC database.

Filtering XML data

When you create an XML data set, you specify what data to retrieve from an XML data source by mapping XML elements and attributes to data set columns. To map an XML element or attribute to a column, you specify an XPath expression. If you are not familiar with XML, XPath is a query language for accessing parts of an XML document. Figure 15-2 shows an example of column mappings defined in an XML data set and the data rows that BIRT returns.

To select only data that meets certain criteria, specify the value to search in the XPath expression that was used to map the column. The following XPath expression, for example, specifies that only rows where the author's name is Sally Bush should be retrieved:

```
author[@name="Sally Bush"]
```

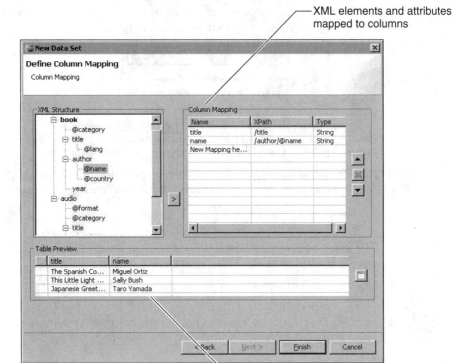

XML elements and attributes mapped to columns

BIRT returns these data rows

Figure 15-2   Column mappings and the data rows returned for an XML document

When filtering data with an XPath expression, observe the following limitations:

- You can specify only one value on which to search. You cannot, for example, search for author names Sally Bush and Miguel Ortiz.

- You can filter only on XML attributes, not XML elements. The XML structure in the Column Mapping page displays XML attributes with the @ symbol. For example, @category is an attribute, and title is an element.

If you need more advanced filtering capabilities, use BIRT Report Designer's filter tool, which is described later in this chapter.

How to define a filter on row retrieval for XML data sets

1 In Data Explorer, double-click the data set to which to add a filter condition.

2 On Edit Data Set, choose Column Mapping. Column Mapping displays the XML structure and the XML elements and attributes that you mapped to data set columns.

3 In XML structure, select the attribute on which to filter, then choose the right arrow. You can select only items that contain the @ symbol in their names.

Column Mapping appears, as shown in Figure 15-3. It displays a default column name, XPath expression, and data type.

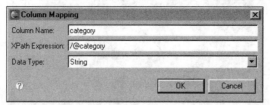

Figure 15-3   Column Mapping, showing default settings

4   Modify the XPath expression to specify the value on which to filter. The following expressions are examples of XPath filtering expressions:

```
[@category="CHILDREN"]
author[@name="Sally Bush"]
```

The value you specify within the double quotation marks (" ") must match exactly the value in the XML document.

5   Choose OK. The column mapping that you defined appears on Column Mapping.

6   In Table Preview, click the preview button to confirm that the filter returns only rows that match the value that you specified.

Filtering data after row retrieval

BIRT provides options for filtering data that complement, and in some cases, replace filtering provided by data sources. It is always recommended to filter at the data source when possible. There are cases, however, when you cannot. For example, if you use flat file data sources and you want to filter data, you must filter data in BIRT.

In addition, if using SQL to modify an existing database query is problematic, you can specify the filter conditions using JavaScript expressions instead of SQL. BIRT Report Designer provides a graphical tool to help you build these filter conditions.

Deciding where to filter in BIRT

There are three places in BIRT you can filter data. You can create a filter in any or all of these places:

- The data set
- A report element, such as a table or list
- A group

The first opportunity to filter data in BIRT is on the data set level. Use this technique if only one report element uses the data set or if you want all report elements that use the data set to use the same set of rows.

Next, you can filter on a report element. You can edit the report element filter properties to specify conditions for displaying only certain data rows. Use this technique if multiple tables, lists, and charts use the same data set, but you want each report element to display a different set of rows.

For example, you create a data set that returns data for all customers in the USA. You use this data set for two elements, such as a table and a list. You can specify a different filter condition for each element to limit further the rows to display. The table element, for example, can filter the rows to display only customers from California. The list element can filter the rows to display only customers from New York. Figure 15-4 illustrates this concept.

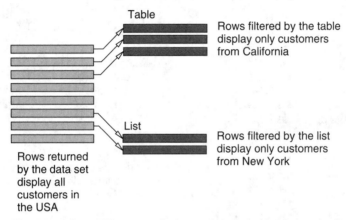

Figure 15-4   Filters applied to a data set, a table, and a list

Finally, you can filter on a group of data. If you group data in a table or list, you can edit the filter properties of each group. Filter at the group level if a table or list displays rows in groups and you want to display only certain groups. For example, a sales report groups orders by customer. Rather than showing data for all customers, you can specify a filter to display only customers that have order totals above a certain amount or specify a filter to display only the top three customers.

Figure 15-5 compares three reports that use the same data set but different group filters. The first report shows all customer groups. The second report uses a filter at the customer group level to show only customers whose order totals exceed $100,000.00. The third report uses a filter at the customer group level to show the top three customers with the highest order totals.

Report shows all customer groups

Report applies a filter on the customer group to show only customers whose order totals exceed $100,000.00

Corporate Gift Ideas Co.	$102,908.44
Order 10159	$37,872.32
Order 10162	$25,345.98
Order 10381	$28,734.69
Order 10384	$10,955.45
Gift Depot Inc.	$83,274.15
Order 10172	$19,318.08
Order 10263	$40,618.93
Order 10413	$23,337.14
Land of Toys Inc.	$105,499.28
Order 10107	$9,347.60
Order 10248	$34,077.36
Order 10292	$23,510.33
Order 10329	$38,563.99
Muscle Machine Inc	$146,063.02
Order 10127	$45,049.74
Order 10204	$47,609.95
Order 10267	$20,314.44
Order 10349	$33,088.89
Online Diecast Creations Co.	$93,495.72
Order 10100	$8,563.71
Order 10192	$40,586.41
Order 10322	$44,345.60
The Sharp Gifts Warehouse	$133,390.92
Order 10250	$40,517.12
Order 10400	$29,589.38
Order 10407	$48,904.14

Corporate Gift Ideas Co.	$102,908.44
Order 10159	$37,872.32
Order 10162	$25,345.98
Order 10381	$28,734.69
Order 10384	$10,955.45
Land of Toys Inc.	$105,499.28
Order 10107	$9,347.60
Order 10248	$34,077.36
Order 10292	$23,510.33
Order 10329	$38,563.99
Muscle Machine Inc	$146,063.02
Order 10127	$45,049.74
Order 10204	$47,609.95
Order 10267	$20,314.44
Order 10349	$33,088.89
The Sharp Gifts Warehouse	$133,390.92
Order 10250	$40,517.12
Order 10257	$14,380.28
Order 10400	$29,589.38
Order 10407	$48,904.14

Report applies a filter on the customer group to show customers with the top three order totals

Land of Toys Inc.	$105,499.28
Order 10107	$9,347.60
Order 10248	$34,077.36
Order 10292	$23,510.33
Order 10329	$38,563.99
Muscle Machine Inc	$146,063.02
Order 10127	$45,049.74
Order 10204	$47,609.95
Order 10267	$20,314.44
Order 10349	$33,088.89
The Sharp Gifts Warehouse	$133,390.92
Order 10250	$40,517.12
Order 10257	$14,380.28
Order 10400	$29,589.38
Order 10407	$48,904.14

Figure 15-5   Three reports using the same data set, but displaying different results, because of filters applied on the group level

You can specify filter conditions at all three levels if your report design needs it. Filtering at each level serves a different purpose, can yield different results, and can have different rules. Use the following guidelines to help you decide where to filter data for a report:

- When you filter at the data set level, BIRT filters all rows that are retrieved from the data source.

- When you filter at the report element level, BIRT filters all rows that are returned by the data set that is bound to the report element.

- When you filter at the group level, BIRT filters only rows in that particular group. In the reports shown in Figure 15-5, you can filter on customer names and order totals only. You cannot, for example, filter on order number, because that data is in a different group. Typically, a filter at the group level uses an aggregate expression.

- Filters that use aggregate expressions can be specified only at the group level. The second report shown in Figure 15-5 uses the following filter condition:

  ```
  Total.sum(row["orderTotal"]) Larger Than 100000
  ```

  The third report uses the following filter condition:

  ```
  Total.sum(row["orderTotal"]) Top n 3
  ```

  If you use an aggregate expression in a filter at the data set or report element level, BIRT Report Designer displays an error message.

- Some filter conditions provide the same results whether they are applied at the data set, report element, or group level. In the reports shown in Figure 15-5, if you want to display only customers whose names start with M or a later letter, you can specify the following filter condition at the data set, table, or group level, and the reports display the same data:

  ```
  row["customerName"] Larger Than "M"
  ```

Types of BIRT filter conditions

Just as with the data source filtering capabilities, you can design different types of filter conditions with BIRT Report Designer depending on how you want to search for data rows. For example, you can specify that BIRT returns rows when the value of a particular field matches a specific value, when the field value falls within a range of values, when the field value matches a string pattern, or when the field value is null.

The filter tool displays operators as English words instead of the actual operators. For example, the tool displays Equal, Larger than, Larger than or Equal, and Not Equal, instead of ==, >, >=, and !=. Table 15-2 describes the types of filter conditions that you can create with the filter tool. The table also contains numerous examples of expressions you can create using the operators. Most operators can be used with different data types. You should be aware that the filter tool provides two pattern-matching operators: Like and Match. The Like operator enables users who are familiar with SQL to specify pattern-matching expressions using SQL syntax. The Match operator enables users who are familiar with JavaScript to specify pattern-matching expressions using JavaScript's regular expression syntax.

Table 15-2   Examples of BIRT filter conditions

Type of filter condition	Description	Example as it appears in the filter tool

Comparison	Compares the value of a field to a specified value.	`row["quantity"] Less than 10`
		`row["custName"] Equal "Acme Inc."`
		`row["custName"] Larger than or Equal "P"`
		`row["custState"] Not Equal "CA"`
		`row["orderDate"] Less than or Equal "06/30/05"`

Null value	Tests whether a field has a value or not.	`row["manager"] Is Null` `row["shipDate"] Is Not Null`

Range	Tests whether the value of a field falls within a range of specified values. The test includes the endpoints of the range.	`row["quantity"] Between 50 and 100`
		(returns all quantities between 50 and 100, including 50 and 100)
		`row["custName"] Between "A" and "B"`
		(returns all names that start with A)
		`row["custName"] Not Between "A" and "M"`
		(returns all names that start with M and later letters)
		`row["orderDate"] Between "06/01/05" and "06/30/05"`
		(returns all dates between these dates, including 06/01/05 and 06/30/05)

Conditional logic	Tests if a complete filter condition evaluates to true or false. Use to create a single filter condition that consists of multiple conditions.	`row["country"] == "USA"││`
		`row["country"] == "Canada"`
		`Is False`
		(returns all countries except the USA and Canada)
		`row["orderStatus"] == "Open"││`
		`row["orderTotal"] > 100000`
		`Is True`
		(returns all orders with open status and all orders with totals exceeding 100000)

Table 15-2 Examples of BIRT filter conditions *(continued)*

Type of filter condition	Description	Example as it appears in the filter tool

Pattern-matching test, using JavaScript syntax	Tests whether the value of a string field matches a specified pattern called a regular expression. For more information about matching patterns with regular expressions, see "Matching string patterns" in Chapter 14, "Writing Expressions."	`row["custName"] Match /Smith/`
		(returns names that contain the substring Smith)
		`row["creditRank"] Match /[AB]/`
		(returns credit ranks A or B)
		`row["productCode"] Match /^S10/`
		(returns product codes that begin with S10)

Pattern-matching test, using SQL syntax	Tests whether the value of a string field matches a specified pattern that uses SQL syntax.	`row["custName"] Like "%Smith%"`
		(returns names that contain the substring Smith)
		`row["productCode"] Like "S10%"`
		(returns product codes that begin with S10)

Top or bottom *n* logic	Tests if the value of a specified field is within the top or bottom *n* values.	`row["age"] Top Percent 5`
		(returns ages in the top five percent)
		`row["age"] Bottom Percent 5`
		(returns ages in the bottom five percent)
		`row["orderTotal"] Top n 10`
		(returns the top ten orders)
		`row["orderTotal"] Bottom n 10`
		(returns the bottom ten orders)

Creating a filter condition

The procedure for creating a filter condition is the same whether you create it at the data set, report element, or group level. The difference is in how you access the filter tool.

When you create a filter condition, you specify the following information:

- The expression to evaluate, typically the field to search, such as row["grade"].

- The operator that specifies the type of filter test, such as Equal.

- The value for which to search, such as "A".

You can create more complex filter conditions that include JavaScript functions or scripts. For example, you can specify calculated values for the expression and value portions of the filter. The following example shows a multiline expression in the expression part. The expression returns a customer's first name from the customerName field, which stores full names:

```
spaceCharPosition = row["customerName"].indexOf(" ");
stringToGet = row["customerName"]substr(0, spaceCharPosition);
```

If you combine this expression with the Equal operator and specify a value of "John", the filter condition extracts the first name from the customerName field, compares the first name to John, and returns only rows where this condition is true.

The expressions and values that you specify in a filter condition in BIRT Report Designer must use JavaScript syntax. If you filter data using both the SQL query and BIRT Report Designer's filter tool, be careful not to confuse SQL syntax with JavaScript syntax when specifying the filter condition.

It is easy, for example, to confuse the use of single quotation marks (' ') and double quotation marks (" "). SQL requires single quotation marks for string and date constants, but JavaScript requires double quotation marks. Another example is the comparison operator. You use = for SQL and == for JavaScript.

How to filter at the data set level

1 In Data Explorer, right-click the data set whose rows you want to filter, then choose Edit. Edit Data Set displays the query for the data set, as shown in Figure 15-6.

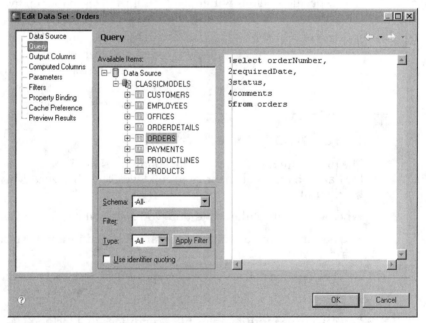

Figure 15-6   Edit Data Set, displaying the query

2 Choose Filters from the left side of the window. Edit Data Set displays filter information, as shown in Figure 15-7.

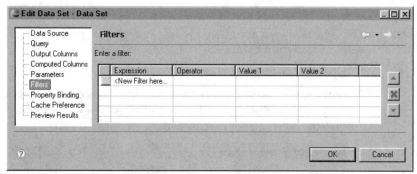

Figure 15-7   Edit Data Set, displaying filtering information

3 Specify the filter condition:

1 Click the cell below Expression. Two buttons appear on the right. The arrow button displays a list of fields you can use in Expression. The ellipsis (...) button launches Expression Builder, which you can use to create a more complex expression.

2 For Expression, select a field. You can also type the filter expression.

3 For Operator, select an operator from the drop-down list.

4 For Value 1, specify the search value. You can type the value, select from the list of values, or use Expression Builder to create a more complex value expression. If you select the Is True, Is False, Is Null, or Is Not Null operator, you do not specify a value.

5 For Value 2, specify a value only if you select the Between or Not Between operator. Figure 15-8 shows some examples of filter conditions.

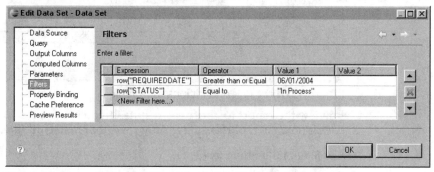

Figure 15-8   Filter conditions in Edit Data Set

4 Choose Preview Results to verify the results that the data set returns. If you specified multiple filter conditions, the report displays only rows that match all filter conditions. To display rows that match any one of the filter conditions, create a single filter condition that contains an OR expression, then select the Is True operator. This task is described later in this chapter.

How to filter at the report element level

These instructions assume you already created a report that uses a table to display data from a data set.

1 Open Property Editor.

2 In the layout editor, select the table or list whose data you want to filter. Property Editor displays the properties of the table or list, as shown in Figure 15-9.

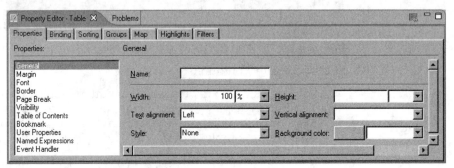

Figure 15-9 Table properties

3 Choose the Filters tab. Property Editor displays the filters page.

4 Choose Add to create a filter condition.

5 Specify the filter condition. For detailed steps, see the previous section. Figure 15-10 shows some examples of filter conditions.

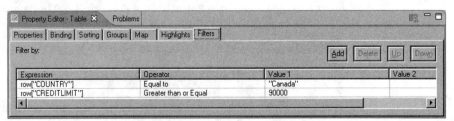

Figure 15-10 Filter conditions for a table

6 Preview the report to verify the results. If you specified multiple filter conditions, the report displays only rows that match all filter conditions.

How to filter at the group level

These instructions assume that you have already created a table that displays data from a data set, and created a group or groups to organize the data.

1 In the layout editor, select the table that contains the data to filter.

2 In Property Editor, choose the Groups tab. Property Editor displays the groups that you defined for the table.

3 Double-click the group whose data you want to filter. Edit Group displays the properties of the group, as shown in Figure 15-11.

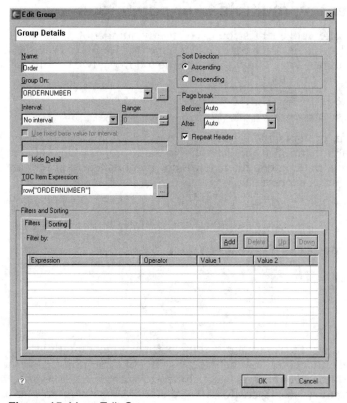

Figure 15-11 Edit Group

4 Under Filtering and Sorting, choose Filters.

5 Choose Add to create a filter condition. A placeholder expression appears in the first row.

6 Specify the filter condition. Figure 15-12 shows an example.

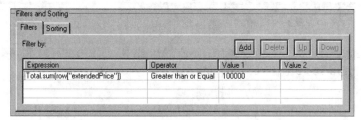

Figure 15-12 Filter condition for a group

7 Choose OK.

8 Preview the report to verify the results. The report displays a different set of group values.

Creating multiple filter conditions

The filter tool enables you to create any number of conditions for filtering data. BIRT evaluates each condition and includes only data rows that meet all the conditions. For example, assume the following two conditions were created with the filter tool:

```
row["orderTotal"] Larger Than 10000
row["country"] Equal "USA"
```

In this example, BIRT includes a row only if the value in the orderTotal field is greater than 10000 and the value in the country field is equal to USA. In other words, creating two filter conditions is equivalent to specifying the following JavaScript expression:

```
row["orderTotal"] > 10000 && row["country"] == "USA"
```

The following rows meet the specified filter conditions:

```
Country    Order ID   Order Total

USA        1010       15000
USA        1035       18500
USA        1155       25000
USA        1200       12000
USA        1455       20500
```

If you want to return a row if it meets any one of multiple conditions, create a single filter condition that uses the OR (| |) operator to combine multiple conditions. For example, to include a row where either orderTotal exceeds 10000 or country is USA, create an expression that compares to true, as follows:

```
row["orderTotal"] > 10000 || row["country"] == "USA" Is True
```

For expressions that compare to true or false, you must use the comparison operator. As the previous example shows, you use ==, not the assignment operator, =. Figure 15-13 shows how the filter condition is specified in the filter tool. Note that you select Is True from the list of operators under Operator.

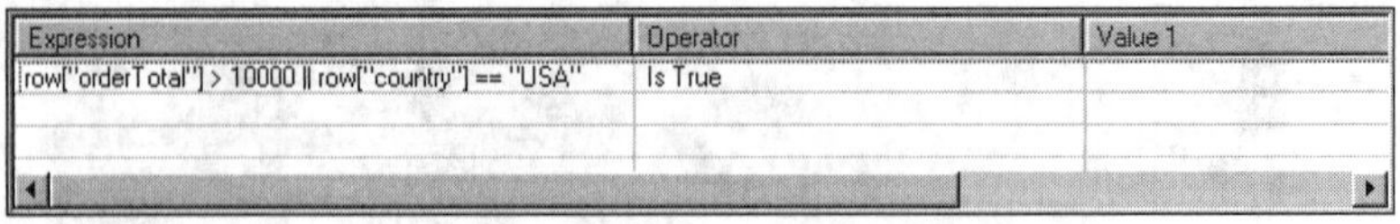

Expression	Operator	Value 1
row["orderTotal"] > 10000 || row["country"] == "USA"	Is True	

Figure 15-13 Filter condition that uses the OR operator

In this example, the following rows meet the specified filter condition:

Country	Order ID	Order Total
Belgium	1020	21000
France	2005	14500
USA	1425	5000
USA	1750	7500
USA	1010	15000
USA	1035	18500
USA	1155	25000
USA	1200	12000
USA	1455	20500

16

Enabling the User to Filter Data

When you create a report, you build a data set and typically specify filter criteria to display specific data in the report. When a user views the report, the user sees the information that you selected. As users become familiar with the report and recognize its potential as an analytical tool, they may want to view the data in different ways. For example, in a sales report, a user may want to view only sales in California, or sales over a certain amount, or sales that closed in the last 30 days.

The solution for this type of ad hoc reporting requirement is for the report to prompt the user to provide information that determines what data to display. Report developers make this solution available by using report parameters.

About report parameters

Report parameters select information that determines the data to display in the report when the report runs. Typically, you use report parameters to prompt a report user to specify what data to display before BIRT generates the report. You can also use report parameters in more creative ways. For example, a web application can use a user's login information to programmatically set the value of an account number report parameter. Then the web application can generate a report for that particular account.

Using report parameters, you can

- Generate on-demand reports.

By using report parameters in a report design, you can create a single report design that generates specialized reports, on demand, to meet the different needs of report users.

- Design a report once, and use the same design to display different data that is based on specific criteria.

  Report parameters are essential tools for time-sensitive reports. Consider a monthly sales report. A report developer generates and publishes a report each month. When the report developer first creates the report, she builds a query to show sales data for the month of January only. To generate a report for February's numbers, she must modify the query to get data for February only. Without using report parameters, the report developer must modify the query manually every month. By creating a report parameter that prompts for the month for which to display sales information, the report developer can create one report and run it each month to refresh its data. The report user gets exactly what he needs to see.

- Manage large reports.

  Report parameters are also useful for managing large reports. Consider a report design that generates a detailed report that is several hundred pages long. It displays, for example, all itemized sales orders for all customers in all cities in every state. That report is comprehensive but includes more information than most users want most of the time. To reduce the size of the report and let the user select only the data that he wants to view, you can use report parameters to generate specific parts of the original report. You can, for example, provide report parameters that ask the user to specify a customer name, a city, or a state for which to display sales orders.

Enter Parameters, shown in Figure 16-1, displays the available parameters to a report user.

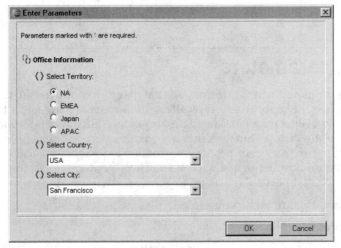

Figure 16-1   Enter Parameters

When the user runs the report, he chooses the parameter values that he wants to see. The report developer must specify default parameter values in order for the report to run even if the user fails to specify any parameters.

Planning to use report parameters

Before you create parameters for a report, decide what field values you want the report user to specify and how to prompt the user for those values:

- Think of the different ways in which a user may need to filter the information. You create one report parameter for each question that you want the user to answer. Theoretically, you can create a parameter for each discrete piece of data in the data source. To ensure that report parameters are not overwhelming for the user, limit the available parameters to important fields.

- If you create more than one report parameter, consider the interaction of the values. For example, if you create two parameters to get the values of state and sales total, decide whether to return rows only if both values in the row match or if either value matches.

- If you create many report parameters, organize them in logical groups. For example, you can create two groups of parameters to organize customer parameters, such as customer name, city, and state, in one group and order parameters, such as order ID, order date, and order amount, in another group.

- Use short, descriptive text prompts, but ensure the text is not ambiguous. For example, Customer State is clearer than State.

- Do not assume that the report user knows how the data is stored in the data source. For example, a user might not know that an order-status field takes three values: Open, Closed, and In Evaluation. Without this knowledge, the user does not know what value to enter for an order-status parameter. To improve usability, create a drop-down list or radio buttons for the user to select a value instead of requiring the user to type a value. Figure 16-1 provides an example of a simple, but effective, parameter presentation.

Ways to enable user filtering

You can enable filtering on user-specified values either at query run time, or after running the query. To enable a user to filter at query run time, you must use a JDBC data source. By defining filters at the table-element level, you can also enable user filtering after the query returns a result set. You can enable user filtering at this level for any data source.

Enabling the user to filter at query run time

As described previously, a report parameter enables or requires users to specify a value that they can easily understand. When they run a report, BIRT updates the SQL query with these values before it retrieves any data. The data source then returns only the rows that match the user-specified values.

To enable users to filter database data, you complete the following tasks in the recommended order. For detailed information about these tasks, see the corresponding topics later in this section.

- Create report parameters to prompt the user to specify values that determine what rows to retrieve.

- Insert parameter markers in the SQL query.

- Create a data set parameter to supply a value for each parameter marker in the SQL query.

- Bind the data set parameter to the report parameter, so the data set parameter gets the user-specified value from the report parameter and passes it to the SQL query.

- Determine how to present the report parameters to a user.

- Test the report parameters.

Task 1: Creating a report parameter

Report parameters provide a mechanism for passing values into a report. You can create a report parameter to prompt the report user to specify a value for a particular field, or you can use a hidden report parameter to pass a value into the report on a programmatic basis. For instance, a hidden parameter might be used to pass a customer's account code into a report if you did not want a customer to look at any account data but her own.

Report parameters have global scope, which means they are available to the entire report and any report element can access a report parameter's value. To enable user filtering, you typically bind the report parameter to a corresponding data set parameter.

When you create a report parameter, you perform two main tasks.

- Define the basic properties of the parameter: its name and data type.

- Design the presentation of the parameter to the report user. The tasks you should consider include:

  - Specifying whether users type a value or select a value from a list box or radio buttons

  - Providing a default value

- Displaying a descriptive text prompt
- Organizing report parameters in logical groups

How to create a simple report parameter

1   In the data explorer, right-click Report Parameters, and choose New Parameter.

New Parameter appears, as shown in Figure 16-2.

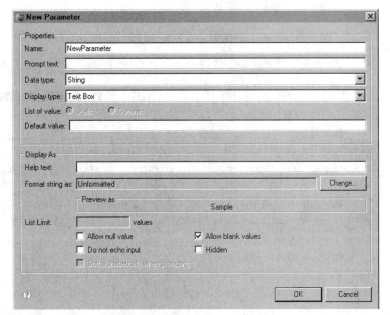

Figure 16-2   New Parameter

2   Specify the following basic properties:

   1   For Name, type a name for the parameter. If you do not specify a value for Prompt text, the report user sees that Name value as the prompt. Instead, it is good practice to supply a user-friendly name for the parameter in Prompt text. Prefix the value you select for Name with RP to help distinguish report parameters from other parameter types, such as data set parameters. For example, a report parameter used to filter quantityinstock might be named RP_quantityinstock.

   2   For Data type, select a data type for the parameter.

      The data type that you select does not have to match the data type of the field in the data source. Values in an orderID field, for example, can be stored as integers in the database, but the report parameter that is associated with this field can be of decimal or string type. The data type that you select for the report parameter determines the formatting options that are available if you choose to provide a default value or a list of values for the report parameter.

For date fields, you can select either Date Time or String. Specifying the string data type provides more flexibility for the user to specify dates in a variety of formats. For example, the user can type 02/04/2004, 2/4/04, or Feb 4, 2004. The trade-off is that you cannot use date-and-time formats to change how dates appear if you choose to provide the user with a list of date values.

3 Choose OK.

The parameter appears in Report Parameters in the data explorer.

If necessary, repeat these steps to create additional report parameters.

Task 2: Inserting a parameter marker in the SQL query

After you create your report parameter, insert a parameter marker in the WHERE clause of the SQL query of the data set that you want to filter with the value of the report parameter. The parameter marker, represented by a question mark (?), indicates where you want BIRT to insert the parameter value.

For example, to ask the user to specify the threshold inventory quantity for a restocking report, insert the ? parameter marker in the WHERE clause, as shown in the following example:

```
WHERE quantityinstock < ?
```

When the report runs, if the user specifies 500 for quantityinstock, BIRT replaces ? with 500 and sends the following filter condition to the data source:

```
WHERE quantityinstock < 500
```

If you write a filter condition that uses more than one field, think about the interaction of the field values. Each of the following WHERE clauses, for example, returns a different set of rows:

```
WHERE quantityinstock < ? AND productvendor = ?

WHERE quantityinstock < ? OR productvendor = ?
```

The first clause returns only those rows in which both the quantityinstock and the productvendor values match the values that replace the ? markers. The second clause returns more rows. It returns rows in which the quantityinstock value is less than the value that replaces the quantityinstock marker and rows in which the productvendor value matches the value that replaces the productvendor ? marker.

It is necessary to write filter conditions that make sense for your report. Before you complete all steps to enable filtering, you should test your filter conditions by specifying actual values in the WHERE clause to verify that the results meet your expectations.

SQL supports many options and operators for specifying filter conditions. For complete information about writing WHERE clauses and SQL statements in general, consult a book about SQL.

How to insert a parameter marker in the SQL query

This procedure assumes that you already created a data set.

1 In the data explorer, right-click the data set whose query you want to edit, then choose Edit. Edit Data Set displays the query.

2 Add a WHERE clause with one or more parameters.

```
WHERE quantityinstock < ?

WHERE quantityinstock < ? AND productvendor = ?

WHERE quantityinstock < ? OR productname LIKE ?
```

Figure 16-3 shows an example of a query with a single parameter marker.

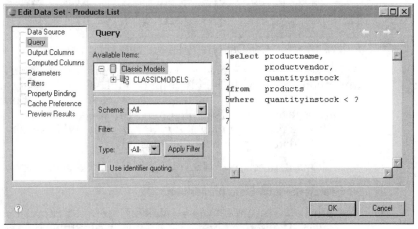

Figure 16-3   Query with one parameter marker

At this point, you are ready to create a data set parameter for each ? parameter marker. The next section describes this task.

Task 3:   Creating a data set parameter and binding it to the report parameter

A data set parameter passes a value that replaces the ? parameter marker in the WHERE clause of the query when the query is run. You must create one data set parameter for each parameter marker in the query's WHERE clause. If you do not, BIRT displays an error.

SQL uses the positions of the ? parameter markers in the WHERE clause to determine which data set parameter matches which ? marker. Therefore, the order of the data set parameters is critical. For example, you must create two data set parameters if you specify the following WHERE clause:

```
WHERE quantityinstock < ? and productvendor = ?
```

The first parameter in the list of data set parameters must pass a value to quantityinstock < ?, and the second parameter must pass a value to productvendor = ?. Figure 16-4 shows these two data set parameters. The order of these parameters matches the order of the parameter markers' appearance in the example WHERE clause.

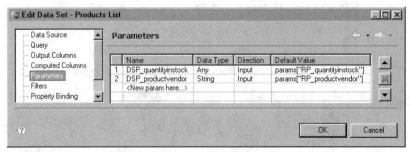

Figure 16-4   Edit Data Set, with two data set parameters

A data set parameter replaces a parameter marker in the query with a value from another part of the report design. Think of the data set parameter as an intermediary—it gets a value from a report element, then it passes the value to the query. To enable users to filter data, you use a data set parameter to get a value from a report parameter. If you change the WHERE clause in the query, update the data set parameters accordingly.

The following procedure tells you how to create a data set parameter.

How to create a data set parameter

This procedure assumes that you already inserted a parameter marker in the SQL query, as described previously. If you use multiple data set parameters, create them in the order in which their corresponding parameter markers appear in the WHERE clause.

1   In the data explorer, choose the data set for which you want to create parameters. Edit Data Set displays the query for the data set.

2   Choose Parameters. Edit Data Set displays default parameter information in the first row.

3   Create a data set parameter by specifying the following required values:

    1   In the first row, in Name, type a name for the parameter. It is good practice to prefix the name you select with DSP for data set parameter to to help distinguish the parameter from other parameter types, such as report parameters. For example, a data set parameter used to filter quantityinstock might be named DSP_quantityinstock.

    2   In Data type, select a data type for the parameter.

3 In Direction, choose Input. This value means that the parameter is an input parameter.

4 Select Default value and a button appears at the right of the empty field.

5 Choose the ellipsis (…) button at the right. Expression Builder appears.

4 Bind the data set parameter to the appropriate report parameter by selecting the report parameter as the data set's default value:

1 In Category, choose Report Parameters, then choose All in Sub-Category. The report parameters that you created appear, as shown in Figure 16-5.

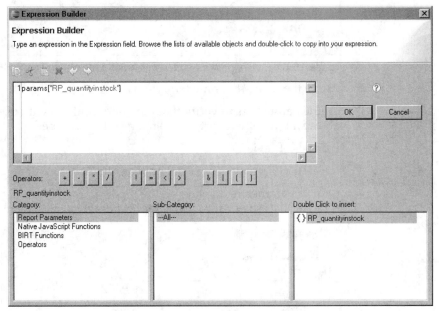

Figure 16-5   Binding a data set parameter to a report parameter

2 Double-click the appropriate report parameter. The report parameter appears in the expression area.

3 Choose OK.

5 Repeat steps 3 and 4 to create additional data set parameters for any other parameter markers that you inserted in your SQL query.

Assuming that you entered a default value for each report parameter, you can choose Preview Results to verify that the query returns rows that match your WHERE condition.

Figure 16-6 shows the results of the previous example where a default value of 999 was entered for the report parameter RP_quantityinstock. It shows all rows for products in stock with a quantity of less than 999.

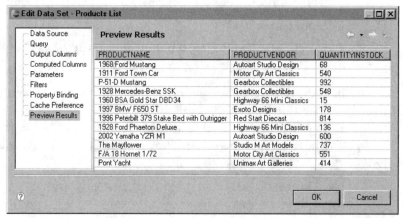

Figure 16-6 Preview Results, with rows that match the WHERE condition

6 To save the data set parameters, choose OK.

7 Test the parameters to verify that the query updates with user-specified values and that the report shows the results you expect:

   1 Choose Preview.

   2 If Enter Parameters does not appear, choose Show Report Parameters.

   Enter Parameters displays all the report parameters that you created. Figure 16-7 shows the simple report parameter RP_quantityinstock.

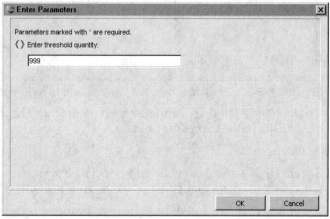

Figure 16-7 Enter Parameters

   3 Specify a value for each parameter, then choose OK.

If you completed all the tasks that were described earlier in this chapter, the WHERE clause of your query updates with the specified values, and the report displays the rows that match the WHERE clause.

Enabling the user to filter after running the query

An alternative to enabling filtering at query run time is to enable filtering at the time the report is rendered. This option is available for all data sources, including JDBC, XML and text-file, but filtering at query run time through the use of data set parameters is usually the preferred approach for JDBC for performance reasons.

Though the goal in enabling users to filter at query run time and after the query runs is the same, the steps are different. To enable users to filter after running the query, you complete the following tasks in the recommended order. For detailed information about these tasks, see the corresponding topics later in this section:

- Create report parameters to prompt a user to specify field values that determine what data to display.
- Create one filter condition for each field for which you want the report user to supply a value. Set the value of each filter condition to a report parameter to dynamically update the filter condition with the parameter value.
- Determine how to present the report parameters.
- Test the report parameters.

Task 1: Creating a report parameter

Just as you create a report parameter to enable user filtering at query run time, you create a report parameter to enable user filtering after the query is executed. As report parameter creation is covered earlier in this chapter, it is not repeated here.

Task 2: Updating a filter condition when the report runs

Typically, when you specify a filter condition to display only certain data in a report, you specify the value on which to search, as in these examples:

```
row["quantityinstock"] Less than 500
row["productvendor"] Equal to "Exoto Designs"
```

To enable a user to filter data when the report runs, specify the report parameter as the filter value. The following expressions are examples of filter conditions whose values are set to report parameters:

```
row["quantityinstock"] Less than params["RP_quantityinstock"]
row["productvendor"] Equal to params["RP_productvendor"]
```

When the user runs the report and supplies a value for the report parameter, BIRT dynamically updates the filter condition with the parameter value and generates a report that displays only the specified data.

How to dynamically update a filter condition when the report runs

This procedure assumes that you already created

- A report that contains a table or list to display data from a data set

- One or more report parameters for the report

1 In the layout editor, select the table element or list element to filter. The property editor displays the properties of the selected table or list.

Figure 16-8 shows an example of a selected table and its properties.

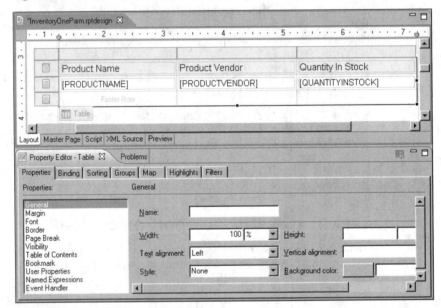

Figure 16-8   Table properties

2 Choose the Filters tab. The property editor displays the Filters page, as shown in Figure 16-9.

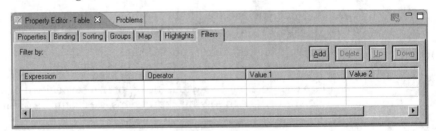

Figure 16-9   The Filters page in Property Editor

3 Choose Add to create a new filter condition.

4 Specify the filter condition:

1 Choose the cell below Expression. Two buttons appear at the right.

2 Choose the arrow button, then select the field for which you want the user to specify a value when the report runs.

3 For Operator, select an operator from the drop-down list.

4 For Value 1, specify the name of the report parameter that you created.

You can use the expression builder to select the report parameter from the list of report parameters that you created for the report. Figure 16-10 shows an example of a filter condition for which the value is set to a report parameter.

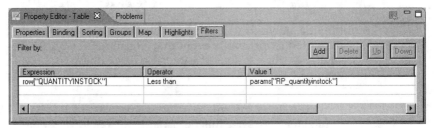

Figure 16-10   Filter condition, set to a report parameter

5 Preview the report.

Enter Parameters appears and displays the report parameters that you created. Figure 16-11 shows an example.

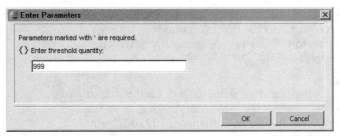

Figure 16-11   Enter Parameters, showing a report parameter

6 Specify values for the report parameters, then choose OK.

The report displays data that matches the values that you specified.

Designing the presentation of report parameters

After you verify that your report parameters generate the report that you expect, remember to improve the presentation of the parameter information. If you used the default options when you created the report parameter, you can make the parameters more user-friendly by setting their display properties when you edit the report parameters. You access these properties by double-clicking a report parameter in Data Explorer. Table 16-1 lists the ways in which you can enhance the usability and appearance of report parameters. Details about each technique are presented in subsequent sections.

Table 16-1   Techniques for enhancing report parameter usability

Technique	Property to set
Use a prompt that describes clearly what values a user can enter. For example, you can display text, such as: `Enter the state's abbreviation`	Prompt text
Provide a default value that results in a well-presented report in the event that a user does not supply a value. A default value also functions as an example.	Default value
Provide helpful information about a report parameter. Users see this information just below the input field for a parameter. For example, for a customer ID parameter, you can provide information, such as: `Type a number between 100 and 500`	Help text
Rather than requiring the user to type a value in a text box, create a list box, a combo box, or a set of radio buttons that provide values from which a user can select.	Display type
If a report parameter displays a default value or a list of values in a list box, a combo box, or radio buttons, display those values in a suitable format. For example, if values for sales totals are stored in #### format in the data source, you can change the display format to $#,###.00.	Format
Provide the user with the option of specifying null values.	Allow null value
Provide the user with the option of specifying blank values.	Allow blank values

Providing a default value

While it is not required, you should provide a default value for each report parameter. If you do not, the user must specify a value to generate the report. It is particularly important to specify a default value if you present the report parameter as a text box in which the user has to type a value, rather than a list box from which the user can select a value.

The default value can be any value from the data set field that is bound to the report parameter. You should, however, specify a value that most users would select, such as Active for an account status. Another option is to specify a value that appears most often. If the field contains unique values, such as an order ID or a customer ID, it is typical to specify the first ID as the default value, particularly when using a list box or combo box to display a list of values.

How to provide a default value for a report parameter

This procedure assumes you are editing a report parameter that you already created.

1 In the data explorer, expand Report Parameters, then choose the report parameter to edit. Edit Parameter displays the current property settings for the selected report parameter. Figure 16-12 shows an example of a report parameter with no value specified for Default value.

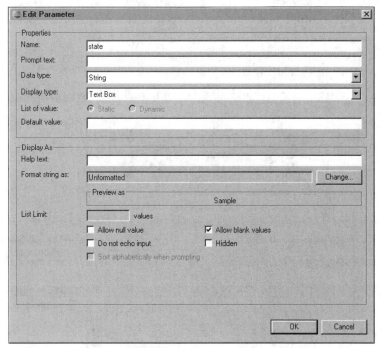

Figure 16-12   Property settings for a report parameter

2 Depending on the display type that you select, complete one of these tasks:

- If the display type is text box, for Default value, type a value. Use a value that exists in the data set field that is bound to this report parameter.

- For all other display types, specify a list of values to display, then select one value as the default value.

3 Choose OK.

Providing the user with a list of values

List boxes, combo boxes, and radio buttons are ideal mechanisms for providing a list of choices to a user. A user can make only one selection from multiple choices. The differences between these user interface elements are:

- Radio buttons occupy as many lines in the Enter Parameters dialog as there are choices, and you must specify one button as a default value. For ease of use, a set of radio buttons should contain fewer than 10 entries.

- The list box and combo box appear identical to the user. Both save space because they take up only one line in the Enter Parameters dialog. For ease of use, a list box and combo box should contain fewer than 100 values.

- Unlike the list box, the combo box auto-completes text that the user types. For example, when the user starts to type Ad, the first matching value, such as Advanced Design Inc., appears.

- The combo box requires you to specify a default value when you create it. A list box does not.

- The combo box does not support the user specifying null values or blank values for string data. The list box does.

Figure 16-13 shows an example of an Enter Parameters dialog that displays a list box, combo box, and radio buttons.

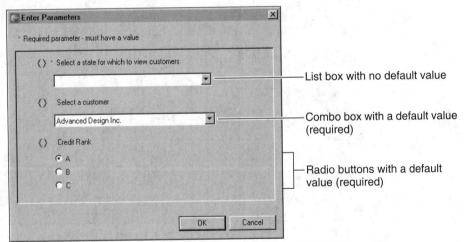

Figure 16-13   Three types of selection elements in Enter Parameters

You create a list of values for a list box or a combo box using one of the following techniques:

- Create a static list of values.
- Create a dynamic list of values.

For radio buttons, you can only create a static list of values. In a static list, you specify the values to display to the report user during report design. In a dynamic list, BIRT retrieves the values from the data source when the report runs. Create a dynamic list for values that are frequently updated in the data source. New customer names or product names, for example, are often added to a data source. If you create a static list of these values, you have to manually update the list to match the values in the data source. Creating a static list, however, provides more control over the list of values to display to the report user. For example, you might not want to present all values to the user.

Creating a static list of values

You can create a static list of values for a list box, combo box, or a set of radio buttons using one or both of the following techniques:

- Import values from a data set field.
- Type each value to display.

To display all the unique values in a data set field, which is the typical case, import the values from the data set field. You can type the values, but this task would be tedious. Type a value only to display a value that is not in the data set field, such as ranges of values (0–100, 101–200, and so on).

To import all values from a data set field, you first create a data set that retrieves the values. The query in the following example retrieves all the values from the state field. You would specify this simple query to populate a parameter list with all the state names.

```
SELECT Customers.state
FROM Customers
```

You do not need to specify SELECT DISTINCT, because BIRT automatically populates the parameter list with unique values.

How to specify static report parameter values for users to select

This procedure assumes that you are editing a report parameter that you already created.

1   In the data explorer, expand Report Parameters, then choose the report parameter to edit. Edit Parameter displays the property settings for the report parameter.

2   For Display type, choose Combo Box, List Box, or Radio Button. Edit Parameter displays the Selection values field and the Import Values button, as shown in Figure 16-14.

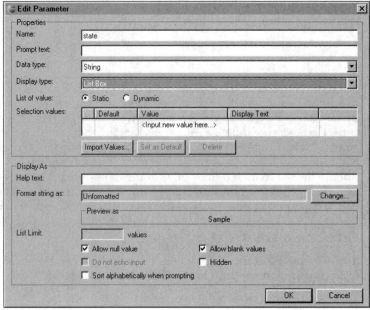

Figure 16-14   Selection values field and Import Values button in Edit Parameter

The Selection values field is where you specify the values to display in the list box, combo box, or radio buttons.

3   Use the default value, Static, for List of value.

4   To import values from a data set field:

   1   Choose Import Values. Import Values displays the first data set in the report and the values of the first field in the data set, as shown in Figure 16-15.

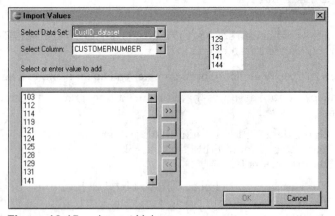

Figure 16-15   Import Values

2 In Select Data Set, choose the data set for which to display the field values in the list box, combo box, or radio buttons. Typically, this data set is one that you create specifically for populating the parameter's list of values.

3 In Select Column, choose the field that contains the values to use. Import Values displays the values for the selected field.

4 Select the values to import:

    ❏ To import all values, choose the double right arrow (>>) button.

    ❏ To import a particular value, select the value, and choose the right arrow (>) button.

Choose OK. Edit Parameter displays the imported values in Selection values—Value and Display Text, as shown in Figure 16-16.

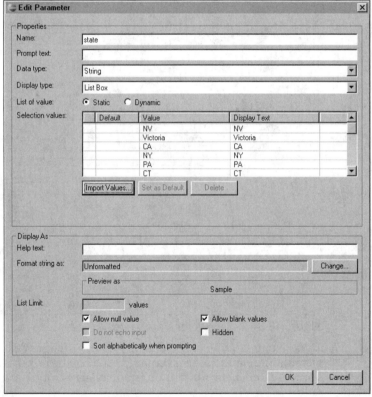

Figure 16-16   Imported values in Edit Parameter

5 To add values manually, complete the following steps for each value:

1 In Value, select the first available row, which displays <Input new value here>.

2 Type the value to add to the list. Press Enter, or select another field. Edit Parameter adds the value to the list.

6 To provide labels for users to choose, other than the value in Display Text, select Display Text beside the value for which you want to provide an alternative label. Then, type the label to display to the user. Press Enter, or select another field.

BIRT Report Designer adds the labels to the list. Figure 16-17 shows examples of labels for field values. The labels, state names, appear for the user instead of the state abbreviation values.

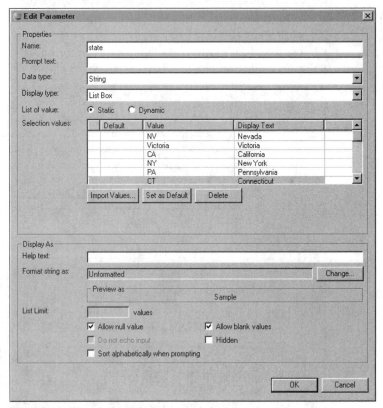

Figure 16-17 Labels for state values

7 To designate a value as the default value, select the value, then choose Set as Default. A default value is required for a combo box or a set of radio buttons. For these items, the OK button is not available until you select a default value.

8 To sort the values in ascending order when the report presents them to the user, choose Sort alphabetically when prompting.

Creating a dynamic list of values

You can create a dynamic list of values for a list box or a combo box. In the same way as you create a static list, you first create a data set that retrieves the values with which to populate the list. The query in the following example retrieves all the values from the name field in the Customers table. You specify this simple query in a data set to populate a parameter list with all the customer names.

```
SELECT Customers.name
FROM Customers
```

With dynamic lists, values are retrieved from the data source when the report runs. You cannot tell during the design process how many values the list box or combo box displays when the user runs the report. If you are concerned about the list getting too long, you can specify a maximum number of values to display.

How to specify dynamic report parameter values for users to select

This procedure assumes that you are editing a report parameter that you have already created.

1 In the data explorer, expand Report Parameters, then choose the report parameter to edit. Edit Parameter displays the property settings for the report parameter.

2 For Display type, choose Combo Box or List Box.

3 For List of value, choose Dynamic. Edit Parameter displays additional fields, as shown in Figure 16-18.

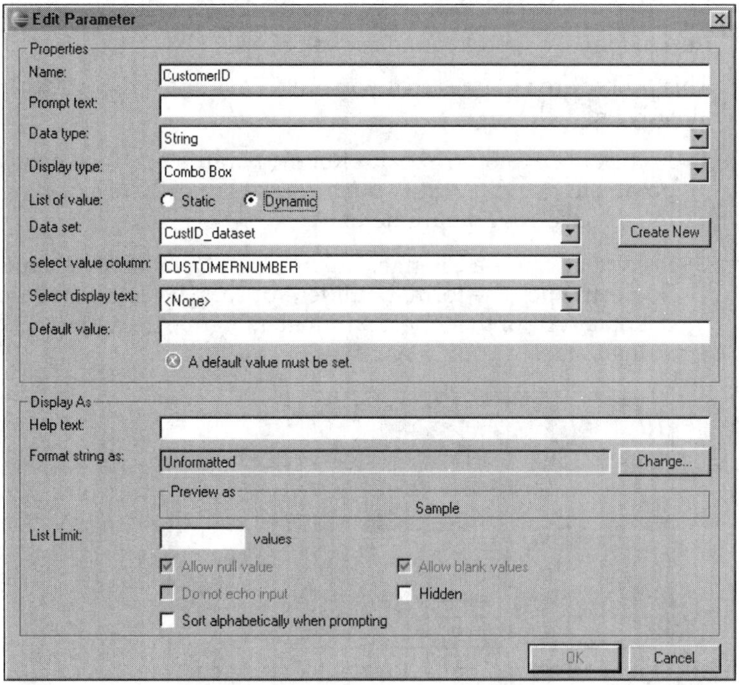

Figure 16-18   Dynamic parameter options in Edit Parameter

4 For Data set, select the data set from which you want to display the field values in the list box or combo box.

5 For Select value column, select the field that contains the values that you want to use. Optionally, for List Limit, specify the maximum number of values to display. Choose OK.

Formatting report parameter values

By default, the default values you specify and the values that you import to display in a list box, combo box, or radio buttons appear exactly as they are stored in the data source. Sometimes, the values are not in a format that is appropriate for display. For example, US telephone numbers might be stored in ########## format. It is preferable to display these values in another format, such as (###) ###-####. Remember also that international telephone numbers will not appear correctly using this format.

You can specify a different format using the Format property. You format a report parameter value in the same way that you format a value that a data element displays. You select from a list of common formats, or you specify a custom format pattern.

Note that you can reformat values for display purposes only. You cannot use the Format property to require a user to type values in a particular format, nor does it affect the format of the data in the generated report.

How to format a report parameter value

This procedure assumes that you are formatting a report parameter that you already created.

1 In the data explorer, expand Report Parameters, then choose the report parameter to edit. Edit Parameter displays the current property settings for the selected report parameter.

2 In Format, choose Change. Change is not available for report parameters of Boolean type. The format builder appears. Its contents differ, depending on the data type of the report parameter. Figure 16-19 shows Format Builder for string data.

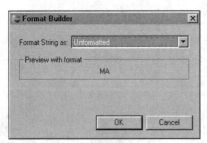

Figure 16-19 Format Builder for string data

3 Specify what format to use. The format choices that are available vary according to the data type of the parameter.

    1 For Format <data type> as, choose one of the predefined formats, or choose Custom to define your own format pattern. Additional fields may appear, depending on the data type and format that you selected. A sample formatted value appears in Preview with format. Figure 16-20 shows the additional fields that are available for a report parameter of decimal type when Currency format is selected.

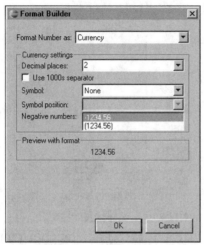

Figure 16-20   Format Builder for Currency data

    2 Type or select values for any additional fields that are available for that parameter data type and format. When you finish specifying the format, choose OK. Edit Parameter appears. Format shows the format that you specified.

Enabling the user to specify null or blank values

You can provide users who are database-savvy with the option of selecting rows when a field has a null value. Databases use a null value to indicate that there is no data in that field. A user might find it useful, for example, to view customer data where a customer's credit-limit field is null, because null in this field means that the customer account is new, and a credit limit has not been set.

For string data, a null value is not the same as an empty string (" "), which is an actual value. You can set properties that determine whether a user can choose to match a null value, an empty string, or both. To enable a user to match a null value or a blank value, you must use a text box or a list box for the report parameter. The combo box and radio buttons require the user to specify an actual value.

Figure 16-21 shows Enter Parameters with two parameters for which null values are enabled. The Threshold Quantity parameter uses a text box, and the Product

Vendor parameter uses a list box. To specify a null value, the user selects Null Value.

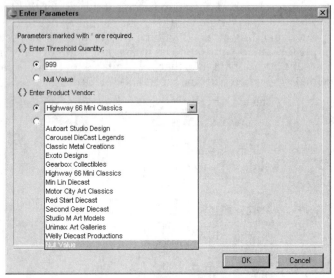

Figure 16-21   Parameters with null values

How to enable a user to specify a null or blank value

This procedure assumes that you are editing a report parameter that you already created.

1   In the data explorer, expand Report Parameters, then choose the report parameter to edit. Edit Parameter displays the current property settings for the selected report parameter.

2   For Display type, select either Text Box or List Box. These are the only items that support the user specifying a null or blank value.

3   To enable a user to specify a null value for the report parameter, select Allow null value. This property applies to data of all types except Boolean. To enable a user to specify an empty string, or blank value, select Allow blank values. This property applies to string data only.

Organizing report parameters in groups

If you create many parameters or want to provide the user with a prompt for certain sets of parameters, consider using parameter groups. Typically, you create parameter groups to organize report parameters logically. For example, you could create a parameter group to contain the report parameters for a specific table or data set.

When prompting the user to supply parameter values, the Enter Parameters dialog displays the parameter group name and the parameters within that group. Figure 16-22 shows two parameter groups, Customer Information and Order Information. Each group contains multiple report parameters.

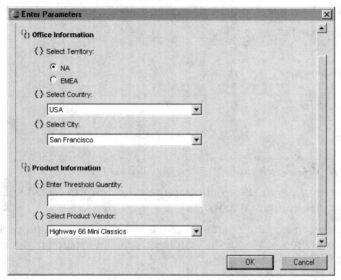

Figure 16-22 Parameter groups with multiple parameters in each group

You can create a parameter group before or after you create the report parameters. If you create the report parameters first, you can drag them from the report parameters list to the parameter group. If you create the parameter group first, you create the report parameters in the parameter group.

How to create a parameter group

1 In the data explorer, right-click Report Parameters, and choose New Parameter Group. New Parameter Group appears.

2 In Name, specify a unique name for this parameter group.

3 In Display Name, specify the name that the Enter Parameters dialog displays when it prompts a user for parameter values.

Figure 16-23 shows an example.

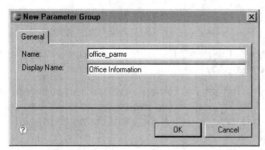

Figure 16-23 Create a display name for a parameter group

4 Choose OK.

BIRT Report Designer creates the new parameter group and displays it in Report Parameters in the data explorer, as shown in Figure 16-24.

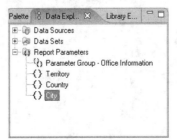

Figure 16-24 New parameter group in Data Explorer

5 Add report parameters to the parameter group. You can add parameters to a parameter group in two ways:

- Move an existing parameter to the parameter group. From the report parameters list in the data explorer, drag an existing parameter, and drop it in the parameter group.

- Create a new parameter in the parameter group. In Report Parameters, right-click the parameter group name, and choose New Parameter.

Figure 16-25 shows the data explorer after you move three report parameters to a parameter group called Office Information.

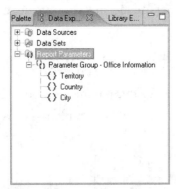

Figure 16-25 Parameter group with three parameters

Figure 16-26 shows the Enter Parameters dialog, which displays the new parameter group and its three report parameters.

Enter Parameters displays parameter groups and report parameters in the order in which they appear in the report parameters list. To display the groups or report parameters in a different order, change the order in the data explorer.

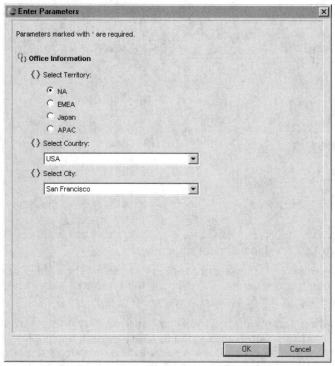

Figure 16-26   Customer Information parameter group on Enter Parameters

Creating cascading report parameters

Cascading parameters are report parameters that have a hierarchical relationship, as shown in the following three examples:

```
Product Type        Territory          Mutual Fund Type
   Product            Country              Fund Class
                        City                  Fund
```

In a group of cascading parameters, each report parameter displays a set of values. When the report user selects a value from the top-level parameter, the selected value determines the values that the next parameter displays, and so on.

The advantages of cascading parameters are obvious when you compare the alternative technique, which is the creation of separate and independent parameters. Consider the Territory-Country-City example. If you create three separate parameters, the territory parameter displays a list of all territories, the country parameter displays all countries, and the city parameter displays all cities. Figure 16-27 shows independent parameters as they appear to the report user.

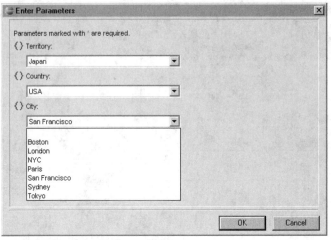

Figure 16-27   Independent parameters

The user has to traverse three long lists to select the values, and there is a potential for user errors. The user can inadvertently select invalid combinations, such as Japan, USA, Paris.

Cascading parameters, on the other hand, display only relevant values based on user selections. For example, the territory parameter displays all the territories, and when the report runs, the user selects a territory, such as NA (North America), then the country parameter displays only countries in the sales territory of NA. Similarly, when the user selects USA, the city parameter displays only cities in the USA. Figure 16-28 shows cascading parameters as they appear to the report user.

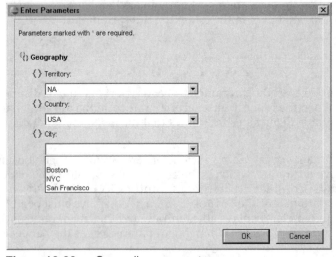

Figure 16-28   Cascading parameters

Cascading parameters can be based on a single data set or multiple data sets. Use cascading parameters with a single data set when the values for all the parameters are contained in a single data set. Use cascading parameters with multiple data sets when the values for the parameter must be retrieved from more than one data set.

Before you create cascading report parameters, you must first create the data set(s) that retrieve the values with which to populate the cascading parameter lists. The query in the following example retrieves all the values from the territory, country, and city fields of the Offices table. You specify this query in a data set to populate the Territory-Country-City parameter lists.

```
SELECT Offices.territory,
Offices.country,
Offices.city
FROM Offices
```

Given that only one data set is required, Territory-Country-City would be a single data set cascading parameter.

When you create cascading parameters based on multiple data sets, you must link the data sets together by adding a data set parameter to the queries for all data sets except for the one used to value the top-level parameter. Each data set parameter must then be bound to the appropriate report parameter from the cascading parameter group in order to form the appropriate dependency relationships.

For example, if you were creating a cascading parameter that prompted the report user to select an office from the Offices table and then prompted the user to select an employee from the Employees table based on the office in which she worked, you would create an Offices data set and an Employee data set. The Employee data set would have a data set parameter bound to the value of the office-report parameter in order to filter rows for employees from the selected office.

After you create cascading parameters, bind the final report parameter in the group to a data set parameter, or specify the report parameter as a filter-condition value, depending on the user-filtering technique that you are using.

How to create single data set cascading parameters

1 In the data explorer, right-click Report Parameters, and choose New Cascading Parameter. New Cascading Parameter appears, as shown in Figure 16-29.

2 For Cascading Parameter Name, you can specify a different name. The name that you specify appears in the list of report parameters in the data explorer.

3 For Prompt text, specify the name for the parameter group that appears in the Enter Parameters dialog.

4 Select Single Data Set.

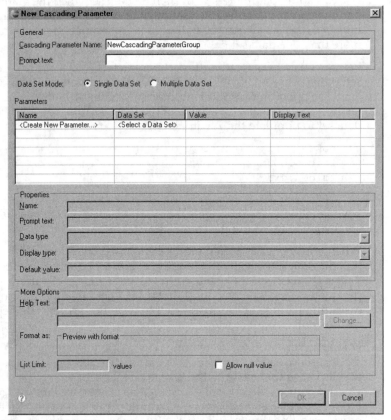

Figure 16-29   New Cascading Single Data Set Parameter

5 Create the report parameters for this group of cascading parameters:

1 In Parameters, choose the first row. <Create New Parameter> appears in Name. Specify the following values:

    1 In Name, type the parameter name.

    2 In Data Set, select the data set from which to retrieve the values for all the parameters.

    3 In Value, select the field for the value of the top-level parameter.

    4 In Display Text, optionally select a field with a more friendly display value to represent the parameter to the report user. For example, if the parameter is based on productcode field, it is better to display the associated productname to the user.

2 In Properties, specify a descriptive name for the parameter, such as Territory.

3 Set the other properties for this report parameter.

4 To create the next report parameter, choose the row below the report parameter that you just created, and follow the same steps until you set up all levels of the cascading parameter group. Figure 16-30 shows sample values in New Cascading Parameter.

Figure 16-30 New Cascading Single Data Set Parameter example

6 When you finish creating all the report parameters in the group, choose OK.

The cascading parameters appear in Report Parameters in the data explorer.

How to create multiple data set cascading parameters

This procedure assumes that you created all the data sets that retrieve the values for the cascading parameter lists.

1 In the data explorer, right-click Report Parameters, and choose New Cascading Parameter.

2 In New Cascading Parameter, for Cascading Parameter Name, you can specify a different name. The name that you specify appears only in the list of report parameters in the data explorer.

3 For Prompt text, specify the name for the parameter group that appears in the Enter Parameters dialog.

4 Select Multiple Data Set.

5 Create the report parameters for this group of cascading parameters:

    1 In Parameters, choose the first row. <Create New Parameter> appears. Specify the following values:

        1 In Name, type the parameter name.

        2 In Data Set, select the data set from which to retrieve the values for the top-level parameter.

        3 In Value, select the field for the value of the top-level parameter.

        4 In Display Text, optionally select a field with a more friendly display value to represent the parameter to the report user. For example, if the parameter is based on productcode field, it is better to display the associated productname to the user.

    2 In Properties, specify a descriptive name for the parameter, such as Territory.

    3 Set the other properties for this report parameter.

    4 To create the next report parameter, choose the next row in Parameters, then repeat steps 1 through 3 to set up all levels of the cascading parameter group.

6 When you finish creating all the report parameters in the group, choose OK. The cascading parameters appear in Report Parameters in the data explorer.

7 Add data set parameters to the dependent data sets and bind them to the appropriate report parameters from the cascading parameter group.

    1 In the data explorer, right-click the data set that supplies the values for the second parameter in the cascading parameter group, then choose Edit. Edit Data Set displays the query.

    2 Insert a parameter marker in the WHERE clause of the SQL query to filter the values of the data set based on the top-level parameter in the cascading group. Figure 16-31 shows an example.

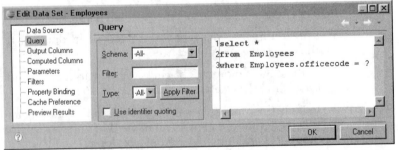

Figure 16-31   Query with parameter marker for cascading parameter group

3 Choose Parameters. Create a data set parameter to supply a value for the parameter marker in the SQL query.

4 Using the expression builder, set the default value of the data set parameter to the top-level parameter in the cascading group, so the data set parameter gets the user-specified value from the top-level parameter and passes it to the SQL query. Figure 16-32 shows an example.

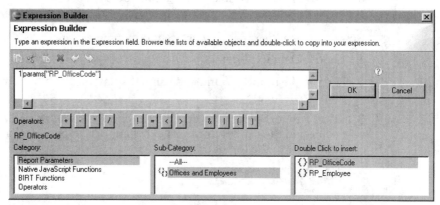

Figure 16-32   Binding a data set parameter to a cascading parameter

5 Choose OK.

6 Follow the same steps for subsequent data sets in the cascading parameter group until you establish dependencies for all levels in the group.

Figure 16-33 shows how Enter Parameters appears to the report user when you create a multiple data set cascading parameter group based on the Office and Employee data sets.

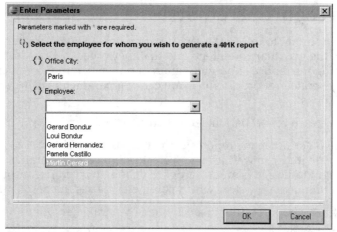

Figure 16-33   Multiple data set cascading parameters

Changing the order in which report parameters appear

By default, report parameter groups and report parameters are displayed to the user in the order in which they appear on Data Explorer—Report Parameters. The list of groups and parameters in the report parameters list, in turn, appear in the order in which you created them. You can change the order of groups and report parameters.

How to change the order in which report parameters appear

1 Choose Data Explorer.

2 Expand the report parameters list to display the list of parameter groups and report parameters.

3 Select a report parameter group or a report parameter, and drag it to a new position in the list. Figure 16-34 shows how to move the State report parameter to the top of the list.

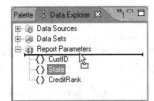

Figure 16-34   Moving a report parameter

4 Repeat step 3 until all the report parameter groups and report parameters appear in the desired order.

Testing the report parameters

It is important to test all the report parameters that you create to verify that they work the way that you intend and that they meet user needs. Testing entails running the report, supplying different report parameter values, and checking the generated report carefully. You can test parameters using the following guidelines:

■ Test each report parameter as you create it.

   If you create many report parameters, it is best to test each parameter as you create it. If you wait until you create all the report parameters before you begin testing, it is much harder to debug errors in the output, because it is not immediately clear which parameter causes the problem.

■ Run the report without specifying any parameter values.

   The result of running a report without specifying any parameter values should be a report with information in it. If the OK button on the Enter

Parameters dialog is unavailable, at least one report parameter that is currently empty requires the user to specify a value. Ensure that you provide a default value for each required parameter. A report parameter requires a value if you do not set its Allow null or Allow blank values properties.

- Test each value in a list box, combo box, or series of radio buttons.

  If you manually created the values that these items display, rather than importing values from the data set field, test each value to confirm that the output is correct. If the report appears with no data, it means that no records matched your selection, which indicates one of three possibilities:

  - There are no rows that contain the value that you selected.

  - The value that you created is not valid. For example, you might have created the value Closed for an order-status field, but the value in the data source is actually Shipped.

  - Another parameter causes the problem.

  To debug the first two possibilities, review the data in the data source. Debugging the third possibility requires more effort if the report contains many other report parameters. As suggested earlier, you can avoid this situation if you always test parameters, one at a time, as you create them.

How to test report parameters

1 In the layout editor, choose Preview. Enter Parameters displays the report parameters that you created.

2 Specify a value for the report parameters. Choose OK. The report appears.

3 Review the report data carefully.

4 Test each report parameter with a different value by first choosing Show Report Parameters, then providing another value.

5 Repeat step 4 until you are certain that the report displays the correct data.

Building a Report That Contains Subreports

You can build a report that contains multiple reports, called subreports, and you can lay out the subreports in a variety of configurations. For example, within a single report, you can

- Display multiple reports, one after another. For example, you can display the top ten customers, top ten sales representatives, and top ten products.

- Display multiple reports next to one another. For example, you can display general employee information and employee salary history.

- Display one report within another. For example, you can display detailed mutual fund performance within general fund information.

Also, you can combine any of the report configurations that are in the preceding list.

A subreport is simply a report that appears inside another report. You already know how to create a report. Basically, it takes one additional step to create a report that contains subreports. You must set up the structure of the main report to organize the subreports.

Each subreport can access a different data source, its own set of tables and fields, and specify its own data selection criteria. Subreports can be linked to one another or be independent of each other. Two reports are linked when the data of one report determines what data appears in another.

Always create, lay out, and test each subreport before you create the next one, and verify that the subreport displays the correct data. If you create all the subreports before you test the entire report, it can be difficult to determine which subreport causes errors.

Creating the report structure

This section describes some general principles and provides a few examples for organizing subreports in a report. The three report elements that you use to organize subreports are the table, list, and grid. Reports with complex layouts typically use all three container elements.

- The table iterates through the rows in a data set and displays the data in row and column format. For some reports, a subreport consists of data that is organized in a table.

- Like the table, the list iterates through the rows in a data set. The list, however, provides much greater flexibility for arranging data. A report that contains multiple linked subreports typically uses a list as the top-level container. Within the list, subreport data can be organized in tables.

- The grid is a static table that organizes elements in rows and columns. In a report with subreports, you can use a grid to align multiple tables horizontally or to add space between tables. For example, to display two subreports next to one another, you can create two tables to display the data for the subreports then insert both tables in a grid to align the subreports.

Building a report with independent subreports

Figure 17-1 shows an example of a report with four unlinked subreports. Each Top 10 subreport displays a different set of data. Each subreport is a table with data elements. The tables are arranged in a grid so they can appear side by side.

Top 10 Products	
1992 Ferrari 360 Spider red	$276,839.98
2001 Ferrari Enzo	$190,755.86
1952 Alpine Renault 1300	$190,017.96
2003 Harley-Davidson Eagle Drag Bike	$170,686.00
1968 Ford Mustang	$161,531.48
1969 Ford Falcon	$152,543.02
1980s Black Hawk Helicopter	$144,959.91
1998 Chrysler Plymouth Prowler	$142,530.63
1917 Grand Touring Sedan	$140,535.60
2002 Suzuki XREO	$135,767.03

Top 10 Sales Representatives	
Gerard Hernandez	$1,258,577.81
Leslie Jennings	$1,081,530.54
Pamela Castillo	$868,220.55
Larry Bott	$732,096.79
Barry Jones	$704,853.91
George Vanauf	$669,377.05
Peter Marsh	$584,593.76
Loui Bondur	$569,485.75
Andy Fixter	$562,582.59
Steve Patterson	$505,875.42

Top 10 Customers	
Euro+ Shopping Channel	$820,689.54
Mini Gifts Distributors Ltd.	$591,827.34
Australian Collectors, Co.	$180,585.07
Muscle Machine Inc	$177,913.95
La Rochelle Gifts	$158,573.12
Dragon Souveniers, Ltd.	$156,251.03
Down Under Souveniers, Inc	$154,622.08
Land of Toys Inc.	$149,085.15
AV Stores, Co.	$148,410.09
The Sharp Gifts Warehouse	$143,536.27

Top 10 Cities	
Madrid	$979,880.77
San Rafael	$591,827.34
NYC	$497,941.50
Auckland	$292,082.87
Singapore	$263,997.78
Paris	$240,649.68
San Francisco	$199,051.34
New Bedford	$190,500.01
Nantes	$180,887.48
Melbourne	$180,585.07

Figure 17-1   Unlinked subreports

Figure 17-2 shows the design for the report that appears in Figure 17-1.

An empty grid column with a fixed width — adds space between the subreports

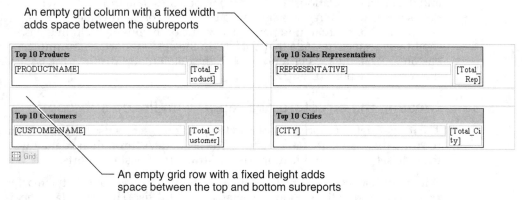

An empty grid row with a fixed height adds space between the top and bottom subreports

Figure 17-2   Report design for unlinked subreports

Building a report with linked subreports

The preceding section described creating subreports that are not linked to each other. The subreports run independently and do not coordinate their data. Sometimes, however, you need to create reports that coordinate data, such as a detailed customer issues report in a customer report, as shown in Figure 17-3.

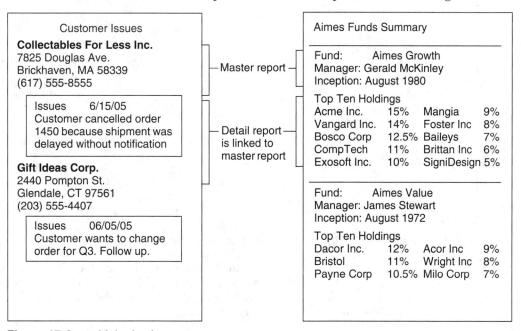

Figure 17-3   Linked subreports

As the example shows, one report is nested in another, creating a master report and detail report relationship. Each report accesses data from a different table or data source, and the reports are linked by a common field value, such as customer ID or mutual fund name. The value of the linking field in the master report determines the data that appears in the detail report. For example, if the customer ID in the master report is 112, the detail report displays the issues for the customer whose ID is 112.

Creating the structure of a report with linked subreports

The master-detail report examples in the previous section use the list element as the primary organizational structure. The list iterates through the data rows that the data set returns, and it supports the structure of nested reports.

Within the list, a grid aligns the data in both reports. The data for the master report is placed in the grid in the detail area of the list. The grid aligns the data in a column, and the list iterates through the master report's data rows. The detail report uses a table to iterate through its data rows.

This structure assumes that the master and detail reports use different data sets and that each data set accesses data from a different table or data source. Figure 17-4 shows the report design for the customer-issue master-detail report that appears in the previous section.

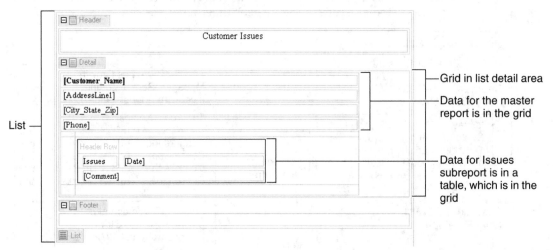

Figure 17-4 Report design for linked subreports, using the list element

An alternate design is to use two tables, one nested in the other. Place data for the master report in the detail rows of the outer table. Place data for the detail report in a table, and place the table in the detail row of the outer table. Figure 17-5 shows this alternate report design.

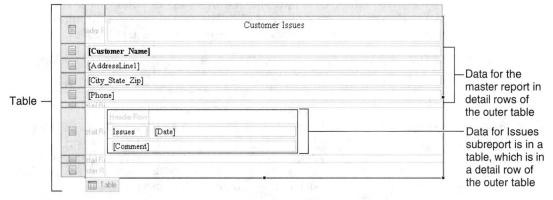

Table ───

Data for the master report in detail rows of the outer table

Data for Issues subreport is in a table, which is in a detail row of the outer table

Figure 17-5   Report design for linked subreports, using nested tables

Linking master and detail reports

Master and detail reports must be linked by a common field. In the customer-issue example report, the linking field is the customer ID. To link the reports, perform the following tasks:

1 For the detail report's data set, create a SELECT statement with a parameter marker in a WHERE clause. For example:

```
SELECT *
FROM issues
WHERE issues.customerNumber = ?
```

2 Create a data set parameter. Figure 17-6 shows the definition of a parameter in the data set that the detail report uses. You must supply a specific value as the parameter's default value so that the query works properly during the report design process.

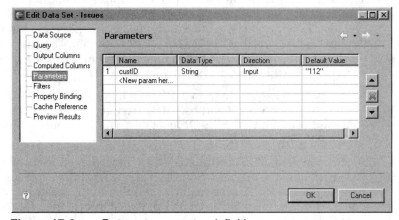

Figure 17-6   Data set parameter definition

3 In the layout editor, bind the detail report's data set parameter to the linking field in the master report. Figure 17-7 shows an example of this binding, which you perform using the property editor for the detail table.

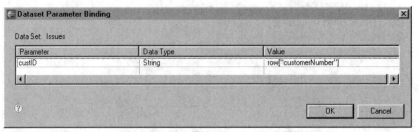

Figure 17-7 Data set parameter, bound to the linking field

When the report runs, BIRT performs the following tasks:

- When the master report processes a customer row, it passes the customer number value to the data set parameter that you defined for the detail report.

- The data set parameter passes this customer number value to the detail report's query and dynamically updates the WHERE clause.

- The detail report displays the issues data for that customer number.

The previous steps repeat until the master report processes all its customer rows.

Tutorial 3: Building a report with side-by-side subreports

This section provides step-by-step instructions for building a report that displays a list of customers. For each customer, the report displays order and payment information. The order information and payment information are in separate subreports that appear next to one another. The customer report is the master report, which is also called the outer report. The order and payment subreports are the detail reports, which are also called the inner reports.

Each report accesses data from a different table in the sample database, Classic Models. The customer report uses data from the Customers table. The orders subreport uses data from the Orders table. The payments subreport uses data from the Payments table.

A common field, CUSTOMERNUMBER, links the reports. The value of the linking field in the master report determines what data appears in the detail reports. For example, if the customer number in the master report is 173, the detail reports display the order and payment information for the customer whose ID is 173.

Figure 17-8 shows a portion of the finished report.

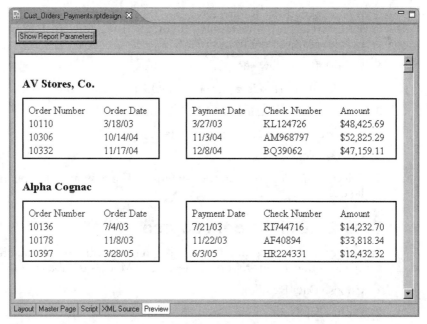

Figure 17-8   Customers master report, with order and payment subreports

In this tutorial, you perform the following tasks:

- Create a new report.

- Build a data source.

- Build a data set for the customer report.

- Build a data set for the orders subreport.

- Build a data set for the payments subreport.

- Create the customer master report.

- Create the orders subreport.

- Link the orders subreport to the customers master report.

- Create the payments subreport.

- Link the payments subreport to the customers master report.

- Display only customers that have orders or payments.

- Display the subreports next to one another.

- Format the report.

Task 1: Create a new report

If you are using BIRT Report Designer, this task assumes you have already created a project for your reports. If you are using BIRT RCP Report Designer, there is no requirement for a project.

1 Choose File➤New➤Report.

2 On New Report, select a project in which to store your report.

3 Type the following text as the file name:

    Cust_Orders_Payments.rptdesign

4 Choose Next.

5 Select Blank Report, then choose Finish. The new report appears in the layout editor.

Task 2: Build a data source

Before you begin designing your report in the layout editor, you create a data source to connect your report to the Classic Models database.

1 Choose Data Explorer.

2 Right-click Data Sources, and choose New Data Source from the context menu.

3 Select Classic Models Inc. Sample Database from the list of data sources, use the default data source name, then choose Next. Connection information about the new data source appears.

4 Choose Finish. BIRT Report Designer creates a new data source that connects to the sample database. It appears within Data Sources in Data Explorer.

Task 3: Build a data set for the customer report

In this procedure, you build a data set to indicate what data to extract from the Customers table. The customer report that you create later uses this data set.

1 In Data Explorer, right-click Data Sets, and choose New Data Set.

2 On New Data Set, type the following text for data set name:

    Customers

3 Use the default values for the other fields:

   ▪ Data Source shows the name of the data source that you created earlier.

   ▪ Data Set Type specifies that the data set uses a SQL SELECT query.

4 Choose Next. Query displays the information to help you create a SQL query. The text area on the right side shows the required keywords of a SQL SELECT statement.

5 Expand the CUSTOMERS table. The columns in the Customers table appear.

6 Use the following SQL SELECT statement to indicate what data to retrieve. You can type the column and table names, or you can drag them from the left side to the appropriate location in the SELECT statement.

```
SELECT Customers.customerName,
Customers.customerNumber
FROM Customers
```

This statement that you created, which is shown in Figure 17-9, gets values from the CUSTOMERNAME and CUSTOMERNUMBER columns in the CUSTOMERS table.

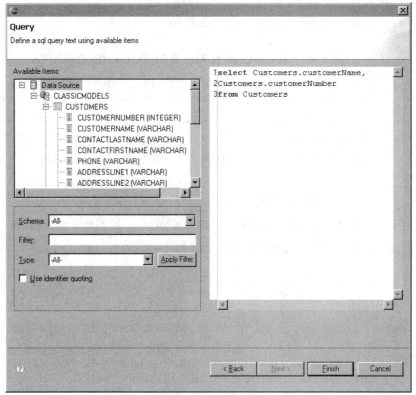

Figure 17-9 Query

7 Choose Finish to save the data set. Edit Data Set displays the columns specified in the query, and provides options for editing the data set.

8 Choose Preview Results to confirm that the query is valid and that it returns the correct data. If you created the SELECT statement correctly, you should see the results that appear in Figure 17-10. These are the data rows that the query returns.

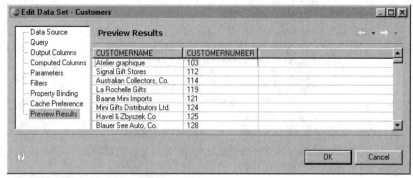

Figure 17-10   Data preview

9 Choose OK to save the data set.

Task 4:   Build a data set for the orders subreport

In this procedure, you build a data set to indicate what data to extract from the Orders table. The orders subreport that you create later uses this data set.

1 In Data Explorer, right-click Data Sets, and choose New Data Set from the context menu.

2 On New Data Set, type the following text for the data set's name:

```
Orders
```

3 Use the default values for the other fields, then choose Next.

4 On Query, expand the Orders table to display the columns in the table.

5 Use the following SQL SELECT statement to indicate what data to retrieve:

```
SELECT Orders.orderNumber,
Orders.orderDate
FROM Orders
WHERE Orders.customerNumber = ?
```

This statement selects the ORDERNUMBER and ORDERDATE columns from the Orders table. The WHERE clause has a parameter marker for the value of CUSTOMERNUMBER. When the report runs, the orders subreport gets the current CUSTOMERNUMBER value from the customers report.

6 Choose Finish to save the data set. Edit Data Set displays the columns specified in the query, and provides options for editing the data set.

7 Create a data set parameter to supply the CUSTOMERNUMBER value in the WHERE clause:

1   Choose Parameters from the left side of the window. Edit Data Set displays parameters information.

2 Specify the following values in the first line of the table:

- ❑ Name: CustID
- ❑ Data Type: Integer
- ❑ Direction: Input
- ❑ Default value: 103

  103 is one of the values in the CUSTOMERNUMBER column. A
  default value is required for BIRT Report Designer to run the query for
  testing purposes.

Edit Data Set should look like the one shown in Figure 17-11.

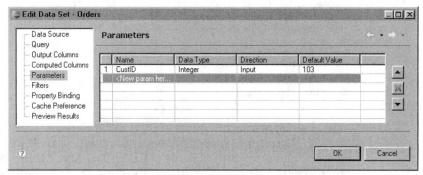

Figure 17-11 Parameter definition in the orders subreport

8 Choose Preview Results to confirm that the query is valid and that it returns
the correct data. If you created the SELECT statement and created the data
set parameter correctly, you should see the results that appear in
Figure 17-12. These are the data rows that the query returns for customer
number 103.

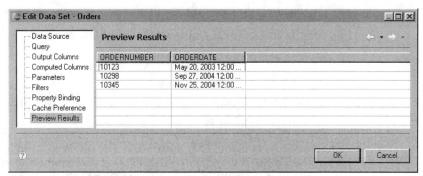

Figure 17-12 Data preview for the orders subreport

9 Choose OK to save the changes to the data set.

Task 5: Build a data set for the payments subreport

In this procedure, you build a data set to indicate what data to extract from the Payments table. The payments subreport that you create later uses this data set.

1   In Data Explorer, right-click Data Sets, and choose New Data Set from the context menu.

2   On New Data Set, type the following text for the data set's name:

```
Payments
```

3   Use the default values for the other fields, then choose Next.

4   On Query, expand the Payments table to display the columns that are in the table.

5   Use the following SQL SELECT statement to indicate what data to retrieve:

```
SELECT Payments.paymentDate,
Payments.checkNumber,
Payments.amount
FROM Payments
WHERE Payments.customerNumber = ?
```

This statement selects the PAYMENTDATE, CHECKNUMBER, and AMOUNT columns from the Payments table. The WHERE clause has a parameter marker for the value of CUSTOMERNUMBER. When the report runs, the payments subreport gets the current CUSTOMERNUMBER value from the customers report.

6   Choose Finish to save the data set. Edit Data Set displays the columns specified in the query, and provides options for editing the data set.

7   Create a data set parameter to supply the CUSTOMERNUMBER value for the WHERE clause:

1   Choose Parameters. Edit Data Set displays parameters information.

2   Specify the following values in the first line of the table:

❑   Name: CustID

❑   Data Type: Integer

❑   Direction: Input

❑   Default value: 103

8   Choose Preview Results to confirm that the query is valid and that it returns the correct data. If you created the SELECT statement and created the data set parameter correctly, you should see the results that appear in Figure 17-13. These are the data rows that the query returns for customer number 103.

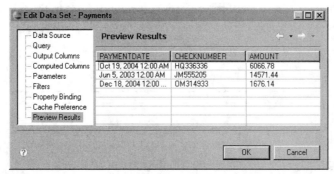

Figure 17-13 Data preview for the payments subreport

9 Choose OK to save the changes to the data set.

Task 6: Create the customer master report

You use a list element to create the master report and organize the orders and payments subreports within it. The list iterates through the customer data rows and creates the related orders and payments subreports for each record. For the sake of simplicity, the customer report displays just the customer name. It can, of course, display additional data, such as customer address, phone number, and credit limit.

1 Choose Palette.

2 Drag a list element from the palette, and drop it in the report. The list element appears in the report, as shown in Figure 17-14.

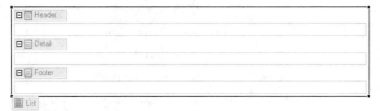

Figure 17-14 List element

3 Associate, or bind, the list with the Customers data set:

   1 In Property Editor, choose the Binding tab.

   2 For Data Set, select Customers from the drop-down list.

4 Choose Data Explorer, expand Data Sets, then expand Customers. The columns that you specified in the query appear below Customers.

5 Drag CUSTOMERNAME from Data Explorer, and drop it in the detail area of the list. BIRT Report Designer creates a named column, which is bound to the data set field. Select Data Binding displays this column binding.

6 Choose OK to accept the default column binding. In the layout editor, the list displays the field that you added, as shown in Figure 17-15.

Figure 17-15   Data set field in the list element

7 Choose Preview to preview the report. The report should look like the one shown in Figure 17-16. The report lists all the customer names in the order in which the query returns them.

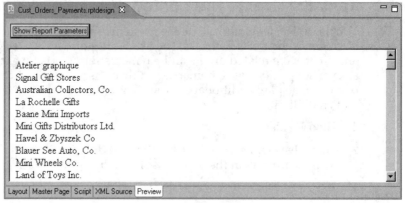

Figure 17-16   Data preview for the master report

8 Sort the customer names in ascending order:

   1 Choose Layout to return to the layout editor.

   2 In the layout editor, select the list element. Hover the mouse pointer over the bottom-left corner until you see the List tab, then choose the tab.

   3 In Property Editor, choose the Sorting tab.

   4 On the Sort page, choose Add to create a sort expression. A row appears under Sort on.

   5 Click the area under Sort Key, then select the arrow button that appears, and select CUSTOMERNAME from the drop-down list.

   6 Use the default value, Ascending, for Sort Direction, as shown in Figure 17-17.

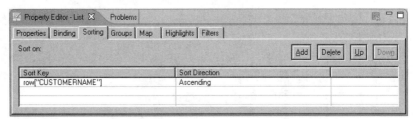

Figure 17-17   Sort expression

9 Preview the report. Customer names appear in ascending order.

Task 7: Create the orders subreport

The orders subreport lists the orders for each customer in a row and column format. It displays the order number and date of each order. To iterate through the orders data set rows and display them in a row and column format, you use the table element.

1 Choose Layout to return to the layout editor.

2 Drag a table element from the palette, and drop it below the [CUSTOMERNAME] data element, in the detail area. Insert Table prompts you to specify the number of columns and detail rows to create for the table.

3 Indicate that you want to create 2 columns and 1 detail row, then choose OK. A table with two columns and one detail row appears in the layout editor.

4 Bind the table with the Orders data set.

   1 In Property Editor, choose Binding.

   2 For Data set, select Orders from the drop-down list.

5 Choose Data Explorer, expand Data Sets, then expand Orders. The columns that you specified in the query appear below Orders.

6 Drag ORDERNUMBER from Data Explorer, and drop it in the first cell of the table's detail row. BIRT Report Designer creates a named column, which is bound to the data set field. Select Data Binding displays this column binding.

7 Choose OK to accept the default column binding. In the layout editor, the table cell in which you dropped the data set field contains a data element that displays [ORDERNUMBER]. Above this data element is a label element that the layout editor automatically adds to the header row. This label displays the field name as static text and serves as the column heading.

8 Drag ORDERDATE from Data Explorer, and drop it in the second cell in the detail row. Choose OK to accept the default column binding. The report page should look like the one shown in Figure 17-18.

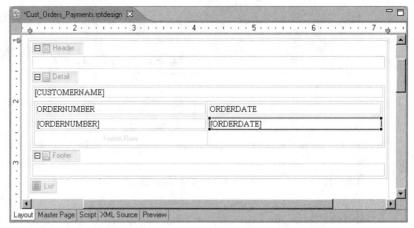

Figure 17-18   Report design includes the orders subreport

9 Sort the order rows by order number.

   1 Select the orders table.

   2 In Property Editor, choose Sorting.

   3 On the Sort page, choose Add to create a sort expression.

   4 Click the area under Sort Key, then select the arrow button that appears, and select ORDERNUMBER from the drop-down list.

   5 Use the default value, Ascending, for Sort Direction.

10 Preview the report. The report should look like the one shown in Figure 17-19.

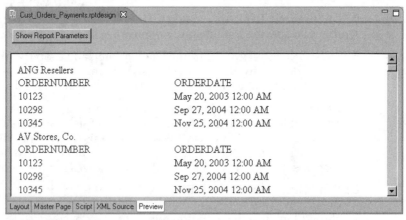

Figure 17-19   Preview of the report shows repeated order records

The same order records appear for every customer, because you specified a default value of 103 for customerNumber when you created the data set parameter, CustID. Because of this default value, the orders subreport always displays the order records for customer 103. The solution is to dynamically update the value of the CustID parameter each time the customer row in the master report changes. This procedure is described in the following task.

Task 8: Link the orders subreport to the customers master report

You link the orders subreport to the customers master report by binding the CustID parameter to the CUSTOMERNUMBER data set field in the customers report. Each time the customers report reaches a new customer row, the CustID parameter is updated with the new CUSTOMERNUMBER value.

Before you can bind the CustID parameter to the CUSTOMERNUMBER data set field, you must create a column binding and bind it with the data set field. Parameters cannot access data set fields directly.

1 Choose Layout to return to the layout editor.

2 Create a column binding that binds to the CUSTOMERNUMBER data set field:

   1 Select the list, and on Property Editor, choose Binding.

   2 On the Binding page, choose Add.

   3 On Expression Builder, choose Available Data Sets, choose Customers, then double-click CUSTOMERNUMBER. Expression Builder displays the expression, dataSetRow["CUSTOMERNUMBER"], as shown in Figure 17-20.

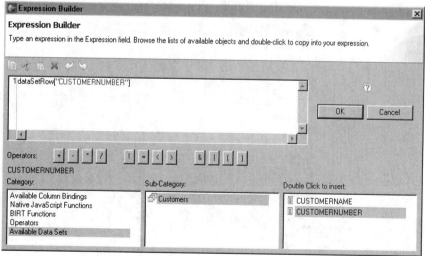

Figure 17-20   Expression Builder shows the column-binding expression

4   Choose OK. The new column binding appears on the binding page of Property Editor with the column name highlighted.

5   Replace the name New Binding with the following name:

    CUSTOMER_NUMBER

3 Select the orders table.

4 In Property Editor, choose Binding.

5 On the Binding page, choose Dataset Parameter Binding. Dataset Parameter Binding displays the CustID parameter, as shown in Figure 17-21. Its value is set to the default, 103, which you specified when you created the data set parameter.

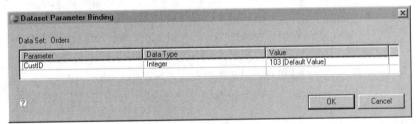

Figure 17-21   Dataset Parameter Binding for the orders table

6 Change the parameter value to the CUSTOMERNUMBER field in the customers report.

1 Click the Value field, then choose the button that appears on the right.

2 On Expression Builder, choose Available Column Bindings, choose List, then double-click CUSTOMER_NUMBER. Expression Builder displays the expression, row["CUSTOMER_NUMBER"], as shown in Figure 17-22.

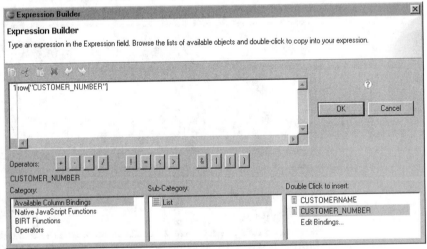

Figure 17-22   CUSTOMERNUMBER field in Expression Builder

3 Choose OK to save the expression. The Dataset Parameter Binding page displays the new value of row["CUSTOMER_NUMBER"] for the CustID parameter.

7 Choose OK to save the changed data set parameter binding.

8 Preview the report, which should look like the one shown in Figure 17-23.

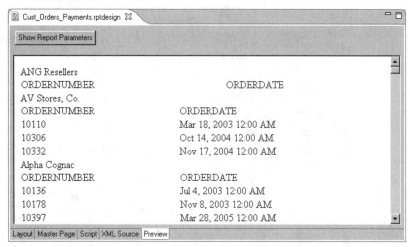

Figure 17-23 Preview of the report shows correct orders data

Now different order records appear for different customers. Not all customers have order records. To display only customers that have orders, you change the query for the customers report. This task is described later in Task 11: "Display only customers that have orders or payments."

Task 9: Create the payments subreport

The payments subreport shows, in a row and column format, the payments that each customer made. It displays the payment date, check number, and amount of each order. To iterate through the payments data set rows and display them in a row and column format, you use a table element.

1 Choose Layout to return to the layout editor.

2 Drag a table element from the palette, and drop it below the orders subreport, in the detail area. Insert Table prompts you to specify the number of columns and detail rows to create for the table.

3 Indicate that you want to create 3 columns and 1 detail row, then choose OK. A table with three columns and one detail row appears in the layout editor.

4 Bind the table with the Payments data set.

   1 In Property Editor, choose Binding.

   2 For Data set, select Payments from the drop-down list.

5 Choose Data Explorer, expand Data Sets, then expand Payments. The columns that you specified in the query appear below Payments.

6 Drag the PAYMENTDATE, CHECKNUMBER, and AMOUNT fields from Data Explorer, and drop them in the first, second, and third cells, respectively, in the detail row of the table. Choose OK to accept the default column bindings for all the fields. The report page should look like the one shown in Figure 17-24.

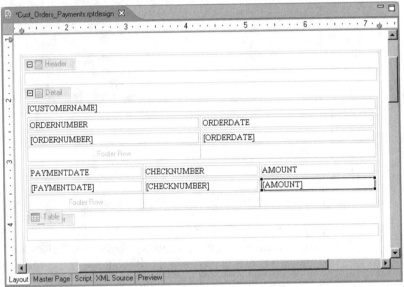

Figure 17-24   Report design includes the payments subreport

The table shows the data set fields that you added. It also shows the labels that the layout editor automatically added to the header row. The labels display the field names as static text and serve as the column headings.

7 Sort the payment rows by payment date.

   1 Select the payments table.

   2 In Property Editor, choose Sorting.

   3 On the Sorting page, choose Add to create a sort expression. A row appears under Sort on.

   4 Click under Sort Key, choose the arrow button that appears, and select PAYMENTDATE from the drop-down list.

   5 Use the default value, Ascending, for Sort Direction.

8 Preview the report. The report should look like the one shown in Figure 17-25.

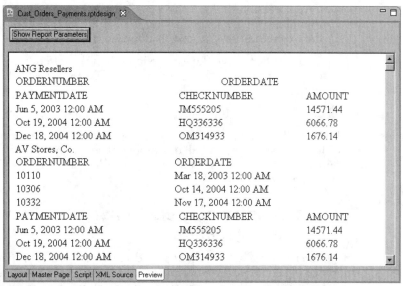

Figure 17-25   Report preview shows repeated payments records

As with the orders subreport when you first created it, the same payment records repeat for every customer, because you specified a default value of 103 for customerNumber when you created the parameter, CustID, for the Payments data set. Because of this default value, the payments subreport always displays the payment records for customer 103. Just as you did for the orders subreport, you need to dynamically update the value of the CustID parameter for each customer in the master report.

Task 10: Link the payments subreport to the customers master report

You link the payments subreport to the customers master report by binding its CustID parameter to the CUSTOMERNUMBER field in the customers report.

1 Choose Layout to return to the layout editor.

2 Select the payments table.

3 In Property Editor, choose the Binding tab.

4 On the Binding page, choose Dataset Parameter Binding. Dataset Parameter Binding displays the CustID parameter. Its value is set to the default, 103, which you specified when you created the data set parameter.

5 Change the parameter value to the CUSTOMERNUMBER field in the customers report:

　1 Click the Value field, then choose the button that appears on the right.

   2 On Expression Builder, choose Available Column Bindings, choose List, then double-click CUSTOMER_NUMBER. Expression Builder displays the expression row["CUSTOMER_NUMBER"].

   3 Choose OK to save the expression. The Dataset Parameter Binding page displays the new value of row["CUSTOMER_NUMBER"] for the CustID parameter.

6 Choose OK to save the changed data set parameter binding.

7 Preview the report. Now the report displays different payment records for different customers. Not all customers have payment records. To display only customers that have payments or orders, you change the query for the customers report.

Task 11: Display only customers that have orders or payments

The database contains customers that do not have orders or payments. The query for the customers report returns all customers. When you run the report, there are customer rows that show only the column headings for the orders and payments tables, as shown in Figure 17-26.

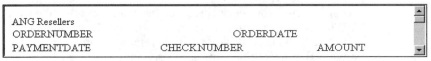

Figure 17-26   Report shows no order or payment data for one customer

You can exclude customers that do not have orders or payments by changing the query for the customers report.

1 Choose Layout to return to the layout editor.

2 In Data Explorer, expand Data Sets, right-click Customers, then choose Edit.

3 Add the following SQL lines to the end of the existing query:

```
WHERE
EXISTS
(SELECT Orders.customerNumber
FROM Orders
WHERE Customers.customerNumber =
Orders.customerNumber)
OR
EXISTS
(SELECT Payments.customerNumber
FROM Payments
WHERE Customers.customerNumber =
Payments.customerNumber)
```

The WHERE EXISTS clause checks the Orders and Payments tables for customerNumber values that match the customerNumber values in the Customers table. Only rows that have matching customerNumber values are selected. The complete query should look like the one shown in Figure 17-27.

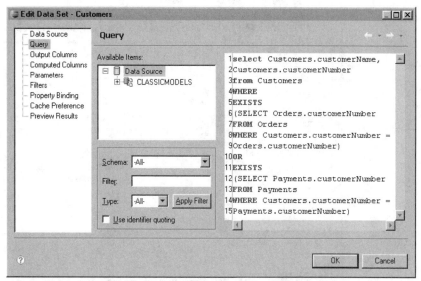

Figure 17-27   Updated SELECT query in Edit Data Set

4 Choose Preview Results to verify that the query returns rows, then choose OK.

5 Preview the report. Scroll down the report to check the output. The report no longer displays customers that do not have orders or payments.

Task 12: Display the subreports next to one another

Now that the subreports display the correct data, you can focus on laying out the subreports next to one another. You cannot place two tables next to one another, because BIRT Report Designer creates block-level elements, which means that each element starts on a new line. To display side-by-side tables, you insert the tables in a grid. The grid enables you to align elements easily.

1 Choose Layout to return to the layout editor.

2 Drag a grid element from the palette, and drop it into the Detail row above the orders table. Insert Grid prompts you to specify the number of columns and rows for the grid.

3 In Number of columns, type 2 and in Number of rows, type 1, then choose OK. A grid with two columns and one row appears in the layout editor.

4 Move the orders table to the first grid cell. To do this, select the Table tab in the bottom-left corner, then drag the table and drop it in the grid cell.

5 Move the payments table to the second grid cell. The report layout should look like the one shown in Figure 17-28.

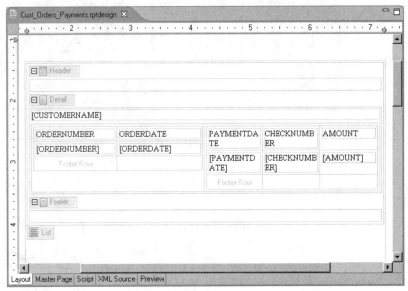

Figure 17-28 Side-by-side subreports in the report design

6 Preview the report. The report should look like the one shown in Figure 17-29.

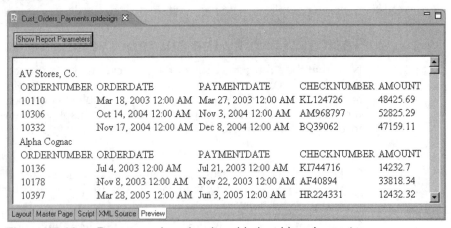

Figure 17-29 Report preview showing side-by-side subreports

Task 13: Format the report

Now that the report displays the correct data and layout, you can turn your attention to improving the report's appearance. You perform the following tasks in this section:

- Highlight the customer names.
- Edit the column headings.
- Change the date formats.
- Change the number formats.
- Increase the vertical space between elements.
- Increase the horizontal space between the orders and payments tables.
- Add borders around the tables.
- Increase the space between the table borders and contents.

Highlight the customer names

1 Choose Layout to return to the layout editor.

2 In the layout editor, select the [CUSTOMERNAME] data element.

3 Choose the Properties tab of Property Editor.

4 Select General from the list under Properties. Property Editor displays the general formatting properties of the data element.

5 For Size, choose Large to display the element's text in a larger size.

6 Choose B to format the data as bold text.

Edit the column headings

When you insert a data set field in a table, BIRT Report Designer automatically adds a label with the data set field name in the header row. Often, data set field names are not in a form that is appropriate for reports, and need to be changed.

1 Double-click the first column heading in the orders table. The text is highlighted.

2 Replace ORDERNUMBER with the following text, then press Enter:

```
Order Number
```

3 Repeat the previous steps to change the rest of the column headings to the following text:

```
Order Date
Payment Date
Check Number
Amount
```

The report layout should look like the one shown in Figure 17-30.

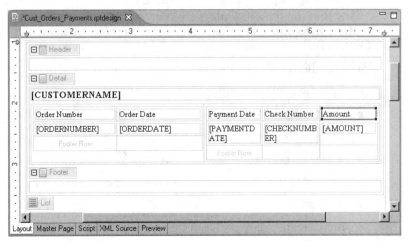

Figure 17-30   Edited column headings in the report design

4 Preview the report. The report should look like the one shown in Figure 17-31.

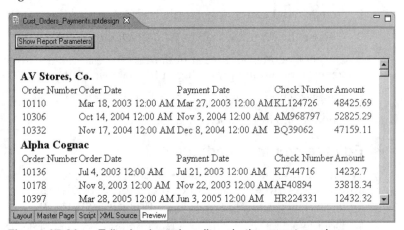

Figure 17-31   Edited column headings in the report preview

Change the date formats

When you insert a data element of date data type, BIRT Report Designer displays dates according to your system's locale setting. BIRT Report Designer provides many different date formats that you can select if you do not want to use the default format. In this procedure, you create a style that changes the format of ORDERDATE and PAYMENTDATE values from Jun 3, 2005 12:00 AM to 6/3/05.

1 Choose Layout to return to the layout editor.

2 Select the data element that displays [ORDERDATE].

3 Choose Element→New Style from the main menu. New Style displays the properties you can set for a style, as shown in Figure 17-32.

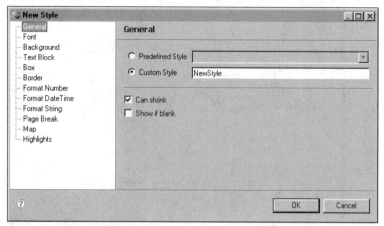

Figure 17-32 New Style

4 For Custom Style, type:

```
Date_data
```

5 Choose Format DateTime from the list of style properties on the left.

6 Choose the m/d/yy format from the drop-down list, as shown in Figure 17-33. The values in the drop-down list dynamically update with the current date.

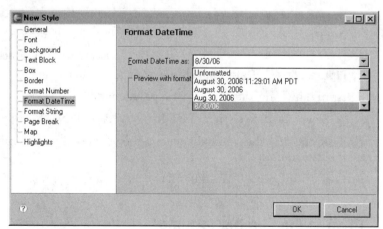

Figure 17-33 DateTime formats

7 Choose OK.

The Date_data style is applied to the [ORDERDATE] data element, as shown in Figure 17-34.

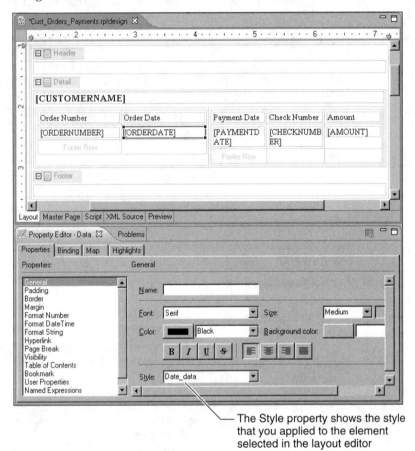

The Style property shows the style that you applied to the element selected in the layout editor

Figure 17-34 Date_data style applied to a data element

8 Apply the Date_data style to the payment date data element.

1 Select the data element that displays [PAYMENTDATE].

2 Right-click the selected element, then choose Style➤Apply Style➤ Date_data.

9 Preview the report. The dates have changed from Jun 3, 2005 12:00 AM format to 6/3/05.

Change the number formats

When you insert a data element of integer data type, BIRT Report Designer displays numbers according to your system's locale setting. BIRT Report

Designer provides many different number formats that you can select if you do not want to use the default format. In this procedure, you create a style that changes the amount values format from 48425.69 to $48,425.69.

1 Choose Layout to return to the layout editor.

2 Select the data element that displays [AMOUNT] in the payments table.

3 Choose Element➤New Style from the main menu. New Style displays properties in the general category.

4 For Custom Style, type:

   Currency_data

5 Choose Format Number from the list of style properties on the left.

6 Specify the following formatting attributes, as shown in Figure 17-35:

   ■ For Format Number as, select Currency from the drop-down list.

   ■ For Decimal places, use the default value of 2.

   ■ Select Use 1000s separator.

   ■ For Symbol, select $ from the drop-down list.

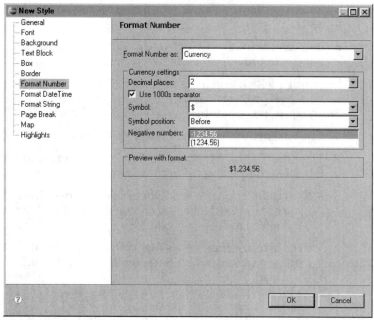

Figure 17-35   Format Number properties

7 Choose OK. The Currency_data style is applied to the [AMOUNT] data element, as indicated by the element's Style property in Property Editor.

8 Preview the report. The numbers appear in the currency format, as shown in Figure 17-36.

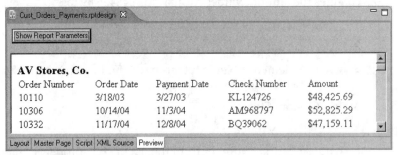

Figure 17-36 Currency format in the report preview

Increase the vertical space between elements

In this procedure, you increase the space between each customer name and the lines before and after it. You can adjust the vertical space between elements in several ways:

- You can increase the top or bottom padding or margins of elements.

- You can organize the elements in a grid and adjust the heights of the grid rows.

- You can organize the elements in a grid and use empty rows with specified heights to provide space between elements.

Formatting with a grid is easier and provides more predictable results. Padding and margins property values can yield different results in different web browsers. In this procedure, you use the third method.

1 Choose Layout to return to the layout editor.

2 Place the [CUSTOMERNAME] data element in the grid that contains the two tables by completing the following steps:

1 Select the grid. Hover the mouse pointer over the bottom-left corner until you see the Grid tab, then choose the tab. Guide cells appear at the top and left of the selected grid.

The layout editor shows the borders of individual data elements, grids, tables, and cells, and it can sometimes be difficult to see where an element is placed. If you need a clearer view of the containers and the elements within the containers, use the Outline view to get a tree view of the report design. You can also use the Outline view to select a particular element if it is too difficult to select. For example, selecting the grid rather than the table within the grid can be difficult. To open the Outline view, choose Window→Show View→Outline.

2 Right-click the guide cell on the left of the grid's first row, then choose
   Insert➤Row➤Above, as shown in Figure 17-37.

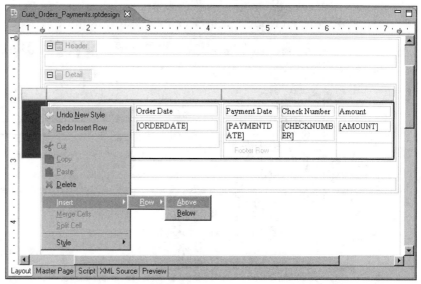

Figure 17-37   Inserting a new row

A new row appears above the selected row.

3 Move the [CUSTOMERNAME] data element from its current location to
   the first cell of the new grid row. Figure 17-38 shows the
   [CUSTOMERNAME] data element in the new location.

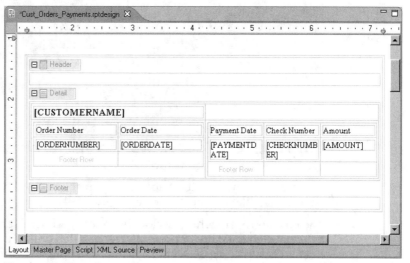

Figure 17-38   Data element moved to the new row

3 Add a new grid row above and below the row that contains the [CUSTOMERNAME] data element, using the procedures that were described earlier.

4 Select the grid, then select the first row in the grid, as shown in Figure 17-39.

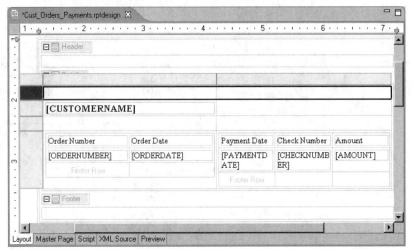

Figure 17-39 Selecting the first row

5 To decrease the size of the row, in the General properties of Property Editor, set the row's height to 0.2 in, as shown in Figure 17-40.

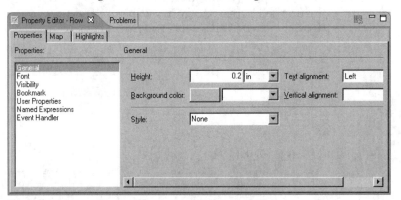

Figure 17-40 Setting the row height property

6 Select the third row in the grid, and set its height to 0.1 in. The report design should look like the one shown in Figure 17-41.

The custom row heights provide the exact amount of space you need between elements. If you prefer to work with a unit of measurement other than inches, you can select mm, points, or even pixels for very precise sizing control.

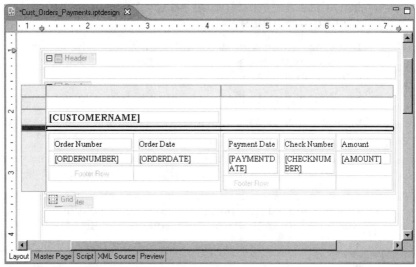

Figure 17-41 New row heights in the report design

7 Preview the report. There is more space above and below the customer name. The report should look like the one shown in Figure 17-42.

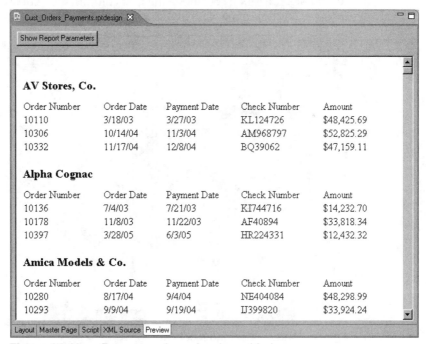

Figure 17-42 Report preview, showing added space

Increase the horizontal space between the orders and payments tables

In this procedure, you increase the space between the orders and payments tables. As with vertical spacing, you can adjust the horizontal space between elements in several ways:

- You can increase the left or right padding or margins of elements.

- You can organize the elements in a grid and adjust the widths of the grid columns.

- You can organize the elements in a grid and use empty columns with specified widths to provide space between elements.

Again, formatting with a grid is easier and provides more predictable results. Padding and margins property values can yield different results in different web browsers. In this procedure, you use the third method.

1 Choose Layout to return to the layout editor.

2 Select the grid. Hover the mouse pointer over the bottom-left corner until you see the Grid tab, then choose the tab. Guide cells appear at the top and left of the selected grid.

3 Right-click the guide cell above the first column, then choose Insert→Column to the Right, as shown in Figure 17-43.

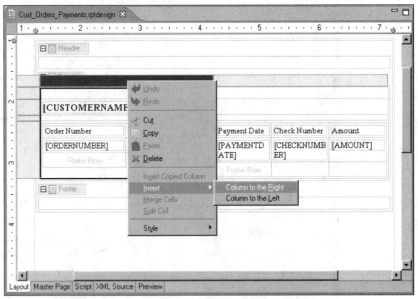

Figure 17-43   Inserting a column

A new column appears between the first and third columns. By default, BIRT Report Designer creates columns with the same widths.

4 Select the column that you just added, and use Property Editor to set its width to 0.4 in, as shown in Figure 17-44.

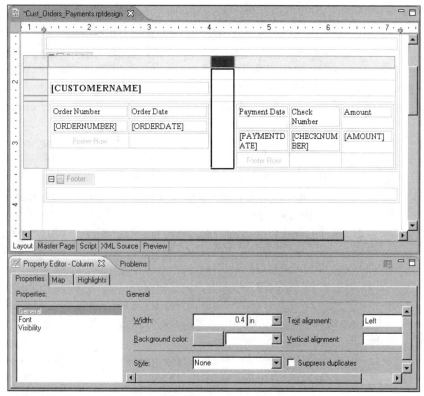

Figure 17-44   Setting a column width

The width of the second column decreases.

5 Preview the report. There is more space between the orders and payments tables, as shown in Figure 17-45.

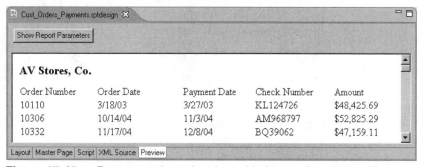

Figure 17-45   Report preview, showing added space between tables

Add borders around the tables

In this procedure, you add a box around the orders and payments tables to clearly identify them as two separate subreports.

1 Choose Layout to return to the layout editor.

2 Select the orders table. Hover the mouse pointer over the bottom-left corner until you see the Table tab, then choose the tab. Guide cells appear at the top and left of the selected table.

3 Choose Border in Property Editor, then set the border properties:

- Set Style to a solid line, the default option.

- Set Width to the thinnest line.

- Set Color to black, the default color.

- Choose all the buttons to add borders around the table, as shown in Figure 17-46.

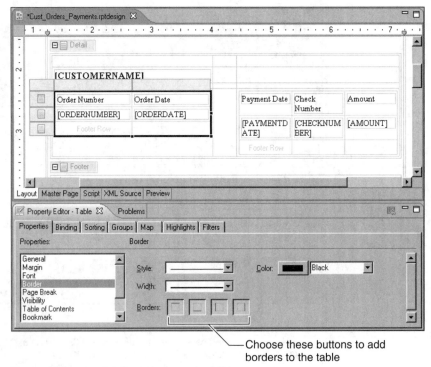

Choose these buttons to add borders to the table

Figure 17-46 Adding borders to a table

4 Repeat the previous steps to draw a border around the payments table.

5 Preview the report. The report should look like the one shown in Figure 17-47.

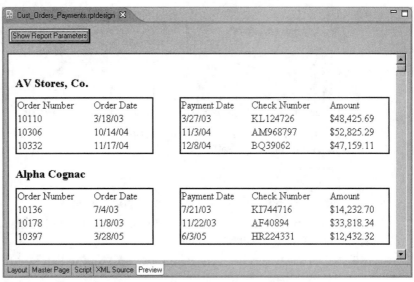

Figure 17-47   Borders around tables in report preview

Increase the space between the table borders and contents

The top and left borders of the tables are too close to the table content. In this procedure, you increase the space between the top and left borders and the content.

1 Choose Layout to return to the layout editor.

2 Select the first cell in the group header row of the orders table. Be careful to select the cell, as shown in Figure 17-48, and not the data element in the cell.

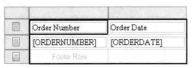

Figure 17-48   Selecting a cell

The title that appears in Property Editor shows the name of the element that you selected. Verify that it displays the following text:

```
Property Editor - Cell
```

3 Choose the Padding properties in Property Editor, then set Top and Left to 6 points. Figure 17-49 shows these property settings.

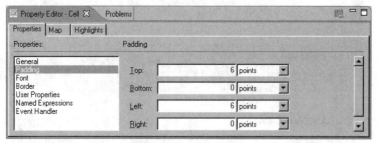

Figure 17-49 Cell padding properties in Property Editor

In the layout editor, extra space appears at the top and left of the cell, as shown in Figure 17-50.

Order Number

Figure 17-50 Cell padding in the report design

4 Select the cell next to the cell that you just formatted, and set its Top and Left padding properties to 6 points.

5 Select the two cells in the detail row, and set the Left padding property to 6 points.

6 Select the cells that are in the same positions in the payments table, and apply the same settings that you used for the cells in the orders table.

7 Preview the report. The report should look like the one shown in Figure 17-51.

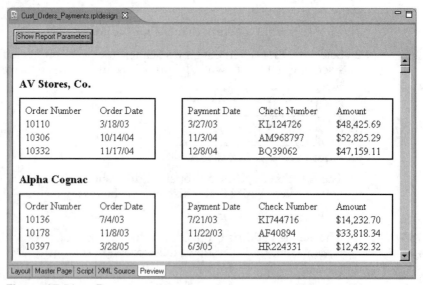

Figure 17-51 Report preview shows more space within the tables

18

Using a Chart in a Report

A chart is a graphical representation of data or the relationships among sets of data. Charts display complex data in an easy-to-assimilate format. You can use a chart as a report in itself or combine a chart with other report elements to enhance or highlight related information.

The guidelines that you should follow when you plan a chart are similar to the guidelines that you use when you plan a report. To create an effective chart, you must decide what data to display, then you select the chart type that best represents that data. For example, to show the growth of a company's business units over time, you use a chart that tracks data along an axis, such as a line chart or a bar chart.

Setting up a chart is different from setting up other report elements. After you select a chart type, you must supply expressions that organize the data in visual elements that are available for that chart type, such as bars in a bar chart. The BIRT Report Designer chart builder walks you through the steps that you need to complete to select a chart type and to create each type of chart.

This chapter introduces BIRT charts. It begins with a tutorial in which you build a chart using the BIRT sample database, Classic Models. As you complete the tutorial, you learn about the essential chart-building tasks.

Tutorial 4: Creating a chart

This section provides step-by-step instructions for building a report that displays order totals that are organized by product line. The report shows the information graphically in a pie chart.

The chart uses data from the sample database, Classic Models. You install that database when you install BIRT. Figure 18-1 shows the chart that you create in the tutorial.

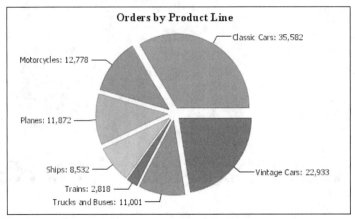

Figure 18-1   Completed tutorial chart

To create this chart, you complete the following tasks:

- Set up the report design file. You create a new report, data source, and data set.

- Add the chart to the report. You insert a chart element and select a chart type.

- Provide data for the report. You link the chart to a data set and set up the expressions that the chart uses.

- Review the chart. You use the previewer to examine the chart.

- Update chart titles. You modify the chart title and remove an unnecessary title beneath the pie.

- Refine the chart appearance. You remove the chart legend and modify the labels that identify each sector.

Task 1:   Set up the report design file

Before you start to design a chart, you must create a report design file in which to display the chart, then set up the data source and data set that the chart uses. These tasks are discussed in detail in earlier sections of this book, including a tutorial in which you build a sample report. This tutorial explains how to select the specific data that you use to build the sample pie chart.

1 Using the Blank Report template, create a new report design called Chart.rptdesign.

2 Build a data source for the report design file using the sample database, Classic Models.

3 Build a data set for the chart. Use the following data set name:

```
ChartData
```

Use the following SQL SELECT statement:

```
SELECT Products.ProductLine,
sum(OrderDetails.QuantityOrdered)
FROM OrderDetails,
Products
WHERE Products.ProductCode=OrderDetails.ProductCode
GROUP BY Products.ProductLine
ORDER BY Products.ProductLine
```

This statement gets values from the ProductLine column in the Products table. Then it groups the results by product line and calculates the sum of the order quantities for each group.

4 Preview the query to validate the data it returns. If you created the SELECT statement correctly, you should see the data rows that appear in Figure 18-2.

Edit Data Set - ChartData	
Data Source	**Preview Results**
Query	
Preview Results	
Computed Columns	
Parameters	
Filters	
Output Columns	
Property Binding	
Cache Preference	

PRODUCTLINE	2
Classic Cars	35582
Motorcycles	12778
Planes	11872
Ships	8532
Trains	2818
Trucks and Buses	11001
Vintage Cars	22933

Figure 18-2   Previewing the data set

The first column lists product-line names. The second column shows the sum of the order totals for each product line. The sum column is called 2.

5 To rename the sum column to something more descriptive, choose Output Columns. Use the following text for the alias for the 2 column:

```
TotalOrders
```

Use the following text for the display name for the 2 column:

```
TOTALORDERS
```

6 Now you are finished setting up the report design file. To close Edit Data Set and open the layout editor, choose OK.

Task 2:   Add the chart to the report

You use the palette to add a chart element, and then select a chart type. In this tutorial, you build a pie chart.

1 Choose Palette, then drag a chart element from the palette to the report, as shown in Figure 18-3. The chart builder, New Chart, appears. If you have an existing chart, the window title is Edit Chart. The Select Chart Type page displays the different types of charts that you can create. Each chart type includes several subtypes, giving you an extensive range of available types. For example, when you first open the chart builder, you see three different bar chart subtypes, as shown in Figure 18-4.

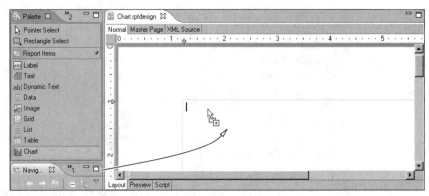

Figure 18-3   Adding a chart element to a report

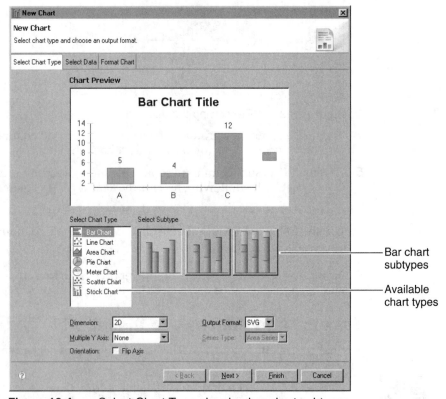

Figure 18-4   Select Chart Type showing bar chart subtypes

Choosing a different type on Select Chart Type displays the available subtypes for that type of chart. These subtypes create two-dimensional charts. Later in this chapter, you learn how to use the Dimension option to show even more subtypes.

2 In the Select Chart Type list, select Pie Chart. The chart builder shows the pie chart in the preview window, as shown in Figure 18-5. Pie charts have only one two-dimensional subtype, so you see only one option in the Subtype area. As you design a chart, the preview window gives you an indication of the progress you are making. For example, if you change the color of the pie chart sectors or replace the default title text with a new title, the preview window reflects your changes.

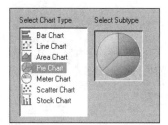

Figure 18-5   Two-dimensional subtype for a pie chart

Task 3: Providing data for a chart

In this tutorial, you already created the data source connection and data set that you need. If necessary, you can use the chart builder to build a new data set or create filters or parameters that refine the chart data. After selecting the data set to use, you must set up the expressions that the chart uses. Each type of chart uses data differently. For a pie chart, you must select data expressions that specify:

- Which sectors appear in the pie. In this tutorial, you use an expression that creates one sector for each product line.

- The size of each sector. In this tutorial, the number of orders determines the size of each product-line sector.

You can use different techniques to provide a data expression in a chart. The easiest way to specify the data to use is to drag a column from Data Preview to a field. You can also type the expression or use Expression Builder to create an expression.

1 To navigate to the page you use to provide data, choose Next. Then, on Select Data, choose Use data set. Figure 18-6 shows the options that appear.

This report file includes only one data set, ChartData. If the file included more data sets, the data set names would appear in the drop-down list. In the lower half of the chart builder, Data Preview displays some of the data from the data set that you are using. You can see the product line and total orders columns. By default, Data Preview shows six data rows.

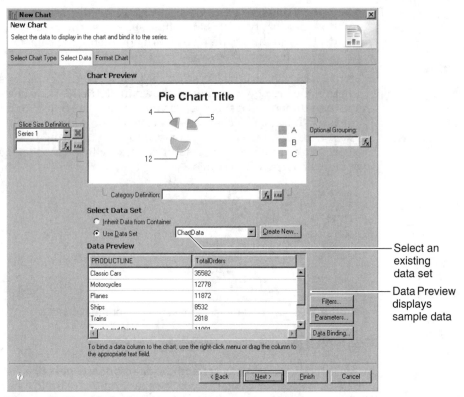

Figure 18-6   Selecting the data set that you created

2 First, to determine which sectors the pie displays, you provide a category
series expression. In Data Preview, select the PRODUCTLINE column
header, and drag it to the empty field to the right of Category Definition, as
shown in Figure 18-7.

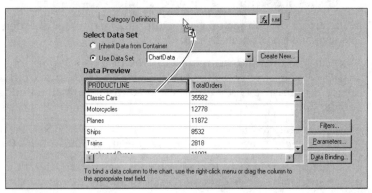

Figure 18-7   Supplying a category series expression

The following expression appears in Category Definition:

```
row["PRODUCTLINE"]
```

In Data Preview, the product-line column now appears colored to show that you have used the column in the chart. Figure 18-8 shows the selected column.

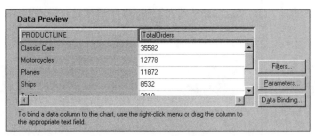

Figure 18-8   Data Preview with selected column

3 To set the size of each sector, select the TOTALORDERS column header, and drag it to the empty field below Slice Size Definition, as shown in Figure 18-9.

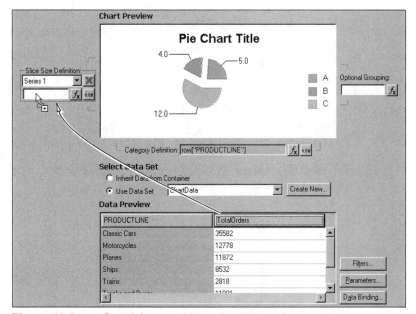

Figure 18-9   Supplying a value series expression

The following expression appears in Slice Size Definition:

```
row["TOTALORDERS"]
```

In Data Preview, the total orders column now appears colored to indicate that the column is used in the chart. The image in Chart Preview also changes to use the data you specified. The product lines are chart categories. Each sector represents one product line. The order totals are chart values. The size of each sector represents the total orders for that product-line category. You can use the preview image to verify that you supplied the correct expressions for the chart. The preview image should look like the one shown in Figure 18-10.

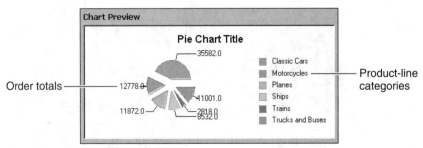

Figure 18-10   Chart preview image

Now you have completed the necessary steps to create a basic pie chart. To confirm that the chart looks correct in the report, you view it in the previewer.

Task 4: View the chart

Testing as you go is an important aspect of the developer process. Reviewing your work at different points in the process ensures that you do not waste time by pushing the report in the wrong direction. The preview image in the chart builder is one way to check your progress. You should also use the previewer to review how the chart looks in a report document.

1   To close the chart builder, choose Finish. The chart element appears in the layout editor. The chart should look similar to the one shown in Figure 18-11.

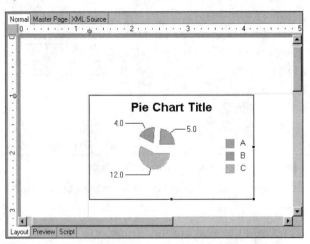

Figure 18-11   Chart element in the layout editor

2 The chart element appears small, relative to the report page. To make the chart bigger so that the data appears more clearly and takes up more of the report page, enlarge the chart element to approximately 5 inches wide and 3 inches tall. To enlarge the chart, select it, then drag the handles that appear in the borders of the chart element, as shown in Figure 18-12.

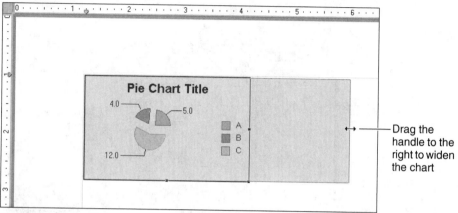

Figure 18-12 Enlarging a chart element

3 Choose Preview to show the chart in the previewer. The chart looks like the one shown in Figure 18-13.

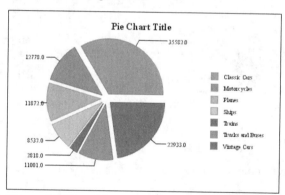

Figure 18-13 Chart in the previewer

The chart uses the correct data, but the layout is not very attractive. You need to refine the chart appearance and organization to emphasize the points that you want. The remaining procedures in this tutorial help you to modify the chart. Some of the changes that you make include creating a new title, adjusting the data labels, and removing the legend.

Task 5: Updating the chart title

Currently, the chart displays a default title. You provide new title text.

1 Choose Layout to return to the layout editor, then double-click the chart design to open the chart builder.

2 Choose Format Chart, then choose Chart Area in the list at the left. Figure 18-14 shows the chart builder.

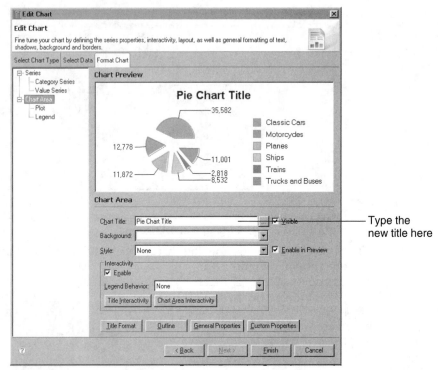

Figure 18-14   Adding a title in the chart area section

3 In Chart Title, type:

```
Orders by Product Line
```

The preview image displays the change, as shown in Figure 18-15.

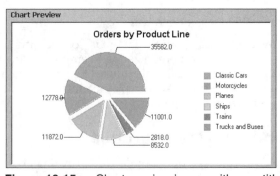

Figure 18-15   Chart preview image with new title

Task 6: Refine the chart appearance

The chart includes labels that identify the value of each sector. A legend identifies which product line a sector represents. While the legend includes useful information, it takes up space and reduces the size of the pie. You can remove the legend and add the legend information to the sector labels to display the same information in a different way. An additional benefit to moving the labels is that, when you print the report, the chart clearly shows which sector represents a product line, even if the colors are not easily distinguished. Each data label will display category information (the sector name) and value information (the total number of orders for the sector). For example, the following label identifies the motorcycles sector:

```
Motorcycles: 12,778
```

1 To navigate to the legend section of the chart builder, choose Legend from the navigation list at the left, as shown in Figure 18-16.

Use the list to open formatting sections

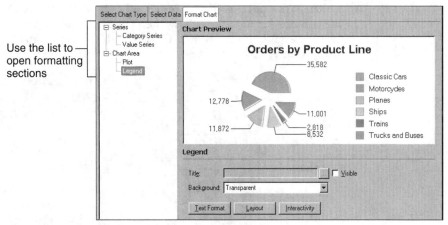

Figure 18-16 Legend section of Format Chart

2 To open the window from which to delete the legend, choose Layout at the bottom of the screen. Layout Legend appears, as shown in Figure 18-17.

Deselect Visible to hide the legend

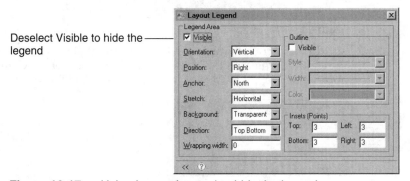

Figure 18-17 Using Layout Legend to hide the legend

3 Deselect Visible, then close the window. Chart Preview reflects the change. The chart looks like the one shown in Figure 18-18.

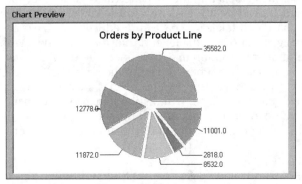

Figure 18-18 Chart with hidden legend

4 Now you can add the legend information to the sector labels. Navigate to the value series formatting section, then choose Labels. Labels shows you what data the sector labels display. You can also use Labels to change the label formatting, such as outlines and text style. Figure 18-19 shows Labels.

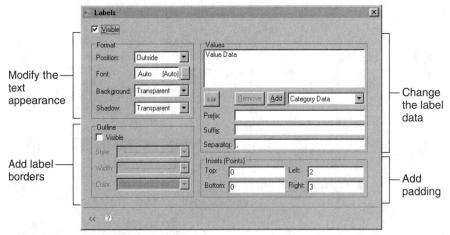

Figure 18-19 Labels

5 To add the section name to the label, ensure that Category Data appears in the drop-down list in the Values area, then choose Add. Category Data appears below Value Data in the list, as shown in Figure 18-20.

Figure 18-20 Adding category data to a label

6 Using this setup, the labels show sector values, then sector names. You want to rearrange the label data so the sector names appear first. Select Value Data, and choose Remove, then, in the drop-down list, select Value Data again, and choose Add. Value Data now appears below Category Data in the list, as shown in Figure 18-21.

Figure 18-21   Labels with rearranged data

Now the labels will display information in the correct order, but you still need to change the label appearance. When you use more than one kind of information in a label, you can use a separator in between the different sections. The current separator is a comma.

7 To change the separator, in Separator, type a colon (:) then a space. Figure 18-22 shows where to type the separator text.

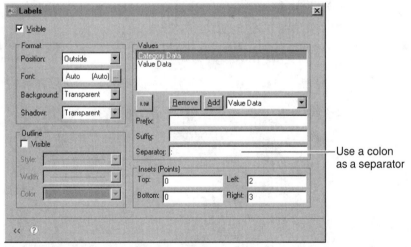

Use a colon as a separator

Figure 18-22   Adding a label separator

8 Because the chart uses data with whole numbers, a number format that shows decimal values is unnecessary. To change the number format of the value part of the label, select Value Data in the list, then select Edit Format. You can use Edit Format to change the number format of date-and-time or numerical data.

9 Select Standard, then change the value in Fraction Digits to 0. At this point, Edit Format appears as shown in Figure 18-23.

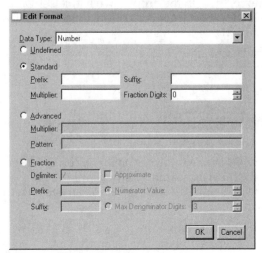

Figure 18-23 Edit Format

Choose OK to close Edit Format.

10 To change the formatting attributes of the label text, choose Invoke Font Editor. Figure 18-24 shows where to find the Font Editor button.

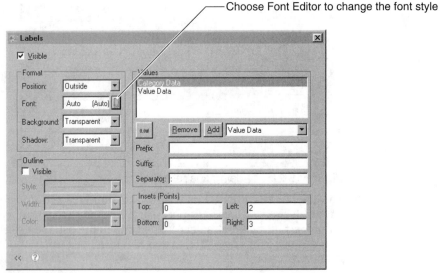

Choose Font Editor to change the font style

Figure 18-24 Opening Font Editor from Labels

Edit Font appears. You use Edit Font to change the text format of the labels.

11 Change the font to Tahoma and the size to 11, as shown in Figure 18-25. Then choose OK, and close Labels.

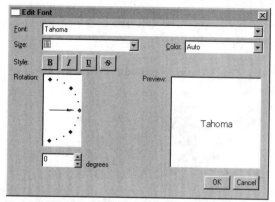

Figure 18-25   Edit Font

Now you set a consistent length for the leader lines that connect the labels to the sectors. Figure 18-26 shows where to find the leader line settings.

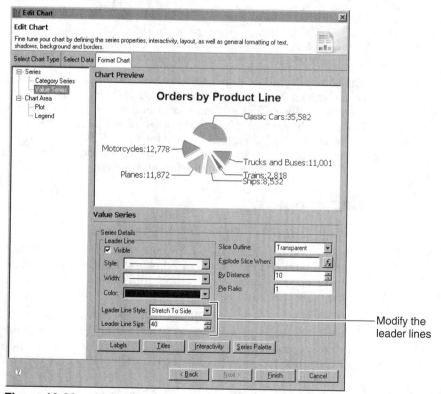

Figure 18-26   Value Series section of Format Chart

12 In Leader Line Style, select Fixed Length. Change Leader Line Size to 20.

13 You have finished creating and formatting the chart. To close the chart builder and see the chart element in the layout editor, choose Finish. Then, for the last time, choose Preview to preview the chart. The chart looks like the one shown in Figure 18-27.

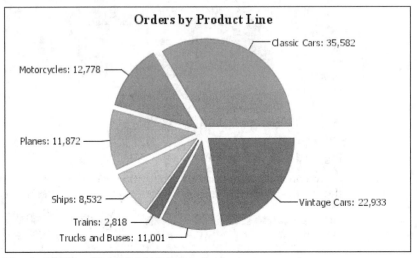

Figure 18-27   Completed tutorial chart

The completed chart shows the category names for each sector as well as the sector values. The size and organization of the chart make quick analysis possible, while still providing more detailed data. For example, the user can immediately see that the largest pie sector is Classic Cars, which has 35,582 orders, followed by Vintage Cars, which has 22,933. The two car sectors are larger than all other sectors combined. Other product-line groups, such as Trains, do not contribute significant numbers of orders.

Next steps

To learn more about charts, review the following topics:

- Exploring the chart builder. You use the chart builder to complete all tasks that are related to creating or adjusting a chart. The chart builder organizes tasks, so you can easily find the settings that you need. The tutorial explored the main chart builder sections and some of the most common settings.

- Positioning a chart. In addition to stand-alone charts like the pie chart that you just created, you can use charts in combination with other report elements, such as lists or tables. You should understand how the position of a chart in a report with other elements can affect the data that the chart displays.

- Chart types and subtypes. You should review the types and subtypes, so you know what formats are available to display your data.

- Chart output formats. By default, the chart builder creates a chart in Scalable Vector Graphics (SVG) format. This format works well in most deployed reports. You can also create a chart in a static image file format, such as BMP or PNG.

- Chart data. Each type of chart uses data differently. You can also manipulate the scale or placement of data on an axis or in a pie or meter to show information more effectively.

- Chart formatting. In the tutorial, you formatted some parts of a pie chart, such as leader lines and data labels, using settings such as text style, position, and visibility. Other chart types offer different formatting options.

- Interactive features. To make the chart more useful to the report users, you can add interactive features, such as hyperlinks and highlighting, which enable users to interact with the chart more effectively.

Exploring the chart builder

The tutorial that you just completed introduced the chart builder. You used the chart builder to complete the tasks that are mandatory when you create a chart, such as selecting data, as well as some tasks that are optional, such as formatting the labels. The structure of the chart builder makes it easy to complete the necessary tasks.

The chart builder has three main pages, which you access by choosing the buttons at the top:

- Select Chart Type, on which you determine the type of chart and basic structural attributes such as orientation and the number of dimensions in which the chart appears.

- Select Data, on which you specify the data that the chart displays.

- Format Chart, on which you modify the appearance of the chart. Format Chart tasks can modify the data that the chart displays, such as the range of values an axis displays, or the visual elements of the chart, such as the color of the lines in a line chart.

This section describes the chart builder pages.

Select Chart Type

The most common task that you complete on Select Chart Type is selecting a chart type and subtype, as you did in the tutorial. You can also use Select Chart Type to modify the subtype you choose. You can show a chart in two dimensions, two dimensions with depth, or three dimensions, and you can flip the axes of a chart so the x-axis is horizontal. Select Chart Type is also where you can determine the output format of the chart. Figure 18-28 shows the options that appear on Select Chart Type.

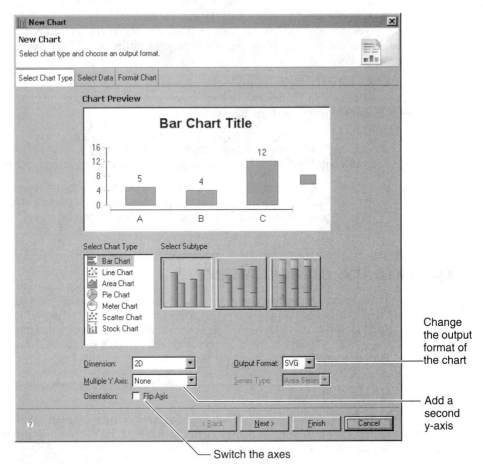

Change
the output
format of
the chart

Add a
second
y-axis

Switch the axes

Figure 18-28   Select Chart Type

Select Data

You use Select Data to determine what data the chart displays. You select a data set, then you select columns from the data set and place them in the data fields.

Select Data appears different for each chart type, making it easy for you to see which expressions you must provide. For example, in Figure 18-29, Select Data displays the fields that you use for a bar chart.

You can also use Select Data to refine the chart data set. Data Preview shows you actual data rows, so you can see if you want to exclude values or use a parameter to return only certain data.

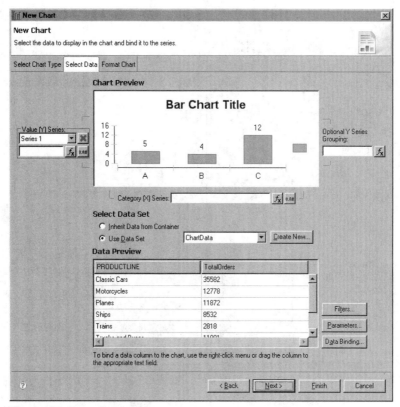

Figure 18-29   Select Data

Format Chart

Every task on the Format Chart page is optional. You can successfully create a chart using only the Select Chart Type and Select Data pages. The options on Format Chart, however, enable you to manipulate and arrange the chart data so that it highlights the most important information. You can also use Format Chart to make a chart more attractive or easier to read.

Format Chart includes several sections. The sections organize formatting tasks by the area of the chart to which they relate, such as the plot and the legend. You use the list on the left of the Format Chart page to navigate among sections. Figure 18-30 shows Format Chart. The Series section is the first section in the list.

Each Format Chart section displays different formatting options. Most sections also include buttons that you can use to open windows that contain more detailed formatting options. For example, on the value series page, you can use the Series Palette button to open a window in which you change the colors a value series uses, as shown in Figure 18-31.

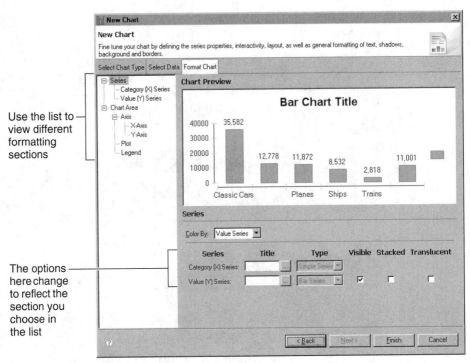

Use the list to view different formatting sections

The options here change to reflect the section you choose in the list

Figure 18-30   Format Chart

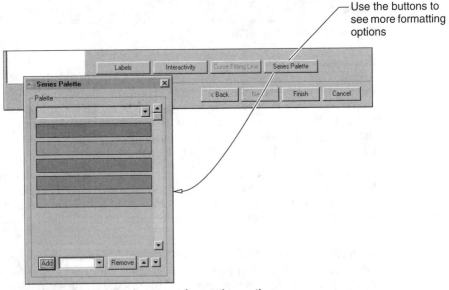

Use the buttons to see more formatting options

Figure 18-31   Accessing more formatting options

Series section

To see the main series section, choose Series in the list, as shown in Figure 18-32.

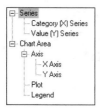

Figure 18-32   Series item in the Format Chart section list

The information that appears provides an overview of the chart series. It lists the series a chart uses and enables you to hide or stack a series, or to make a series appear translucent against the plot. You can also provide a title for a series. Figure 18-33 shows the series section.

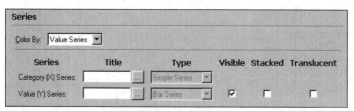

Figure 18-33   Series section options

To see options for the category series or the value series, choose the relevant item in the list. You use the category series and value series sections to modify series details. For example, you can use the category series section to set up grouping or sorting of category data. Figure 18-34 shows the category series section.

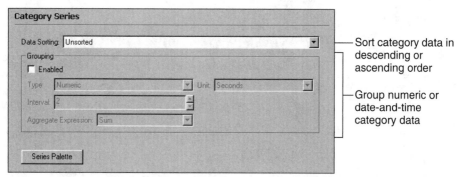

Sort category data in descending or ascending order

Group numeric or date-and-time category data

Figure 18-34   Category series options

You can use the value series section to change the appearance of the value series, such as the bars in a bar chart or the lines in a line chart. For example, Figure 18-35 shows the options that you can change in a stock chart value series.

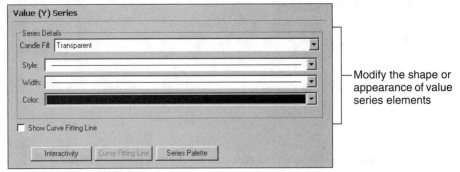

—Modify the shape or appearance of value series elements

Figure 18-35   Value series options

Chart area section

To see the chart area section, choose Chart Area in the list, as shown in Figure 18-36.

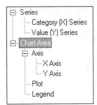

Figure 18-36   Chart Area item in the Format Chart section list

The section that appears displays options that you use to change the appearance of the entire chart element. For example, you can apply a style that modifies all the text in a chart or change the background color of the chart area. Figure 18-37 shows the chart area section.

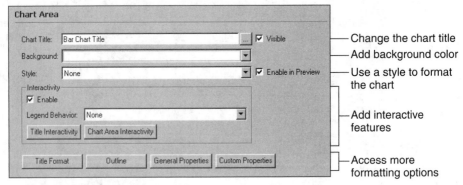

—Change the chart title
—Add background color
—Use a style to format the chart

—Add interactive features

—Access more formatting options

Figure 18-37   Chart area options

Axis section

To see the main axis section, choose Axis in the list, as shown in Figure 18-38.

Figure 18-38   Axis item in the Format Chart section list

The information that appears provides an overview of the chart axes. Pie charts and meter charts do not use axes, so this section is not available for those chart types. You can use options in the main axis section to hide an axis, change the axis type, or modify the color of an axis. Figure 18-39 shows the axis section.

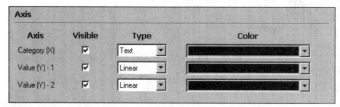

Figure 18-39   Axis options

To see the section for the x-axis or the y-axis, choose the relevant item in the list. The options that appear are the same for an x-axis or a y-axis. You can change axis details, such as line color, labels, or scale. Figure 18-40 shows x-axis and y-axis options.

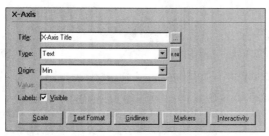

Figure 18-40   X-axis and y-axis options

Plot section

To see the plot section, choose Plot in the list, as shown in Figure 18-41.

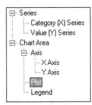

Figure 18-41 Plot item in the Format Chart section list

The section shows formatting options for the plot area, which is where the series elements, such as bars or lines, appear. You can set a background color or add an outline. To set more advanced plot options such as positioning and padding, choose Client Area. Figure 18-42 shows the plot section.

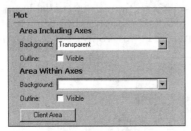

Figure 18-42 Plot options

Legend section

To see the legend section, choose Legend in the list, as shown in Figure 18-43.

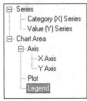

Figure 18-43 Legend item in the Format Chart section list

The section includes options that you can use to change the style, position or organization of the legend text, or to add a legend title. Figure 18-44 shows the legend section.

Figure 18-44 Legend options

Positioning a chart

The chart in the tutorial is a stand-alone chart, meaning that it does not appear in a report with other data. You also can insert a chart in a section of a report that uses other report items, such as grids and lists, to display data.

You can specify a chart data set that is different from the data set that you use in the rest of the report. For example, a chart that you place in a customer list could show the total sales for each customer. The customer list might use one set of data, such as customer names and addresses, while the chart uses a data set that returns the sales totals.

A chart that you place in a table typically uses the same data set as the table. A table often groups data, and a report designer wants the chart data to use the same grouping setup as the table in which it appears. Where a chart appears in a table determines what data the chart displays. For example, in a table that includes grouping, you can place a chart element in the following places:

- A table header or footer. The chart displays data for the entire data set.

- A group header or footer. Each group section includes a chart, and each chart displays data for the group section in which it appears.

- A detail row. Each detail row in the completed report includes a chart, and each chart displays data for the detail row in which it appears.

For example, Figure 18-45 shows the design for a report that includes Classic Models order information that is grouped by product line, such as Vintage Cars and Motorcycles. The report uses a chart to show the order totals graphically.

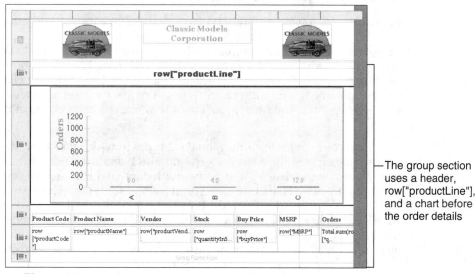

The group section uses a header, row["productLine"], and a chart before the order details

Figure 18-45 Report design with a chart in a group section

When you preview the chart, the data for a product-line group composes one section. Each group shows a chart before listing the order details, as shown in Figure 18-46.

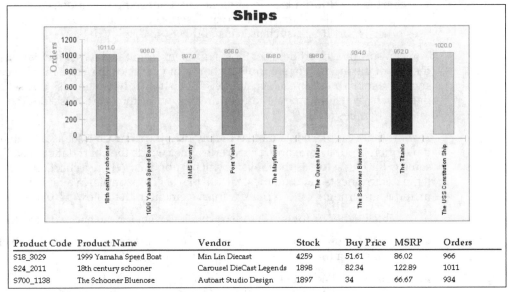

Product Code	Product Name	Vendor	Stock	Buy Price	MSRP	Orders
S18_3029	1999 Yamaha Speed Boat	Min Lin Diecast	4259	51.61	86.02	966
S24_2011	18th century schooner	Carousel DieCast Legends	1898	82.34	122.89	1011
S700_1138	The Schooner Bluenose	Autoart Studio Design	1897	34	66.67	934

Figure 18-46   Report with a chart in a group section

Understanding types of charts

BIRT supports several different types of charts. Some chart types, such as bar and line charts, use axes to arrange data. Other chart types, such as pie charts, do not use axes. The main difference between the two types is that charts without axes cannot use time values to plot data. A pie chart that shows sales by month does not help you see if sales are rising or falling, but a bar chart that shows the same information clearly shows not just the monthly values but any trends in the data. You learn more about how axes work in charts in the next chapter.

All chart types offer two-dimensional subtypes in which the chart shape appears flat against the chart background. BIRT charts are not limited to two dimensions. You can also use subtypes with depth, which use the appearance of depth to enhance a chart, and three-dimensional subtypes, which arrange series elements along a third axis in addition to the typical x- and y-axes. Figure 18-47 shows the difference between a bar chart with depth and a three-dimensional bar chart. In the first chart, the bars have the appearance of three-dimensional objects, but they are arranged on the x- and y-axes only. The second chart places bars back along the z-axis as well as on the x- and y-axis.

A chart with depth plots data
on two axes, x and y

A three-dimensional chart
uses an x-, a y-, and a z-axis

Figure 18-47   Depth and three-dimensional bar charts

The charts in the previous illustration show each value as a separate bar. You can also stack the elements of an area, bar, or line chart to show series data as it contributes to a category total:

- A stacked chart arranges the data points from one series on top of the data points of another series.

- A percent stacked chart is similar to a stacked chart, except the total of the data points in a category fills the entire plot area for a category. The value of each data point is a percentage of the total of all data points for that category.

Figure 18-48 shows examples of a stacked bar chart series and a percent stacked bar chart series. The two options offer different ways to compare series contributions while still reviewing exact totals.

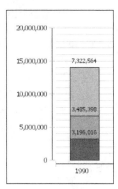
Stacked

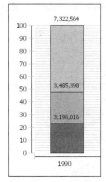
Stacked percent

Figure 18-48   Stacked and percent stacked bar charts

The following sections describe the main chart types.

About area charts

An area chart displays data values as a set of points that are connected by lines. If you include several series on an area chart, the chart displays filled areas that overlap. For example, the area chart in Figure 18-49 shows product types as overlapping areas.

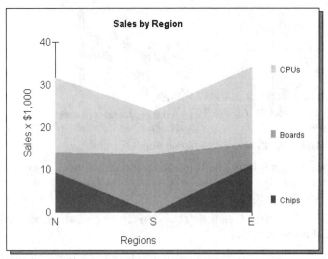

Figure 18-49   Area chart

An area chart emphasizes change over time. A stacked or percent stacked area chart also shows the relationship of parts to a whole.

About bar charts

A bar chart typically displays data values as a set of vertical columns. You can flip the axes of a bar chart to display data values as a set of horizontal bars. For example, the bar chart in Figure 18-50 shows internet usage in the United States by connection speed and region.

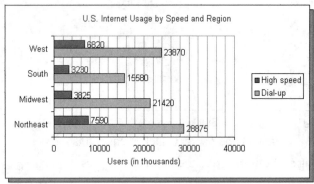

Figure 18-50   Bar chart

A bar chart is useful to show data changes over a period of time or illustrate comparisons among items. When you flip the axes, as in the chart in the previous illustration, the chart emphasis is more on comparing values, typically with less emphasis on time. Stacked and percent stacked bar charts can also show the relationship of individual items to a whole.

About line charts

A line chart displays data as a sequence of points, connected by a line. For example, the line chart in Figure 18-51 shows sales values for chips and boards.

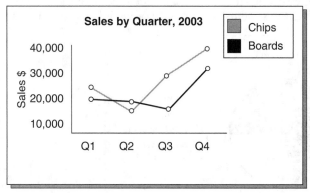

Figure 18-51   Line chart

You use a line chart to show trends in data at equal intervals, such as over a period of time. A stacked or percent stacked bar chart can show the contribution of individual items to a whole.

About meter charts

A meter chart shows a value as a needle pointer on a circle or semicircle. You use a meter chart to create a gauge or dashboard display. Dividing the meter background into sections, called dial regions, enables you to highlight the needle values. You can adjust the dial settings in the same way you adjust an axis, giving you many options for arranging and emphasizing the dial data. Figure 18-52 shows a meter chart that contrasts the speed of two products.

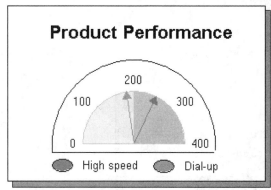

Figure 18-52   Meter chart

A meter chart is best used to show a small number of values in a visually impressive way.

About pie charts

You use a pie chart to show data as part of a total. For example, the chart in Figure 18-53 shows price quote totals for different product lines. Each sector shows total price quotes for an item as a percentage of the total for all items. For example, DSP is the smallest sector, with only eight percent of total sales.

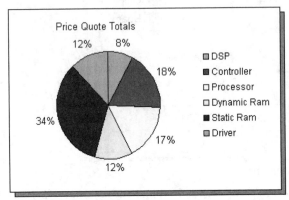

Figure 18-53 Pie chart

A pie is useful to show the relationship of parts to a whole.

About scatter charts

A scatter chart shows data as points. Scatter charts display values on both axes and do not use a category-axis. For example, the chart in Figure 18-54 compares two sets of numerical data for certain sports cars: the top speed and the price. You can use the chart to see how performance increases in relation to price.

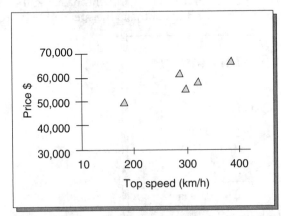

Figure 18-54 Scatter chart

A scatter chart shows the relationships among the numeric values of multiple data series. Scatter charts typically display scientific data.

About stock charts

A stock chart shows data as points on a time continuum, such as a business day. Stock values appear as a candlestick, a box with lines extending up and down from the ends. Open and close values mark the upper and lower edges of the box. High and low values mark the upper and lower points of the line. The default appearance of the bar depends on the chart values. If the open value is higher than the close value, the box is shaded. If the close value is higher than the open value, the box is white. You can change the color of the shaded boxes. Figure 18-55 shows a sample stock chart.

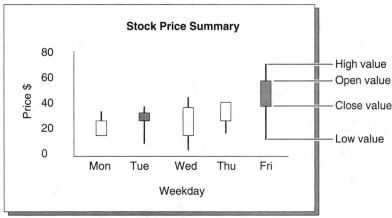

Figure 18-55   Stock chart

Although a stock chart typically displays stock price data, you can also use a stock chart to show scientific data, such as indicating temperature changes.

Understanding chart output formats

By default, the chart builder creates a chart in SVG format. SVG is a language that is used to describe two-dimensional graphics and graphical applications in XML. SVG enables report developers to include more accessible, searchable, and interactive images in their reports. For example, the legend interactive features that BIRT charts include use the SVG format to enable highlighting and hiding series data.

SVG output is appropriate for most charts. SVG files are typically smaller than image files in other formats and produce high-resolution images. You can also produce a chart in other image formats, such as PNG or BMP. For example, if your chart uses a photograph as a background image, you will likely want to use JPEG or PNG format, because those formats display photographic images particularly well. Some web browsers do not currently support SVG images. You must use the SVG format, however, if you want your chart to be interactive.

The following procedure explains how to change the chart output format.

How to change the chart output format

1   On the chart builder, choose Select Chart Type. Select Chart Type appears as shown in Figure 18-56.

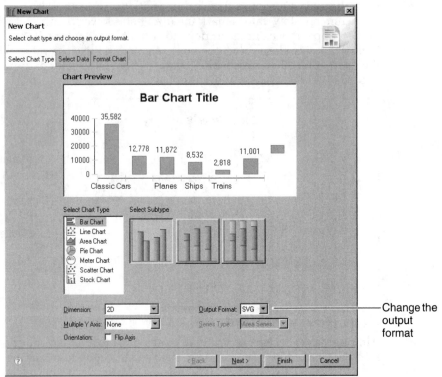

Change the
output
format

Figure 18-56   Output format option on Select Chart Type

2   In Output Format, select an option, such as PNG or BMP.

Choose Finish.

Now you have created a sample chart and become familiar with the different types of charts and the output formats a chart can use. The next chapter describes in detail how to use data in a chart.

19

Displaying Data in Charts

You use the same sorts of data sources for a chart as you do for other report elements. Connecting with data sources and creating data sets are topics that are discussed earlier in this book.

How you return and arrange chart data is often different from the way in which you use data elsewhere in BIRT. One important difference is the data set that you create for a chart. Charts do not aggregate data. To use totals in a chart, you must create a data set that returns total information, which is why we showed you how to do that in the tutorial that appears earlier in this book.

Another difference is the way in which you can manipulate chart data to make it more effective or visually appealing. You provide expressions that organize the data into visual elements, such as bars or lines. After you preview the chart, you may feel that you need additional or different data to make the meaning of the chart more complete or clear. For example, you can group data values or use chart axis settings to modify the range, scale, or formatting of the data that the chart displays.

Understanding chart data concepts

A chart displays data as one or more sets of points. In most chart types, you arrange points along the chart axes. For example, the basic bar chart in Figure 19-1 displays a set of bars that show budget values. The chart arranges the budget totals by year and enables a user to see the total budget growth for a group of cities.

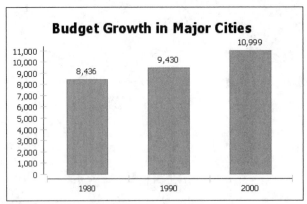

Figure 19-1   Bar chart using one set of bars

To build a chart, you organize your data points into sets of values that are called series. The two types of series are category and value. The category series determines what text, numbers, or dates you see on the x-axis. In the chart in Figure 19-1, the category series shows years. The value series, in a bar chart, determines the height of each bar, relative to the y-axis. In this chart, the values are budget values. The chart shows only one set of bars, so it uses only one value series.

The chart in Figure 19-2, however, displays three sets of bars. Each set displays the budget values for one city. This chart offers a different analysis from the single-series chart, showing that the New York budget dropped while the Chicago and Los Angeles budgets grew. The category series is the same as it was in the first chart. The chart still organizes the data on the x-axis by years. The three value series organize the budget totals by city.

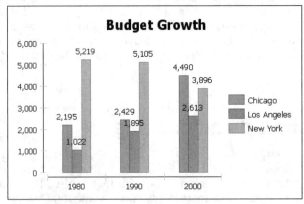

Figure 19-2   Bar chart using three value series

The same principles of data organization apply to series in charts without axes. Figure 19-3 shows population information in a pie chart. The category series divides the pie into cities and the value series uses population values to determine the size of each city sector. The chart shows only one set of pie sectors, so it uses only one value series.

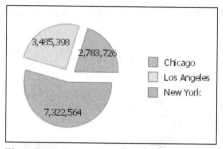

Figure 19-3   Pie chart using one value series

The chart in Figure 19-4, however, organizes the data into three sets of pie sectors. The three value series, one for each year, create three pies. The category series is the same as in the previous chart. The categories separate each pie into city sectors.

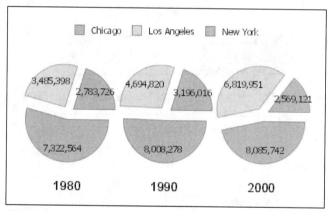

Figure 19-4   Pie chart using three value series

Now that you understand the series concepts, you learn how to specify the data to use for the series in your chart.

Using expressions to set up chart series

To define a series, you provide an expression. You add the expression to the chart builder. The expressions that you use in a chart are similar to the expressions that you use in a data field. For example, row["Totals"] returns the value of the Totals column. This section assumes that you have read the information about expressions that appears earlier in this book.

Selecting a chart data set

Before you start to define expressions, you must link the chart element to a data set, as you did in the tutorial in Chapter 18, "Using a Chart in a Report."

How to select a chart data set

1 Navigate to the Select Data page of the chart builder. Figure 19-5 shows Select Data for a meter chart.

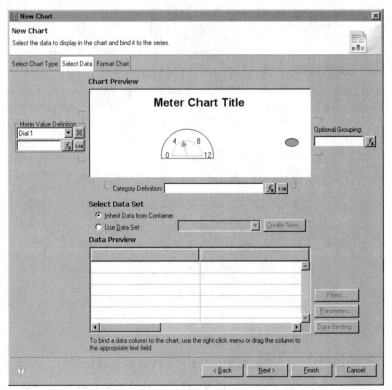

Figure 19-5   Select Data

2 In Select Data Set, select an option:

- To use the data set that is bound to the container element, such as a grid or table, in which the chart appears, select Inherit Data from Container.

- To use a different data set, select Use Data Set, then select a data set from the drop-down list.

- To build a new data set, select Use Data Set, and choose Create New.

Data Preview shows some of the data for the data set. Reviewing sample data can help you decide which column to use for a series. For example, in Figure 19-6, Data Preview shows several columns of stock data.

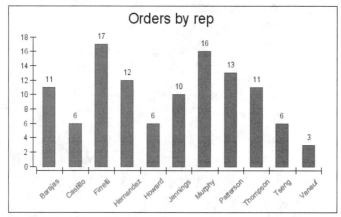

Figure 19-6 Data Preview with data for a stock chart

You can limit the data that the chart displays. To filter the data set, choose Filters. If you use a data set in which you defined parameters, you can review or change a parameter value. To see data set parameters, choose Parameters. You can also modify the column binding for the data in a chart. To see current binding settings, choose Binding.

Aggregating information for a chart

BIRT charts process basic expressions, such as row["Population"]. You cannot use an aggregate expression in a chart element. To use summary information in a chart, you must use a data source that includes summary data or create a query that calculates summary data from the values in the data source. After you retrieve or calculate the summary data, you can use a basic expression to set up that data in the chart. For example, the chart in Figure 19-7 displays the number of orders that sales representatives secured in one month.

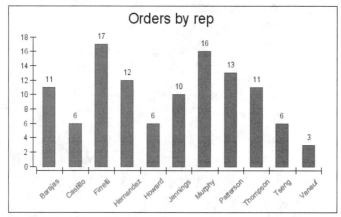

Figure 19-7 Chart that displays orders by sales representative

The data for the chart appears in detail rows in the data source. Each order appears in a detail row that lists order information, such as the order number, the order date, the customer name, and the name of the sales representative who set up the order. To return the summary information, the query selects the sales representative names and aggregates the count of the order rows for each representative. Table 19-1 shows some sample rows from the data set that BIRT returns. For example, Barajas has eleven order rows in the original data. Castillo has six order rows. To create the chart, you include the aggregate field, COUNTofOrderID, in an expression, row["COUNTofOrderID"].

Table 19-1   Aggregated data

RepLast	COUNTofOrderID
Barajas	11
Castillo	6
Firrelli	17

Setting up an expression in the chart builder

The Select Data page in the chart builder is where you set up the series for a chart. You use one of three methods to provide a series expression:

- Type an expression in the field, as shown in Figure 19-8.

Figure 19-8   Typing an expression

- Use Expression Builder to build an expression, as shown in Figure 19-9. You use Expression Builder to build chart expressions in the same way that you use it to build expressions for other report elements, such as data elements.

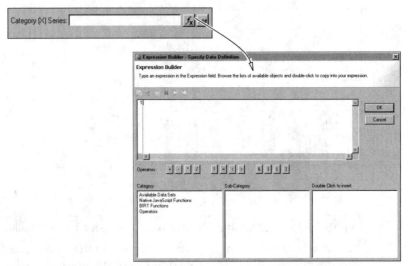

Figure 19-9   Using Expression Builder to supply an expression

- Select a column in the data preview, then drag it to the desired series field, as shown in Figure 19-10. You used this method in the tutorial.

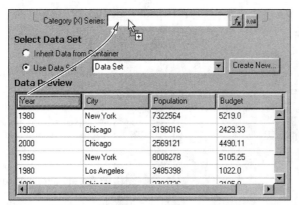

Figure 19-10 Dragging an expression

Formatting the data that an expression returns

An expression can include text, numeric, or date-and-time values. When you use a numeric or a date-and-time expression, you can apply number formatting to the values that the expression returns.

For a numeric expression, you can change the format in the following ways:

- Add a prefix, such as a currency symbol, before the returned values.

- Multiply values by a number, such as 100.

- Add a suffix to a number value, such as the word million.

- Determine the number of decimal places that numbers include.

- Specify a number format pattern, such as #,###, which formats numbers with a thousands separator.

For a date-and-time expression, you can define one or more of the following attributes:

- Type. You can use a standard date-and-time format, including Long, Short, Medium, and Full.

- Details. You can specify that the format is Date or Date and Time.

- Pattern. You can specify a date-and-time format pattern, such as MMMM to show only the month value or dddd to show only the day value, such as Wednesday.

How to format a numeric expression

 1 In the chart builder, to the right of the expression to format, choose Edit Format.

2 From the Data Type drop-down list, choose Number to see the number format options. Figure 19-11 shows the options.

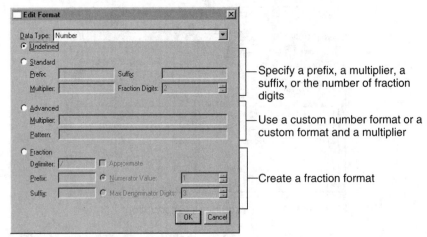

Figure 19-11   Format options for numeric data

3 To add a prefix, multiplier, or suffix, or to specify the number of decimal places to display, select Standard, then specify the format settings:

- To add a number prefix, type the value in Prefix.

- To multiply values by a number, type the number by which to multiply expression values in Multiplier.

- To add a number suffix, type the value in Suffix.

- To specify the number of decimal places to use, select the number in Fraction Digits.

4 To use a custom number pattern, select Advanced, then specify the format settings:

- To multiply values by a number, type the number by which to multiply expression values in Multiplier.

- To specify a number format pattern, type the pattern string in Pattern.

5 To use a custom fraction format, select Fraction, then specify the format settings:

- Specify a delimiter symbol, such as / or :.

- To add a prefix, type the value in Prefix.

- To add a suffix, type the value in Suffix.

- To define guidelines for representing fractions rather than using the default, select Approximate, then provide a suggested numerator or the suggested maximum number of denominator digits. For example, to show fractions with single-digit denominators, such as 1/2 or 3/8, supply 1 as the maximum number of denominator digits.

6   When you finish defining the format, choose OK.

How to format a date-and-time expression

1   In the chart builder, to the right of the expression, choose Edit Format.

2   From the Data Type drop-down list, choose Date and Time to see the date-and-time format options. Figure 19-12 shows the options.

3   To use a predefined date or time format type, select Standard, then specify format options:

   ▪ Select a format value in Type.

   ▪ In Details, select Date or Date and Time.

4   To use a custom format pattern, select Advanced, then type the custom format string in Pattern.

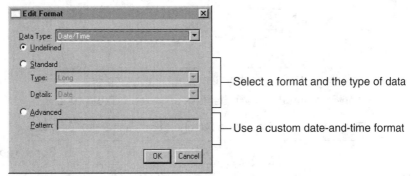

Figure 19-12   Format options for date-and-time data

5   When you finish defining the format, choose OK.

Defining series expressions in different chart types

Each chart type uses series in a different way. For example, the value series in an area chart determines the upper border of a colored area, while the value series in a meter chart determines where a needle appears on a dial. The procedures in this section describe how to set up series expressions in each of the different chart types.

Defining series in an area, bar, or line chart

Area, bar, and line charts use series in similar ways. The category series determines how the chart arranges data on the x-axis. The expression that you choose determines what values the x-axis displays. The value series determines which values the chart plots on the y-axis. Each value series represents a set of data points, such as a colored section of the plot, a set of bars, or a line that connects data points.

To set up multiple sets of data points, such as multiple lines in a line chart or a number of colored plot sections, you can use multiple value series definitions. You can also use a grouping key to set up multiple sets. For example, the chart in Figure 19-13 uses a grouping key to define multiple sets of bars.

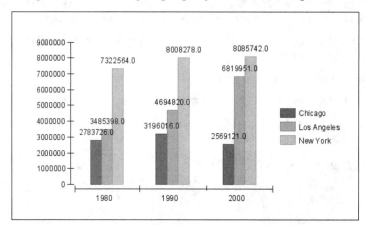

Figure 19-13   Bar chart that uses a grouping key

The data that the chart displays appears in Table 19-2.

Table 19-2   Data for a bar chart that uses a grouping key

Year	City	Population
1980	Los Angeles	3485398
1980	Chicago	2783726
1980	New York	7322564
1990	Los Angeles	4694820
1990	Chicago	3196016
1990	New York	8008278
2000	Los Angeles	6819951
2000	Chicago	2569121
2000	New York	8085742

Figure 19-14 shows the expressions to use to create the chart using data stored in this arrangement. The chart uses the category series expression to plot each year as a section on the x-axis and the values series expression to plot each population value as the top of a bar. The grouping key arranges values for each city in a set of bars of one color. The legend identifies the sets.

Value series expression is
row["Population"]

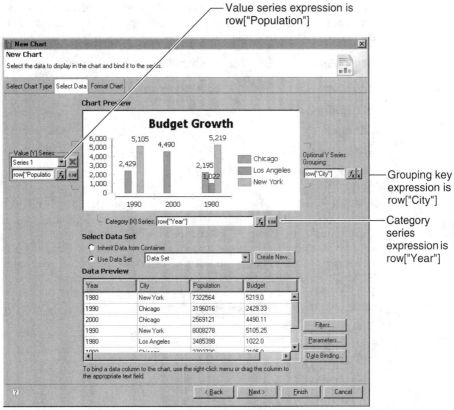

Grouping key
expression is
row["City"]

Category
series
expression is
row["Year"]

Figure 19-14　Data expressions for the bar chart in Figure 19-15

You can also create an area, bar, or line chart that uses multiple value series expressions. Multiple value series expressions enable you to organize all the data from one expression in one set of bars. For example, Figure 19-15 shows a chart with two sets of bars.

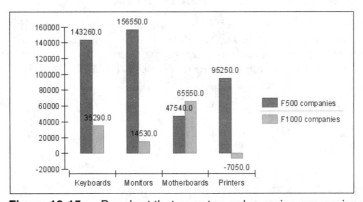

Figure 19-15　Bar chart that uses two value series expressions

The chart in Figure 19-15 shows sales figures for different product categories at Fortune 500 companies and Fortune 1000 companies. The data that the chart displays appears in Table 19-3.

Table 19-3   Data for a bar chart that uses two value series expressions

Category	F500 companies	F1000 companies
Keyboards	143260	35290
Monitors	156550	14530
Motherboards	47540	65550
Printers	95250	–7050

The category series expression is row["Category"]. Each product category is a section on the x-axis. The two value series expressions are row["F500 companies"] and row["F1000 companies"]. The chart shows F500 values as one set of bars and F1000 values as a different set of bars. To provide more than one value series expression, you use the value series drop-down list. Select New Series, then use the expression field to supply the series expression, as shown in Figure 19-16. After you add one or more series, you use the drop-down list to navigate among the value series definitions.

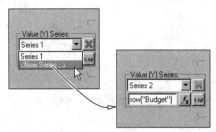

Figure 19-16   Adding a value series expression

Defining series in a meter chart

A meter chart shows a data value as a needle that marks a position on a dial. You can create a chart that shows one or more needles on one dial or one that shows multiple dials, each displaying one needle. You cannot use multiple needles on multiple dials. Figure 19-17 shows two sample meter charts.

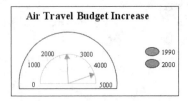
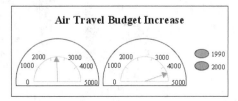

Figure 19-17   Meter charts with one and two meters

The meter value series specifies the needle value. The expression that you choose determines where on the dial the needle appears. To show multiple needles or meters, you can either use multiple meter value series expressions or use a grouping key.

A category series is not essential to a meter chart. You must, however, provide an expression in the category field. You can type a space that is enclosed by quotation marks in this field to satisfy this requirement.

For example, the chart in Figure 19-18 is a standard meter chart. Standard meter charts use only one needle for each meter. The chart uses population as the needle value and city as a grouping field. Because the chart builder requires a value in the category field, the chart designer provided " " as the category expression, even though it does not contribute to the chart.

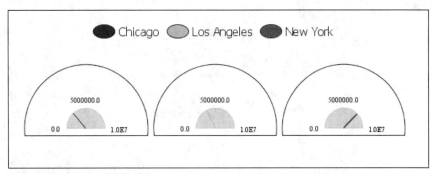

Figure 19-18   Meter chart that uses a grouping key

The chart in Figure 19-18 uses the data in Table 19-4.

Table 19-4   Data for a meter chart that uses a grouping key

City	Population
Chicago	2783726
Los Angeles	3485398
New York	7322564

Figure 19-19 shows the expressions to use to create the chart. The chart uses the meter value series expression to plot each population value as a needle's position on a dial. The chart uses the grouping key to set up a meter for each city. The legend identifies the meters. The category series expression is a blank string, " ".

You can also use multiple series definitions to create multiple meters or a meter with multiple needles. For example, the chart in Figure 19-20 is a superimposed meter chart that shows multiple needles in one meter. One needle shows interior temperature, and the other needle shows exterior temperature.

Meter value expression is
row["Population"]

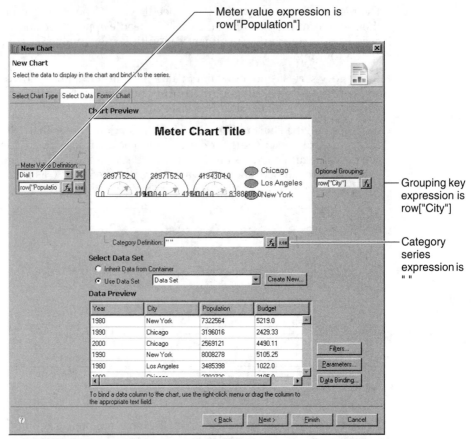

Figure 19-19   Data expressions for the meter chart in Figure 19-18

Grouping key
expression is
row["City"]

Category
series
expression is
" "

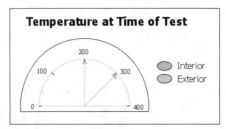

Figure 19-20   Superimposed meter chart

The chart in Figure 19-20 uses the data in Table 19-5.

Table 19-5   Data for a meter chart that uses two meter value expressions

InteriorTemp	ExteriorTemp
201	303

The first meter value series expression is row["InteriorTemp"]. The second meter value series expression is row["ExteriorTemp"]. The chart does not use a grouping key. Because the chart builder requires category field input, the chart designer used a blank expression, " ", in the category field.

To provide more than one meter value series expression, you use the meter value series drop-down list. Select New Series, then use the expression field to supply the series expression, as shown in Figure 19-21. After you add one or more series, you use the drop-down list to navigate among the meter value series definitions.

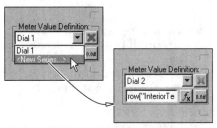

Figure 19-21   Adding a meter value series expression

Defining series in a pie chart

In a pie chart, the category series defines how the chart divides the pie into sectors. The expression that you choose for the category series definition determines which sectors each pie displays. The value series is called a slice size series and determines the size of each sector in a pie. To show multiple pies, you can either use multiple slice size series definitions or use a grouping key that creates multiple pies from the values in one data column.

For example, the pie chart in Figure 19-22 shows product categories as pie sectors and uses sales totals to determine the size of each sector. The entire pie represents total overall sales.

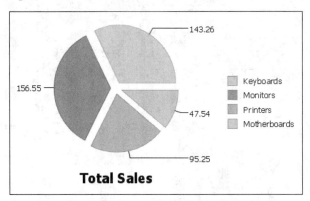

Figure 19-22   Pie chart with one value series

The chart uses the data from the first two columns of Table 19-6.

Table 19-6   Data for a pie chart that uses one or two value series expressions

Category	Value1	Value2
Keyboards	143260	35290
Monitors	156550	14530
Motherboards	47540	65550
Printers	95250	47050

Figure 19-23 shows the expressions to use to create the chart. The chart uses the category series expression to plot each product category as a sector of the pie. To determine the size of a pie sector, the chart uses the slice size expression. The chart legend identifies the sectors. You can also add the legend information to the data labels, as you did in the tutorial earlier in this book.

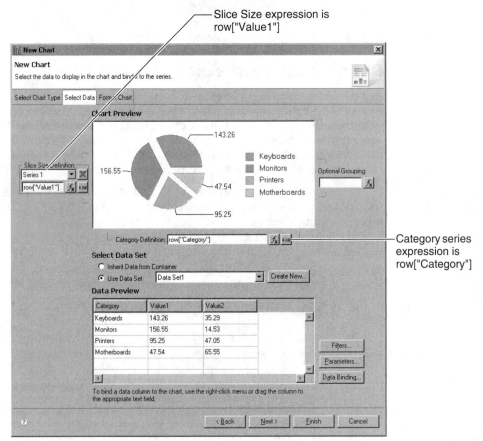

Figure 19-23   Data expressions for the pie chart in Figure 19-22

To display more than one pie, you can use a second slice size series expression. For example, to add data from the Value2 column as a second pie, you use row["Value2"] as a second slice size series. The chart then shows one pie for the Value1 data and one pie for the Value2 data.

To provide more than one slice size expression, you use the slice size series drop-down list. Select New Series, then use the expression field to supply the series expression, as shown in Figure 19-24. After you add one or more series, you use the drop-down list to navigate among the slice size series.

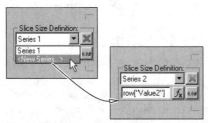

Figure 19-24   Adding a slice size series expression

You can also use a grouping key to show multiple pies. For example, the chart in Figure 19-25 shows a different pie for each year of sales data.

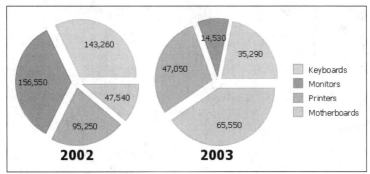

Figure 19-25   Pie chart that uses a grouping key

Table 19-7 shows the data that this chart displays.

Table 19-7   Data for a pie chart that uses a grouping key

Category	Year	Sales
Keyboards	2002	143260
Monitors	2002	156550
Motherboards	2002	47540
Printers	2002	95250
Keyboards	2003	35290
Monitors	2003	14530

(continues)

Table 19-7 Data for a pie chart that uses a grouping key *(continued)*

Category	Year	Sales
Motherboards	2003	65550
Printers	2003	47050

To create a pie for each year and separate each pie into product category sectors, you use the row["Category"] as the category series expression, row["Sales"] as the slice size expression, and row["Year"] as the grouping expression.

Defining series in a scatter chart

A scatter chart displays values along both the x-axis and the y-axis. A scatter chart data point represents the intersection of the two values. To show multiple sets of data points, you can either use multiple value series definitions or use a grouping key. For example, the chart in Figure 19-26 uses one value series to show budget and population values in different school districts in two cities.

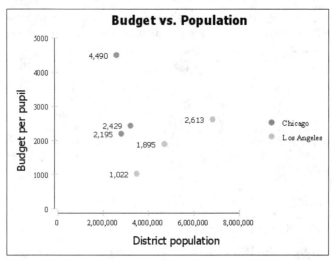

Figure 19-26 Scatter chart that uses one value series

The data for the chart appears in Table 19-8.

Table 19-8 Data for a scatter chart

City	Population	Budget
Los Angeles	3485398	1022
Los Angeles	4694820	1895
Los Angeles	6819951	2613
Chicago	2783726	2195

Table 19-8   Data for a scatter chart *(continued)*

City	Population	Budget
Chicago	3196016	2429
Chicago	2569121	4490

Figure 19-27 shows the expressions to use to set up the chart.

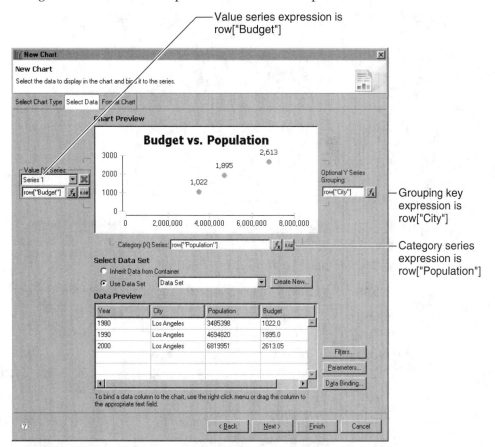

Figure 19-27   Data expressions for the scatter chart in Figure 19-26

The chart uses the value series expression to place the dots on the y-axis and the category series expression to plot the dots along the x-axis. Each dot marks the intersection of a budget and population value. The grouping key creates two sets of dots, one for the districts in Chicago and one for the districts in Los Angeles.

Defining series in a stock chart

In a stock chart, four different value series expressions provide the high, low, open, and close data. The category series expression arranges the values along the x-axis, typically along a date or time scale. To set up multiple sets of candlesticks, you can either define multiple value series definitions or use a grouping key. For example, the stock chart in Figure 19-28 shows stock data for two companies.

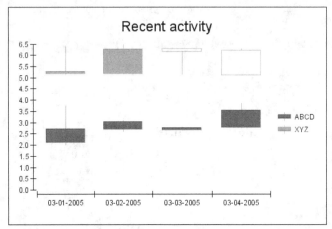

Figure 19-28   Stock chart that uses a grouping key

The data for the chart appears in Table 19-9.

Table 19-9   Data for a stock chart that uses a grouping key

Company Name	DateOf Entry	High	Close	Low	Open
ABCD	3/1/2005	3.77	2.73	2	2.1
ABCD	3/2/2005	3.1	3.04	2.6	2.71
XYZ	3/1/2005	6.41	5.28	5.13	5.19
XYZ	3/4/2005	6.3	5.13	5.13	6.21
XYZ	3/2/2005	6.48	6.26	5.16	5.19
ABCD	3/4/2005	3.86	3.56	2.74	2.79
XYZ	3/3/2005	6.31	6.17	5.14	6.3
ABCD	3/3/2005	2.8	2.78	2.65	2.66

Figure 19-29 shows the expressions to use to create the chart. The chart uses the value series expressions to set up the candlesticks and the category series expression to arrange the candlesticks in chronological order along the x-axis. The grouping key creates one set of candlesticks for each company.

Value series expressions are row["High"],
row["Low"], row["Open"], and row["Close"]

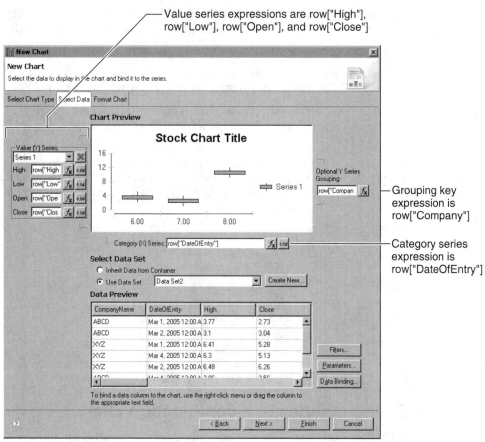

Grouping key
expression is
row["Company"]

Category series
expression is
row["DateOfEntry"]

Figure 19-29   Data expressions for the stock chart in Figure 19-28

You can also use multiple sets of value series expressions to create multiple sets of candlesticks. For example, you can create the same chart using data in a structure that looks similar to Table 19-10.

Table 19-10   Data for a stock chart that uses two sets of value series expressions

DateOf Entry	XYZHigh	XYZLow	XYZOpen	XYZClose	ABCD High
3/1/2005	6.41	5.13	5.19	5.28	3.77
3/2/2005	6.48	5.16	5.19	6.26	3.1
3/3/2005	6.31	5.14	6.3	6.17	2.8

The table must also include fields for ABCDHigh, ABCDLow, and ABCDClose. Using this data, you use the following expressions to set up the chart:

- The category series definition is row["DateOfEntry"].

- The first set of value series expressions uses row["ABCDHigh"], row["ABCDLow"], row["ABCDOpen"], and row["ABCDClose"].

- The second set of value series expressions uses row["XYZHigh"], row["XYZLow"], row["XYZOpen"], and row["XYZClose"].

To define multiple sets of value series expressions in a stock chart, you use the value series drop-down list. Select New Series, then use the expression fields to supply the series expressions, as shown in Figure 19-30. After you add one or more sets of series expressions, you can use the drop-down list to navigate among the value series.

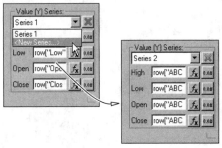

Figure 19-30   Adding a stock chart value series

Defining series in a combination chart

A combination chart displays value series of different types. You must use at least two value series. For example, the chart in Figure 19-31 uses a line chart series and a bar chart series.

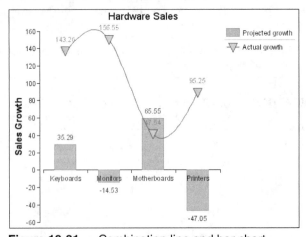

Figure 19-31   Combination line and bar chart

The chart must use multiple value series definitions to define the value series for each chart type. For example, the chart in Figure 19-31 uses one bar chart value series and one line chart value series. Both series use the same category series definition.

You can combine only area, bar, line, and stock chart series in a chart. To create the combination chart, you first create a chart of one type, such as a line chart. Next, you define the series expressions, and then you change the type of one of the series, as described in Chapter 20, "Laying Out and Formatting a Chart."

Sorting category series or base series data

When you create a chart, the category data appears in the order in which the query returns it. You can sort the data so that it appears in a different order on an axis or dial or in a pie. For example, you can show cities along the x-axis in alphabetical order or customer ranks in descending numeric order around a pie. You can sort the data in an ascending or a descending sort order. To sort data, navigate to the category series section of Format Chart, then select Ascending or Descending. Figure 19-32 shows the category series section of Format Chart for a bar chart.

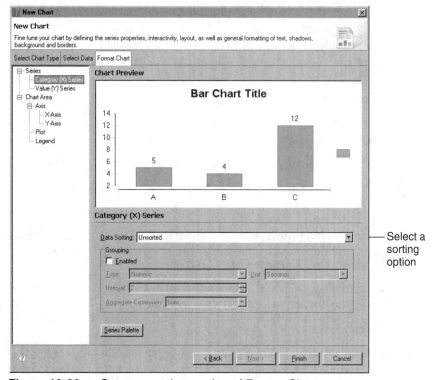

Figure 19-32   Category series section of Format Chart

Grouping category data

You can group category data in a chart. Grouping data enables you to plot chart data using different category values from those that the expression returns. You can group text, numeric, or date-and-time data.

When you group text data, you use an interval to set up the groups. The interval that you choose determines how many rows compose each group. For example, if you use an interval of 20, each group contains 20 rows.

When you group numeric data, you use a value to set up the groups. The value that you choose determines how the chart builder selects rows for a group. The chart builder uses a base value of 1 to create numeric groups. For example, if you use a value of 20, the first group contains rows with values between 1 and 20, the second group contains rows with values between 21 and 40, and so on. If the chart does not include a value in a group section, that section does not appear in the report. If you group order numbers 150–300 using a value of 20, the first group section that appears in the chart is 141–160.

For example, Table 19-11 displays budget data for three cities.

Table 19-11   Data for a chart that uses category series grouping

Year	City	Budget
1998	Los Angeles	3485398
1998	Chicago	2783726
1998	New York	7322564
1999	Los Angeles	4694820
1999	Chicago	3196016
1999	New York	8008278
2000	Los Angeles	6819951
2000	Chicago	2569121
2000	New York	8085742

To group using the Year field, you enable grouping, specify the data type of the field, and define a grouping interval. The data type that you select determines how the chart builder creates the groups:

- If Year is a text field, selecting an interval value of 3 creates three groups. The first group includes the first three rows in the table, the second group contains rows four through six, and the third group contains the last three rows.

When you group text values, you must use a regular grouping interval. You cannot create groups of varied sizes or use a field value to create a group. To create sensible groups in the chart, you must arrange the data in your data source before you create the chart. To use more complicated grouping, you should use your query to group data, then you can use those grouped values in the chart.

- If Year is a numeric field, selecting an interval value of 3 creates two groups. The first group includes the 1998 rows, because grouping by three from a base value of 1 creates one group that ends with 1998. The second group contains the 1999 rows and the 2000 rows.

After you define how to create the groups, you must select an aggregate expression that determines how the chart builder combines the values in each group. You can average or sum the group values.

How to group category series data

Navigate to the category series section of Format Chart. In Grouping, select Enabled to see the grouping options shown in Figure 19-33.

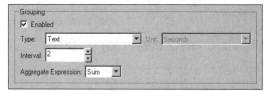

Figure 19-33   Category series grouping options

Use the following options to set up a group:

- In Type, select Text, Numeric, or Date and Time. If you select Date and Time, you can specify the units to use to form the groups, such as Minutes.

- In Interval, select a number that represents the size of the groups to create. For example, to group three-row sequences of text data, select 3. To group numeric data in sections of four, select 4.

- In Aggregate Expression, select the function to use to aggregate the data in the group. You can select Average or Sum.

Working with data on a chart axis

All types of charts except pie and meter charts use an x-axis and at least one y-axis. Pie and meter charts do not use visible axes. Typically, a y-axis is vertical and displays values, and an x-axis is horizontal and displays categories. Figure 19-34 shows the parts of an axis. You can make the following changes to the way axes display data:

- Make an x-axis a value axis so it displays a value scale.

- Change the number format of the divisions and labels on a numerical axis.

- Change the scale of the axis to compress or expand the data.

- Change where an axis intersects an opposing axis.
- Modify the scale of the data an axis displays.
- Add a second y-axis.
- Switch the x- and y-axes, so the x-axis is vertical, and the y-axis is horizontal.

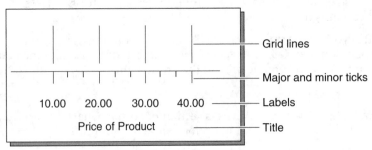

Figure 19-34   Parts of an axis

Understanding value and category axes

Area, bar, line, pie, scatter, and stock charts use two types of axes:

- A value axis positions data relative to the axis marks. The value of a data point determines where it appears on a value axis. You plot numeric and date-and-time data on a value axis. You do not plot text data on a value axis.
- A category axis does not use a value scale. The segments of a category axis are regular and do not correspond to numerical values. Typically, the values on a category axis appear in the order in which they appear in the data source. You can also sort category data in ascending or descending order.

In most charts with axes, the y-axis is a value axis, and the x-axis is a category axis. By default, the x-axis of a scatter chart is a value axis, but you can make it a category axis. Navigate to the x-axis section of Format Chart, then choose Gridlines and select Is Category Axis. Figure 19-35 shows the Gridlines settings.

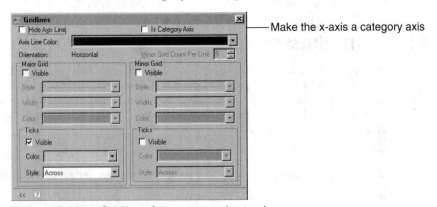

Figure 19-35   Gridlines for a scatter chart axis

Defining the axis data type and number format

The axis data type and format determine how the axis arranges the data that appears on the axis. To set the axis type, you select one of the following settings:

- Linear. A linear axis spaces values evenly. The distance between ticks and the numeric value that the distance represents are regular.

- Logarithmic. A logarithmic axis spaces values on a scale that is based on multiplication rather than addition. Each step on a logarithmic plot is a multiple of 10.

- Date and time. A date-and-time axis shows data on a date or time scale.

- Text. A text axis displays text values only. A text axis spaces values evenly, and the location of a data point on a text axis does not indicate its size or value. Typically, a text axis is a category axis.

On axes that display numeric or date-and-time data, you can set the number format of the axis. The number format determines the format of the axis labels.

How to set the data type and format of an axis

On Format Chart, navigate to the axis section, then use the Type settings to change the data type of the axis. Figure 19-36 shows axis options.

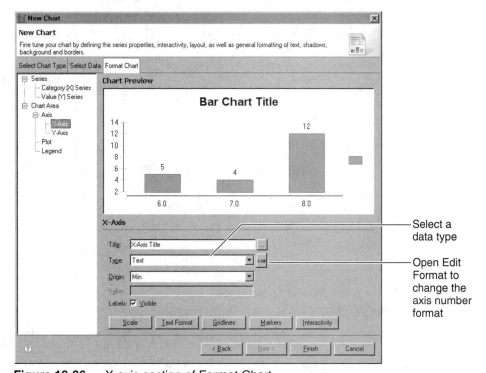

Figure 19-36   X-axis section of Format Chart

Defining where one axis intersects the other

When you set an axis intersection setting, you define at what value the axis joins the opposing axis. You can select one of the following values:

- To have the axis intersect the opposing axis at the opposing axis's minimum value, select Min.

- To have the axis intersect the opposing axis at the opposing axis's maximum value, select Max.

- To have the axis intersect the opposing axis at a value that you specify, select Value.

Typically, a chart displays each axis intersecting the opposing axis at the minimum value. Figure 19-37 shows the results of selecting Min, Max, and Value for the y-axis of a scatter chart.

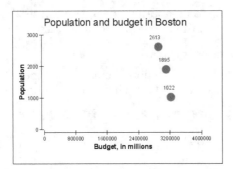

X-axis intersects y-axis at minimum value

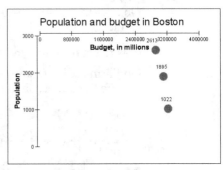

X-axis intersects y-axis at maximum value

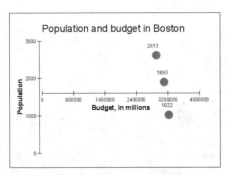

X-axis intersects y-axis at 1500

Figure 19-37   Y-axis intersection options

To set the intersection of an axis, on Format Chart, navigate to the page for that axis. In Origin, select Min, Max, or Value as the intersection setting. If you select Value, you must provide a value at which to join the axes.

Defining the scale of an axis

The scale of an axis determines the range of values that a linear or logarithmic axis displays. When you first create a chart, the chart builder selects a maximum and a minimum axis value to fit the data that the axis displays. Typically, the chart builder selects a minimum value that is just below the lowest axis value and a maximum value that is just higher than the highest axis value, rounding down or up to the nearest major unit, so the markings on the axis span the range of data that it displays.

You can use axis scale to change the following settings:

- The minimum and maximum values for an axis.

- The span between major grid values and the number of minor grid marks between major grid values on the axis. The distance between major grid marks is the step value. The number of minor grid marks is the minor grid count.

For example, in Figure 19-38, the axis on the left shows values from 0 to 1200. The step value is 200, so the major grid marks indicate values of 200, 400, and so on. The minor grid count is five grid marks for each major unit. The axis on the right shows values from 0 to 800. The step value is 100, so the major grid marks indicate 100, 200, and so on. The minor grid count is two grid marks for each major unit.

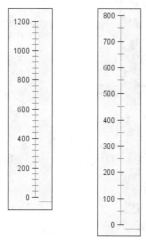

Figure 19-38   Axes using different scale options

You can set the scale of value axes only. Category axes do not support scale changes. The following procedures describe how to set the scale of an x-axis. To set the scale of a y-axis, complete the same steps on the y-axis page. Most scale items appear in the Scale dialog. To set the number of minor grid marks per major unit, you use the Gridlines dialog.

How to define the scale of an axis

On Format Chart, navigate to the section for the axis to modify, then choose Scale. Use the Scale options to change the range and divisions of data on an axis. Figure 19-39 shows the scale options.

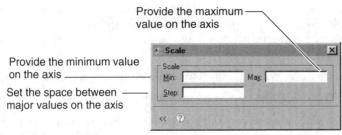

Provide the maximum value on the axis

Provide the minimum value on the axis

Set the space between major values on the axis

Figure 19-39   Scale options

How to define the minor grid count

On Format Chart, navigate to the section for the axis to modify, then choose Gridlines. Use Minor grid count per unit to set the number of minor grid marks between two major grid marks, as shown in Figure 19-40.

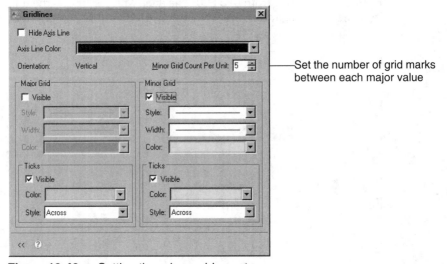

Set the number of grid marks between each major value

Figure 19-40   Setting the minor grid count

Using multiple y-axes

You can use more than one y-axis in a chart. Additional y-axes can use a different scale from the first y-axis. After you add the second axis, you must define the data that appears on that axis. Both y-axes use the same category expression and grouping key. To create a second y-axis, you use Select Chart Type. In Multiple Y Axis, select More Axes. Figure 19-41 shows Select Chart Type.

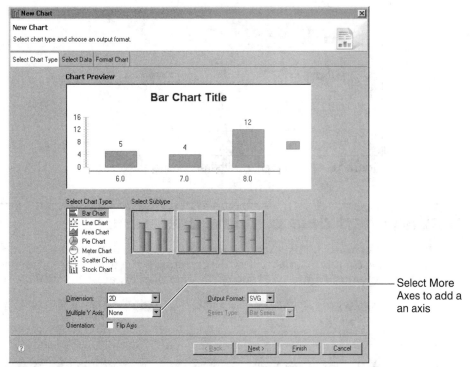

Figure 19-41   Using Select Chart Type to add a y-axis

After you enable multiple axes, you must specify what data the additional axis displays. You must add a series expression for the axis. The category and grouping expressions apply to all y-axes. Figure 19-42 shows how to provide the data expression for the second y-axis.

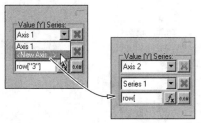

Figure 19-42   Using Chart Data to add data for a second y-axis

Transposing the chart axes

You can switch the chart axes, so the x-axis is vertical and the y-axis is horizontal. Figure 19-43 shows a bar chart with transposed axes. You can transpose the axes of two-dimensional charts and charts with depth. You cannot transpose the axes in a three-dimensional chart. To transpose axes, navigate to Select Chart Type, then select Flip Axis.

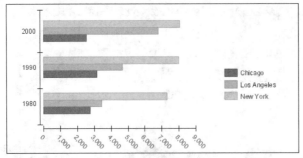

Figure 19-43 Bar chart with transposed axes

Setting chart data preview preferences

As you set up the expressions that specify the data for your chart, you can use the chart builder to review the current chart setup and the available data columns. Figure 19-44 shows the data preview areas for a bar chart.

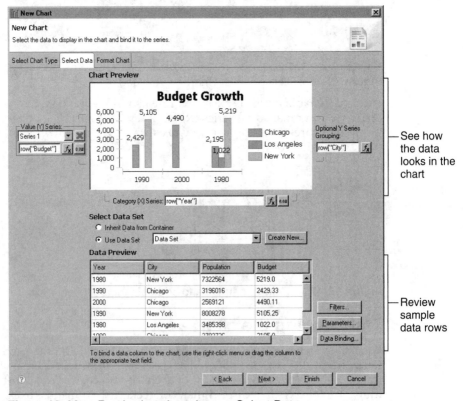

Figure 19-44 Previewing chart data on Select Data

You can change the behavior of the sample chart that the chart builder displays. By default, the sample chart uses data from the data set that you have selected, as in the previous illustration. You can make the chart builder display randomly generated sample data, as in Figure 19-45. For example, if you want to design a chart before you connect to a production data source, you can use this option to see how a chart might appear using the settings that you choose.

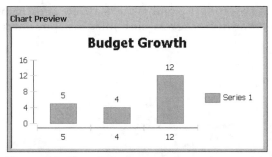

Figure 19-45   Bar chart preview using random data

You can also change the number of data rows that appear in chart builder. By default, the data preview section shows six rows of data. You can display more or fewer rows.

How to change chart preview preferences

1   Choose Window→Preferences.

2   Expand the Report Design list item, then choose Chart to see the options shown in Figure 19-46.

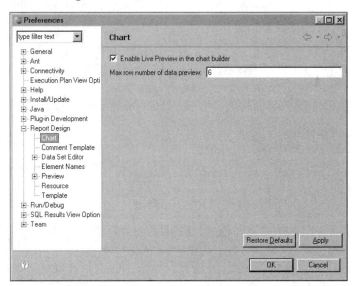

Figure 19-46   Chart page of Preferences

3 To have the chart builder use randomly selected data in the chart preview window, deselect Enable Live Preview.

4 To set the number of rows that Data Preview displays, type a value in the field.

5 Choose Finish.

Now you understand how to set up and manipulate the data that you use in a chart. The next chapter describes how to customize the appearance of a chart.

Chapter

20

Laying Out and Formatting a Chart

Charts include many different visual elements. You can customize the appearance of most chart elements. To clarify the presentation of data or to create a more pleasing composition, you can rearrange the chart layout. For example, you can change where the chart title appears or add padding between a series of bars and the axis on which they are arranged.

You can also change the color and style of the chart parts. For example, you might need to modify a chart to use your company's standard color scheme. You can outline or add a background color to most chart parts, such as the plot, legend, or labels. You can also change the color and shape of the series elements, such as the pies in a pie chart or the candlesticks in a stock chart.

Figure 20-1 identifies some parts of a basic bar chart that uses default settings.

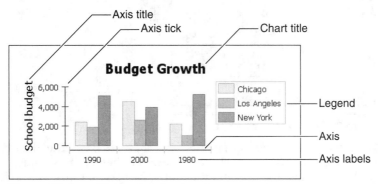

Figure 20-1   Parts of a chart

The titles and markers in Figure 20-1 are typical of most charts. These elements often help users to interpret the information that the chart displays, but you can remove or move them if necessary. You can also add elements, such as gridlines, that extend across the plot or data point labels to show the exact value of each bar. You can make the following types of changes to the chart appearance:

- Laying out and formatting the chart area. You can change the background color or outline of different chart areas or modify the padding between chart areas.

- Formatting an axis. You can adjust the line style of an axis. You can also modify the text style, position, coloring, or outline of axis labels or titles.

- Formatting a series. You can change the type of a series, such as line or bar, and the color or style of the series markers. You can also change attributes that are specific to each series type.

- Using styles to format a chart. You can use the property editor to apply a style to a chart.

Laying out and formatting the chart area

You can adjust the formatting, such as coloring and outlines, of the chart background and peripheral areas. Figure 20-2 shows the chart areas to which you can apply color or line-style formatting or layout changes.

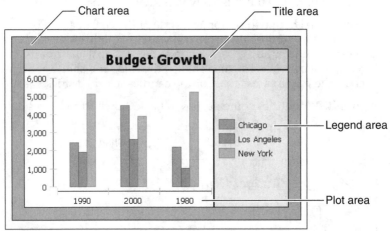

Figure 20-2   Areas of a chart

To change the size and placement of the chart area, the title, the legend, and the plot, you can adjust the inset spaces between them. For example, you can add padding between the title and the plot or increase the size of the chart area without increasing the size of the other areas.

In a chart with depth or a three-dimensional chart, you can also modify the color of the walls and floor, which stretch between the axes. When you first create a chart, the walls and floor are transparent.

Setting the background color for a chart

The chart background can display a standard color, a custom color, a color gradient, or an image. You can also use a transparent background. A transparent background displays the background color of the report page on which it appears.

How to set a chart's background color

1 In the chart builder, choose Format Chart, then navigate to the Chart Area section. Use the list on the left to navigate among sections. Figure 20-3 shows the Chart Area section.

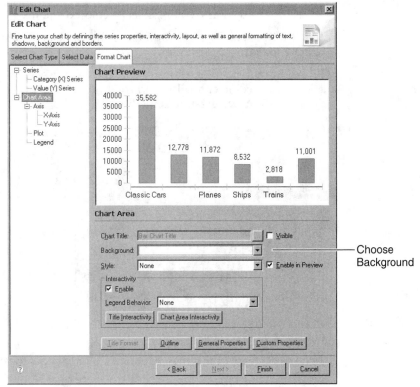

Figure 20-3   Background option in the Chart Area section

2 Choose Background to open the color picker.

Figure 20-4 shows the color picker.

Figure 20-4   Color picker

3 Use the color picker to select a background color or image:

- To use one of the basic colors, select a colored square.

- To use a transparent background, use the Opacity scroll tool to set the opacity to 0, then press Enter.

- To use a gradient color, choose Gradient, then use the gradient editor to select a start color, end color, and rotation for the gradient pattern. Figure 20-5 shows the gradient editor.

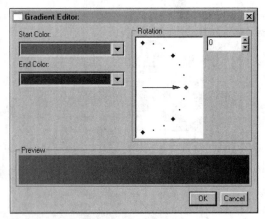

Figure 20-5   Gradient Editor

- To use a custom color, choose Custom Color to show the custom color list, then select a color.

- To use a background image, choose Image, then use Open to navigate to and select the image to use.

The background color or image appears in Background on the chart builder.

4 To apply the color to the chart, choose Finish.

How to define a custom color

On the color picker, choose Define Custom Colors to show the custom color picker, as shown in Figure 20-6.

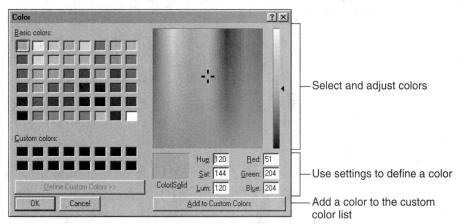

Figure 20-6   Color picker with custom color options

Use the color picker options to select or define a custom color. When you finish, choose Add to Custom Colors, then choose OK.

Outlining a chart

An outline can highlight the chart area. To add an outline, navigate to the Chart Area section of Format Chart, then choose Outline to see the outline options, as shown in Figure 20-7.

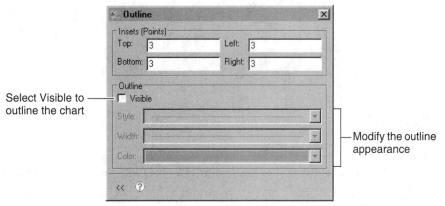

Figure 20-7   Outline

Select Visible to add the outline, then use the Style, Width, and Color fields to change the appearance of the outline.

Setting the wall or floor color of a chart

In a chart with depth or a three-dimensional chart, you can modify the color of the chart wall or floor. The default wall and floor color setting is transparent. Figure 20-8 shows where the wall and floor appear in a sample bar chart with depth.

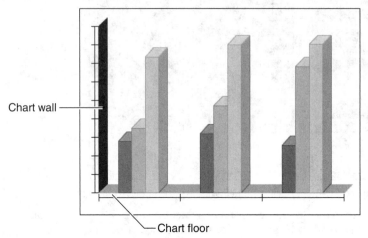

Chart wall

Chart floor

Figure 20-8   Wall and floor of a chart with depth

Figure 20-9 shows where the wall and floor appear in a three-dimensional chart.

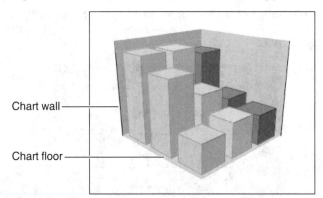

Chart wall

Chart floor

Figure 20-9   Walls and floor of a three-dimensional chart

How to set the wall or floor color of a chart with depth or a three-dimensional chart

Navigate to the Chart Area section of Format Chart, then choose General Properties. Use the settings shown in Figure 20-10 to set a wall or floor color.

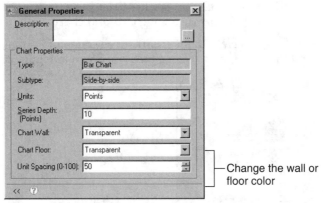

Figure 20-10 Wall and floor color options

Adding padding around the chart

You can change the spacing around a chart area or between two chart areas. The settings around and between chart areas are called inset settings. To add more space, use a higher inset setting. For example, Figure 20-11 shows the effect of using two different chart top inset settings. In the second chart, the top section of the chart area is larger.

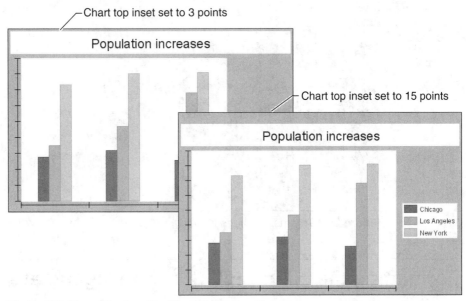

Figure 20-11 Charts with different inset settings

By default, inset values appear in points. To specify chart insets in a different unit, such as pixels, inches, or centimeters, use the chart builder to select the chart unit. The unit that you choose applies to chart settings, such as insets, or the width of series in three-dimensional charts and charts with depth.

To set the chart unit, navigate to the Chart Area section of Format Chart, then choose General Properties and select a unit, as shown in Figure 20-12.

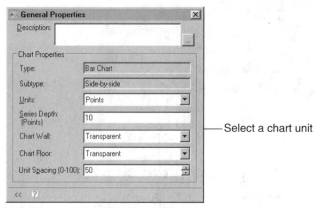

Select a chart unit

Figure 20-12   Chart unit option

How to set chart area insets

Navigate to the Chart Area section of Format Chart, then choose Outline to see inset options, as shown in Figure 20-13. Type a value in one or more of the Insets fields.

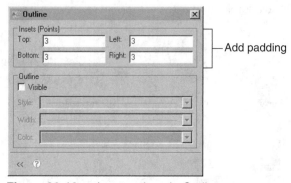

Add padding

Figure 20-13   Inset options in Outline

Formatting the chart plot, title, and legend areas

You can rearrange or format the plot, legend, or title area in a chart. Each area includes a client or text section in which data or text appears. For example, Figure 20-14 shows a chart with the legend area outlined. The text area in the legend uses a colored background.

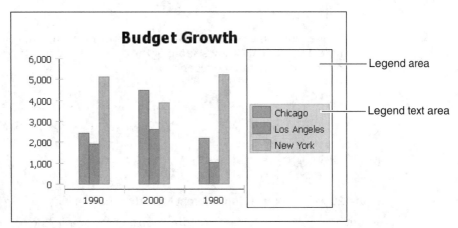

Figure 20-14 Legend areas

You can set the background color and outline attributes of a chart area. To highlight the plot, legend, or title, you can add a shadow behind that area. For example, Figure 20-15 shows a shadow behind title text. A shadow uses basic or custom colors. You cannot use a gradient color as a shadow.

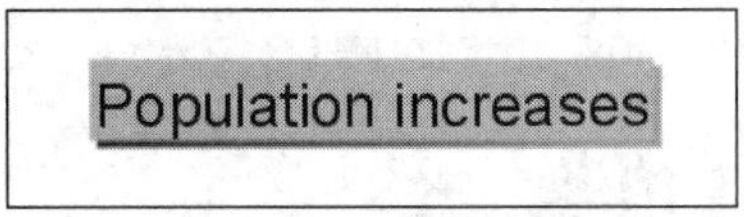

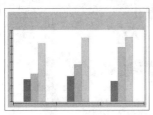

Figure 20-15 Title with shadow

When you create a chart, the chart builder inserts the plot, legend, and title using default placement and size. You can change the location of these chart parts, add inset padding to separate a part from another part, or change the way a part resizes when the chart expands or contracts. You adjust the layout using the following settings:

- Visibility

  To hide a chart area, make the area invisible. For example, Figure 20-16 shows a chart that hides the title and the legend.

![Chart without title or legend]

Figure 20-16 Chart without title or legend

- Anchoring

  To change where the plot, legend, or title appears, change the anchoring. For example, Figure 20-17 shows some of the different anchoring options for the legend text area within the legend area.

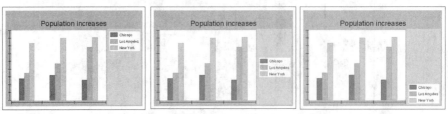

Figure 20-17   Charts using different legend anchor settings

  Anchor positions are based on directions. For example, the first example chart in Figure 20-17 uses North_East.

- Insets

  To adjust the padding around a chart area, modify the inset settings. For example, Figure 20-18 shows the effect of increasing the top inset setting for the plot. The chart on the right uses a higher inset setting, so there is more space between the top of the plot and other chart parts, such as the title.

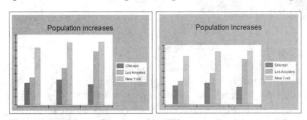

Figure 20-18   Charts with different plot inset settings

  You also use inset settings to modify where the client area or text area appears within a chart area. For example, to change where series markers, such as bars in a bar chart, appear within the plot, change the plot client area insets. Figure 20-19 shows the effect of increasing the left inset for a bar chart plot client area. The chart on the right uses a higher inset setting, so more space appears between the plot client area, where the bars appear, and the edge of the rest of the plot.

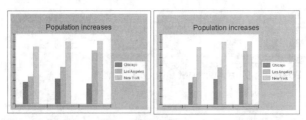

Figure 20-19   Charts with different plot client area inset settings

The following sections describe how to arrange and format the chart plot, legend, and title.

Working with the plot area

When you adjust the plot area, you can modify the entire plot area, which includes the axes, or only the area that appears within the axes. Figure 20-20 shows the two sections of the plot in a sample bar chart. The lighter area shows the area including axes. The smaller, darker area shows the area within the axes. To use one color across the entire plot, you must select that color in both areas.

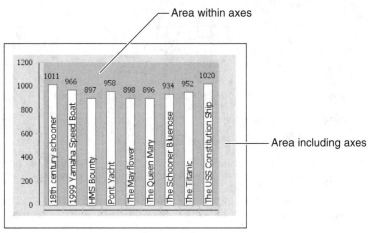

Figure 20-20   Plot areas

Setting the color, outline, or shadow for the plot

The default background color for the plot is transparent. You can also use a standard color, a custom color, a color gradient, or an image. Also, you can outline the plot and change the line color, style, and width. To highlight the plot area within the axes, you can use a shadow, similar to the one in Figure 20-21.

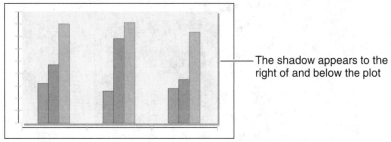

Figure 20-21   Plot with a shadow

The following procedures describe how to set the plot color, outline, or shadow.

How to set a background color for the plot

Navigate to the Plot section of Format Chart. Figure 20-22 shows the Plot section options. Choose Background for either Area Including Axes or Area Within Axes, then use the color picker to select a background color. To apply the color to the plot, choose Finish.

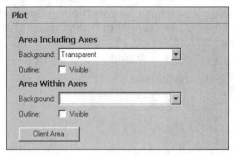

Figure 20-22 Background color options in the Plot section

How to outline the plot area

1 Navigate to the Plot section of Format Chart.

2 Select Visible in Outline for either the Area Including Axes or the Area Within Axes.

3 To change the outline attributes, choose Area Format to see the options shown in Figure 20-23. Use the settings to modify the outline.

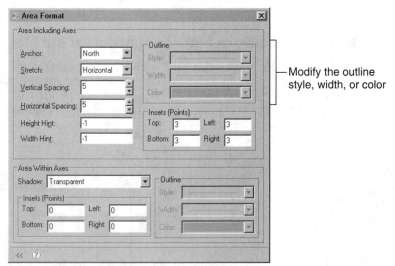

Figure 20-23 Outline options in Area Format

4 When you are done, close Area Format, then choose Finish on the chart builder to save your changes.

How to shadow the plot area within the axes

Navigate to the Plot section of Format Chart, then choose Area Format, which is shown in Figure 20-24. Choose Shadow, then use the color picker to select a shadow color.

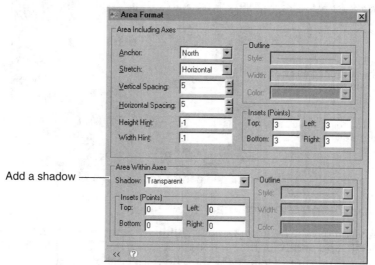

Figure 20-24   Shadow option in Area Format

Placing and adding space around the plot

You can use anchor settings to modify where the plot appears within the chart and inset settings to determine how much padding appears between the plot and other chart features. You can use plot spacing settings to modify the space between the plot area and the chart axes. Plot spacing includes horizontal and vertical settings. For example, Figure 20-25 shows the effect of increasing the horizontal spacing in a bar chart. In the second chart, the space between the horizontal axis and the bottom edge of the plot is much larger.

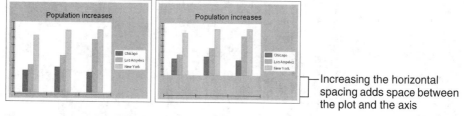

Figure 20-25   Charts with different horizontal plot spacing

How to adjust the placement and padding of a chart plot

Navigate to the Plot section of Format Chart, then choose Area Format to see the options that are shown in Figure 20-26. Use Area Format to modify the padding or spacing settings.

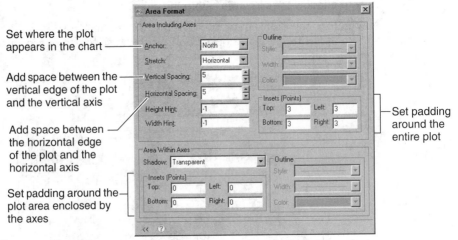

Set where the plot appears in the chart ———

Add space between the vertical edge of the plot and the vertical axis ———

Add space between the horizontal edge of the plot and the horizontal axis

Set padding around the plot area enclosed by the axes

Set padding around the entire plot

Figure 20-26   Placement and padding options in Area Format

Specifying the plot size

You can use the height hint and width hint settings to suggest a minimum height and width for the plot. In most cases, BIRT Report Designer uses the values you supply to size the plot. If you set a plot size that is too large to fit in the chart, or if other chart elements such as the legend or a title are too large to accommodate the suggested plot size, BIRT Report Designer ignores the settings.

A height or width hint is most useful in a report that uses multiple charts, such as a report with different chart elements or a report that includes a chart element in a group section. Because chart sizing is dynamic, one chart element can produce multiple charts with plots of different sizes, as shown in Figure 20-27.

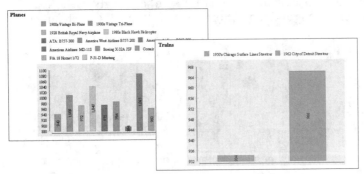

Figure 20-27   Charts created without a height hint

Height and width hints help you to regulate the plot sizes in a group of charts. For example, the illustrations in Figure 20-28 show the result of setting a height hint in a bar chart.

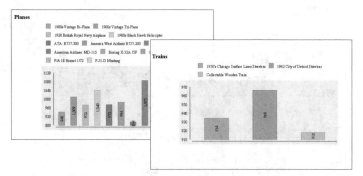

Charts from a design with a height hint are the same height

Figure 20-28   Effect of setting a height hint

To set a height or width hint, navigate to the Plot section of Format Chart, then choose Area Format. Use the settings to provide a value for Height Hint or Width Hint, as shown in Figure 20-29.

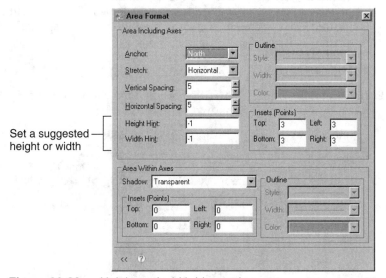

Set a suggested height or width

Figure 20-29   Height and width hint settings

Working with the chart title

When you first create a chart, it displays a title using default text. The title uses a transparent background and does not include an outline or a shadow.

To hide or change the title text, navigate to the Chart Area section of Format Chart. Figure 20-30 shows the Chart Area options. Type a new title in the text box. To hide the title, deselect Visible.

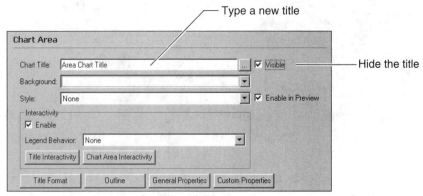

Figure 20-30   Chart title options in the Chart Area section

Formatting title text

You can modify the appearance of the title text. For example, you can change the font, size, color, style, or alignment of the text. You can also set the format to strike through text or change the rotation of the title to display text at an angle.

How to modify title text

1   Navigate to the Chart Area section of Format Chart.

2   To format the title, choose Title Format, then choose Invoke Font Editor to open the font editor, as shown in Figure 20-31.

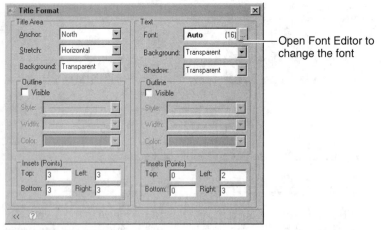

Figure 20-31   Title Format

3 Use the font editor settings shown in Figure 20-32 to modify the font.

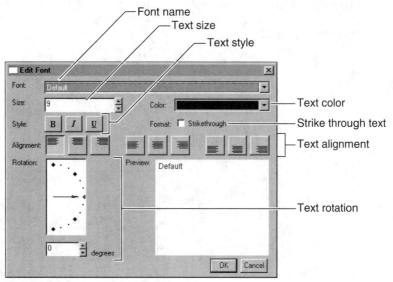

Figure 20-32 Font Editor

4 To accept your changes, choose OK, close Title Format, and choose Finish on the chart builder.

Setting a background color, outline, or shadow for the title

When you apply a background color or outline to a chart title, you can work with the entire title area or with only the text area. Figure 20-33 shows the difference between the two areas in a sample chart. If you apply a background color to the title area, the same color appears in the text area unless you set a new background color for the text. You can add a shadow only to the text area. You cannot shadow the entire title area.

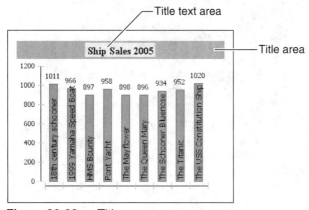

Figure 20-33 Title areas

To add a background color, outline, or shadow to the chart title, navigate to the Chart Area section of Format Chart, then choose Title Format to see the options that are shown in Figure 20-34. Use the settings to modify the entire title area or only the text area.

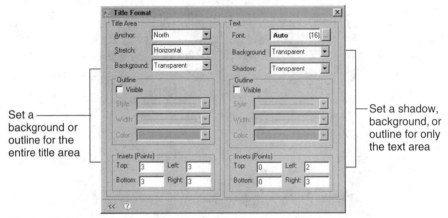

Set a background or outline for the entire title area

Set a shadow, background, or outline for only the text area

Figure 20-34   Color, outline, and shadow options in Title Format

Placing or adding padding around a chart title

You can use anchor settings to modify where the title appears within the chart. To determine how much padding appears between the title or title text areas and other chart features, use the inset settings.

To adjust the placement and padding of a chart title, navigate to the Chart Area section of Format Chart, then choose Title Format to see the options shown in Figure 20-35. Use the settings to adjust the title.

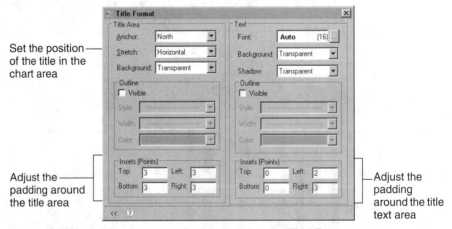

Set the position of the title in the chart area

Adjust the padding around the title area

Adjust the padding around the title text area

Figure 20-35   Placement and padding options in Title Format

Working with the legend

By default, a chart displays a legend. The legend uses a transparent background and does not include an outline or a shadow. To highlight the legend area, you can add a background color, outline, or shadow. You can hide the legend or change its position in the chart area, and you can add a legend title or modify legend-text properties, such as the font size.

Setting the color, outline, or shadow for the legend

When you apply a background color or outline to a chart legend, you can work with the entire legend area or with the text area only. Figure 20-36 shows the difference between the two areas in a sample chart. If you apply a background color to the legend area, the color also appears in the text area, unless you set a background color in the text area that overrides the legend-area settings. You can add a shadow only to the text area. You cannot shadow the entire legend area.

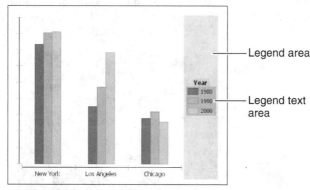

Figure 20-36   Legend areas

How to set the background color of a legend

To set the background color of the legend text area, use the Legend section of Format Chart. Figure 20-37 shows the Legend section options.

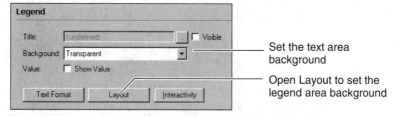

Figure 20-37   Background options in the Legend section

To set the background color of the entire legend area, choose Layout from the Legend section, then use Layout Legend, as shown in Figure 20-38.

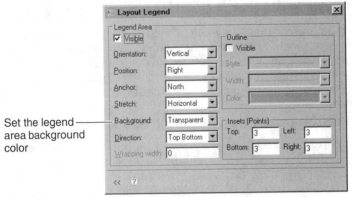

Set the legend
area background
color

Figure 20-38   Background option in Layout Legend

How to add an outline or a shadow to a legend

To outline or shadow the legend text area, navigate to the Legend section of
Format Chart, then choose Text Format. Use the settings on Format Legend Text
to add an outline or shadow, as shown in Figure 20-39.

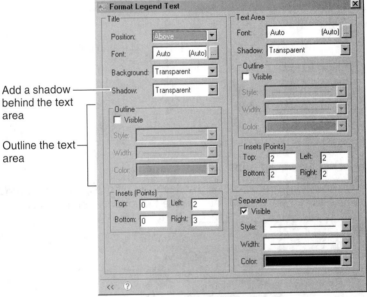

Add a shadow
behind the text
area

Outline the text
area

Figure 20-39   Shadow and outline options on Format Legend Text

To add an outline to the legend area, navigate to the Legend section of Format
Chart and choose Layout, then use the settings on Layout Legend to add or
modify the outline, as shown in Figure 20-40.

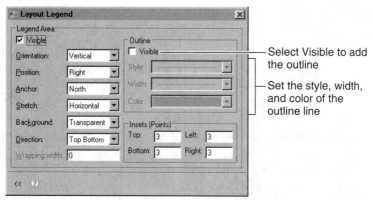

Figure 20-40   Outline options in Layout Legend

Hiding a legend

To hide the legend, navigate to the Legend section of Format Chart, then choose Layout. Deselect Visible, as shown in Figure 20-41.

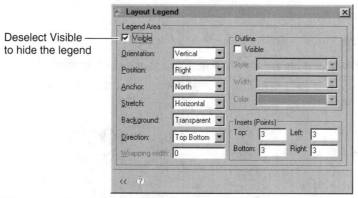

Figure 20-41   Visible option on Layout Legend

Placing and adding space around a legend

You use anchor settings to modify where the legend appears within the chart. To determine how much padding appears between the legend or legend text areas and other chart features, use the inset settings.

To adjust the position of the entire legend area, rather than the client area where the legend items appear, change the legend-position setting. You position a legend relative to the plot. For example, Figure 20-42 shows different legend positions in a sample chart.

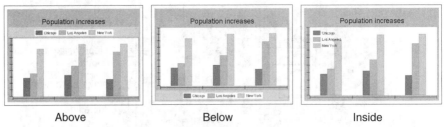

| Above | Below | Inside |

Figure 20-42   Legend positions

You can also organize legend items within the legend client area. For example, in Figure 20-43, the chart on the left shows legend items arranged horizontally. The chart on the right shows legend items arranged vertically. To adjust the positions of legend items in the legend-client area, set the legend orientation.

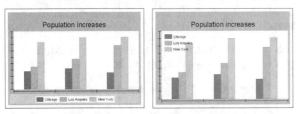

Figure 20-43   Horizontal and vertical legend orientation

How to adjust the placement and padding of a chart legend

Navigate to the Legend section of Format Chart, then choose Layout. Use the settings on Layout Legend to pad or place the legend, as shown in Figure 20-44.

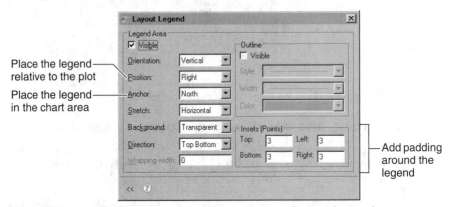

Figure 20-44   Placement and padding options on Layout Legend

How to arrange legend items horizontally or vertically

Navigate to the Legend section of Format Chart, then choose Layout. Select an option in Orientation, as shown in Figure 20-45.

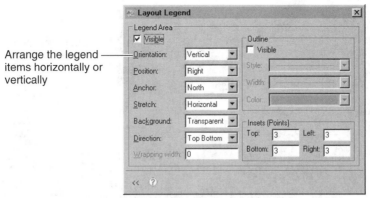

Arrange the legend items horizontally or vertically

Figure 20-45   Orientation option on Layout Legend

Showing series item values in a legend

In a legend, you can display the value of a series item as well as the item name. To add value information to a legend, navigate to the Legend area of Format Chart, then select Show Value, as shown in Figure 20-46.

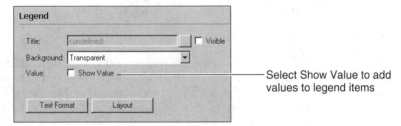

Select Show Value to add values to legend items

Figure 20-46   Adding values to legend text

Formatting the text that appears in the legend

You can change the font style and size of the legend text. If you use more than one series, you can add a separator line between the items in one series and the items in the next. You can also enable text wrapping. To wrap legend text, you specify a maximum width for legend items. Items that extend beyond the wrapping width appear on multiple lines in the legend.

How to wrap legend text

Navigate to the Legend section of Format Chart and choose Layout. On Layout Legend, provide a Wrapping Width value to determine the maximum width for legend items.

How to format the legend text

Navigate to the Legend section of Format Chart and choose Text Format, then choose Invoke Font Editor to open the font editor, as shown in Figure 20-47. Use the font editor to modify the font attributes.

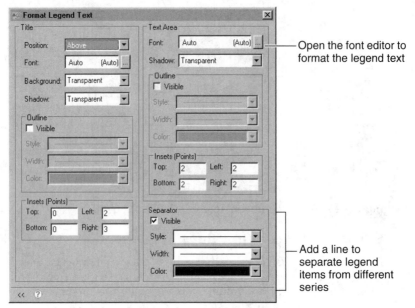

Open the font editor to format the legend text

Add a line to separate legend items from different series

Figure 20-47   Font Editor button on Format Legend Text

Adding a legend title

You can use a title for the chart legend. When you first add the title, it uses default font settings and appears above the list of legend items. You can change the font style and color of the title. You can also add a title outline, background color, or shadow, or position the title below, to the left, or to the right of the legend text.

How to add and format the title of the legend

Navigate to the Legend section of Format Chart. Figure 20-48 shows the Legend section options. Select Visible to show the title, then type the title text.

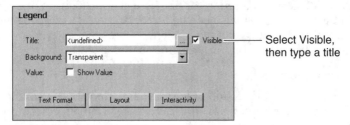

Select Visible, then type a title

Figure 20-48   Title options in the Legend section

To format the title, choose Text Format. Then use the settings that are shown in Figure 20-49 to modify the title position or appearance.

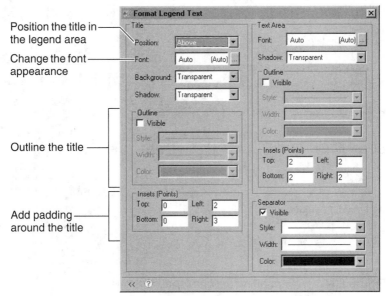

Position the title in the legend area

Change the font appearance

Outline the title

Add padding around the title

Figure 20-49   Title formatting options on Format Legend Text

Formatting an axis

When you format an axis, you work with titles, markers, lines, and labels. You can hide or reposition an axis element. For example, you can delete the title for an axis or move the axis tick marks. You can also change the color or style of an element, add an outline, or change the padding.

Working with an axis title

In an area, bar, line, scatter, or stock chart, you can add an x-axis or y-axis title. Navigate to the Format Chart section for the axis, as shown in Figure 20-50, then provide the title text. After you add a title, you can modify the title position, outline, padding, or text style. Navigate to the Format Chart section for the axis, and choose Text Format to see the options in Figure 20-51. Select Visible, then position and format the text.

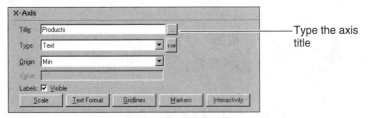

Type the axis title

Figure 20-50   Title field in an axis section

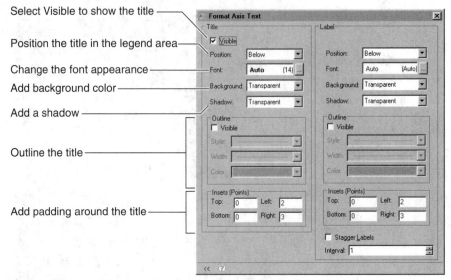

Select Visible to show the title

Position the title in the legend area

Change the font appearance

Add background color

Add a shadow

Outline the title

Add padding around the title

Figure 20-51 Formatting options for an axis title

Working with axis markers

Axis markers highlight numbers or ranges on two-dimensional charts or charts with depth. You can use the following types of markers:

- A marker line is a line that extends across the plot from a point on the axis. You specify on what axis and from what value to draw the line.

- A marker range is a rectangular area that highlights a range of values. You specify on what axis and between what values to draw the rectangle.

For example, Figure 20-52 shows a marker line and a marker range. Both markers highlight points on the y-axis. The marker line uses a label to show the marker value. You can change the style or color of the marker, change label text, or hide labels. You should only add a marker to an x-axis if it shows numeric or date-and-time data. Adding a marker to an axis that shows text values as categories does not help users read the chart.

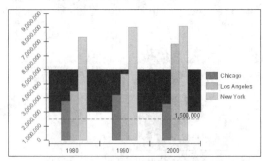

Figure 20-52 Chart with a marker line and a marker range

Adding an axis marker

To create and format an axis marker, you use Markers. Navigate to the Format Chart section for the axis to which you want to add a marker, then choose Markers to see the options shown in Figure 20-53.

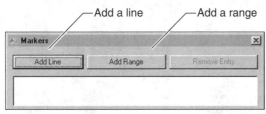

Figure 20-53   Adding a marker line or range

To create a marker line, choose Add Line. The marker appears in the marker list, as shown in Figure 20-54. In Value, type the value at which the line should start. To create an axis marker range, choose Add Range, then set the span of values the marker covers. In Start Value, type the value at which to begin the range. In End Value, type the value at which to end the range.

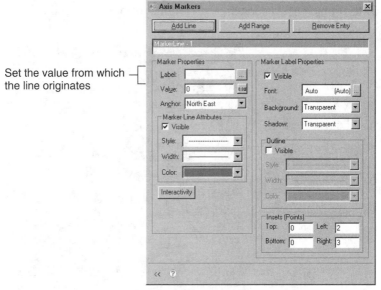

Figure 20-54   Markers with a marker line

Formatting axis markers

When you first create a marker, the marker uses default formatting and displays a label to identify the axis point or range that the marker highlights. You can adjust the attributes of a marker line, or change the fill color or outline of a marker range. You can also hide or format the label. To format a marker line, use the line-format settings, which are shown in Figure 20-55.

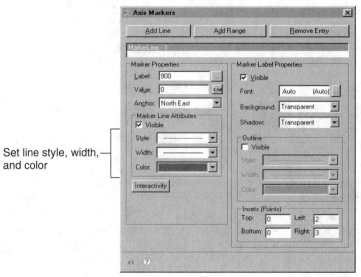

Figure 20-55 Marker line formatting options

To format a marker range, use the range format settings that are shown in Figure 20-56.

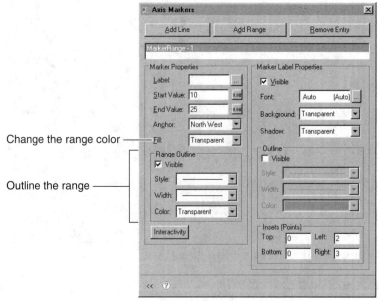

Figure 20-56 Marker range formatting options

To hide or format a marker label, select the name of the line or range to format in the marker list, then use the settings to modify the label text, as shown in Figure 20-57.

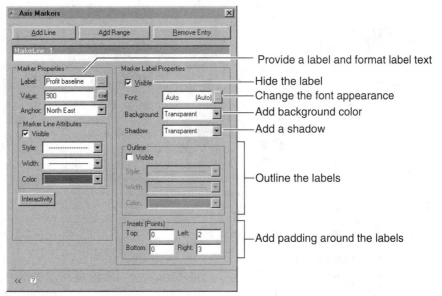

Figure 20-57   Marker label options

Working with an axis line

When you first create a chart with axes, the axes use default line styles. You can modify the line style of an axis. Tick marks, which highlight points on the axis, also use default line styles and colors. You can modify the line style and position of the axis tick marks. Major ticks mark large intervals on the axis. Minor ticks mark smaller intervals. Typically, when you first create a chart, the axes use major ticks that are positioned across an axis. You can also position ticks to the left or right of a vertical axis or above or below a horizontal axis. Figure 20-58 shows different tick settings for a y-axis.

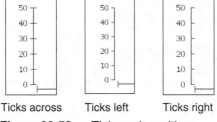

Figure 20-58   Tick mark positions

You can also add gridlines, which extend from an axis and span the plot area. For example, Figure 20-59 shows a chart that uses y-axis gridlines to clarify the data points. When you add major or minor gridlines to an axis, the chart includes a gridline for each major or minor interval on the axis.

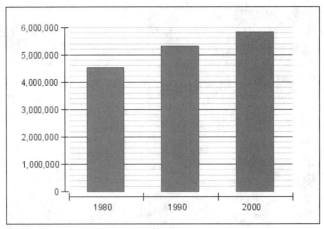

Figure 20-59   Y-axis gridlines

How to modify an axis line

Navigate to the Format Chart section for the axis, then choose Gridlines. Use the Gridlines settings to format the axis line, as shown in Figure 20-60.

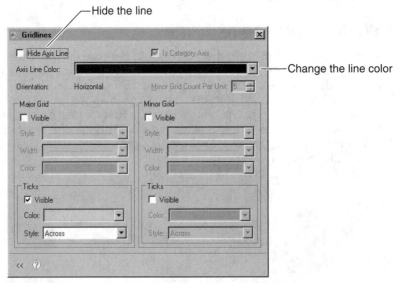

Figure 20-60   Axis line formatting options

How to modify axis tick marks

Navigate to the Format Chart section for the axis, then choose Gridlines. Use the Gridlines settings to format the tick marks, as shown in Figure 20-61. You can modify major or minor tick mark settings.

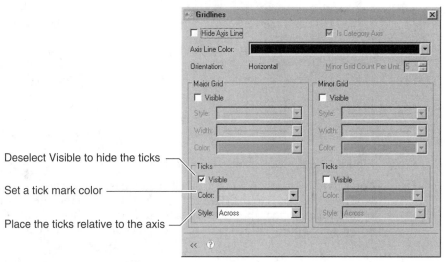

Deselect Visible to hide the ticks

Set a tick mark color

Place the ticks relative to the axis

Figure 20-61   Tick mark options

How to add or modify gridlines

Navigate to the Format Chart section for the axis, then choose Gridlines. Use the settings to add or change the axis gridlines, as shown in Figure 20-62. You can modify major or minor division settings.

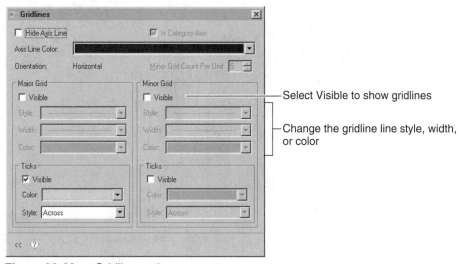

Select Visible to show gridlines

Change the gridline line style, width, or color

Figure 20-62   Gridline options

Working with axis labels

By default, a chart displays labels to the left of a vertical axis and below a horizontal axis, as shown in Figure 20-63.

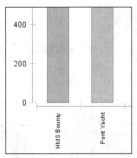

Figure 20-63   Default axis label positions

You can hide or reposition the labels on an axis. For example, you can show the labels on the y-axis to the right of the axis rather than the left, or rotate the labels on the x-axis so that they are easier to read. You can also modify the label font; add a background color, shadow, or outline; or change the padding around the labels.

Sometimes, a chart displays so many values on an axis that the label text overlaps and becomes illegible. In this case, the chart builder drops some of the axis labels. Figure 20-64 shows a chart in which labels have dropped. In the chart, only three of four x-axis labels appear. The chart dropped the second label, because it overlapped the neighboring labels.

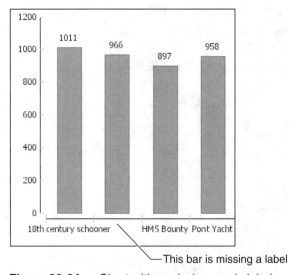

Figure 20-64   Chart with a missing x-axis label

To fix this problem, you can rotate the labels or stagger them, so they do not overlap. Figure 20-65 shows the two solutions on an x-axis. In the chart on the left, the chart developer rotated the x-axis labels to fit all the labels in the space. The chart on the right uses staggered labels to display all axis categories.

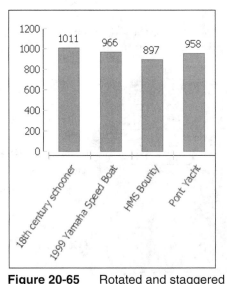
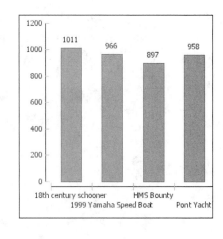

Figure 20-65 Rotated and staggered x-axis labels

You can also skip labels. For example, in Figure 20-66, the chart on the left shows all labels. The chart on the right skips every other label. To skip labels, set the interval at which labels should appear. For example, to show every other label, use an interval of 2. To show every fifth label, use an interval of 5.

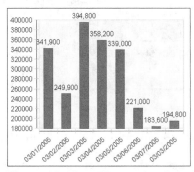
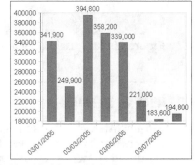

Figure 20-66 Charts showing all labels and skipped labels

To hide the axis labels, navigate to the Format Chart section for the axis, then deselect Visible. Figure 20-67 shows the Format Chart options for an axis.

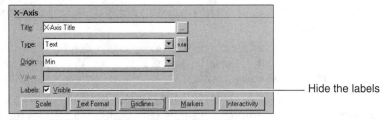
Hide the labels

Figure 20-67 Visible option for axis labels

How to format axis labels

Navigate to the Format Chart section for the axis, then choose Text Format. Use the Text Format options to update the position or style of the labels, as shown in Figure 20-68.

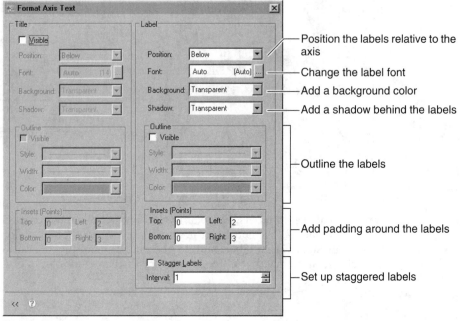

Figure 20-68 Axis label formatting options

Formatting a series

Most charts use value series of the same series type. For example, you can display three value series as three lines on a line chart. To create a combination chart that shows different series types in the same chart, you change the type of a series. You can also hide a series, so the chart includes data for that series but does not display it.

Some series changes apply to series of all chart types:

- In value or category series of all chart types, you can set the color palette that series items use.

- To value series of all chart types, you can add a trendline. You can also add a trendline to the category series in a scatter chart, because a scatter chart category series displays values.

Otherwise, the type of series determines what formatting options you can apply for that series. For example, in a series with depth, you can set the depth of the series, such as the depth of bars in a bar chart with depth. In a pie chart, you can explode the pie sectors from the center of the pie or add a pie sector outline.

To identify the data points in a series, you use data point labels. You format data point labels as you do other labels, specifying the position, style, outline, and insets settings. You can also determine which data the labels display and select a number or text format.

Setting the series type

You can change the type of a value series in an area, bar, line, or stock chart. To change all the value series in a chart, change the chart type. To create a combination chart that displays value series of different types, you change the type of one of the series. You can combine only area, bar, line, and stock-chart series in a chart. To change the type of a series, navigate to the Series section of Format Chart, and select a new series type, as shown in Figure 20-69.

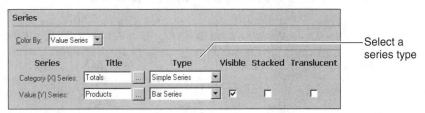

Select a series type

Figure 20-69   Series type option in the Series section

Hiding a series

You can hide a series in a chart. A hidden series contributes data but does not appear in the chart. For example, you might want to use a series to contribute to a trendline without displaying the series data points. Typically, you hide a value series rather than a category series.

To hide a series, navigate to the Series section of Format Chart, and deselect Visible for the series, as shown in Figure 20-70.

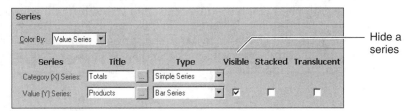

Hide a series

Figure 20-70   Visible option in the Series section

Making a series translucent

You can make a chart series translucent so you can see an image or color behind the chart data. For example, Figure 20-71 shows two versions of a chart that uses an image as the plot background. The chart on the left uses a solid series. The chart on the right uses a translucent series.

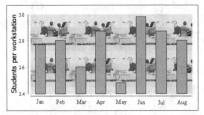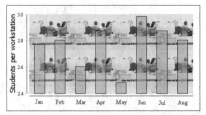

Figure 20-71   Bar chart with an opaque series and a translucent series

To make a series translucent, navigate to the Series section of Format Chart, and select Translucent for the series.

Setting the color palette for a series

You can specify which colors a series uses. Charts with axes, such as line and stock charts, use varied colors to distinguish between different value series. When a bar chart uses more than one set of bars, the default behavior is to show each set in a different color. If a bar chart uses only one set of bars, the bars are the same color. Figure 20-72 shows charts using the default settings.

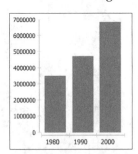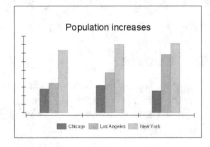

Figure 20-72   Default series colors

In charts with axes, you can choose to color the chart by category series instead. This is useful when you have only one value series, but you want to show variously colored series elements, as in the chart in Figure 20-73. The chart uses one value series but shows each bar in the series in a different color. Note that coloring the chart by category series also displays the category series items, rather than the value series items, in the legend.

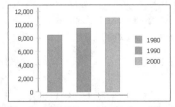

Figure 20-73   Varied colors in a chart with one value series

Pie charts and meter charts work differently. By default, a bar or a meter chart varies the category series colors to show each pie sector or needle in a different color, as shown in Figure 20-74.

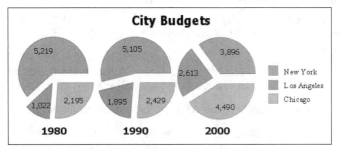

Figure 20-74   Pie chart colored by value series

Coloring by category series enables you to show all the sectors in a pie or all the needles on a meter in the same color. For example, Figure 20-75 shows a similar pie chart, colored by category series.

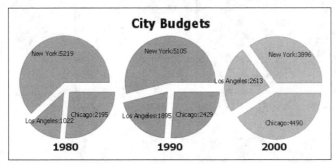

Figure 20-75   Pie chart colored by category series

To determine which data the legend displays, navigate to the Series section of Format Chart, then use Color By to select Value Series or Categories, as shown in Figure 20-76.

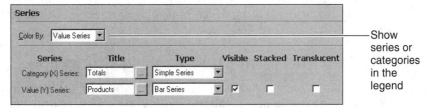

Figure 20-76   Color By option in the Series section

When you create a chart, it uses default colors for series elements. To select different colors, you modify the series palette. The chart uses the colors that you select in the order in which they are in the palette list. If the chart displays more series elements than there are colors in the palette, it uses some colors more than once.

How to specify the palette for a category series

Navigate to the Category Series section of Format Chart, then choose Series Palette to see the options that are shown in Figure 20-77. Use the settings to modify the series palette:

- To add a new color, select the color drop-down list to the right of Add, and use the color picker to select or create a color. When you finish, choose Add.

- To remove a color, select the color in the list, and choose Remove.

- To modify a color, select it, then use the color picker to select or create a color.

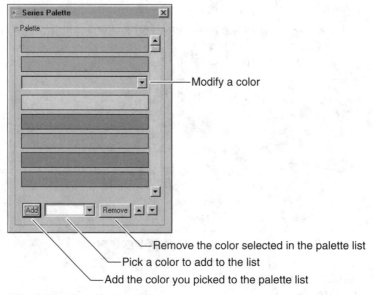

Figure 20-77   Series Palette

When you finish adjusting the color palette, close Series Palette, then choose Finish in the chart builder.

Adding and formatting a curve-fitting line

A curve-fitting line is a graphical representation of a trend in data. You can use a curve-fitting line to detect patterns in data or to predict future values. For example, the chart in Figure 20-78 uses curve-fitting lines to highlight population trends in several cities. You can use the trendlines to estimate population in the years after 2000. The population for Los Angeles, for example, is growing sharply, while the population in New York has increased less dramatically.

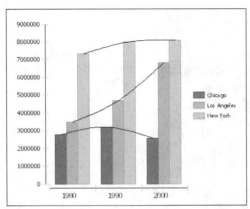

Figure 20-78   Chart with curve-fitting lines

You use curve-fitting lines in two-dimensional and two-dimensional with depth area, bar, line, scatter, and stock charts. You cannot use curve fitting with a three-dimensional chart. A curve-fitting line in a BIRT chart places each curve-fitting point based on two factors:

- The location of the neighboring data points

- A weight function that takes into account all the data points that the curve-fitting line includes

A curve-fitting line can look very different depending on the span and amount of data that you use. Before adding curve fitting to your chart, ensure you have enough data to show a meaningful trend.

To add a curve-fitting line, navigate to the Value Series section of Format Chart, then select Show Curve Fitting Line, as shown in Figure 20-79. By default, a curve-fitting line uses a thin black line. You can change the line style or color.

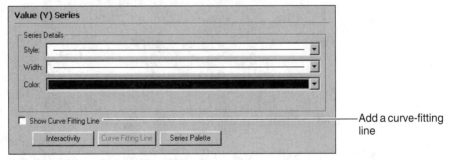

Add a curve-fitting line

Figure 20-79   Show curve-fitting line option

How to format a curve-fitting line

Navigate to the Value Series section of Format Chart, and choose Curve Fitting Line, then use the settings to change the style, width, or color of the line, as shown in Figure 20-80.

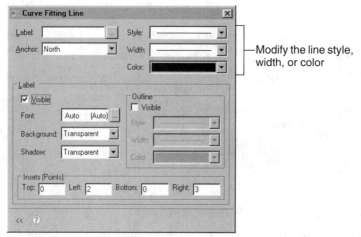

Modify the line style, width, or color

Figure 20-80   Formatting options for a curve-fitting line

How to add labels to a curve-fitting line

Navigate to the Value Series section of Format Chart, and choose Curve Fitting Line. In Label, select Visible, then use the settings on Curve Fitting Line to format the labels, as shown in Figure 20-81.

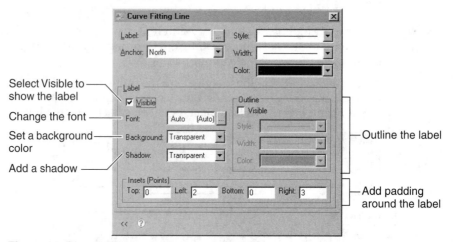

Select Visible to show the label

Change the font

Set a background color

Add a shadow

Outline the label

Add padding around the label

Figure 20-81   Label options for a curve-fitting line

Stacking series

You can stack the value series that you display in a chart. In a stacked chart, the data points from one value series are arranged on top of the data points of another series. Stacking helps to show each data point's contribution to the total of all the data points in a category.

You can stack only area, bar, and line series. To stack a series, navigate to the Series section of Format Chart, then select Stacked for the series.

Working with different series types

Different series types offer different formatting options. The procedures in this section describe how to modify the formatting of series with depth; three-dimensional series; and area, bar, line, scatter, meter, pie, and stock series.

To tell what type of series a chart uses, use the Series section of Format Chart. For example, in Figure 20-82, the Series section shows that a chart uses a standard series, called a simple series, for categories and a bar series for values. You can use the Type drop-down list to change the type of a series.

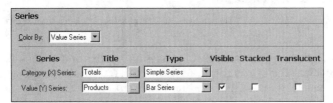

Figure 20-82   Series information in the Series section

Setting the series depth of a chart with depth or a three-dimensional chart

In a chart with depth or a three-dimensional chart, you can specify how far back the chart markers stretch. For example, you can specify the depth of lines in a three-dimensional line chart. You set the series depth in the chart unit, such as points.

How to set the depth of series elements in a chart with depth

Navigate to the Chart Area section of Format Chart, then choose General Properties. Provide a value in Series Depth, as shown in Figure 20-83.

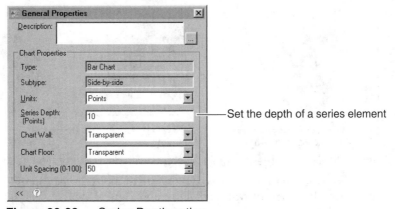

Set the depth of a series element

Figure 20-83   Series Depth option

Formatting a three-dimensional chart

When you format a three-dimensional chart, you can use axis rotation to change the orientation of the chart or use unit spacing to set the space between series.

Working with chart rotation

You can rotate the axes of a three-dimensional chart. When you rotate axes, you use the following settings:

- The x-axis rotation controls how the chart tilts toward or away from the viewer.

- The y-axis rotation controls how the chart pivots left and right on the y-axis in the center of the chart.

- The z-axis rotation controls how the chart tilts up and down on the central z-axis.

By default, a three-dimensional chart uses an x-axis rotation of –20, a y-axis rotation of 45, and a z-axis rotation of zero. A chart that uses default rotation settings appears oriented like the one shown in Figure 20-84.

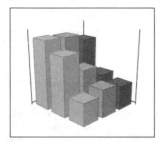

Figure 20-84   Three-dimensional chart using default axis rotation

Figure 20-85 shows the effects of changing each setting in the sample chart.

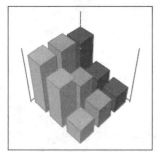  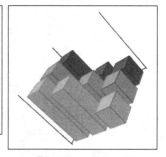

X rotation set to –45   Y rotation set to –45   Z rotation set to –45

Figure 20-85   Three-dimensional charts with different rotation settings

To change the rotation of an axis, navigate to the Axis section of Format Chart, then provide a rotation value, as shown in Figure 20-86.

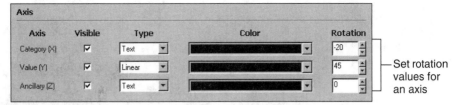

Figure 20-86   Rotation options in the Axis section

Working with the space between elements in a three-dimensional series

To control the space between the series in a three-dimensional chart, you use unit spacing. The unit-spacing value is the percentage of the series width that appears between each series. For example, the default unit spacing is 50. This means that the space between two series elements in the chart, such as two sets of bars, is approximately 50 percent of the width of one series element. For example, Figure 20-87 shows the difference between two unit-spacing settings in a sample three-dimensional bar chart.

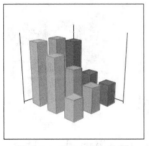   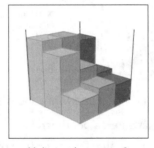

Unit spacing set to 100   Unit spacing set to 0

Figure 20-87   Charts that use different unit-spacing settings

To change the spacing, navigate to the Chart Area section of Format Chart, then choose General Properties. In Unit Spacing, provide a value. The value indicates the percentage of the series width to use to separate series elements.

Formatting an area-chart series

When you format an area chart, you can change the style or color of the lines that border the areas or hide the lines altogether. To change the appearance of the areas, you can curve the lines between data points. Curved lines can help to show trends in the data.

For example, Figure 20-88 shows the difference between a chart with standard lines and a chart with curved lines.

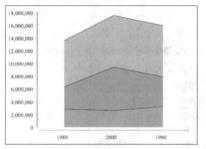 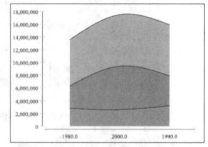

Figure 20-88   Area chart with default lines and curved lines

You can also add point markers that identify the data points that an area encloses. The legend uses the markers to identify the areas. In a chart without markers, the legend uses lines. Figure 20-89 shows an area chart with and without markers.

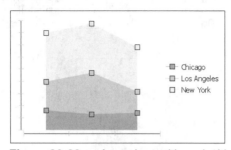 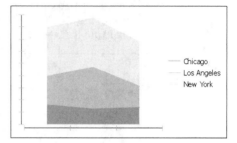

Figure 20-89   Area chart with and without markers

How to format an area-chart series

Navigate to the Value Series section of Format Chart, then use the settings to modify the area chart lines or markers, as shown in Figure 20-90.

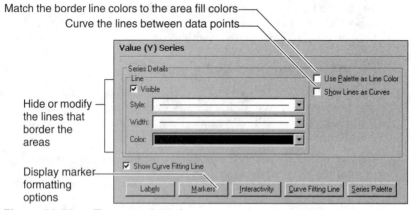

Figure 20-90   Format options for an area-chart series

Formatting a bar-chart series

When you first create a bar chart, the chart uses default formatting. For example, bars typically appear as rectangles without outlines. You can show the bars as triangles or add a bar outline.

To format a bar-chart series, navigate to the Value Series section of Format Chart. Use the settings to modify the bars, as shown in Figure 20-91.

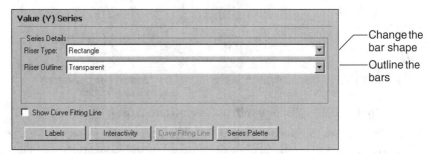

Figure 20-91   Format options for a bar-chart series

Formatting a line or a scatter-chart series

Line and scatter charts use the same formatting attributes. The default formatting of line and scatter charts is also similar, except that a line chart shows lines between data points, but a scatter chart does not. In either a line or a scatter chart, you can add shadows to the lines and data point markers, change the size and shape of the markers, or change the shape, line style, or color of the lines that connect the data points.

To format a line or scatter-chart series, navigate to the Value Series section of Format Chart. Use the settings to modify the chart lines and markers, as shown in Figure 20-92.

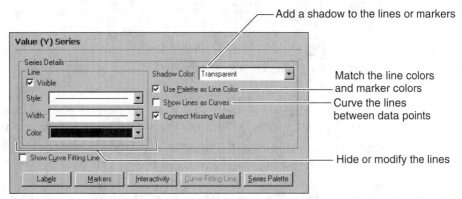

Figure 20-92   Format options for a line or scatter-chart series

Sometimes, line charts include categories for which no data exists. You can define how the chart treats the empty values. The chart can either connect the line between the existing points or represent the empty value as a blank space in the chart. Figure 20-93 shows the two options in a line chart.

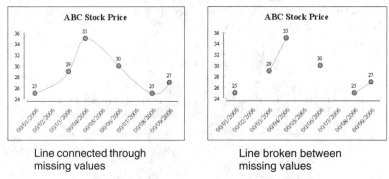

Line connected through missing values   Line broken between missing values

Figure 20-93   Charts with connected and broken lines

By default, the chart connects lines. To change the missing value setting, navigate to the Value Series section of Format Chart, then deselect Connect Missing Values.

Formatting a meter-chart series

When you format a meter-chart series, you work with the chart parts that are shown in Figure 20-94.

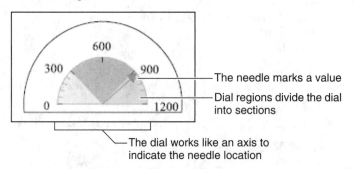

Figure 20-94   Parts of a meter chart

You can modify the following meter-chart attributes:

- Dial size. You can determine the radius of the dial. You can also use start- and stop-angle settings to determine if the dial is circular or semicircular.

- Dial scale and tick marks. Working with the dial scale and tick settings is similar to working with the same settings on an axis.

- Needle formatting. You can modify the style and width of the needle or change how the pointer end of the needle appears.

- Dial placement. If you create a chart that displays multiple dials, you can arrange the dials in a row or in columns.

- Label settings. You can show or hide labels for regions and for the chart data point, which is where the needle falls on the meter.

- Dial-region size, color, and placement. Working with dial-region settings is similar to working with axis-marker settings.

Working with dial size

When you create a meter chart, the dial uses default sizing. To enlarge or shrink the distance between the center of the chart and the outside of the dial, you change the dial radius. Use percentage settings to size the dial relative to the meter that surrounds it. For example, a setting of 50 will create a dial radius that is half the distance from the center of the meter to its outer boundary. In a chart that uses more than one value-series definition, you can set the dial radius for either series, and it applies to both series. If different series contain different dial radius values, the dial uses the larger value.

A default dial is a semicircle. To change the shape of a dial to encompass more or less of a circle, you change the dial start- and stop-angle settings. The angles are measured counter-clockwise from the right. For example, in Figure 20-95, the dial uses a start setting of 20 and a stop setting of 160.

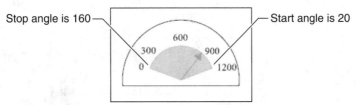

Figure 20-95 Start- and stop-angle settings in a semicircular meter

To show a full circle, use values that produce 360 degrees. For example, the chart shown in Figure 20-96 uses a start angle of –90 and a stop angle of 270. The first value in the dial, 0, appears at –90 degrees, and the last, 1200, is not labeled but appears at 270 degrees.

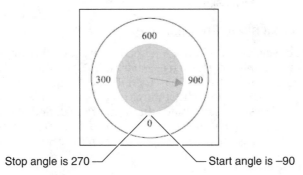

Figure 20-96 Start- and stop-angle settings in a full meter and full dial

The start and stop settings of the dial define the size of the meter that surrounds it. If you use an angle setting that is less than 0 degrees or greater than 180 degrees, the chart displays a full circle. If you use angle settings between 0 and 180, the chart displays a half-circle. For example, the chart shown in Figure 20-97 uses a start angle of –45 and a stop angle of 90.

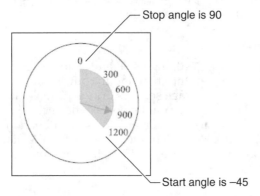

Figure 20-97   Start- and stop-angle settings in a full meter and semicircular dial

How to set the size of a dial

Navigate to the Value Series section of Format Chart. Use the settings to modify the dial size, as shown in Figure 20-98.

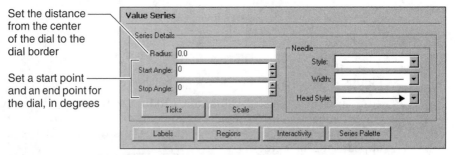

Figure 20-98   Dial size settings

Working with dial scale and markings

The chart builder sets up a dial for a meter chart in much the same way that it sets up an axis in another chart, such as a bar chart. The chart builder uses the available data to set a span for the dial, then it places tick marks at appropriate intervals along it. Working with the settings on a dial is similar to working with axis settings. The dial scale determines the span of the data that the dial displays in the same way that the scale of an axis determines which data the axis displays. Tick marks on a dial work in the same way as on an axis.

How to change the scale of a dial

Navigate to the Value Series section of Format Chart, then choose Scale. Use the Scale settings to change the range or spacing of the data the dial displays, as shown in Figure 20-99.

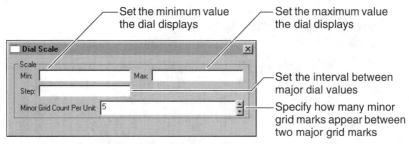

Set the minimum value the dial displays

Set the maximum value the dial displays

Set the interval between major dial values

Specify how many minor grid marks appear between two major grid marks

Figure 20-99   Dial scale options

How to modify the tick marks on a dial

Navigate to the Value Series section of Format Chart, then choose Ticks. Use the settings to modify the major or minor grid ticks, as shown in Figure 20-100.

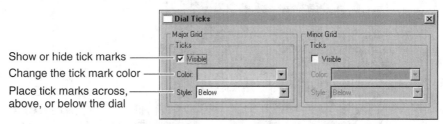

Show or hide tick marks

Change the tick mark color

Place tick marks across, above, or below the dial

Figure 20-100   Dial tick mark options

Working with needle settings

You can change the line style, width, and end settings of a needle. Navigate to the Value Series section of Format Chart, then use the settings in Needle to modify the needle appearance, as shown in Figure 20-101. To change the color of a needle, change the value-series palette.

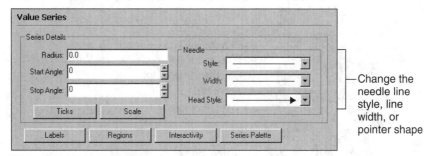

Change the needle line style, line width, or pointer shape

Figure 20-101   Needle formatting options

Arranging multiple meters

To include all the dials in a meter chart in one meter, you must use the superimposed subtype. In a meter chart that displays multiple meters, you can position the meters and specify how many columns to use to display them. For example, in Figure 20-102, the chart on the left uses three columns. The chart on the right uses two columns.

Figure 20-102   Different column arrangements in a meter chart

To arrange the dials, navigate to the Chart Area section of Format Chart, then choose General Properties. Use Grid Column Count to supply the number of columns in which to display the meters, as shown in Figure 20-103.

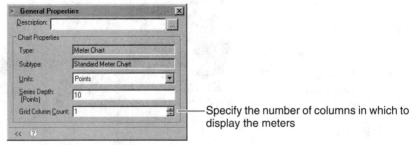

Figure 20-103   Grid Column Count option

Working with meter-chart labels

By default, a meter chart displays labels, similar to axis labels, that identify points on the dial. To format the labels, navigate to the Value Series section of Format Chart and choose Labels. Use the settings to hide or format the labels, as shown in Figure 20-104.

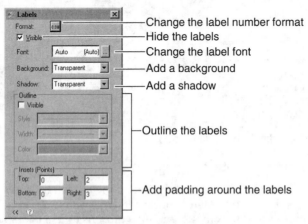

Figure 20-104   Dial label options

Working with dial regions

To highlight the values on the dial, you use dial regions. Dial regions are similar to axis markers. You determine a start and an end value for each region. After you set up the regions, you can change the region color or outline. If regions overlap, the last region that you create takes precedence in formatting. You can also change the radius of a region to determine where it starts or ends in relation to the position of the dial. For example, Figure 20-105 shows a chart with two regions. The region on the left has an outer radius of 50. The region on the right has an outer radius of 75.

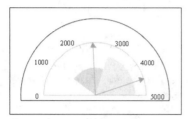

Figure 20-105   Regions in a dial

How to add a dial region

Navigate to the Value Series section of Format Chart, then choose Regions to see the options that are shown in Figure 20-106.

Add a region ———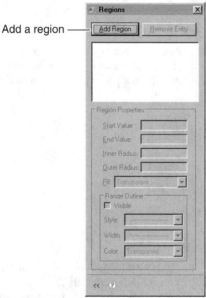

Figure 20-106   Regions

Choose Add Region. The region appears in the list at the top of the window. Provide a start and an end value for the region, as shown in Figure 20-107.

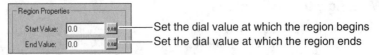

— Set the dial value at which the region begins
— Set the dial value at which the region ends

Figure 20-107   Dial region settings

How to format a dial region

Navigate to the Value Series section of Format Chart, then choose Regions. Select the name of the region to format, then use Region Properties to modify the region settings, as shown in Figure 20-108.

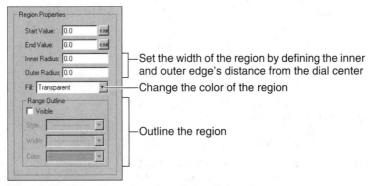

— Set the width of the region by defining the inner and outer edge's distance from the dial center
— Change the color of the region

— Outline the region

Figure 20-108   Format options for a dial region

Formatting a pie chart series

When you first create a pie chart, the chart is a circle. The pie sectors appear exploded, or pulled away from the pie, and leader lines connect sectors and associated data labels. Figure 20-109 shows a pie chart that uses default settings.

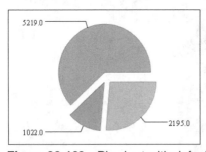

Figure 20-109   Pie chart with default settings

If you minimize or expand the chart, it maintains a circular shape. You can change the ratio setting so that the pie adjusts to fit all the available horizontal or vertical space. In this case, resizing can produce an oval pie. You can format the pie sectors to change the color or outline properties. To control the size of the pie sectors, you can define a minimum value for sectors. Sectors below that value combine with other below-minimum sectors in a remainders sector.

You can also change the explosion settings that determine how the chart pulls sectors away from the center of the pie. To change how the chart identifies each sector, you can modify the leader lines that connect data labels and sectors. If a chart displays multiple pies, the formatting applies to each pie. In a pie chart that displays multiple pies, you also can arrange the pies in rows or columns.

Changing the shape of a pie

You can change the height and width ratio so that the pie stretches to fit the horizontal or vertical space in the chart area. If you make the pie wider than it is tall or taller than it is wide, the chart can appear as an oval. For example, Figure 20-110 shows a sample chart that was widened into an oval.

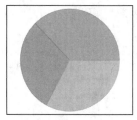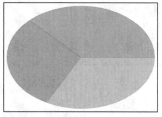

Figure 20-110   Pie chart as a circle and an oval

To shape the chart as a circle or an oval, navigate to the Value Series section of Format Chart, then supply a value in Pie Ratio, as shown in Figure 20-111. Use 1 to retain the circular shape or 0 to allow the chart to stretch into an oval.

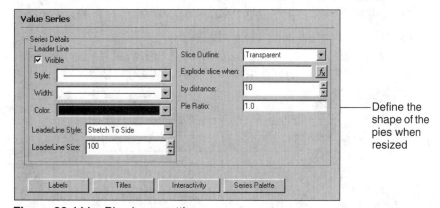

Figure 20-111   Pie shape setting

Working with pie sectors

When you format a pie chart, you can modify the following features:

- Pie sector formatting. You can outline each sector and change the outline properties. You can also select a color palette for the sectors.

- Minimum sectors. You can set a minimum value for pie sectors. A sector with a value equal to or greater than the minimum appears as usual. Sectors with values below the minimum are combined in a new remainders sector. You can create a label for the remainders sector to display in the legend.

You can set the minimum as a static value or as a percentage of the pie value. For example, you can show sales totals for a group of customers and combine customers with sales below $1,000,000.00 in a sector called Infrequent Orders, or you can combine customers with sales below two percent of the total sales.

How to outline pie-chart sectors

Navigate to the Value Series section of Format Chart, then use Slice Outline to select an outline color, as shown in Figure 20-112.

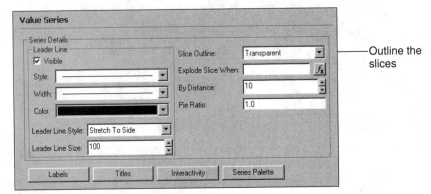

Figure 20-112   Slice outline option

How to specify a minimum sector size

Navigate to the Category Series section of Format Chart, then use the settings to set up a minimum sector, as shown in Figure 20-113.

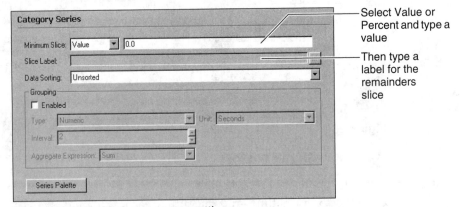

Figure 20-113   Minimum sector settings

Working with explosion settings for a pie chart

You can specify how far from the center of the pie the exploded sectors appear. You can also decide how a pie selects sectors to explode. Typically, you explode all sectors. You can also explode based on an expression. For example, you can explode only those sectors that compose more than 20 percent of the pie. To explode all pie chart sectors, do not provide an explosion expression.

When you create an explosion expression, you can type an expression. You can also use Edit Expression, which includes a Chart Variables category, as shown in Figure 20-114. You use this category to add elements such as Value Data or Category Data to your expression. For example, you can use an expression such as ValueData>200 to explode sectors that have a value greater than 200.

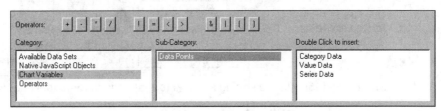

Figure 20-114   Edit Expression for exploding pie sectors

How to explode pie sectors based on an expression

Navigate to the Value Series section of Format Chart. In Explode Slice When, provide an expression. When the expression is true for a sector, that sector pulls away from the pie.

For example, to explode sectors for which the category value is California, use the following expression:

```
CategoryData="California"
```

How to set the explosion distance

Navigate to the Value Series section of Format Chart. In By Distance, provide an explosion value. The explosion value represents the percentage of the original chart size by which to separate each sector from the pie center. For example, an explosion value of 50 pulls out exploded sectors half the distance of the original pie.

Working with leader lines

As with other lines in a chart, you can modify the line style, width, or color for leader lines in the same way as you modify the formatting attributes of other lines in a chart. You can also modify the length of the leader lines. When you first create a pie chart, the chart uses leader lines of a default length. To change the length, you change the leader line's style setting. The leader-line style Stretch to Side indicates that the chart uses the default leader length. A chart with the leader-line style Fixed Length can use the length that you specify. You can also hide the leader lines.

How to modify leader lines

Navigate to the Value Series section of Format Chart, then use the settings that are shown in Figure 20-115 to hide the lines, change the line style, or adjust the line length.

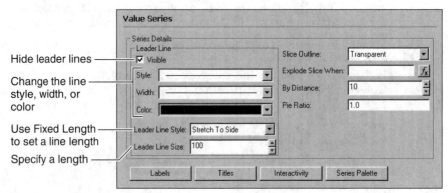

Figure 20-115 Visible setting and line format options for leader lines

Arranging multiple pies in a pie chart

When you use multiple pies in a pie chart, you can specify how to arrange the pies. To arrange the pies, you specify how many columns to use to display them. For example, in Figure 20-116, the chart on the left uses one column. The chart on the right uses two columns.

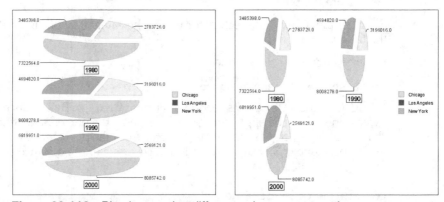

Figure 20-116 Pie charts using different column-count settings

How to arrange multiple pies in a pie chart

Navigate to the Chart Area section of Format Chart, then choose General Properties. In Grid Column Count, select the number of columns in which to display the pies.

Formatting a stock-chart series

To display values, a stock chart uses a candlestick, a box with lines extending up and down from the ends. The upper and lower edges of the box are the stock open and close values. The upper and lower points of the line are the high and low values. If the open value is higher than the close value, the box is shaded. If the close value is higher than the open value, the box is transparent. For example, in the chart in Figure 20-117, the marker for 03/01/2005 indicates that day's close value was lower than the open value.

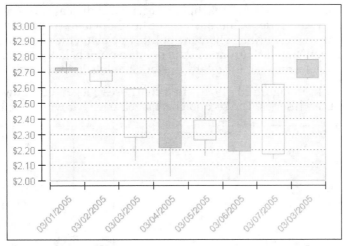

Figure 20-117   Stock chart

When you format a stock chart, you can change the color of the shaded boxes. You can also change the color and style of the box outline and the candlestick lines.

How to format a stock-chart series

Navigate to the Value Series section of Format Chart, then use the settings to change the appearance of the stock series, as shown in Figure 20-118.

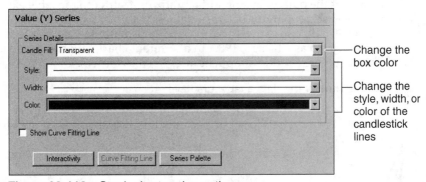

Figure 20-118   Stock-chart series options

Working with data points and data point labels

By default, a chart displays labels that identify value-series values, such as the height of a bar in a bar chart or the size of a sector in a pie chart. You can hide labels; reposition the labels; add a background, shadow, or outline; or change the label font. You can also use inset settings to add padding around the labels to separate them from other chart elements, such as leader lines or the chart border.

To display different data in the labels, you change the data point settings. The data point settings determine what text each label displays. Typically, the label shows the value-series value, such as the height of a line chart point on the y-axis. You can also show where the point appears on the x-axis, use the series value to show to which group of data points a point belongs, or display the value as a percentage of the total value of all points in the chart.

For example, in Figure 20-119, the first chart uses a legend to show which bar represents each series. The second chart labels each bar with the city name.

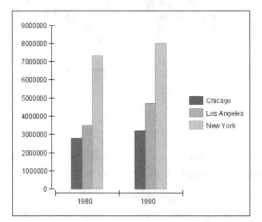 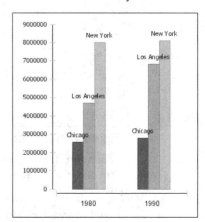

Figure 20-119　Bar charts using different label settings

After you decide what data to show in the labels, you can change the number format of the data points or add a prefix or a suffix to the label expression. You can also use a separator between values. For example, in the chart in Figure 20-119, you can display the city value and the year value, separated by a comma, such as Chicago, 1980. In a different chart, you could add a currency symbol before a value or append text, such as Orders.

How to modify the data a label displays

Navigate to the Value Series section of Format Chart, then choose Labels. Use the settings in Values to set up the data the label displays, as shown in Figure 20-120.

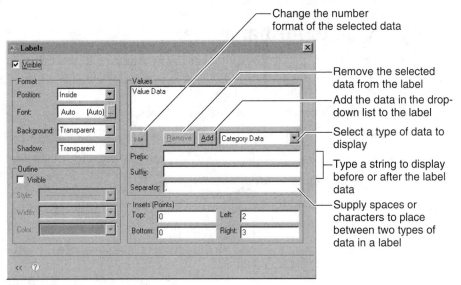

Change the number
format of the selected data

Remove the selected
data from the label

Add the data in the drop-
down list to the label

Select a type of data to
display

Type a string to display
before or after the label
data

Supply spaces or
characters to place
between two types of
data in a label

Figure 20-120   Label data settings

How to format data point labels

Navigate to the Value Series section of Format Chart, then choose Labels. Use
the settings in Values to set up the data the label displays, as shown in
Figure 20-121.

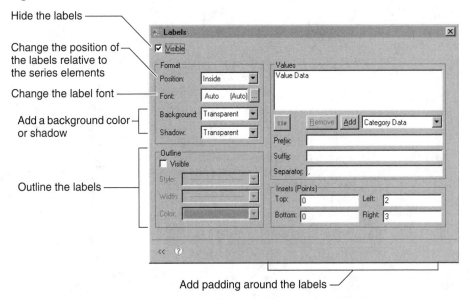

Hide the labels

Change the position of
the labels relative to
the series elements

Change the label font

Add a background color
or shadow

Outline the labels

Add padding around the labels

Figure 20-121   Label formatting, position, and placement options

Using styles to format a chart

You can use a style to apply several formatting attributes to the chart in one step or to apply the same attribute to several chart elements. Using a style in a chart is similar to using styles for other report elements.

BIRT supports the following style features for charts:

- Font
- Color
- Background Color
- Background Image
- Padding

To apply a style to a chart, in the property editor, choose Properties, and, in Style, select the style to apply.

Enhancing Reports

21

Designing a Multipage Report

Most reports display and print on multiple pages. When you design a report, consider how a multipage report displays and prints. You can, for example, design a report so that page breaks occur at logical places. For a report that contains a series of subreports, you can specify page breaks to start each subreport on a new page.

You can also design a page layout that enhances the report's appearance and usability. A page layout specifies the style of the pages on which report data appears. You can specify, for example, that all pages display the report title in the top-left corner, the company logo in the top-right corner, a page number in the bottom-right corner, and a report-generation date in the bottom-left corner. You can also design special effects, such as a watermark that appears in the background. To design a page layout, you customize the report's master page.

Planning the page layout

Before you design a page layout, preview the report in the desired output format, and decide what changes, if any, to make to the default page layout. Consider the following design issues:

- Decide whether you are designing a page layout for a PDF or HTML report or a page layout that is suitable for both. A report design renders differently in PDF and in HTML.

  - For an HTML report, an important decision is whether the report appears on a single scrollable page or on multiple pages. A single page is typical for online viewing, but, if the report is very long, displaying the report on multiple pages might be more suitable. If you choose to display an HTML report on a single page, decide if a master page is necessary. It does not make sense, for instance, to display a page number for a one-page report.

- For a PDF report, decide the page dimensions, including paper size, margin sizes, header size, footer size, and page orientation. The default master page uses US letter size (8.5" by 11"). If you are developing a report for a locale that typically uses A4 paper, change the page size.

- Decide the design of the master page. The default page layout displays the report-generation date in the bottom-left corner of every page. Report designers typically customize the master page to reflect a corporate style or to provide additional information, such as page numbers or confidentiality statements. You can design a different master page for PDF and HTML output by displaying elements for one output and hiding them for the other. You can also design and use different master pages in a single report.

Controlling pagination

By default, an HTML report displays on a single scrollable page and a PDF report appears on multiple pages as necessary. A PDF report also displays as much data as can fit on each page. This behavior can result in key sections that appear in the middle or at the bottom of a page. For most reports, you will want to start certain sections at the top of a new page or avoid breaking a section across two pages.

Note that an HTML report appears on multiple pages only when viewed in the report viewer (File→View Report in Web Viewer). When you preview a report in the layout editor or as HTML (File→View Report as HTML), the entire report appears in a scrollable window.

Inserting page breaks

Reports that consist of a series of documents or distinct sections typically look more organized if each document or section appears on a separate page. For example, if a report consists of a cover letter, disclaimer information, and a summary report that is followed by a detailed report, you can insert page breaks to display each type of information on a separate page. Similarly, if a report groups sales data by state, then by customer, you can start the data for each state on a new page.

You can specify page breaks for these elements:

- Top-level elements

These are elements that are not placed in another element.

- Second-level elements

  These are elements that are placed in a top-level list, table, or grid. For example, if table A contains table B, and table B contains table C, you can specify a page break for table A and table B, but not for table C.

- Groups

  You can specify page breaks for data groups defined in top-level and second-level tables or lists.

You specify page breaks using the Page Break Before and Page Break After properties. Table 21-1 describes the values you can select for these properties.

Table 21-1   Values for Page Break Before and After properties

Page Break Before, Page Break After value	Description
Always	Always insert a page break before or after the selected element.
Auto	Insert a page break before or after the element as necessary. Auto is the default value.
Avoid	Avoid inserting a page break before or after the selected element.
Always Excluding First	Applies only to groups and Page Break Before. Always insert a page break before each instance of the selected group, but not before the first instance.
Always Excluding Last	Applies only to groups and Page Break After. Always insert a page break after each instance of the selected group, but not after the last instance.

The rest of this section provides examples of inserting page breaks for various elements.

Inserting page breaks in a report with multiple sections and groups

Figure 21-1 shows a PDF report with default page breaks. In this report, the page break properties are set to Auto. Figure 21-2 shows the same report with page breaks after the Top Products and Top States reports and after each state group in the Sales By State and Product report. Notice in Figure 21-2 that the title, Sales By State and Product, repeats at the top of every page of that report. The Repeat Header option is set by default. If you want the report header to appear only once, at the beginning of the report, deselect the Repeat Header option.

Top Products

S10_1949	$78,860.11
S10_4698	$74,524.35
S10_2016	$50,719.68
S10_4962	$50,248.48
S10_4757	$48,402.40

Top States

California	$139,321.53
Massachusetts	$64,194.11
New York	$47,336.15
Pennsylvania	$33,979.95
Connecticut	$26,015.12

Sales By State and Product

California		$139,321.53	40.67%
Product Code	Total Units	Amount	% of Total Amount
S10_1678	152	$12,652.59	9.08%
S10_1949	214	$42,223.67	30.31%
S10_2016	125	$13,044.24	9.36%
S10_4698	146	$25,475.89	18.29%
S10_4757	186	$24,579.28	17.64%
S10_4962	156	$21,345.86	15.32%

Connecticut		$26,015.12	7.59%
Product Code	Total Units	Amount	% of Total Amount
S10_1678	34	$3,026.00	11.63%
S10_1949	34	$6,630.34	25.49%
S10_2016	40	$4,282.00	16.46%
S10_4698	41	$7,940.06	30.52%
S10_4962	28	$4,136.72	15.90%

Massachusetts		$64,194.11	18.74%
Product Code	Total Units	Amount	% of Total Amount
S10_1678	78	$6,821.58	10.63%
S10_1949	70	$14,210.11	22.14%
S10_2016	97	$11,145.67	17.36%

8.50 x 11.00 in

Figure 21-1   PDF report with default pagination

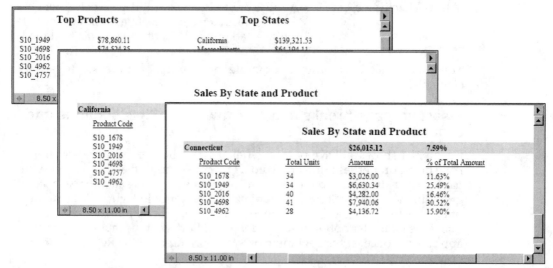

Figure 21-2   PDF report with custom pagination

Figure 21-3 shows the output when the same report is displayed in the previewer in the layout editor or in the window when you choose File→View Report as HTML. You can see from the page numbers that page breaks are inserted. All the pages, however, appear on one screen. If you choose File→View Report in Web Viewer, the BIRT report viewer displays each page on a separate screen.

Top Products

S10_1949	$78,860.11
S10_4698	$74,524.35
S10_2016	$50,719.68
S10_4962	$50,248.48
S10_4757	$48,402.40

Top States

California	$139,321.53
Massachusetts	$64,194.11
New York	$47,336.15
Pennsylvania	$33,979.95
Connecticut	$26,015.12

Page: 1

Sales By State and Product

California		$139,321.53	40.67%
Product Code	Total Units	Amount	% of Total Amount
S10_1678	152	$12,652.59	9.08%
S10_1949	214	$42,223.67	30.31%
S10_2016	125	$13,044.24	9.36%
S10_4698	146	$25,475.89	18.29%
S10_4757	186	$24,579.28	17.64%
S10_4962	156	$21,345.86	15.32%

Page: 2

| Connecticut | | $26,015.12 | 7.59% |

Figure 21-3   HTML output with pagination, viewed in the previewer

Figure 21-4 shows the report design and indicates where and how page breaks are set. In this report design:

- The Page Break After property of the grid at the top of the report is set to Always, which inserts a page break after the grid. Alternatively, selecting the top-level table element that appears after the grid and setting its Page Break Before property to Always achieves the same result.

- The Page Break After property of the state group is set to Always Excluding Last. This setting inserts a page break after each state group, except for the last group. If the Page Break After property is set to Always, the report displays a blank page after the last group. Alternatively, you can set the state group's Page Break Before property to Always Excluding First. This setting inserts a page break before each state group, except for the first group, and prevents a blank page from appearing before the first group.

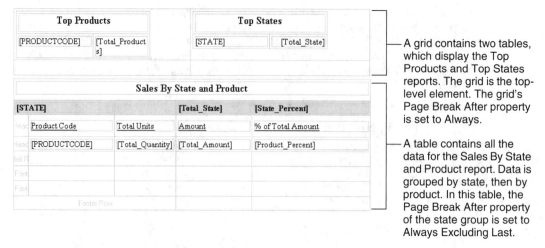

A grid contains two tables, which display the Top Products and Top States reports. The grid is the top-level element. The grid's Page Break After property is set to Always.

A table contains all the data for the Sales By State and Product report. Data is grouped by state, then by product. In this table, the Page Break After property of the state group is set to Always Excluding Last.

Figure 21-4   Page break property settings in a report design

Figure 21-5 shows a partial view of the group editor where you set the state group's Page Break After property.

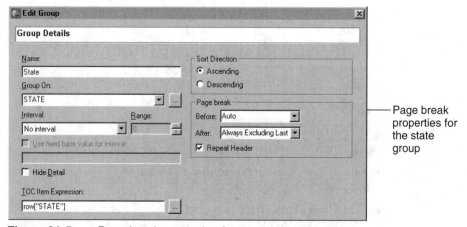

Page break properties for the state group

Figure 21-5   Page break properties for a group

Inserting page breaks in a master-detail report

In the next example, a report displays data with a master-detail relationship. An outer, top-level table contains two inner tables. The top-level table displays customer information. For each customer, the inner tables display order information and payment information, respectively. Figure 21-6 shows the PDF report with page breaks inserted so that each customer starts on a new page.

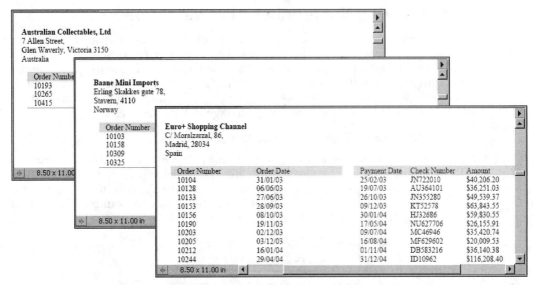

Figure 21-6   PDF output with each customer's data starting on a new page

Figure 21-7 shows the report design and indicates where and how the page break is set. The Page Break After property of the second-level table is set to Always.

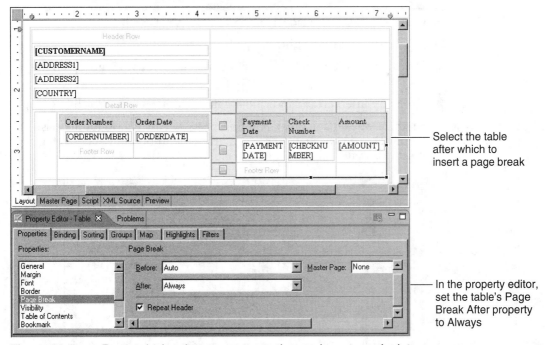

Select the table after which to insert a page break

In the property editor, set the table's Page Break After property to Always

Figure 21-7   Report design that supports starting each customer's data on a new page

Specifying the number of rows per page

Specifying page breaks before or after selected sections or groups in a report is the typical way to control pagination. For some reports, however, you might want to insert a page break after a specified number of data rows. In a simple listing report that does not contain groups or multiple sections, you could, for example, display twenty rows on each page. To do so, group data rows by the desired number of rows, and insert a page break after each group.

How to specify the number of rows to display per page

1   Select the table that contains the data, and on Property Editor, choose Binding to create a new column binding. Specify Total.runningCount( ) as the expression. This aggregate function returns the current row number as BIRT processes each data row. Figure 21-8 shows an example of a column binding that uses Total.runningCount( ).

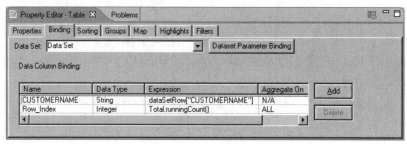

Figure 21-8   Column binding using Total.runningCount( )

2   Select Groups to create a group.

1   Instead of grouping on a data set field, which is typical, group on the column binding you just created.

2   Group by interval, and indicate the number of rows by which to group.

3   Set the group's Page Break After property to Always Excluding Last. Figure 21-9 shows an example of a group definition in which each group is set to an interval of 20 rows.

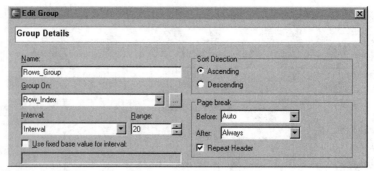

Figure 21-9   Property settings for grouping by a number of rows

3 In the layout editor, delete the data element that BIRT automatically adds to the group header. If you do not, the report displays the row number at the beginning of every group.

Customizing the master page

The master page specifies the dimensions and style of the pages on which report data appears. You can specify, for example, that the page size is 7" x 9", the printable area is 6" x 8", the company logo always appears in the top-right corner, and the page number appears in the bottom-right corner.

The page size and margin settings apply only to PDF reports, where these dimensions matter because PDF documents are page-oriented. For HTML reports, data appears directly in the BIRT report viewer or web browser, and the layout of data adjusts to the size of the viewer or browser window.

Viewing the master page

When you create or open a report design, the layout editor always shows the report layout. To view the master page, use one of the following options:

■ Choose Page➤Master Page➤Simple Master Page.

■ Choose the Master Page tab at the bottom of the layout editor.

You can view either the report layout or the master page but not both at the same time. Figure 21-10 shows the default master page.

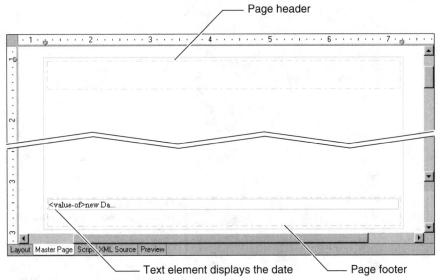

Page header

Text element displays the date   Page footer

Figure 21-10   Master page

Designing the page header and footer

The default master page includes a text element that displays the current date in the page footer. If you preview your report, you see that the current date appears on the bottom left of every report page. You can delete or edit this text element. You can add other elements to the master page by dragging them from the palette and dropping them in the page footer or header.

Observe the following rules:

- You can place elements in the header and footer only. You do not place elements in the report content area, because the contents of those elements would overlap report data.

- You cannot place more than one element directly in the header or footer. To place multiple elements, insert a grid, then insert the elements in the grid.

Displaying page numbers, the current date, and other text

Common header and footer information includes the page number, report-generation date, company name, author name, copyright information, and confidentiality statements.

As Figure 21-11 shows, BIRT Report Designer provides predefined text elements for displaying some of these common items, including the current date, page number, author name, and file name. These items are available on the palette when the master page is displayed.

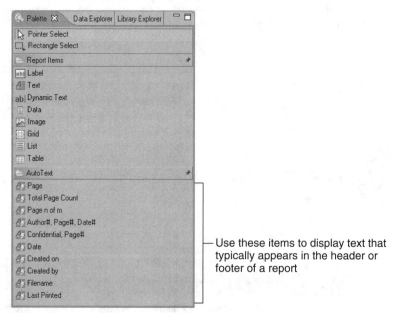

Use these items to display text that typically appears in the header or footer of a report

Figure 21-11   Text elements for common header and footer items

For example, the date element is a text element that contains the following dynamic value:

```
<value-of>new Date()</value-of>
```

After you insert a predefined text element in the page header or footer, you can edit the text to display different information. For example, you can edit the date element to display the date in a different format. By default, the report displays the date according to the locale that is set on the machine on which the report is generated. You can use the format tag to display the date in a custom format, as shown in the following expression:

```
<value-of format="MM-dd-yy">new Date()</value-of>
```

To display other text in the header or footer, you can use the other predefined text elements in the palette and edit the text content or insert a regular text or label element and type the text from scratch.

Remember, to display more than one element in the header or footer, you must first insert a grid, then insert the elements in the grid. The predefined Author#, Page#, Date# element creates a grid and three text elements, so you might find it convenient to insert this element, then edit the individual text elements.

As with any text element, you can also customize the appearance of the predefined elements, for example, to display text in a different style or color, or to align text in the center or right of the page.

How to display text in the header and footer

1   In the layout editor, choose the Master Page tab. The layout editor displays the master page. The palette displays additional elements under AutoText, specifically for use in the master page.

2   To display a single text element in the header or footer, drag the desired element from the palette, and drop it in the header or footer. For example, to display the page number, insert either the Page element or the Page n of m element.

3   To display multiple text elements in the header or footer:

   1   Insert the grid element in the header or footer. Delete the date element from the default footer first.

   2   On Insert Grid, specify the number of columns and rows for the grid. If, for example, you want to display two elements on the same line, specify 2 columns and 1 row.

   3   Insert each text element in a grid cell.

Displaying an image

You can insert static and dynamic images in a master page. You insert an image in a master page the same way you insert an image in the report layout. The difference is that you cannot insert an image inside a table in the master page.

Therefore, when you insert a dynamic image directly on the master page, the same image—the image in the first data row—appears on every page.

Specifying a header size

The size of the header in the generated report can be different when rendered in PDF and in HTML. For an HTML report, the header dynamically resizes to accommodate its contents, and the header always appears directly above the report content. In an HTML report, the header height property is ignored.

For a PDF report, the header also dynamically resizes to accommodate its contents. Unlike the HTML report, you can specify a fixed size for the header. If you specify a header size of one inch, and you insert an image that is half an inch in height, the report displays half an inch of space between the image and the report data. If the header size you specify, however, is not sufficient to display a large image, the report overrides the specified header size and resizes the header to display the image in its entirety.

Increasing the header size is one way to increase the space between the header content and the report content. However, because header size applies only to PDF output, this technique is not recommended if you want to create a master page that serves both PDF and HTML output equally well.

The preferred technique to add space between the header content and report content is to increase the padding at the bottom of the text or label element placed in the header. Alternatively, if you use a grid to organize multiple elements, you can add a row at the bottom of the grid and set the row size. Using either of these techniques, the extra space appears in both PDF and HTML output.

Specifying a footer size

Like the header, the size of the footer in the generated report can be different for PDF and HTML reports. In both types of reports, the footer dynamically resizes to fit its content. If you specify a footer size, the PDF report displays a footer section of the specified size, except when the contents exceed the specified size. The HTML report ignores the specified footer size.

How to specify a header or footer size

1 In the layout editor, choose the Master Page tab. The layout editor displays the master page.

2 In the property editor, choose General properties. The property editor displays the master page's general properties, as shown in Figure 21-12.

3 Specify a size for the header height, the footer height, or both.

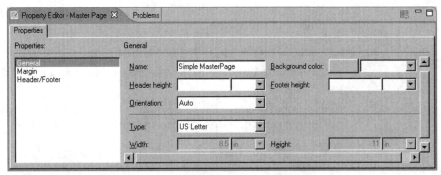

Figure 21-12 Master page properties in the property editor

Excluding header content from the first page

It is common practice to display header content on every page except the first. For example, a report displays a title in bold and large font on the first page, but in a smaller font at the top of the other pages, as shown in Figure 21-13.

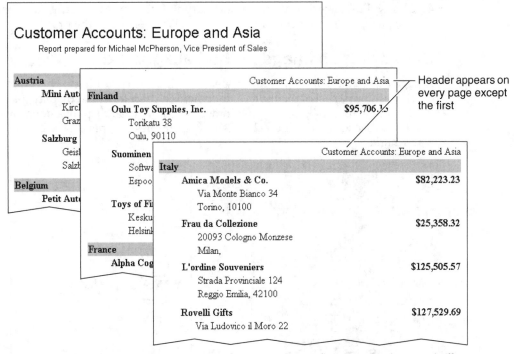

Figure 21-13 Report output when the Show header on first property is turned off

When you insert an element in the page header, it appears, by default, on every page in the report. You control this behavior by turning off the property that controls whether headers appear on all pages or all except the first, as described in the following procedure.

How to exclude header content from the first page

1   In the layout editor, choose Master Page. The layout editor displays the master page.

2   In the property editor, choose Header/Footer. The property editor displays the header and footer properties, as shown in Figure 21-14.

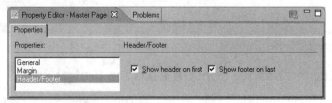

Figure 21-14   Header and footer properties

3   Deselect Show header on first.

4   Choose Preview to verify the report output. If the report contains more than one page, the header content appears on all pages except the first.

Displaying an image in the background

A page can contain an image that appears behind the report data. This effect is called a watermark. For example, a document in draft form can display the word Draft across the page. A government document can display a department seal in the background. Figure 21-15 shows examples of reports with watermarks.

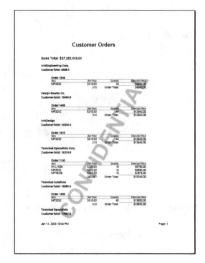

Figure 21-15   Reports with watermarks

When you design a watermark:

- Make sure the image recedes into the background and does not interfere with the readability of the report.

- You can use a small image and repeat it so that it fills the entire page. In Figure 21-15, the report on the left shows this effect. Use this technique judiciously. As the example report shows, filling the page with colored images can reduce the readability of the report.

- You can use a large image that fills the page. In Figure 21-15, the report on the right shows this effect.

- Bear in mind that if any report elements in the report layout have background color, this color appears on top of the background image. Figure 21-16 shows this effect. If you want to display a watermark, limit the use of color in the report layout; otherwise the report could look cluttered.

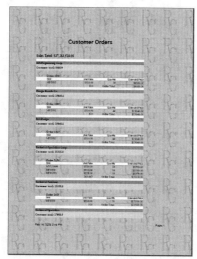

Figure 21-16   Report with colors and a watermark

To use an image as a watermark, select the master page. In the properties view, which is shown in Figure 21-17, expand Simple Master Page, then expand Background. Set the background image to the URL of the image file, such as:

```
http://mysite.com/images/logo.jpg
```

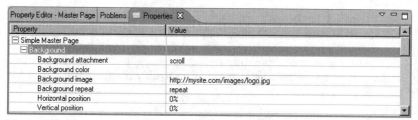

Figure 21-17   Properties view, showing properties for the master page

You can specify a local file-system location, such as c:/images/logo.jpg. You should, however, use a local path for testing purposes only. When you deploy the report, the report will not be able to find the image on the local machine.

Designing the appearance of the background image

By default, a background image repeats to fill the page. You can change this behavior by setting the value of the background repeat property:

- Specify no-repeat to display the image once.
- Specify repeat-x to repeat the image across the page horizontally.
- Specify repeat-y to repeat the image across the page vertically.

Figure 21-18 shows the results of setting the property to different values.

Figure 21-18   Reports with different values for the background repeat property

Positioning the background image

If you set the Background repeat property to no-repeat, repeat-x, or repeat-y, you can reposition the image to display it on a different part of the page by using the Horizontal position and Vertical position properties. For Horizontal position, you can select the center, left, or right values. For Vertical position, you can select the bottom, center, or top values.

Figure 21-19 shows the results of setting the background repeat, Horizontal position, and Vertical position properties to different values. For both properties, you can also specify a precise position or a percentage. For example, setting Horizontal position to 3 in displays the image three inches from the left of the page. Setting Vertical position to 25% displays the image at the top 25% of the page.

Background repeat = repeat-x
Vertical position = center

Background repeat = repeat-y
Horizontal position = 75%

Background repeat = no-repeat
Horizontal position = right
Vertical position = top

Figure 21-19   Reports with different background property values

Displaying different content in a PDF and HTML report

You can design a master page that differs for PDF and HTML. Simply select the element or elements on the master page that you want to display in one output format only, then set the element's visibility property accordingly. Figure 21-20 shows a picture element's visibility property set to hide the picture for HTML output.

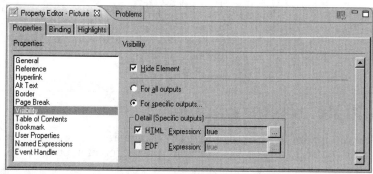

Figure 21-20   Hiding an element in HTML output

You also have the option of applying the master page to PDF output only. If, for example, you choose to display a report on a single HTML page, you might not want the report to display any header or footer information. To disable the master page for HTML reports, choose Window➤Preferences, then choose BIRT—Preview, and deselect Enable master page content. Note that this option takes effect at the application level, not at the report level.

Specifying page size, orientation, and margins

As explained earlier, these page settings apply to PDF reports only. An HTML report displays directly in the BIRT viewer and its size adjusts to the size of the viewer window.

The default master page uses the following settings:

- US letter size, 8.5" x 11"

- Portrait orientation

- Top and bottom margins of 1"

- Left and right margins of 1.25"

You can change these page settings in the property editor, as shown in Figure 21-21.

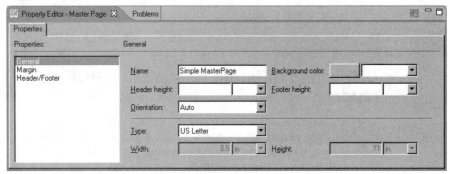

Figure 21-21   Master page properties

If you are designing a report for PDF, specify the page settings before you begin laying out report data. If, for example, you set the page width to a smaller size after you lay out the report data, you most probably have to adjust the report contents to fit in the new page size.

Using multiple master pages

You can use multiple master pages in a single report. A report can use different master pages to display, for example, one section of a report in portrait mode, and another section in landscape mode. Using multiple master pages, you can also specify different background color, or different header and footer content for different sections of a report. Figure 21-22 shows a report that uses two master pages. The first page uses a master page that has portrait mode and a watermark. The second page uses a master page that has landscape mode and text in the footer.

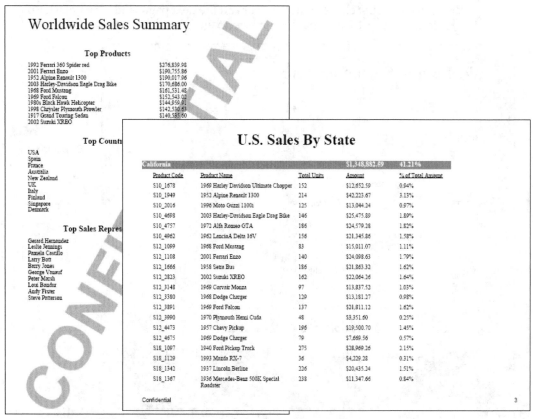

Figure 21-22   Report using two master pages to display different page styles

To use multiple master pages in a report:

- Create the master pages. You can create as many master pages as you wish through the Outline view. Right-click MasterPages and choose Insert to add a new master page to the report design.

- Specify a page break for each report section that uses a different master page.

- Assign a master page to each report section.

For example, to design the report in Figure 21-22, two master pages, named Portrait and Landscape, were created. The Portrait master page was applied to the first report page, and the Landscape master page to the rest of the report, using the following procedure:

- Select the report section that you want to appear on the title page, and set its Master Page property to Portrait. Then set the Page Break After property to Always. Figure 21-23 shows a grid selected, and its master page and page break properties set. The grid contains all the elements whose data appears on the first page.

- Select the first element that appears on the next page, and set its master page to Landscape. The Landscape master page is used for the rest of the pages.

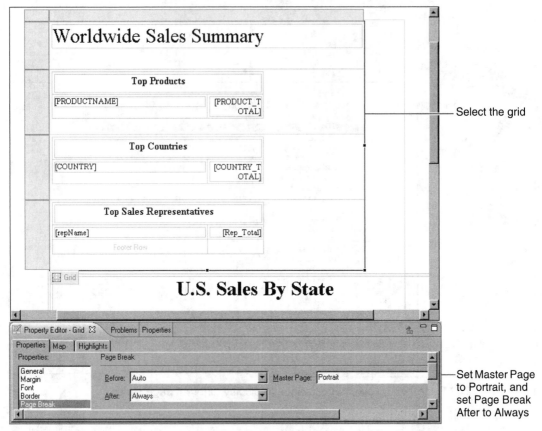

Figure 21-23 Reports with different background property values

22

Adding Interactive Viewing Features

Some reports are long and complex, which can make it difficult for readers to locate and use the information that they need. In these cases, you can add interactive features that help users to navigate and explore reports. Hyperlinks and tables of content offer different ways for a user to find information or drill down to more detailed data. Interactive chart features enable you to customize the data that a chart displays and provide links to additional information. To review information in a different format, a report user can export some or all of the data from a report.

Creating hyperlinks

You can create a hyperlink that links one report element to another element, either in the same report or in a different report. These links are commonly referred to as master-detail or drill-through links. A report, for example, can contain a summary listing with hyperlinks to detailed information. The report element that acts as the link is called the source report element. It must be a data, label, image, or chart element. The report element to which you link is called the target report element.

As an example, a report might contain all the sales for a company aggregated by region. Each region total could then be linked to the detailed sales transactions for that region. The transaction detail may reside in the same report or in a separate report, and if the detail report is separate, it can be a previously executed report or one that is run on demand when the link is traversed. Using a cached detail report can be useful when the report is very large or changes infrequently.

Linking two sections in a report

To create a link from one report element to another element in the same report, you use a bookmark and a hyperlink. First, you create a bookmark for the target report element. The bookmark can be text, such as "My Bookmark", or an expression. For example, you can use row["CUSTOMERNAME"] within a table to generate a dynamic bookmark for each customer in the table. Use the Bookmark property in the property editor to add the bookmark, as shown in Figure 22-1. You can type the expression in the text area or use the expression builder.

Figure 22-1   Bookmark the target element

After you create the bookmark, you create a hyperlink for the source element. Include the bookmark or expression in the hyperlink expression for the source element. To create the hyperlink, you use the hyperlink property of the source report element. In the property editor, choose Hyperlink to display the hyperlink properties, as shown in Figure 22-2, then choose the Hyperlink Options button that is marked with an ellipsis.

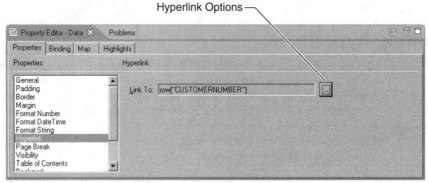

Figure 22-2   Hyperlink the source element

When Hyperlink Options appears, use the settings shown in Figure 22-3 to create the link. Select Internal Bookmark for Hyperlink Type, which indicates you are linking two sections within the same report. Then select a bookmark from the drop-down list, which is automatically generated from all the bookmarks you created earlier.

Linked Expression is populated with the bookmark you select. If you want to link to bookmarks conditionally, you may choose the Expression Builder button to enter script that changes the selected bookmark dynamically based on such things as parameters, sessions values, or data values.

For example, the details to which you link for each customer in a customer listing report may be different depending on the role of the person viewing the report. Someone in the sales department may need to drill to purchase order details, while someone in the shipping department may need to drill to bill of lading information. Adding script in the expression builder to change the bookmark based on user role accomplishes this result.

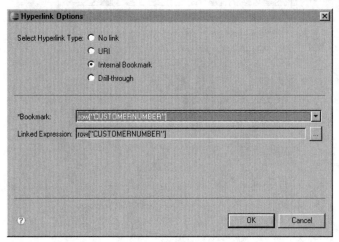

Figure 22-3   Hyperlink Options

Linking to a section in a different report

Creating a link from one report to a different report is very similar to creating a link between elements in the same report. Again, begin by creating a bookmark in the target report. Then use the hyperlink property to open Hyperlink Options and create a hyperlink in the source report. This type of hyperlink is called a drill-through link. After you create the bookmark in the target report, use the settings on Hyperlink Options, as shown in Figure 22-4, to create the hyperlink in the source report.

The most important difference between creating a link within the same report and creating a link to a different report is that the hyperlink expression must contain the name of the report file in which the target element resides when you link to a different report. On Hyperlink Options, you can type a file name or navigate to and select the correct file.

You must also indicate whether the target report opens in the same window or a new one, and whether it is formatted in HTML or PDF.

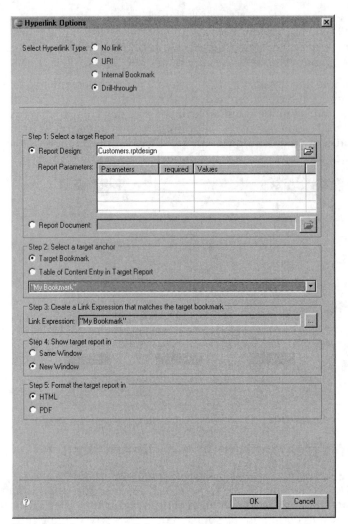

Figure 22-4   Hyperlink options for linking two reports

You can also use a report parameter with a hyperlink to open a customized version of a different report. The hyperlink expression takes a report parameter value and opens a version of the target report that is based on the parameter value. The value for the parameter that is passed to the target report can be set using the expression builder. If the parameter value is left blank and it is a required parameter, the report user is prompted for the value when the link is selected.

After you create the report parameter in the target report, use the settings on Hyperlink Options to create the link in the source report, as shown in Figure 22-5.

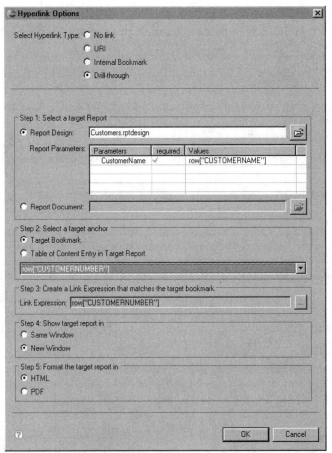

Figure 22-5   Hyperlink options for a link that passes a parameter

When the report user follows the link, the generated detail report displays the page where the target bookmark is found if the format is HTML. If the format is PDF, or if the bookmark entry is blank, the detail report opens at the first page.

An alternative to using a bookmark as a target anchor is using a table of contents entry in the target report. Building table of contents entries is described in a later section of this chapter.

It is also possible to link to a previously executed report. This task can be done by selecting Report Document instead of Report Design and entering a report document name with the .rptdocument extension.

Linking to external content using a URI

You can use a hyperlink to open a document or a web page. These links provide users with easy access to additional sources of information, creating more interactive reports. You can, for example, use a link to:

- Open a company web page when a user chooses a label.

- Open a text file that contains detailed copyright information when a user chooses a label that displays a copyright statement.

- Open an image file or play a movie clip when a user chooses a thumbnail image in the report.

This type of link uses a Uniform Resource Identifier (URI). You provide the document, image, or web page location on the hyperlink properties page, using the settings shown in Figure 22-6.

You must use a URI to specify the location, as shown in the following examples:

```
"http://www.mycompany.com"
"http://mysite.com/legal_notices/copyright.html"
"http://mysite.com/images/executives.jpg"
"file:/C:/copyright/statement.txt"
```

The quotation marks are required. You can type a URI, navigate to and select a file, or use the expression builder to create an expression that evaluates to a URI. Using the expression builder means that the URI is constructed dynamically, which is useful when the full URI is not known at design time or when the URI changes depending on data retrieved from a data source.

Target corresponds to a target attribute for an HTML anchor tag. For example, "Blank" opens the target in a new window.

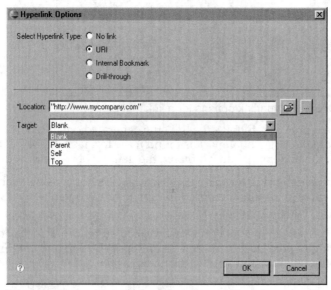

Figure 22-6   Hyperlink options for a URI

Creating a table of contents

A table of contents allows large or congested reports to be more easily navigated by the report user. In the report viewer, the table of contents appears to the left of the report when you choose the table of contents button, and selecting any entry within the table of contents automatically loads the desired section of the report. When viewing the report in PDF format, the table of contents entries appear as bookmarks to the left of the report.

By default, a grouped report includes a table of contents that displays the group values. For example, if the group key is a data set field named PRODUCTLINE, the table of contents expression in the group editor is row["PRODUCTLINE"], as shown in Figure 22-7.

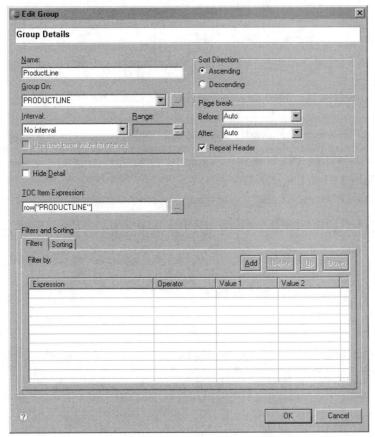

Figure 22-7   Edit Group with the default TOC item expression

In the report viewer, the table of contents lists all the values in the PRODUCTLINE field, as shown in Figure 22-8.

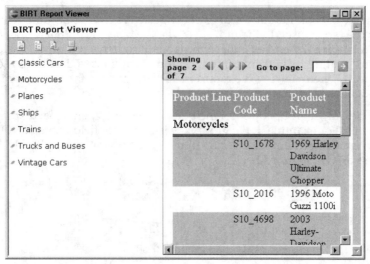

Figure 22-8   Report viewer with Product Line table of contents

In some cases, you may not want the table of contents to display field values exactly as they are saved. For example, the values might be obscure. You can customize the table of contents expression to create a more informative table of contents entry. For example, to display a product name on a separate line after a product code, the TOC Item Expression in Edit Group would be:

```
row["PRODUCTCODE"] + " \n" + row["PRODUCTNAME"]
```

You can provide any valid JavaScript expression as a TOC Item Expression. For example, to show that a product is obsolete, you can check the value of the OBSOLETE database field, as shown in the following example:

```
if ( row["OBSOLETE"] == "yes" ) {
   row["PRODUCTCODE"] + " (Obsolete)"
} else {
   row["PRODUCTCODE"] + " \n" + row["PRODUCTNAME"]
}
```

Table of contents entries may also be nested to reflect the relationship of report elements. For example, you can add a nested table of contents to the report shown in Figure 22-8 to display product codes under each product line. To do so, select the [PRODUCTCODE] report data element and use Property Editor to add a Table of Contents property with the value row["PRODUCTCODE"], as shown in Figure 22-9.

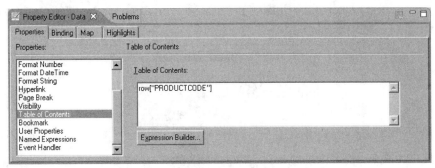

Figure 22-9 Table of contents properties

In the report viewer, the table of contents displays product codes within the product line entries, as shown in Figure 22-10.

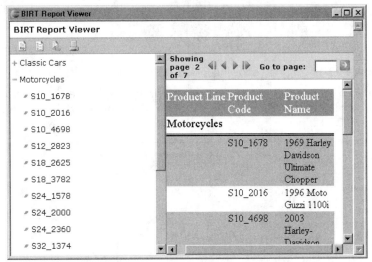

Figure 22-10 Report viewer with nested table of contents

To include a table of contents entry for other report elements, such as charts or images, you would also use Property Editor to add a Table of Contents property.

Adding interactive chart features

You can bookmark or link to a chart or include a chart in the table of contents, as described earlier in this chapter. You can also use additional interactive features to enhance the behavior of a chart in the report viewer. An interactive chart feature supports a response to an event, such as the report user choosing an item or moving the mouse pointer over an item. The response can trigger an action, such as opening a web page, drilling to a detail report, or changing the appearance of the chart. For example, you can use a ToolTip to display the series total when a user places the mouse over a bar in a bar chart, as shown in Figure 22-11.

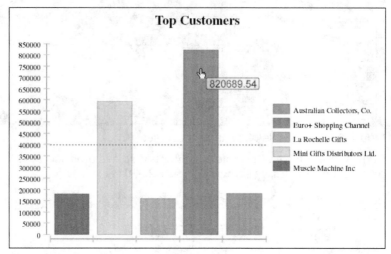

Figure 22-11   Chart showing a ToolTip

You can add an interactive feature to a value series, the chart area, the legend, marker lines, the x- and y-axis, or a title. These areas are illustrated in Figure 22-12.

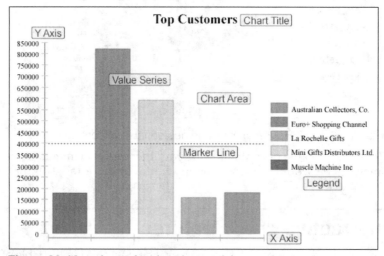

Figure 22-12   Areas for chart interactivity

Start the process of adding interactivity to a chart by choosing Format Chart in the Chart Builder and selecting the chart element you wish to make interactive. Select the appropriate interactivity button, and the interactivity editor appears. Figure 22-13 shows the selection of the Interactivity button for a chart legend.

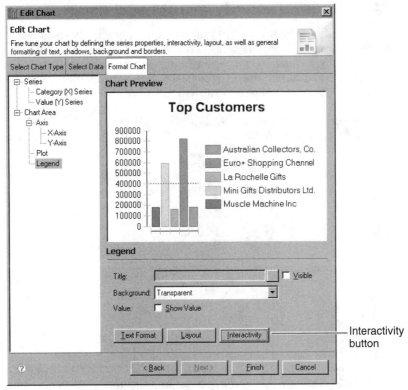

Figure 22-13   Interactivity for chart legend

The location and name for the button to invoke the interactivity editor varies by chart element. Table 22-1 lists the procedure used to invoke the interactivity editor for each element. Not all chart types have all elements.

Table 22-1   Accessing chart interactivity options

Chart element	How to invoke the interactivity editor
Chart Area	Choose Chart Area Interactivity on the Chart Area formatting page
Chart Title	Choose Title Interactivity on the Chart Area formatting page
Legend Area	Choose Interactivity on the Legend formatting page
X-Axis and Y-Axis	Choose Interactivity on the X-Axis or the Y-Axis formatting page
Marker	Choose Markers on the X-Axis or the Y-Axis formatting page. Axis Markers appears. Choose Interactivity.
Value Series	Choose Interactivity on the Value Series

Adding interactivity events and actions

You specify the type of event that triggers interactivity for the selected chart element and indicate the action you wish to perform in Interactivity. For example, in a chart legend, you can use a mouse click to toggle the visibility of the associated data point. Figure 22-14 shows the event type and action in Interactivity required to accomplish this event.

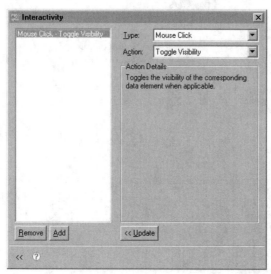

Figure 22-14   Toggle visibility on legend with mouse click

There are a variety of event types that can be used to trigger interactivity. Table 22-2 lists the type options available in the interactivity editor, and describes the UI gesture associated with each.

Table 22-2   Event types

Event type	Description
Mouse Click	Click the selected chart element.
Mouse Double-Click	Double-click on the selected element.
Mouse Down	Press and hold the mouse button down over the selected element.
Mouse Up	Release the mouse button above the selected chart element.
Mouse Over	Move the mouse pointer onto the selected element and leave it there.
Mouse Move	Pass the mouse pointer over the selected element.
Mouse Out	Move the mouse pointer off the selected element.

Table 22-2   Event types *(continued)*

Event type	Description
Focus	Put UI focus on the selected element with the mouse or tab navigation.
Blur	Remove UI focus from the selected element using either the mouse or tab navigation.
Key Press	Press a key while the mouse pointer is over the selected element.
Key Down	Press and hold a key down while the mouse pointer is over the selected element.
Key Up	Release a key while the mouse pointer is over the selected element.
Load	Load the chart in the viewer.

Table 22-3 lists the action options associated with each event type in the interactivity editor. Not all actions are available in all chart output formats.

Table 22-3   Interactive features

Action name	Result	Available in
URL Redirect	Sends the browser to a URL for a web page, a document, or an image. Also used to link to another report.	SVG, SWT, Swing, HTML
Show ToolTip	Displays explanatory text over a chart element.	SVG, SWT, Swing, HTML
Toggle Visibility	Changes the visibility of a chart element, typically a series.	SVG, SWT, Swing
Invoke Script	Invokes a client-side script inside the viewer.	SVG, HTML
Highlight	Highlights a chart element, such as a data point.	SVG, SWT, Swing
Callback	Invokes a callback class.	SWT, Swing
Toggle Data Point Visibility	Changes the visibility of a data point.	SVG, SWT, Swing

After selecting the event type and associated action in Interactivity, choose Add. Remove an existing event type and action pair by selecting the pair and choosing Remove. To update, select an existing pair and select a new event type or action, then choose Update. You can add multiple interactive features to a chart element, but a particular event can produce only one action.

To use some interactive features, such as highlighting, the chart must be formatted in SVG rather than in an image file format, such as GIF or BMP. In addition, the report user must view the report in a browser that has an SVG plug-in and supports JavaScript. To see how an interactive feature works in a chart, you must preview the report in the report viewer.

Linking a chart to a report

One special type of interactivity involves linking a chart value series to a detailed listing of the associated data from the series in another report. To link a chart in this fashion, an event type and action pair must be added to the Value Series element in the interactivity editor. The event type can be set to any UI gesture, but is most often a mouse click, and the action must be set to URL Redirect.

For example, Figure 22-15 shows a URL redirect that has been set up on a bar chart illustrating sales by customer. When the report user clicks the bar associated with a particular customer's sales, the URL redirect action triggers.

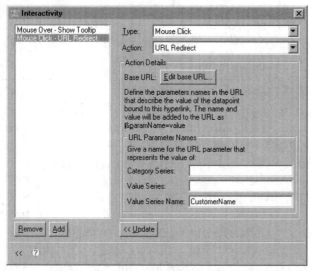

Figure 22-15   The interactivity editor for URL Redirect

A URL redirect action on a value series relies upon the same hyperlink mechanism described earlier in the chapter. In particular, choosing Edit Base URL in Interactivity causes Hyperlink Options to appear to specify the target report and other details. The only difference is in the way that values needed for report parameters are passed. Chart data points can be used to populate report parameters, but because they cannot be accessed directly, you can associate them with the name of the report parameter by supplying the name of the parameter in the interactivity editor, next to the appropriate chart data point.

For example, in Figure 22-15, the value for the chart value series is passed as the report parameter CustomerName. If the report user were to click the bar for a customer named "Acme", the customer would be appended to the target report hyperlink URL as &CustomerName=Acme, and the report would be generated with data associated only with Acme.

Figure 22-16 shows Hyperlink Options with the information required to invoke a drill-through link to the target report, Customers.rptdesign, including the required report parameter CustomerName.

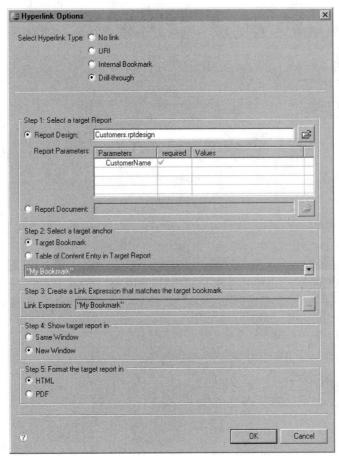

Figure 22-16   Hyperlink options linking a chart to a report

Exporting report data

You can export report data from the report viewer to a comma-separated values (.csv) file by choosing Export data. You can use Export data to quickly extract some or all of the data from a report, then you can use this data in another document or format. For example, you could export customer sales data from a report for a previous quarter, then use the numbers in a spreadsheet to create a forecast for an upcoming one.

How to export report data

1 In the report viewer, choose Export data, as shown in Figure 22-17.

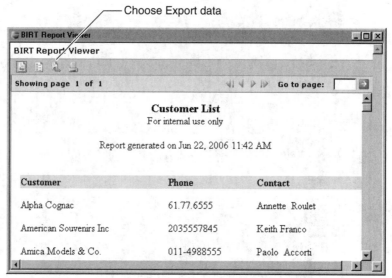

Figure 22-17   Export data button in the report viewer

2 When Export Data appears, select a result set from the drop-down list, then move the data that you want to export from Available Columns to Selected Columns. Figure 22-18 shows selected columns in Export Data.

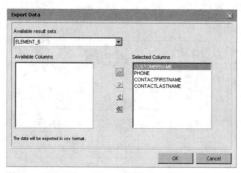

Figure 22-18   Export Data

3 Choose OK. File Download appears.

4 Choose Save, then choose Save As and indicate where to save the file.

Available result sets in Export Data shown in Figure 22-18 lists the container elements that use data, such as tables, charts, and data elements. By default, the name that is displayed in the list is a derivative of the "ELEMENT" string, such as ELEMENT_10. To make it easier for report users to identify the section of the report they wish to export data from, you can give each report element a more meaningful name in Property Editor.

For example, to give a more meaningful name to the main table in a customer report, select the table in the layout editor, and update Name for the General property with "Customer Data", as shown in Figure 22-19.

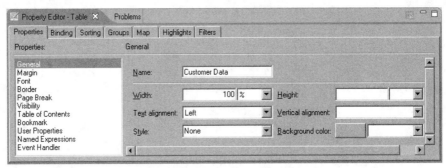

Figure 22-19   Changing result set name in Property Editor

23

Building a Shared Report Development Framework

Previous chapters describe how to create and use data sources and data sets and lay out and format report items. A single report developer with a requirement for only a few reports can use these approaches effectively. For a larger project, either one with more developers or one that requires more reports, many designs need to use the same elements or layouts. In these cases, manual techniques are cumbersome. Developing the same components repeatedly wastes time and is prone to errors. Even if you use the copy-and-paste features of BIRT Report Designer, a report design does not provide convenient access to standard elements and layouts.

BIRT provides the following solutions for designing reports that must conform to standards, including using common design elements and data sources:

■ A library

This type of file stores customized report features, such as data sources, data sets, visual report items, styles, and master pages. Use a library in a report design to access the customized report elements. You can use multiple libraries in a single report design. By using multiple libraries, you can separate the styles and functionality that different projects or processes need.

A library is a dynamic component of a report design. When a library developer makes changes to a library, the report design synchronizes itself with the changed library. In this way, changes propagate easily within a suite of report designs.

■ A template

This type of file provides a structure for a standard report layout. BIRT Report Designer provides a set of standard templates, such as Simple Listing and Grouped Listing report templates. A template can contain visual report items that appear in the report's layout, data sources and data sets, and master page layouts. A template can also use one or more libraries in the same way that a report design does.

A template is a static framework on which to build a new report design. For this reason, a report design can derive from only one template. Additionally, when a template developer changes a template, report designs that are based on that template do not automatically reflect the changes to the template.

Comparing report designs, libraries, and templates

By reading the earlier chapters in this book, you became familiar with the concepts of developing a report design. Developing a library or a template uses similar skills. All these file types use the same report elements from the palette, the data explorer, and the outline view in BIRT Report Designer, but you use each type for a different purpose. Figure 23-1, which illustrates the simplest outlines for each file type, shows the structural differences.

Figure 23-1   Basic structures of report designs, libraries, and templates

The following sections clarify the differences between these file types.

About the report design file type

The main purpose of a report design file is to generate reports by retrieving data from a data set and formatting that data into a layout. The file-name extension for a report design file is .rptdesign.

A report design can contain any number of report features. Data sources, data sets, and report parameters are non-visual elements that you access in the data explorer. You place visual elements in the design by dragging them from the palette and dropping them in the layout. A report design can also include embedded images. You can access any element in a report design by using the outline view. To affect the appearance of the pages in a paginated report, you use the master page, and to ensure a consistent appearance for multiple parts of a report design, you can create and apply styles.

About the library file type

The main purpose of a library is to provide developers of report designs with a shared repository of predesigned report elements. The file-name extension for a library file is .rptlibrary.

Like a report design, a library can include any number of report elements and any type of report element. You add elements to a library by using the palette and the data explorer or by copying them from a report design. If you have a report design that contains all the report elements that you need in a particular library, you can even create a library directly from that report design. Because a library is not a design, there is no Body node in the outline. Instead, a library has a Report Items node, which contains all the visual report items in the library.

When you have added the components to the library, you group related styles into a theme. This grouping provides quick access to all of the necessary styles for that theme. The Themes node in a library takes the place of the Styles node in the other file types.

To share a library across a team of report developers, set the resource folder for each developer to the same shared location, then publish the library to that folder. The developer uses the library explorer to access report elements from the libraries.

About the template file type

The main purpose of a template is to provide a standard start position for a new report design. As such, the structure of a template file is identical to the structure of a report design file. The file-name extension for a template file is .rpttemplate.

A template includes the master pages that the report design uses and any number of report elements. In addition to standard report elements, a template file can include template report elements. These elements display instructions to the report developer about how to use the template. Designing a template is just the same as designing a report design. Indeed, you can create a report design, then save it as a template.

To share a template across a team of report developers, set the template folder for each developer to the same shared location, then publish the template to that folder. When a developer chooses File➙New➙Report, BIRT Report Designer lists all templates in that folder as well as the standard BIRT templates.

Sharing report elements in a library

A library provides a straightforward way to use custom styles and report elements. You can make any change to the properties of a report element and copy the element to a library. When you do, the customized element is available to any report design that uses the library directly. When you use an element from a library in a report design, you can change any properties, but you cannot change the structure of the element. For example, if you use a table from a library, you can change the table's style or data binding, but you cannot add or remove columns or groups.

Figure 23-2 shows the structure of a report design that uses a library. The expanded Libraries item shows all the libraries that the report design uses. In this example, the report design uses three libraries.

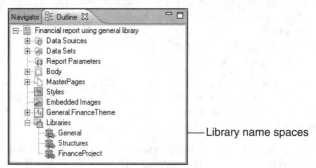

Figure 23-2   The outline view, showing included libraries

A report design can use multiple libraries, so you can separate logical sets of report elements. BIRT uses the concept of name space to identify the sets of report elements that each library contains. Using a separate name space for each library ensures that BIRT distinguishes between items that have the same name but appear in different libraries.

Table 23-1 describes some of the many possible uses of elements from a library. The table gives only one example use for each type of report element. When you start to design a suite of reports, you will find many more reasons to share report items.

Table 23-1   Examples of uses for shared report elements

Report element	Shared use
Data source	Typically, provides data sources for a whole reporting project. Change the data source in the library from a test data source to the live data source when the project is deployed.
Data set	Provides a data set for multiple reports that use the same data. For example, a suite of profit-and-loss reports can use the same tables. Take care when using a shared data set. You must ensure that a shared data set efficiently provides the correct rows for each report design that uses it. In some cases, using different data sets improves performance or accuracy.

Table 23-1 Examples of uses for shared report elements *(continued)*

Report element	Shared use
Label	Provides simply formatted, standard text for a report design. For example, a shared label can be a legal notice, such as "Company confidential" with the required font and size.
Text	Provides standard text that needs complex formatting. For example, a text element can display your company's standard terms and conditions of sale.
Dynamic text	Provides formatted text from a data field or expression. For example, a dynamic text element can display notes about a customer's order.
Data	Provides data or expressions. For example, a data element can display the result of a common calculation, such as the extended price of a line item in a purchase order.
Image	Provides a standard image, such as a company logo.
Grid	Provides a container for other report items. For example, a grid can display a number of static items, such as a company logo in an image element or an address in a label or text element.
List	Provides a container for data-driven report items. For example, a list can bind to a standard data set, such as customers or orders.
Table	Provides a container for data-driven report items in columns. For example, a table can bind to a data set for orders and contain data elements that display order number, order status, and order date.
Chart	Provides a graphical summary of data. For example, a bar chart can display its categories and series in a preferred arrangement. A report developer can use that chart from a library and bind the data fields without needing to know everything about how to design a chart.
Style	Supports using standard style properties, such as company colors and fonts.

Dynamic library behavior

A key feature of a library is that it is dynamic. This means that when you change a library, the same changes occur in report designs that use the library. For example, if the preferred font for your company changes from Times New Roman to Arial Unicode, you make the changes to styles in a library. When you generate a report from any design that uses styles from that library, or when you open or refresh the design in BIRT Report Designer, the changes take effect.

This dynamic behavior ensures that all report elements that derive from a library always use the current styles and properties. For this reason, when you implement a policy of using libraries, you must ensure that every custom element that more than one report design uses derives from a library element. If you use an element directly from the palette and customize it in the same way in multiple designs, the benefits of dynamic library updating are not available.

Sometimes, BIRT cannot apply changes from a modified library to a report design without additional action on the part of a report developer. The following list describes these situations:

- The name of the library changes or the library no longer exists.

- The library no longer contains an element that the report design uses.

- The name of the element in the library changes.

- The name of the element in the library refers to a different type of element.

If BIRT Report Designer opens a report design that has any of these problems, a warning message appears in the layout in place of the affected report element, as shown in Figure 23-3. To repair any of these conditions, you must delete the element that is causing the problem. Alternatively, if you are familiar with XML, you can edit the XML source of the report design. If you choose to edit the XML, you should back up the report design first.

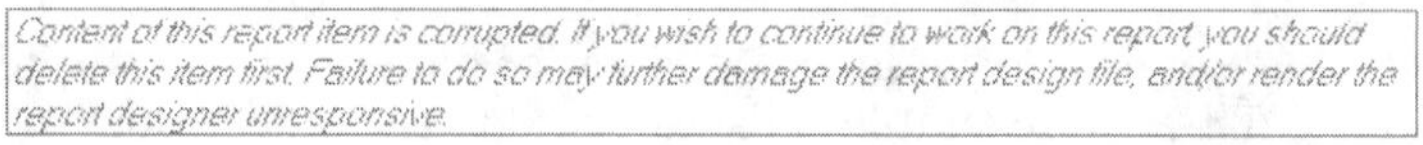

> Content of this report item is corrupted. If you wish to continue to work on this report, you should delete this item first. Failure to do so may further damage the report design file, and/or render the report designer unresponsive.

Figure 23-3   A report item that cannot access a library definition

Sharing styles

A library provides a flexible way to share sets of styles. A library groups styles into themes. In the outline view for a library, instead of Styles, you see Themes. In a newly created library, Themes contains one theme, defaultTheme. By default, the library uses the styles in this theme to display report items in the layout.

When you use a library in a report design, you can assign a single theme to the report design. The property editor shows the theme that the report design is using, as shown in Figure 23-4. To assign a theme to a report design, you drag the theme from the library in the library explorer and drop it onto the report design. This action makes all the styles in that theme available to items in the report design. Any predefined styles, such as grid, table, and so on, take effect immediately on items in the design. You can use custom styles from the theme in the same way that you use custom styles that are defined in the report design itself. If you define a style with the same name in the report design as one in the library, BIRT uses the style that you define in the report design.

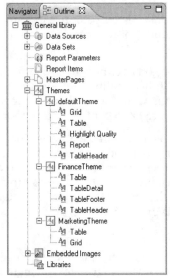

Figure 23-4 Properties for a report design that uses a theme

You can create multiple themes in a single library. For example, you can create styles in the default theme for use in most report designs, then make special themes for financial and marketing report designs, as shown in Figure 23-5.

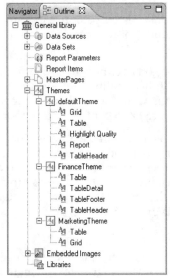

Figure 23-5 Multiple themes in a library

As discussed earlier in this section, a report design can use styles from only one theme. For this reason, if you need some styles to be the same for all themes, you can copy the style from the theme in which you create the style to the other themes.

Because a library is dynamic, when you add styles to a theme, they become available to a report design that uses that theme. For example, consider a theme that does not have a style called table. Tables in a report design that uses this theme use the default style. Later, a library developer adds a style called table to the theme. Now the appearance of the tables in that design match the style that is defined in the theme.

Understanding library name space

When you use a library in a report design, BIRT assigns a name space to the library. This name space identifies every report element from the library that the report design uses. By default, BIRT Report Designer bases the name space on the file name of the library. For example, if the name of the library is FinanceProject.rptlibrary, the name space is FinanceProject. In Figure 23-2, earlier in this chapter, you see an example of how BIRT Report Designer displays the name space in the outline view of a report design.

If you use more than one library with the same default name space, BIRT Report Designer prompts you for a name space for the second and subsequent libraries. In this case, provide a name space that distinguishes the library from the others but shows a relationship to the original library name.

Designing libraries for a shared environment

A library is a key tool for achieving consistent appearance in a suite of report designs. A library also reduces the amount of repetitive work that report developers must complete.

To use libraries effectively, you should consider how to structure the libraries to make best use of their properties and functionality. Although you can use a single library that contains every custom component that your report designs need, this library could become very large and confusing for report developers.

One way to design a suite of libraries is first to make libraries that contain elements that are common to all reporting projects. After you create these general libraries, you can create a project-specific library for each reporting project. These project libraries can contain elements that are simple modifications of the standard report elements. They can also contain complex elements, such as tables nested within grids or lists.

For example, you can create the following libraries:

- A general library that contains standard items that all projects use, such as themes, an image element for the company logo, a text element that contains a confidentiality agreement, and grid elements with standard contents for page headers and footers

- A library that all projects use for complex items, for example, a table element with predefined behavior, such as highlighting

- For each project, one or more libraries that contain elements that are specific to the project, such as data sources

By building suites of libraries in this way, you provide the building blocks for a standard appearance for all reports, then you package the behavior and appearance of report elements that are appropriate to each reporting project. You make the suite of libraries available to report developers by placing them in a repository that is known as the resource folder.

The final step in implementing libraries is to use a library in a report design. A report design can use any library in its project and in the resource folder. The design has access to all the customized elements in these libraries. Figure 23-6 shows a representation of an architecture for libraries and report designs.

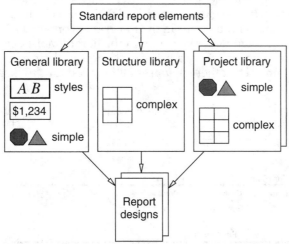

Figure 23-6   Project architecture using libraries

Defining a general library

The purpose of a general library is to provide a foundation for common elements that can appear in any report designs in any reporting project. A general library contains standard, simple items, such as a company logo image element. This library also contains a default theme that includes settings for predefined styles and any custom styles for all report designs. If multiple reporting projects need to use a different theme, place that theme in this library. Figure 23-5, earlier in this chapter, shows an example of such a library.

Defining a structures library

A structures library provides grids, lists, and tables to report designs. For example, imagine that most of your report designs use a table element. Initially, the table element in your library is identical in behavior to the table from the palette. Later, you discover a need to alternate the row colors for every table in every report design. You make the change to the tables in the library, and every report design that uses the table from the library now has the new feature. If your structures library did not contain table elements, you would have to make this change manually.

When you create grid, list, and table elements in a library, you need to consider the contents of the cells as well as the layout and behavior of the element itself. As discussed earlier in this chapter, when a report design uses an element from a library, the structure of the element is not modifiable. You can change only the properties of an element that is derived from an item in a library. For this reason, the recommended practice is to place a report item in every cell in a grid, list, or table that you define in a library. By changing the properties of the labels or data items after you place the element in a report design, you can use the same structure to achieve many different results.

Figure 23-7 shows an example of this approach. The table in the library has four columns. The cells in the header row contain labels, the cells in the detail row contain data elements, and the cells in the footer row contain a label and data elements. A report design uses two copies of the library table. One copy modifies the cell contents to show a list of customers in three columns with a fourth empty column. The other copy uses all four columns to display order information.

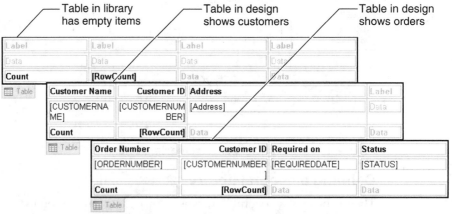

Figure 23-7   Customizing a table from a library

Defining a project library

The purpose of a project library is to provide customized report elements for report designs within a single reporting project.

The most common elements that are specific to a project are data sources. You can also include data sets in a project library, but, for best report generation speed, a report design should use a data set that is designed for its specific needs. A data set that a library provides is often too general for optimum efficiency, because it retrieves more fields from that data source than most report designs require.

Other simple elements that a project library can contain are project-specific image elements and text elements with standard wording and formatting. A project library can also contain complex, structured elements, such as tables with custom layout or behavior.

There are two ways to set up a project library:

- Customizing only the project-specific report elements

  Report developers use this library and the general libraries in every new report design for this project. They use the report items from the project library or from the palette.

  Use this technique if the project customizes only a few elements or provides only complex structures to complement the elements from the palette.

- Customizing every type of report element

  Report developers use this library in every new report design for the project. Instead of using report items directly from the palette or the general libraries, they use report items from the project library.

  Use this technique if the project customizes many elements or if the project's requirements are likely to change frequently.

Understanding the resource folder

BIRT Report Designer uses the resource folder as a repository for libraries. The location of the resource folder is specified in the Preferences page, which you access by choosing Windows→Preferences from the main menu, then choosing the Report Design Resource item. Place general and project libraries in the resource folder. This folder should be one that all report developers can access, such as a directory on a shared network drive.

If you have a large number of libraries, you can use subfolders to organize the libraries in a logical way. For example, the \\SharedServer\Resource\General folder can contain the general libraries, and \\SharedServer\Resource\Finance can contain the Finance libraries.

To place a library into the resource folder, you can publish a library from your current workspace or you can add a library from an external location. Make sure that your library has a meaningful file name because BIRT Report Designer displays this name to the report developers who use the resource folder.

How to publish a library from your workspace

1 Open the library in BIRT Report Designer.

2 Choose File→Publish Library to Resource Folder.

3 On Publish Library, as shown in Figure 23-8, make changes to the file name and folder. For example, change the file name of the library if you need to make the name more meaningful. Use Browse if you want to place the library in a subfolder of the resource folder. Choose Finish.

4 On the context menu in the library explorer, choose Refresh. The new library appears in the list of available libraries.

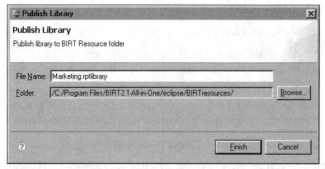

Figure 23-8   Publishing a library

How to add an external library to the resource folder

1 On the context menu in the library explorer, choose Add Library.

2 On Add Library, choose Browse to navigate to and select a library from the file system, as shown in Figure 23-9. You can also make changes to the file name and folder in the same way as for publishing a library from your workspace. Choose Finish.

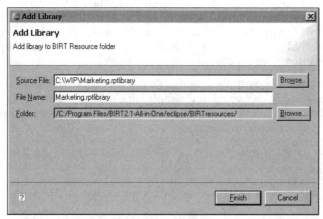

Figure 23-9   Adding an external library

3 On the context menu in the library explorer, choose Refresh. The new library appears in the list of available libraries.

Using a library

BIRT Report Designer provides a tool, the library explorer, which supports access to all libraries in the resource folder and its subfolders. Figure 23-10 shows the appearance of the library explorer.

Figure 23-10   The library explorer

The library explorer shows all the elements in each library in a tree structure, the same as the structure of an open library in the outline view. Because a library does not have a Body slot to order report sections in the report layout, visual report elements are in a Report Items slot. Figure 23-11 shows an example of how the elements in a library appear in the library explorer.

The main difference between the outline view and the library explorer is that you cannot open a library or modify the elements in a library from the library explorer. You can only change elements in a library that you open in the editor. You open a library in the editor in the same way that you open a report design, by using the navigator or, in BIRT RCP Report Designer, by choosing File→Open.

Figure 23-11   The library explorer, showing elements in a library

When you open a library in BIRT Report Designer, no layout appears in the layout editor. Unlike a report design, a library has no Body slot that orders the sections in the layout. Instead, you design each report item separately by selecting an item from Report Items in the outline view. Figure 23-12 shows an example of editing a table element in a library.

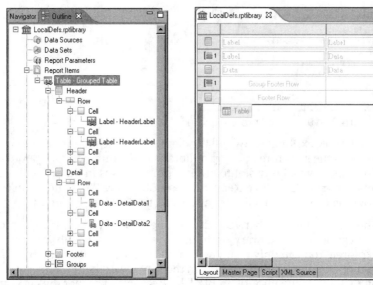

Figure 23-12 Library report item structure and layout

The library explorer does not check actively for changes to libraries. For this reason, it does not immediately display changes to the list of available libraries or the items in an individual library. To update the view in the library explorer, right-click inside it, and choose Refresh.

Creating a library

BIRT Report Designer provides two ways to create a library. Use whichever technique best suits your requirements. The creation options are:

- Creating an empty library

  From the Eclipse main menu, choose File→New→Library. Use this technique if you have no existing report designs or if you have many existing designs that use different styles or property settings. You can create a set of related report elements that do not depend on existing designs.

- Creating a library from an existing report design

  In the outline view, right-click the report design root, and choose Export. Use this technique if you have an existing report design that contains report elements that use the desired properties and styles.

When you name a library file, BIRT uses this name to build the name space when you use the library in a report design. The name space appears in the Libraries node in the outline view for the report design and in the names of themes, styles, and unmodified library report items that the report design uses.

After you create the library, you add report elements to the library. In many ways, this process is similar to adding elements to a report design. You add data sources and data sets to the library in exactly the same way as to a report design.

You add styles to a theme in the outline view, rather than directly to Styles. To add visual report items, you drag the item from the palette to the layout editor or to the Report Items node in the outline view.

How to add an element to a library

Creating an element in a library uses the same wizards and dialogs as when you create an element in a report design. After you add an element to a library, you make changes to it in the same way as you do in a report design.

1   Open or create a library.

2   In the data explorer, create any required data sources and data sets.

3   To add a style, in the outline view, expand the Themes node.

4   Right-click a theme, then choose New Style.

5   To add a theme, in the outline view, right-click the Themes node, and choose New Theme.

6   To add a report item, drag an item from the palette to Report Items in the outline view. The item appears both in Report Items and in the layout editor.

Accessing report items from a library in a report design

Using report items from a library is as straightforward as using items from the palette. In the library explorer, you expand the library that you need, and you expand Report Items inside that library. Then, you drag the report item to the layout of your report design. If this item is the first use that you make of a library, BIRT Report Designer displays a message to let you know that you added the library to the report design. In the outline view of your report design, the icon of an item from a library appears with a link, as shown in Figure 23-13.

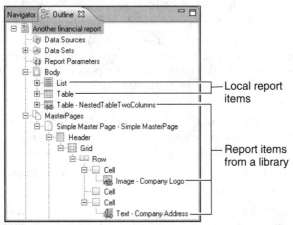

Figure 23-13   The outline view showing report items from a library

When you select an item in your report design that comes from a library, the property editor displays the extra field, Library, as shown in Figure 23-14. This field shows the full path of the library that provides the definition of the item.

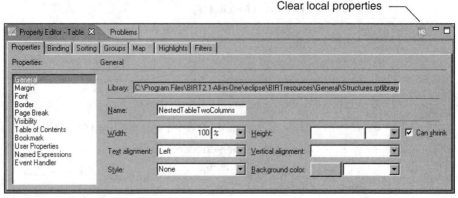

Figure 23-14   The property editor for a table element from a library

To add a data source from a library to a report design, you drag the data source from the library in the library explorer to Data Sources in the outline view or the data explorer. You can then create data sets that use the data source. If you need to use a data set from a library, you first add its data source to the report design, then you drag the data set to the outline view or the data explorer.

Making local changes to a library element in a report design

Typically, when you use a library element in a report design, you need to modify the element's properties in some way. For example, you might want to increase the size of the text in a text element that contains a confidentiality agreement. As shown earlier in this chapter in Figure 23-7, you can also change the values and expressions in labels and other report items in a table.

You make changes to the item's properties in the same way that you change any other item in the report design. The report design stores only the changes that you make to the report item. BIRT takes all other properties from the item in the library. In this way, BIRT retains the dynamic nature of the library item while supporting your local changes.

As discussed earlier in this chapter, you can only change the properties of a report item, not its structure, so you cannot add or remove columns or groups in a grid, list, or table element that comes from a library.

You can also make changes to the query in a data set from a library. To open the data set editor, you double-click the data set.

If you need to revert to the original properties of the element, you select the Clear local properties button on the property editor's tool bar. Figure 23-14 shows the location of this button. When you select this button, BIRT Report Designer prompts you to confirm that you want to discard your changes.

Using themes and styles from a library

To use a style from a library, you first set the Themes property of the report design to the library theme that contains the style that you need. The report design then has access to all the styles in that theme. As shown in Figure 23-15, the styles in the theme appear in the outline view in a new item, Themes.

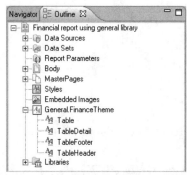

Figure 23-15   Theme styles in the outline view

A report design has access to the themes in all the libraries that it uses, but it can use styles from only one theme. For this reason, the library developer must place all the necessary styles in each theme. Predefined styles in the theme, such as table or grid, take effect when you select the theme in the property editor. Custom styles from the library are available in the list of styles in the property editor for a report item.

If the report design contains styles that have the same names as styles in the current theme, the report design's styles take effect. To revert a report design to use only its local styles, set the Themes property of the report design to None. When you do this, the outline view no longer shows a Themes item.

How to set a theme for a report design

1   In the library explorer, expand the library that contains the theme. Expand the Themes node in the library.

2   Drag the theme that you want to use from the library explorer and drop it in the layout editor.

    Any predefined styles in the theme take effect in the report design immediately. The appearance of any report items in the layout editor changes to match the styles in the theme. The library appears in the Libraries node of the outline view.

How to drop a theme from a report design

You drop a theme from a report design by changing the Theme property of the report root item.

1   To access the report design's properties, in the outline view, select the report root item.

Figure 23-16 shows this item selected. This item shows either the report design's file name or its title property value, if it has one.

Figure 23-16   Report root item

2 In the property editor, select None from the list in Themes, as shown in Figure 23-17.

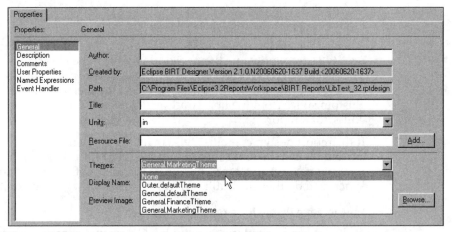

Figure 23-17   Selecting a theme in the property editor

Now, the theme that the report design uses is None, which means that it uses only its own styles, not styles from a theme in a library.

Sharing a report layout as a template

A template provides a straightforward way to use a custom layout and master pages for a suite of reports. You design a template in the same way that you design a report. A template can contain data sources, data sets, master pages, and any type of report item.

Just like a report design, a template can use report elements and themes from a library. In this way, templates extend the shared development effort that libraries provide. Libraries provide access to sets of individual report elements, but templates assemble them into a standard report layout. For example, a template for a bulk marketing letter can use a company logo from a general library and the marketing theme and a data source from the marketing project library. The report designs that build on the template get the addressees and the content for the letter from a report-specific data set.

You can develop a template directly or use an existing report design as the basis for a template. Figure 23-18 shows how the library architecture extends to building templates.

After you design a template, you publish the template to a shared location. You define this location on the Report Design Preferences Template page, which you access by choosing Windows→Preferences. BIRT Report Designer checks this location when a report developer creates a new report design. The new template appears in the list of report templates in the New Report wizard.

To provide visual assistance to the report developer, you can associate an image with the template. This image appears in the preview area of the wizard when the developer selects the template.

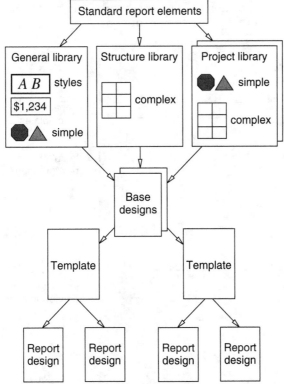

Figure 23-18 Project architecture using templates

Developing a custom template

BIRT Report Designer provides two ways to create a template. Use whichever technique best suits your requirements. The creation options are:

- Creating an empty template

  From the Eclipse main menu, choose File→New→Template. Use this technique if you have no existing report designs that have the required structure.

- Creating a template from an existing report design

  Open the report design. From the Eclipse main menu, choose File→Save As. Change the file type of the report design to .rpttemplate. Use this technique if you have an existing report design that has the structure that you need.

When you create a template, the New Template wizard prompts you for template-specific properties. Figure 23-19 shows the properties and describes where they appear in the wizard. These properties appear in the template selection page of the New Report wizard when the report developer selects the template as the start position for a report design. You must always supply a Display Name. The other properties are optional.

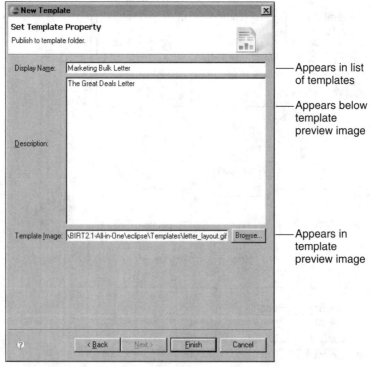

Figure 23-19   Template-specific properties

When the report developer selects a custom template in the New Report wizard, its preview image appears, if you supplied one. Figure 23-20 shows an example of a custom template that has a preview image.

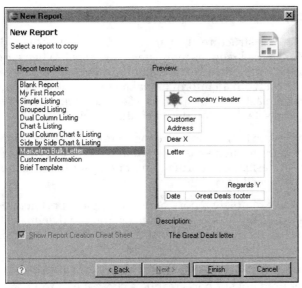

Figure 23-20   Using a custom template

If you do not supply some of the optional template properties, the New Report wizard displays default values. Figure 23-21 shows how such a template appears.

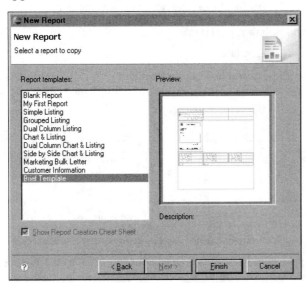

Figure 23-21   Template with no description or template image

No description appears for the template. Because you have not supplied a template image, BIRT Report Designer creates a thumbnail image of the layout of the report design in Preview.

Designing template report items

After you develop the structure of a template, you can choose to identify some or all of the items in the layout as template report items. When a report developer uses the template to create a report design, a template report item appears in the layout with an informational message. Double-clicking the template report item activates the item as a standard report item with the properties that you set when you designed the template.

A template can contain both template report items and normal report items. Use template report items for items that you want the report developer to modify for the new report design. Use normal report items for items that the report developer does not need to change.

Typically, you create template report items on simple report items, such as text or data elements inside a table or grid element. You can then make the container into a template element, with overall instructions for the items inside it.

If you need to provide complex instructions for using a template, you can create a set of instructions for the template that is called a cheat sheet. BIRT RCP Report Designer does not support creating a cheat sheet. You need to use BIRT Report Designer, which includes the Eclipse Plug-in Development Environment. To create a cheat sheet, choose Help→Help Contents. In the Eclipse online help, see the Advanced Workbench Concepts topic inside the Platform Plug-in Developer Guide book's Programmer's Guide. The cheat sheet property is available in the Properties view for a template.

How to create a template report item

1 Create or open a template.

2 Add a report item to the layout, or select an existing item in the layout. For example, Figure 23-22 shows a text item inside a table item.

Figure 23-22 Standard appearance of text element

3 Right-click the report item, and choose Create Template Report Item.

4 On Create Template Report Item, type instructions to the report developer. These instructions explain how to use the report item. Figure 23-23 shows an example of some instructions.

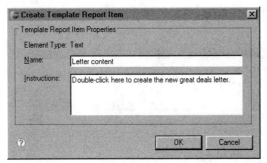

Figure 23-23 Providing instructions for a template report item

5 Choose OK.

The report item now appears in the layout as a template report item. The template report item displays an icon that is appropriate to the type of report item and the instructions that you provided.

Figure 23-24 shows how a text element appears.

Figure 23-24 Text element as a template report item

Publishing a template

To make a template available to report developers, you publish the template to a template folder. The default location of the template folder is the folder in the BIRT report designer user interface plug-in that contains the standard templates. Typically, this folder is not in a shared location, so you need to change it. You define the template folder within your Eclipse preferences. Next, you publish the template. If the template has a preview image, copy the image to the template folder. You must also ensure that the preview image's location in the template is the shared template folder.

How to set up a template folder

1 From the Eclipse main menu, choose Window➤Preferences.

2 In Preferences, expand Report Design, and choose Template.

3 To navigate to the template folder, choose Select, then choose OK.

How to publish a template

1 Open the report template, then choose File➤Publish to Template Folder.

2 In Publish to Template Folder, check the properties, as shown in Figure 23-25.

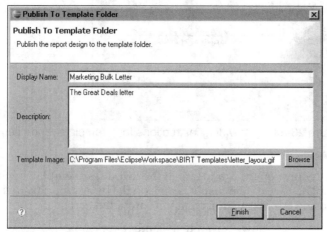

Figure 23-25 Publishing a template

3 Make any corrections to the properties, then choose Finish.

Using a custom template

To use a custom template as a starting point for a report design, you must define the template folder, following the instructions from earlier in this chapter. After you set up the template folder, the New Report wizard includes the custom template in the list of available templates.

After you choose Finish in the New Report wizard, BIRT Report Designer displays the layout of the template in the layout editor. All the report elements in the template, such as data sources, data sets, and visual report items, are available for editing in the same way that you edit a predefined template.

A template can include template report items as well as standard report items in the layout. You can see the appearance of a template report item in Figure 23-24, earlier in this chapter.

How to use a template report item

To use a template report item, you must create a report design from a template that contains a template report item. This example uses the predefined Chart and Listing template.

1 Create a report design. In the New Report wizard, choose the Chart and Listing predefined template.

2 In the layout editor, follow the instructions in the cheat sheet.

The final instruction is to edit the chart. The chart item is a template report item. This item appears in the layout with an appropriate icon and instructional text, as shown in Figure 23-26. The text supplements the instructions in the cheat sheet. In this case, the instructions are similar.

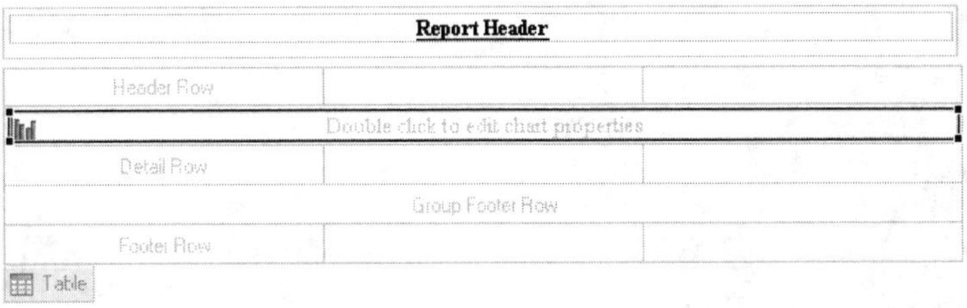

Figure 23-26   Using a template report item

When you double-click the template report item, the chart builder appears.

3 Set up the chart as described earlier in this book.

The chart now appears as a standard chart element in the layout.

4 To discard the changes that you made to the chart, right-click the chart element, and choose Revert to Template Item. The chart now appears as the original template report item, as shown in Figure 23-26.

Chapter

24

Localizing Text

When you insert label and text elements in a report, you typically type the text that you want to display. Use literal, or static, text if a report will always be viewed in one language or locale. If, however, a report will be translated into multiple languages, BIRT Report Designer enables you to use resource keys rather than static text. The resource keys are translated, or localized, in resource files.

If you are not familiar with resource keys or resource files, think of resource keys as variables and resource files as text files in which the variables are set to their values. If a report needs to appear in four languages, you create four resource files to define text values for each language. When a report runs, BIRT uses the machine's current locale, the resource keys, and the resource files to find the appropriate text value to display. Figure 24-1 shows the functions of resource files and resource keys in a localized report.

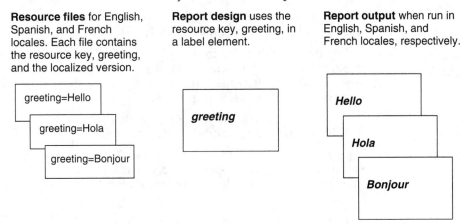

Resource files for English,
Spanish, and French
locales. Each file contains
the resource key, greeting,
and the localized version.

Report design uses the
resource key, greeting, in
a label element.

Report output when run in
English, Spanish, and
French locales, respectively.

greeting=Hello

greeting=Hola

greeting=Bonjour

greeting

Hello

Hola

Bonjour

Figure 24-1   Resource keys in resource files, the report design, and the report

You can specify resource keys for these items:

- Static text in label, text, and chart elements. For example, you can localize report titles, column headings, chart titles, and other static labels. You cannot localize text values that come from a data set.

- Report parameters.

Overview of the localization process

The localization process for BIRT reports is similar to the localization process for Java applications. This section provides an overview of the entire process. Steps that you perform using BIRT Report Designer are described in more detail in later sections. The basic steps are as follows:

- Create the default resource file. The resource file is a text file with a .properties file-name extension. In this file, you define all the resource keys in key=value format:

  ```
  hello=Hello
  thanks=Thank you
  ```

  If you know the text strings that you want to localize, you can create the resource file in an external text editor and define the keys before you build your report. Alternatively, you can create the resource file in BIRT Report Designer and define keys as you add label and text elements to the report.

- If you create the default resource file in an external text editor, place the file in the resource folder. If you create the resource file in BIRT Report Designer, the file is created in the resource folder. The location of the resource folder is specified in the Preferences page, which you access by choosing Windows➤Preferences from the main menu, then choosing the Report Design Resource item.

- For each report parameter, label, text, or chart element that you want to localize, indicate which resource key to use.

- When you finish defining the keys in the default resource file, create a resource file for each language that the report will support. The file name must include the language code and, if necessary, the region code. The file name must be in the following format:

  ```
  <filename>_<ISO 639 language code>_
     <ISO 3166 region code>.properties
  ```

  For example, MyResources_en_US.properties is for U.S. English, and MyResources_en_UK.properties is for British English. For a list of supported language and region codes, see the Java reference documentation at the following URL:

  ```
  http://java.sun.com
  ```

- In the localized resource files, use the same set of keys that are defined in the default resource file, and set their values to the translated strings. A quick way to create the keys is to make a copy of the default resource file then, edit the values. Unless you are multilingual, this task is typically done by a team of translators.

  The following examples show resource keys and values that could appear in two localized versions of the same information:

  ```
  MyResources_fr.properties:

      hello=Bonjour
      thanks=Merci

  MyResources_es.properties:

      hello=Hola
      thanks=Gracias
  ```

- Use the native2ascii command to convert the localized resource files to a format that the Java platform can use. The command requires an input file name and an output file name, so copy the resource file to a temporary file, then use the correct file name as the output file name.

  The following example converts a Japanese resource file:

  ```
  copy MyResource_ja.properties temp.properties
  native2ascii -encoding SJIS temp.properties
      MyResource_ja.properties
  ```

  For more information about native2ascii and the list of supported encoding character sets, see the Java reference documentation at the following URL:

  ```
  http://java.sun.com
  ```

- Place all the localized resource files in the resource folder. When a report runs, BIRT uses the appropriate resource file to find the localized text values to display. If BIRT cannot find a resource file for a specific locale, it uses the default resource file.

Assigning a resource file to a report

You can add as many resource files as you need to the resource folder. Different reports in a project can use different resource files. However, you can assign only one resource file to a report. You assign a resource file to a report by completing one of the following tasks:

- Select a resource file that currently resides in the resource folder.

- Create a new resource file in BIRT Report Designer, then assign it to the report.

If you select an existing file, you can assign the keys that are defined in that file to report parameters, label, text, or chart elements. If you create a new resource file, it contains no keys. You define the keys as you add report parameters, label, or text elements to the report.

How to assign a resource file to a report

1 In the layout editor, select the report by clicking in an empty area on the report page.

2 In the property editor, choose General properties. The property editor displays the general properties for the report, as shown in Figure 24-2.

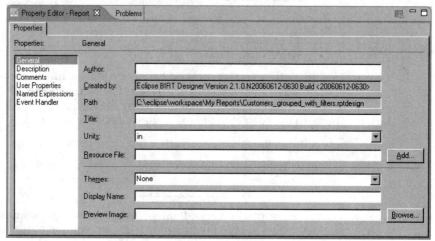

Figure 24-2   General properties for a report

3 Choose Add, next to the Resource File field.

4 On Browse Resource Files, indicate which resource file to use by completing one of the following tasks:

 ■ To use a resource file that currently exists in the resource folder, select the resource file displayed under the resource folder.

 ■ To create a new resource file using BIRT Report Designer, in New File Name, type a name for the new resource file, such as SalesReportResources.properties. You must type the .properties file-name extension.

5 Choose OK.

The name of the resource file appears in Resource File on the general properties page. The report uses the selected resource file. You can, at any time, specify a different resource file to use. You can also specify no resource file by deleting the file name from the Resource File on the general properties page for the report.

Assigning a resource key to a label or text element

After you assign a resource file to a report, you can localize the text in label and text elements by assigning a resource key to each label or text element. You can assign a resource key that you defined earlier, or you can define a new resource key, then assign it to the label or text element.

How to assign an existing resource key to a label or text element

1   In the layout editor, select the label or text element that you want to localize.

2   In the property editor, choose Localization.

 3   Choose the ellipsis (...) button that is next to the Text key field. This button is enabled only if you have already assigned a resource file to the report. Select Key displays the current list of keys and values that are defined in the resource file that the report uses, as shown in Figure 24-3.

Figure 24-3   Select Key

4   Select the key to assign to the label or text element, then choose OK. In the layout editor, the label or text element displays the value that corresponds to the key.

How to define a new resource key

1   Select the label or text element that you want to localize.

2   In the property editor, choose Localization.

 3   Choose the ellipsis (...) button that is next to the Text key field. This button is enabled only if you have already assigned a resource file to the report. Select Key displays the list of keys and values that are defined in the resource file that the report uses.

4   If the key you want to assign is not in the list, add a new key:

    1   In Quick Add, provide a key and value, then choose Add. The key is added to the resource file and appears in the list of keys.

2   To assign the key to the label or text element, select the key from the list, then choose OK. In the layout editor, the label or text element displays the value that corresponds to the key.

Changing localized text in a label or text element to static text

If you change your mind about localizing a label or text element, you can remove the resource key and use static text instead.

How to remove a resource key from a label or text element

1   Select the label or text element.

2   In the property editor, choose Localization. The property editor displays localization information for the selected element, as shown in Figure 24-4.

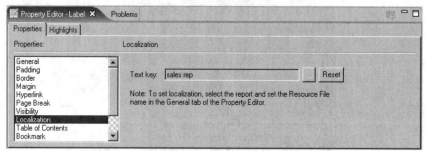

Figure 24-4   Localization properties for an element

3   Choose Reset. The label or text element displays either nothing or the default static text, if you specified any default text when you inserted the element.

Assigning a resource key to chart text

After you assign a resource file to your report, you can localize static text in a chart, such as the chart title and axis titles, by assigning a resource key to the chart text.

How to assign a resource key to chart text

1   In the layout editor, double-click the chart element to open the chart builder, then choose Format Chart.

2   Navigate to the section for the chart part that you want to localize. For example, to localize the chart title, navigate to the Chart Area section. To localize the y-axis title, navigate to the Y-Axis section. Figure 24-5 shows the portion of the chart builder that you use to work with the y-axis.

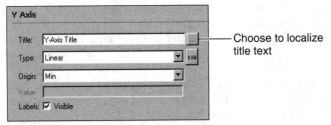

Figure 24-5 Localizing title text on the y-axis

3 Choose the ellipsis (...) button that is next to the field to localize. Externalize Text appears, as shown in Figure 24-6.

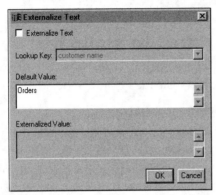

Figure 24-6 Externalize Text, displaying default settings

4 Assign a resource key to the chart text:

1 Select Externalize Text. The list of resource keys is enabled in the drop-down list that is next to Lookup Key.

2 From the drop-down list, select a key to assign to the chart text. The value that corresponds to the key that you selected appears in Externalized Value, as shown in Figure 24-7.

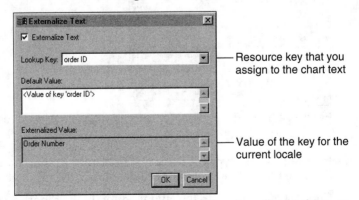

Figure 24-7 Resource key and its externalized value

If the key and value pair that you want to use for the chart text is not available, you can edit the resource file to add a new key. Information about this task appears later in this chapter.

3 Choose OK.

The title field in Edit Chart shows the title's display value in read-only format. To use a different resource key, choose the ellipsis (...) button to open the Externalize Text editor, and select a different key from the list.

5 Choose Finish to close the chart builder and return to the layout editor. In the report design, the chart text displays the value that corresponds to the key that you selected.

Changing localized chart text to static text

If you change your mind about localizing text in a chart, you can remove the resource key and use static text instead.

How to remove a resource key from chart text

1 Navigate to the Format Chart section for the chart part that you want to change.

2 Choose the ellipsis (...) button that is next to the field that you want to change.

Externalize Text displays the resource key that is assigned to the chart part, as shown in Figure 24-8.

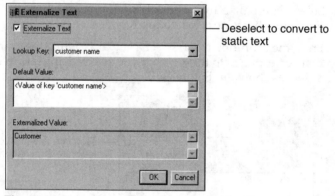

Figure 24-8   Externalize Text, displaying the assigned resource key

3 Deselect Externalize Text.

4 In Default Value, type the static text to display for the chart part, then choose OK. The title field in the chart builder shows the title's new display value.

5 Choose OK to return to the layout editor. In the report design, the chart displays the static text that you typed.

Assigning a resource key to a report parameter

You assign a resource key to a report parameter to localize the text that prompts report users to supply a value for the report parameter. Figure 24-9 shows the dialog box, Enter Parameters, that displays report parameters to the report user. You can localize only the name of a report parameter. In Enter Parameters, the report parameter name appears next to the curly braces symbol, { }.

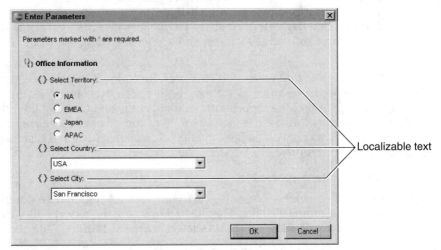

Figure 24-9   Text that can be localized in Enter Parameters

How to assign a resource key to a report parameter

These instructions assume you have already created the report parameters.

1   In Data Explorer, under Report Parameters, select the report parameter that you want to localize.

2   In the property editor, choose Localization.

3   Choose the ellipsis (...) button that is next to the Text key field. This button is enabled only if you have already assigned a resource file to the report. Select Key displays the current list of keys and values that are defined in the resource file that the report uses.

4   Perform one of the following steps:

   ▪   Select an existing key to assign to the report parameter.

   ▪   Under Quick Add, create a new key, choose Add, then select the key from the list.

5   Choose OK.

Editing a resource file

You often need to change the values of keys or add new keys as you design your report. You can accomplish these tasks through the localization properties page of the property editor for a label or text element, but it is easier to edit the resource file directly.

When you edit the values of keys, the values in the report are updated automatically. If, however, you change a key name or delete a key, report text that uses that key will not display a value, because BIRT cannot find the key. It is best to limit your edits to adding new keys or editing the values of the existing keys.

Be aware, too, that when you edit a resource file after it has been translated into locale-specific resource files, those locale-specific resource files must be updated also. Otherwise, the report will not display the text that you intended when it runs in other locales. For this reason, you should create localized resource files only after you have finalized the default resource file and finished creating and testing the report.

How to edit a resource file

Choose File→Open File, navigate to the resource folder, then double-click the resource (.properties) file. The file that opens in the report editor displays the list of keys and their values, as shown in Figure 24-10.

Edit the file as needed, then save and close it.

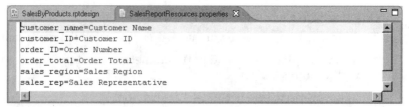

Figure 24-10   Resource file opened in the report editor

Previewing a report in different locales

When you have completed all the localization tasks, preview the report in all the locales that it supports to verify that the localized text appears properly. BIRT Report Designer provides an easy way for you to preview a report in any locale without changing your machine's locale. You can test the report in a different locale by setting the locale option in BIRT's preview preferences.

How to preview a report in a different locale

1 Choose Window➤Preferences. Figure 24-11 shows Preferences as it appears in BIRT Report Designer. If you are using BIRT RCP Report Designer, Preferences displays only BIRT options.

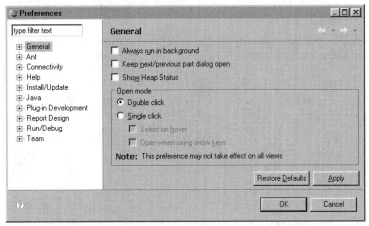

Figure 24-11   General preferences in BIRT Report Designer

2 On the left side of the dialog, expand Report Design, then choose Preview. The preview properties appear, as shown in Figure 24-12.

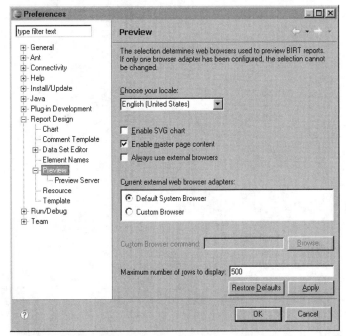

Figure 24-12   Preview preferences in BIRT Report Designer

3 Under Choose your locale, select a locale in which to preview your reports, then choose OK. The locale that you select applies only to previewed reports. It does not change the locale that your machine uses, nor does it change the localized text that appears in the report design.

4 Preview the report. The localized text appears in the language for the locale that you selected.

5 To preview your report in another language, repeat the previous steps to select a new locale.

abstract base class

A class that organizes a class hierarchy or defines methods and variables that apply to descendant classes. An abstract base class does not support the creation of instances.

Related terms
class, class hierarchy, descendant class, object, method, variable

Active Server Page (ASP)

A web server technology that Microsoft Corporation developed. ASPs support the creation of dynamic, interactive sessions. The technology contains both HTML and embedded programming code that is written in VBScript or JavaScript.

Related terms
hypertext markup language (HTML), JavaScript, VBScript (Visual Basic Script Edition), web server

Contrast with
JavaServer Page (JSP)

aggregate expression

An expression that uses an aggregate function to produce an aggregate value. For example, the expression, Total.max(row["SPEED"]), produces an aggregate value that is the maximum value of the field, SPEED, in the data rows.

Related terms
aggregate function, aggregate value, data row, expression, field, value

Contrast with
regular expression

aggregate function

A function that performs a calculation over a set of data rows. For example, Total.ave( ) calculates the average value of a specified numeric field over a set of data rows. An aggregate expression can contain one or more of the following aggregate functions: Total.ave( ), Total.count( ), Total.countDistinct( ), Total.first( ), Total.last( ), Total.max( ), Total.median( ), Total.min( ),

Total.mode( ), Total.movingAve( ), Total.runningSum( ), Total.stdDev( ), Total.sum( ), Total.variance( ), and Total.weightedAve( ).

Related terms
aggregate expression, data row, function
Contrast with
aggregate value

aggregate value

The result of applying an aggregate function to a set of data rows. For example, consider a set of data rows with a field, SPEED, which has values: 20, 10, 30, 15, 40. The aggregate expression, Total.max(row["SPEED"]), produces the aggregate value, 40, which is the maximum value for the field.

Related terms
aggregate expression, aggregate function, data row, field, value

alias

1   In a SQL SELECT statement, an alternative name given to a database table or column.

2   An alternative name that is given to a table column for use in an expression or in code in a script method. This name must be a valid variable name that begins with a letter and contains only alphanumeric characters.

Related terms
column, expression, method, SQL SELECT statement, table, variable
Contrast with
display name

ancestor class

A class in the inheritance hierarchy from which a particular class directly or indirectly derives.
Related terms
class, inheritance
Contrast with
class hierarchy, descendant class, subclass, superclass

applet

A small desktop application that usually performs a simple task, for example, a Java program that runs directly from the web browser.
Related terms
application, Java

application

A complete, self-contained program that performs a specific set of related tasks.
Contrast with
applet

application programming interface (API)

A set of routines, including functions, methods, and procedures, that exposes application functionality to support integration and extend applications.

Related terms
application, function, method, procedure

argument   A constant, expression, or variable that supplies data to a function or method.

Related terms
constant, data, expression, function, method, variable

array   A data variable that consists of sequentially indexed elements that have the same data type. Each element has a common name, a common data type, and a unique index number identifier. Changes to an element of an array do not affect other elements.

Related terms
data, data type, variable

assignment statement

A statement that assigns a value to a variable. For example:

```
StringToDisplay = "My Name"
```

Related terms
statement, value, variable

BIRT   *See* Business Intelligence and Reporting Tools (BIRT).

BIRT extension

See Business Intelligence and Reporting Tools (BIRT) extension.

BIRT Report Designer

See Business Intelligence and Reporting Tools (BIRT) Report Designer.

BIRT technology

See Business Intelligence and Reporting Tools (BIRT) technology.

bookmark   An expression that identifies a report element. A bookmark is used in a hyperlink expression.

Related terms
expression, hyperlink, report element

Boolean expression

An expression that evaluates to True or False. For example, Total > 3000 is a Boolean expression. If the condition is met, the condition evaluates to True. If the condition is not met, the condition evaluates to False.

Related term
expression

Contrast with
numeric expression

breakpoint

In BIRT Report Designer, a place marker in a program that is being debugged. At a breakpoint, execution pauses so that the report developer can examine and edit data values as necessary.

Related terms
Business Intelligence and Reporting Tools (BIRT) Report Designer, data, debug, value

bridge class

A class that maps the functionality of one class to the similar behavior of another class. For example, the JDBC-ODBC bridge class enables applications that use standard JDBC protocol to access a database that uses the ODBC protocol. BIRT Report Designer and BIRT RCP Report Designer use this type of class.

Related terms
application, Business Intelligence and Reporting Tools (BIRT) Report Designer, Business Intelligence and Reporting Tools (BIRT) Rich Client Platform (RCP) Report Designer, class, Java Database Connectivity (JDBC), open database connectivity (ODBC), protocol

Business Intelligence and Reporting Tools (BIRT)

A reporting platform that is built on the Eclipse platform, the industry standard for open source software development. BIRT provides a complete solution for extracting data, processing data to answer business questions, and presenting the results in a formatted document that is meaningful to end users.

Related terms
data, Eclipse, report

Contrast with
Business Intelligence and Reporting Tools (BIRT) extension

Business Intelligence and Reporting Tools (BIRT) Chart Engine

A tool that supports designing and deploying charts outside a report design. With this engine, Java developers embed charting capabilities into an application. BIRT Chart Engine is a set of Eclipse plug-ins and Java archive (.jar) files. The chart engine is also known as the charting library.

Related terms
application, Business Intelligence and Reporting Tools (BIRT), chart, design, Eclipse platform, Java, Java archive (.jar) file, plug-in, report

Contrast with
Business Intelligence and Reporting Tools (BIRT) Report Engine

Business Intelligence and Reporting Tools (BIRT) Demo Database

A sample database that is used in tutorials in online help for BIRT Report Designer and BIRT RCP Report Designer. This package provides this demo database in Derby, Microsoft Access, and MySQL formats.

Related terms
Business Intelligence and Reporting Tools (BIRT), Business Intelligence and Reporting Tools (BIRT) Report Designer, Business Intelligence and Reporting Tools (BIRT) Rich Client Platform (RCP) Report Designer

Business Intelligence and Reporting Tools (BIRT) extension

A related set of extension points that adds custom functionality to the BIRT platform. BIRT extensions are:

- Charting extension

- Open data access (ODA) extension

- Rendering extension

- Report item extension

Related terms
Business Intelligence and Reporting Tools (BIRT), charting extension, extension, extension point, rendering extension, report, report item extension

Business Intelligence and Reporting Tools (BIRT) Report Designer

A tool that builds BIRT report designs and previews reports that are generated from the designs. BIRT Report Designer is a set of plug-ins to the Eclipse platform and includes BIRT Chart Engine, BIRT Demo Database, and BIRT Report Engine. A report developer who uses this tool can access the full capabilities of the Eclipse platform.

Related terms
Business Intelligence and Reporting Tools (BIRT), Business Intelligence and Reporting Tools (BIRT) Chart Engine, Business Intelligence and Reporting Tools (BIRT) Demo Database, Business Intelligence and Reporting Tools (BIRT) Report Engine, design, Eclipse platform, plug-in, report

Contrast with
Business Intelligence and Reporting Tools (BIRT) Rich Client Platform (RCP) Report Designer

Business Intelligence and Reporting Tools (BIRT) Report Engine

A component that supports deploying BIRT charting, reporting and viewing capabilities on an application server. BIRT Report Engine consists of a set of Java archive (.jar) files, web archive (.war) files, and web applications.

Related terms
application, Business Intelligence and Reporting Tools (BIRT), Java archive (.jar) file, report, web archive (.war) file

Contrast with
Business Intelligence and Reporting Tools (BIRT) Chart Engine

Business Intelligence and Reporting Tools (BIRT) Rich Client Platform (RCP) Report Designer

A stand-alone tool that builds BIRT report designs and previews reports that are generated from the designs. BIRT RCP Report Designer uses the Eclipse Rich Client Platform. This tool includes BIRT Report Engine, BIRT Chart Engine, and BIRT Demo Database. BIRT RCP Report Designer supports report design and preview functionality without the additional overhead of the full Eclipse platform. BIRT RCP Report Designer does not support the Java-based scripting and the report debugger functionality it provides. BIRT RCP Report Designer can use, but not create, BIRT extensions.

Related terms
Business Intelligence and Reporting Tools (BIRT), Business Intelligence and Reporting Tools (BIRT) extension, Business Intelligence and Reporting Tools (BIRT) Chart Engine, Business Intelligence and Reporting Tools (BIRT) Demo Database, Business Intelligence and Reporting Tools (BIRT) Report Engine, debug, design, Eclipse platform, Eclipse Rich Client Platform (RCP), extension, JavaScript, library (.rptlibrary) file, plug-in, report

Contrast with
Business Intelligence and Reporting Tools (BIRT) Report Designer

Business Intelligence and Reporting Tools (BIRT) Samples

A sample of a BIRT report item extension and examples of BIRT charting applications. The report item extension sample is an Eclipse platform plug-in. The charting applications use BIRT Chart Engine. Java developers use these examples as models of how to design custom report items and embed charting capabilities in an application.

Related terms
application, Business Intelligence and Reporting Tools (BIRT), Business Intelligence and Reporting Tools (BIRT) Chart Engine, chart, design, Eclipse, Eclipse platform, Java, plug-in, report, report item, report item extension

Business Intelligence and Reporting Tools (BIRT) technology

A set of Java applications and APIs that support the design and deployment of a business report. BIRT applications include BIRT Report Designer, BIRT RCP Report Designer, and a report viewer web application servlet. The BIRT Java APIs provide programmatic access to BIRT functionality.

Related terms
application, application programming interface (API), Business Intelligence and Reporting Tools (BIRT), Business Intelligence and Reporting Tools (BIRT) Report Designer, Business Intelligence and Reporting Tools (BIRT) Rich Client Platform (RCP) Report Designer, Java, report viewer servlet

Business Intelligence and Reporting Tools (BIRT) Test Suite

A set of test packages for BIRT. BIRT developers use these test packages to perform regression testing when they modify BIRT source code. Report developers and application developers do not need to install this BIRT Test Suite.

Related terms
application, Business Intelligence and Reporting Tools (BIRT), report

cascading parameters

Report parameters that have a hierarchical relationship. For example, the following parameters have a hierarchical relationship:

```
Country
   State
      City
```

In a group of cascading parameters, each report parameter displays a set of values. When a report user selects a value from the top-level parameter, the selected value determines the values that the next parameter displays, and so on. Cascading parameters display only relevant values to the user. Figure G-1 shows cascading parameters as they appear to a report user.

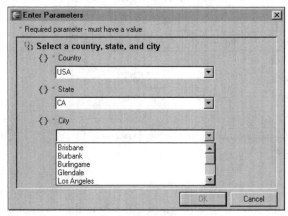

Figure G-1   Cascading parameters

Related terms
hierarchy, parameter, report, value

Contrast with
cascading style sheet (CSS)

cascading style sheet (CSS)

A file that contains a set of rules that attach formats and styles to specified HTML elements. For example, a cascading style sheet can specify the color, font, and size for an HTML heading.

Related terms
element, font, hypertext markup language (HTML), style

Contrast with
template

case sensitivity

A condition in which the letter case is significant for the purposes of comparison. For example, "McManus" does not match "MCMANUS" or "mcmanus" in a case-sensitive environment.

category

In an area, bar, line, step, or stock chart, one of the discrete values that organizes data on an axis that does not use a numerical scale. Typically, the x-axis of a chart displays category values. In a pie chart, category values are called orthogonal axis values and define which sectors appear in a pie.

Related terms
chart, data, value

Contrast with
series

cell

An intersection of a row and a column in a grid element, or table element. Figure G-2 shows a cell.

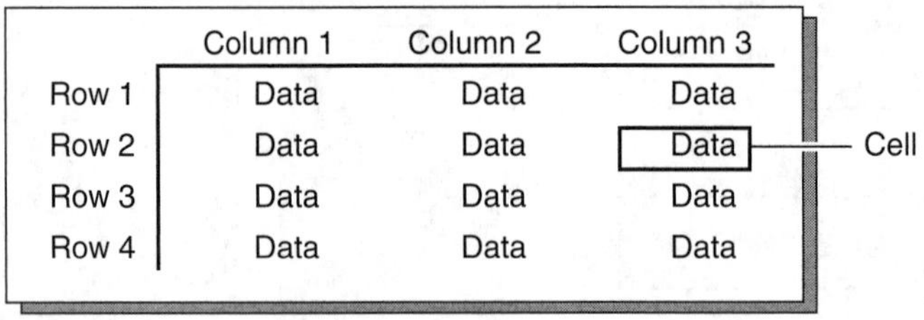

Figure G-2   Cell

Related terms
column, grid element, row, table element

character

An elementary mark that represents data, usually in the form of a graphic spatial arrangement of connected or adjacent strokes, such as a letter or a digit. A character is independent of font size and other display properties. For example, an uppercase C is a character.

Related term
data

Contrast with
character set, glyph

character set

A mapping of specific characters to code points. For example, in most character sets, the letter A maps to the hexadecimal value 0x21.

Related terms
character, code point

Contrast with
locale

chart

A graphic representation of data or the relationships among sets of data.

Related term
data

chart element

A report item that displays values from data rows in the form of a chart. The chart element can use data rows from the report design's data set or a different data set. A report item extension defines the chart element.

Related terms
chart, data, data row, data set, design, element, report, report item, report item extension, value

Contrast with
charting extension

chart engine

See Business Intelligence and Reporting Tools (BIRT) Chart Engine.

charting extension

A BIRT extension that adds a new type of chart, a new component to an existing chart type, or a new user interface component to the BIRT chart engine.

Related terms
Business Intelligence and Reporting Tools (BIRT), Business Intelligence and Reporting Tools (BIRT) extension, Business Intelligence and Reporting Tools (BIRT) Chart Engine, chart, extension

charting library

See Business Intelligence and Reporting Tools (BIRT) Chart Engine.

class

A set of methods and variables that defines the attributes and behavior of an object. All objects of a given class are identical in form and behavior but can contain different data in their variables.

Related terms
data, method, object, variable

Contrast with
subclass, superclass

class hierarchy

A tree structure that represents the inheritance relationships among a set of classes.

Related terms
class, inheritance

class name

A unique name for a class that permits unambiguous references to its public methods and variables.

Related terms
class, method, variable

class variable

A variable that all instances of a class share. The run-time system creates only one copy of a class variable. The value of the class variable is the same for all instances of the class, for example, the taxRate variable in an Order class.

Related terms
class, object, value, variable

Contrast with
class variable, dynamic variable, field variable, global variable, instance variable, local variable, member variable, static variable

code point

A hexadecimal value. Every character in a character set is represented by a code point. The computer uses the code point to process the character.

Related terms
character, character set

column

1 A named field in a database table or query. For each data row, the column has a different value, called the column value. The term column refers to the definition of the column, not to any particular value. Figure G-3 shows a column in a database table.

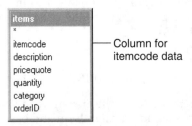

Figure G-3   Column in a database table

2 A vertical sequence of cells in a cross tab, grid element, or table element. Figure G-4 shows a column in a cross tab.

	Column 1	Column 2	Column 3
Row 1	Data	Data	Data
Row 2	Data	Data	Data
Row 3	Data	Data	Data
Row 4	Data	Data	Data

— Column of cells

Figure G-4   Column in a cross tab

Related terms
cell, cross tab, field, grid element, query, data row, table, table element, value

column binding

A named column that defines an expression that specifies what data to return. For each piece of data to display in a report, there must be column binding. Column bindings form an intermediate layer between data-set data and report elements.

Related terms
column, data, data set, expression, report, report element

Common Gateway Interface (CGI)

An internet standard that describes how a web server accesses external programs to return data to the user as a generated web page. When a web user fills out a form, a CGI program handles the data and calls other programs as necessary.

Related terms
data, web page, web server

computed column

See computed field.

computed field

A field that displays the result of an expression rather than stored data.

Related terms
field, data, expression

Contrast with
computed value

computed value

The result of a calculation that is defined by an expression. To display a computed value in a report, use a data element.

Related terms
data element, expression, report, value

Contrast with
computed field

conditional expression

See Boolean expression.

configuration file

In open data access (ODA), a file that specifies the ODA interface version of the driver and defines the structure, contents, and semantics of requests and responses between the open data source and the design tool.

Related terms
data source, interface, open data access (ODA), open data access (ODA) driver, request, response

Connection

A Java object that provides access to a data source.

Related terms
data source, Java, object

constant An unchanging, predefined value. A constant does not change while a program is running, but the value of a field or variable can change.

Contrast with
field, value, variable

constructor code

Code that initializes an instance of a class.

Related terms
class, object

container **1** An application that acts as a master program to hold and execute a set of commands or to run other software routines. For example, application servers provide containers that support communication between applications and Enterprise JavaBeans.

2 A data structure that holds one or more different types of data. For example, a grid element can contain label elements and other report items.

Related terms
application, data, Enterprise JavaBean (EJB), grid element, label element, report item

containment

A relationship among instantiated objects in a report. One object, the container, incorporates other objects, the contents.

Related terms
container, instantiation, object, report

containment hierarchy

A hierarchy of objects in a report.

Related terms
hierarchy, object, report

converter A tool that converts data from one format to another format.

Related terms
data, format

cross tab A report that summarizes data from database table columns into a concise format for analysis. Data appears in a matrix with rows and columns. Every cell in a cross tab contains an aggregate value. A cross tab shows how one item relates to another, such as order totals by credit rating and order status. Figure G-5 shows a cross tab.

Order Totals by Credit Rating and Order Status

	A			B			C			Totals		
	Quantity	Ave Qty	Amount	Quantity	Ave Qty	Amount	Quantity	Ave Qty	Amount	Quantity	Ave Qty	Amount
Open	98,205	349	9,870,799	40,472	283	4,673,517	4,980	332	636,555	143,657	327	15,180,871
Closed	171,813	365	20,633,175	131,183	497	14,465,314	21,790	198	2,591,731	324,786	384	37,690,220
In Evaluation	90,969	469	12,135,326	22,168	411	2,596,936	0		0	113,137	456	14,732,262
Cancelled	23,944	855	3,029,520	0		0	0		0	23,944	855	3,029,520
Selected	10,540	527	1,375,204	0		0	0		0	10,540	527	1,375,204
Totals	395,471	398	47,044,024	193,823	420	21,735,767	26,770	214	3,228,286	616,064	390	72,008,077

Figure G-5   Cross tab

Related terms
aggregate value, cell, column, data, grid, report, row, table, value
Contrast with
aggregate function

CSS   *See* cascading style sheet (CSS).

custom data source

See open data access (ODA).

data   Information that is stored in databases, flat files, or other data sources that can appear in a report.

Related terms
data source, flat file, report
Contrast with
metadata

data element

 A report item that displays a computed value or a value from a data set field.
Related terms
computed value, data set, element, field, report item, value
Contrast with
label element, Report Object Model (ROM) element, text element

Data Explorer

An Eclipse view that shows the data sources, data sets, and report parameters that were created for use in a report. Use Data Explorer to create, edit, or delete these items. Figure G-6 shows Data Explorer.

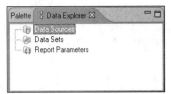

Figure G-6   Data Explorer

Related terms
data set, data source, Eclipse view, parameter, report

data point

A point on a chart that corresponds to a particular pair of x- and y-axis values.

Related terms
chart, value

Contrast with
data row, data set

data row

One row of data that a data set returns. A data set, which specifies the data to retrieve from a data source, typically returns many data rows.

Related terms
data, data set, data source, row

Contrast with
data point, filter

data set

A description of the data to retrieve or compute from a data source.

Related terms
data, data source

Contrast with
data point, data row

data set field

See column.

data set parameter

A parameter that is associated with a data set column and passes an expression to extend dynamically the query's WHERE clause. A data set parameter restricts the number of data rows that the data set supplies to the report.

Related terms
column, data row, data set, expression, parameter, query, report

Contrast with
report parameter

data source

1 A SQL database or other repository of data. For example, a flat file can be a data source.

2 An object that contains the connection information for an external data source, such as a flat file, a SQL database, or another repository of data.

Related terms
data, flat file, SQL (Structured Query Language)

Contrast with
data row, data set

data type   **1**   A category for values that determines their characteristics, such as the information they can hold and the permitted operations.

2   The data type of a value determines the default appearance of the value in a report. This appearance depends on the locale in which a user generates the report. For example, the order in which year, month, and day appear in a date-and-time data value depends on the locale. BIRT uses three fundamental data types: date-and-time, numeric, and string. Data sources such as relational databases support more data types, which BIRT maps to the appropriate fundamental data type.

Related terms
Business Intelligence and Reporting Tools (BIRT), date-and-time data type, locale, numeric data type, report, String data type, value, variable

database connection

See data source.

database management system (DBMS)

Software that organizes simultaneous access to shared data. Database management systems store relationships among various data elements.

Related term
data

database schema

See schema.

date-and-time data type

A data type for date-and-time calculations. Report items can contain expressions or fields with a date-and-time data type. The appearance of date-and-time values in the report document is based on locale and format settings specified by your computer and the report design.

Related terms
data type, design, expression, field, format, locale, report, report item

debug   To detect, locate, and fix errors. Typically, debugging involves executing specific portions of a computer program and analyzing the operation of those portions.

declaration

The definition of a class, constant, method, or variable that specifies the name and, if appropriate, the data type.

Related terms
class, constant, data type, method, variable

derived class

See descendant class.

descendant class

A class that is based on another class.

Related term
class

Contrast with
subclass, superclass

design   1 To create a report specification. Designing a report includes selecting data, laying out the report visually, and saving the layout in a report design file.

2 A report specification. A report design (.rptdesign) file contains a report design.

Related terms
data, layout, report, report design (.rptdesign) file

DHTML (dynamic hypertext markup language)

See dynamic hypertext markup language (DHTML).

display name

An alternative name for a table column, report parameter, chart series, or user-defined ROM property. BIRT Report Designer displays this alternative name in the user interface, for example, as a column heading in a report. This name can contain any character, including spaces and punctuation.

Related terms
Business Intelligence and Reporting Tools (BIRT) Report Designer, character, chart, column, Data Explorer, report, report parameter, Report Object Model (ROM), table, value

Contrast with
alias

document object model (DOM)

A model that defines the structure of a document such as an HTML or XML document. The document object model defines interfaces that dynamically create, access, and manipulate the internal structure of the document. The URL to the W3C document object model is:

```
www.w3.org/DOM/
```

Related terms
extensible markup language (XML), hypertext markup language (HTML), interface, Uniform Resource Locator (URL), World Wide Web Consortium (W3C)

Contrast with
document type definition (DTD), structured content

document type definition (DTD)

A set of markup tags and the interpretation of those tags that together define the structure of an XML document.

Related terms
extensible markup language (XML), tag

Contrast with
document object model (DOM), schema, structured content

domain name

A name that defines a node on the internet. For example, the Eclipse Foundation's domain name is eclipse. The URL is:

```
www.eclipse.org
```

Related terms
node, Uniform Resource Locator (URL)

driver An interface that supports communication between an application and another application or a peripheral device such as a printer.

Related term
interface

dynamic hypertext markup language (DHTML)

An HTML extension that provides enhanced viewing capabilities and interactivity in a web page without the necessity for communication with a web server. The Document Object Model Group of the W3C develops DHTML standards.

Related terms
document object model (DOM), hypertext markup language (HTML), web page, web server, World Wide Web Consortium (W3C)

dynamic text element

 A data element that displays text data that contains multiple style formats and a variable amount of text. A dynamic text element adjusts its size to accommodate varying amounts of data. Use a dynamic text element to display a data source field that contains formatted text. A dynamic text element supports plain or HTML text.

Related terms
data, data source, field, format, hypertext markup language (HTML)

Contrast with
text element

dynamic variable

A variable that changes during program execution. The program requests the memory allocation for a dynamic variable at run time.

Related term
variable

Contrast with
class variable, field variable, global variable, instance variable, local variable, member variable, static variable

Eclipse

An open platform for tool integration that is built by an open community of tool providers. The Eclipse platform is written in Java and includes extensive plug-in construction toolkits and examples.

Related terms
Eclipse platform, Java, plug-in

Contrast with
Business Intelligence and Reporting Tools (BIRT) extension

Eclipse Modeling Framework (EMF)

A Java framework and code generation facility for building tools and other applications that are based on a structured model. EMF uses XML schemas to generate the EMF model of a plug-in. For example, a BIRT chart type uses EMF to represent the chart structure and properties.

Related terms
application, Business Intelligence and Reporting Tools (BIRT) technology, chart, Eclipse, extensible markup language (XML), framework, Java, plug-in, property, schema

Eclipse perspective

A predefined layout of the Eclipse Workbench, including which Eclipse views are visible and where they appear. A perspective also controls what appears in certain menus and toolbars. A user can switch the perspective to work on a different task and can rearrange and customize a perspective to better suit a particular task. Figure G-7 shows the Eclipse perspective.

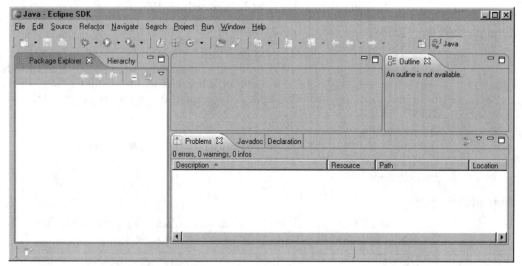

Figure G-7   Eclipse perspective

Related terms
Eclipse, Eclipse view, Eclipse Workbench

Eclipse platform

The core framework and services in which Eclipse plug-in extensions exist. The Eclipse platform provides the run time in which plug-ins load and run. The Eclipse platform consists of a core component and a user interface component. The user interface component is known as the Eclipse Workbench. The core portion of the Eclipse platform is called the platform core or the core.

Related terms
Eclipse, Eclipse Workbench, extension, framework, plug-in

Eclipse Plug-in Development Environment (PDE)

An integrated design tool for creating, developing, testing, and deploying a plug-in. The Eclipse PDE provides wizards, editors, views, and launchers that support plug-in development. The Eclipse PDE supports host and run-time instances of a workbench project. The host instance provides the development environment. The run-time instance enables the launching of a plug-in for testing purposes.

Related terms
design, Eclipse, Eclipse project, Eclipse Workbench, object, plug-in

Eclipse project

A user-specified directory within an Eclipse workspace. An Eclipse project contains folders and files that are used for builds, version management, sharing, and resource organization.

Related terms
Eclipse, Eclipse workspace

Eclipse Rich Client Platform (RCP)

The Eclipse framework for building a client application that uses a minimal set of plug-ins. Eclipse Rich Client Platform (RCP) uses a subset of the components that are available in the Eclipse platform. An Eclipse rich client application is typically a specialized user interface that supports a specific function, such as the report development tools in the BIRT Rich Client Platform.

Related terms
application, Business Intelligence and Reporting Tools (BIRT), Eclipse, Eclipse platform, framework, plug-in, report

Eclipse view

A panel on the Eclipse Workbench, similar to a pane in Windows. An Eclipse view can be an editor, the Navigator, a palette of report items, a graphical report designer, or any other functional component that Eclipse or an Eclipse project provides. A view can have its own menus and toolbars. Multiple views can be visible at one time.

Related terms
design, Eclipse, Eclipse perspective, Eclipse project, Eclipse Workbench, Navigator, Palette, report, report item

Eclipse Workbench

The Eclipse desktop development environment, which consists of one or more Eclipse perspectives.

Related terms
Eclipse, Eclipse perspective

Contrast with
Eclipse Plug-in Development Environment (PDE), Eclipse workspace

Eclipse workspace

A user-specified directory that contains one or more Eclipse projects. An Eclipse workspace is a general umbrella for managing resources in the Eclipse platform. The Eclipse platform can contain one or more workspaces. A user can switch between workspaces.

Related terms
Eclipse platform, Eclipse project

Contrast with
Eclipse Workbench

EJB   *See* Enterprise JavaBean (EJB).

element   1 In Report Object Model (ROM), a component that describes a piece of a report. A ROM element typically has a name and a set of properties.

2 A tag-delimited structure in an XML or HTML document that contains a unit of data. For example, the root element of an HTML page starts with the beginning tag, <HTML>, and ends with the closing tag, </HTML>. This root element encloses all the other elements that define the contents of a page. An XML element must be well-formed, with both a beginning and a closing tag. In HTML, some tags, such as <br>, the forced line break tag, do not require a closing tag.

Related terms
data, extensible markup language (XML), hypertext markup language (HTML), property, report, Report Object Model (ROM), Report Object Model (ROM) element, tag, well-formed XML

Contrast with
report item

ellipsis button

 A button that opens tools that you use to perform tasks, such as navigating to a file, building an expression, or specifying localized text.

encapsulation

A technique of packaging related functions and subroutines together. Encapsulation compartmentalizes the structure and behavior of a class, hiding the implementation details, so that parts of an object-oriented system need not depend upon or affect each other's internal details.

Related terms
class, function, object

Contrast with
object-oriented programming

enterprise A large collection of networked computers that run on multiple platforms. Enterprise systems can include both mainframes and workstations that are integrated in a single, managed environment. Typical software products that are used in an enterprise environment include web browsers, applications, applets, web tools, and multiple databases that support a warehouse of information.

Related terms
applet, application

Contrast with
Enterprise JavaBean (EJB), enterprise reporting

Enterprise JavaBean (EJB)

A standards-based server-side component that encapsulates the business logic of an application. An EJB can provide access to data or model the data itself. Application servers provide the deployment environment for EJBs.

Related terms
application, data, JavaBean

Contrast with
Java

enterprise reporting

The production of a high volume of simple and complex structured documents that collect data from a variety of data sources. A large number of geographically distributed users who are working in both client/server and internet environments receive, work with, and modify these reports.

Related terms
data, data source, report

Contrast with
enterprise, structured content

event An action or occurrence recognized by an object. Each object responds to a predefined set of events that can be extended by the developer.

Related term
object

Contrast with
event handler, event listener

event handler

A Java or JavaScript method that is executed upon the firing of a BIRT event. BIRT fires events at various times in the report generation process. By writing custom code for the associated event handlers, the BIRT report developer can provide special handling at the time the events are fired. Report items, data sets, and data sources all have event handlers for which the report developer can provide custom code.

Related terms
Business Intelligence and Reporting Tools (BIRT), data set, data source, event, Java, JavaScript, method, report, report item

Contrast with
event listener

event listener

An interface that detects when a particular event occurs and runs a registered method in response to that event.

Related terms
event, method

Contrast with
event handler

exception

An abnormal situation that a program encounters. In some cases, the program handles the exception and returns a message to the user or application that is running the program. In other cases, the program cannot handle the exception, and the program terminates.

Related term
application

expression

A combination of constants, functions, literal values, names of fields, and operators that evaluates to a single value.

Related terms
constant, field, function, operator, value

Contrast with
aggregate expression, regular expression

expression builder

A tool for selecting data fields, functions, and operators to write JavaScript expressions. Figure G-8 shows the expression builder.

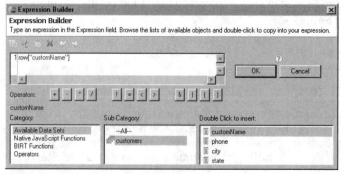

Figure G-8   Expression builder

Related terms
data, expression, field, function, JavaScript, operator

extensible markup language (XML)

A markup language that supports the interchange of data among data sources and applications. Using XML, a wide variety of applications, legacy systems, and databases can exchange information. XML is content-oriented rather than format-oriented. XML uses tags to structure data into nested elements. An XML schema that is structured according to the rules that were defined by the W3C describes the structure of the data.

XML documents must be well formed.

Related terms
application, data, data source, element, schema, tag, well-formed XML, World Wide Web Consortium (W3C)

Contrast with
hypertext markup language (HTML)

extension   A module that adds functionality to an application. BIRT consists of a set of extensions, called plug-ins, which add functionality to the Eclipse development environment.

Related terms
application, Business Intelligence and Reporting Tools (BIRT), Eclipse, plug-in

Contrast with
Business Intelligence and Reporting Tools (BIRT) extension,extension point

extension point

A defined place in an application where a developer adds custom functionality. The APIs in BIRT support adding custom functionality to the BIRT framework. In the Eclipse Plug-in Development Environment (PDE), a developer views the extension points in the PDE Manifest Editor to guide and control plug-in development tasks.

Related terms
application, application programming interface (API), Business Intelligence and Reporting Tools (BIRT), Eclipse Plug-in Development Environment (PDE), extension, framework, plug-in

Contrast with
Business Intelligence and Reporting Tools (BIRT) extension

field   The smallest identifiable part of a database table structure. In a relational database, a field is also called a column.

Related terms
column, table

field variable

In Java, a member variable with public visibility.

Related terms
Java, member, variable
Contrast with
class variable, dynamic variable, field variable, global variable, instance variable, local variable, member variable, static variable

file types   Table G-1 lists the report designer's file types.

Table G-1   File types

Display name	Glossary term	File type
BIRT Report Design	report design (.rptdesign) file	RPTDESIGN
BIRT Report Design Library	library (.rptlibrary) file	RPTLIBRARY
BIRT Report Design Template	report template (.rpttemplate) file	RPTTEMPLATE
BIRT Report Document	report document (.rptdocument) file	RPTDOCUMENT

filter   To exclude any data rows from the result set that do not meet a set of conditions. Some external data sources can filter data as specified by conditions that the query includes directly or through the use of report parameters. In addition, BIRT can filter data after retrieval from the external data source. Report developers can specify conditions for filtering in either the data set or a report item.

Related terms
Business Intelligence and Reporting Tools (BIRT), data, data row, data set, data source, query, report, report item, report parameter, result set

flat file   A file that contains data in the form of text.
Related term
data
Contrast with
data source

font   A family of characters of a given style. Fonts contain information that specifies typeface, weight, posture, and type size.
Related term
character

footer   A unit of information that appears at the bottom of a page.
Contrast with
header

format   1   A set of standard options with which to display and print currency values, dates, numbers, and times.

2   A specification that describes layout and properties of report data or other information, for example, PDF or HTML.

Related terms
data, hypertext markup language (HTML), layout, property, report, value
Contrast with
style

forms-capable browser

A web browser that handles hypertext markup language (HTML) forms. HTML tags enable interactive forms, including check boxes, drop-down lists, fill-in text areas, and option buttons.

Related terms
hypertext markup language (HTML), tag

framework

A set of interrelated classes that provide an architecture for building an application.

Related terms
application, class

function

A sequence of instructions that are defined as a separate unit within a program. To invoke the function, include its name as one of the instructions anywhere in the program. BIRT provides JavaScript functions to support building expressions.

Related terms
Business Intelligence and Reporting Tools (BIRT), expression, JavaScript,
Contrast with
method

global variable

A variable that is available at all levels in an application. A global variable stays in memory in the scope of all executing procedures until the application terminates.

Related terms
application, procedure, scope, variable
Contrast with
class variable, dynamic variable, field variable, global variable, instance variable, local variable, member variable, static variable

glyph

1   An image that is used in the visual representation of a character.

2   A specific letter form from a specific font. An uppercase C in Palatino font is a glyph.

Related terms
character, font

grandchild class

See descendant class.

grandparent class

See ancestor class.

grid   *See* grid element.

grid element

 A report item that contains and displays other report elements in a static row and column format. A grid element aligns the cells horizontally and vertically.

Figure G-9 shows a report title section that consists of an image element and two text elements that are arranged in a grid element with one row and two columns.

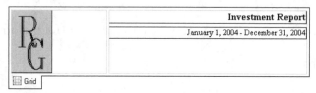

Figure G-9   Grid element

Related terms
cell, column, element, image element, report, report item, row, text element

Contrast with
list element, table element

group   A set of data rows that have one or more column values in common. For example, in a sales report, a group consists of all the orders that are placed by a single customer.

Related terms
column, data row, report, value

Contrast with
group key, grouped report

grouped report

A report that organizes data in logical groups. Figure G-10 shows a grouped report.

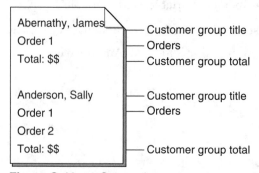

Figure G-10   Grouped report

Related terms
data, group, report

group key   A data set column that is used to group and sort data in a report. For example, a report developer can group and sort customers by credit rank.

Related terms
column, data, data set, group, report, sort

header   1   A unit of information that appears at the top of every page.

2   A group header is a unit of information that appears at the beginning of a group section.

Related terms
group, section
Contrast with
footer

hexadecimal number

A number in base 16. A hexadecimal number uses the digits 0 through 9 and the letters A through F. Each place represents a power of 16. By comparison, base 10 numbers use the digits 0 through 9. Each place represents a power of 10.
Contrast with
character set, octal number

hierarchy   Any tree structure that has a root and branches that do not converge.

HTML   *See* hypertext markup language (HTML).

HTML element

See element.

HTTP   *See* hypertext transfer protocol (HTTP).

hyperlink

   A connection from one part of a report to another part of the same or different report. Typically, hyperlinks support access to related information within the same report, in another report, or in another application. A change from the standard cursor shape to a cursor shaped like a hand indicates a hyperlink.

Related terms
application, report

hypertext markup language (HTML)

A specification that determines the layout of a web page. HTML is the markup language that tells a parser that the text is a certain portion of a document on the web, for example, the title, heading, or body text. A web browser parses HTML to display a web page.
Related terms
layout, web page

Contrast with
dynamic hypertext markup language (DHTML), extensible markup language (XML)

hypertext markup language page

See web page.

hypertext transfer protocol (HTTP)

An internet standard that supports the exchange of information using the web.

Contrast with
protocol

identifier   The name that is assigned to an item in a program such as a class, function, or variable.

Related terms
class, function, variable

image   A graphic that appears in a report. BIRT Report Designer supports .bmp, .gif, .jpg, and .png file types.

Related terms
Business Intelligence and Reporting Tools (BIRT) Report Designer, report

Contrast with
image element

image element

 A report item that adds an image to a report design.

Related terms
design, element, image, report, report item

inheritance

A mechanism whereby one class of objects can be defined as a special case of a more general class and includes the method and variable definitions of the general class, known as a base or superclass. The superclass serves as the baseline for the appearance and behavior of the descendant class, which is also known as a subclass. In the subclass, the appearance and behavior can be further customized without affecting the superclass. Typically, a subclass augments or redefines the behavior and structure of its superclass or superclasses. Figure G-11 shows an example of inheritance.

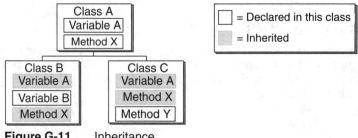

Figure G-11   Inheritance

Related terms
class, descendant class, file types, method, object, subclass, superclass, variable
Contrast with
abstract base class

inner join   1   A type of join that returns records from two tables that are based on their having specified values in the join fields. The most common type of inner join is one in which records are combined and returned when specified field values are equal. For example, if customer and order tables are joined on customer ID, the result set contains only combined customer and order records where the customer IDs are equal, excluding records for customers who have no orders.

2   When creating a joint data set in BIRT, a type of join that returns all rows from both data sets if the specified field values are equal. For example, if customer and order data sets are joined on customer ID, the joint data set returns only combined customer and order rows where the customer IDs are equal.

Related terms
Business Intelligence and Reporting Tools (BIRT) technology, data set, field, join, result set, row, table, value
Contrast with
outer join

input source

See data source.

instance   *See* object.

instance variable

A variable that other instances of a class do not share. The run-time system creates a new copy of an instance variable each time the system instantiates the class. An instance variable can contain a different value in each instance of a class, for example, the customerID variable in a Customer class.
Related terms
class, value, variable
Contrast with
class variable, dynamic variable, field variable, global variable, local variable, member variable, static variable

instantiation

The action of creating an object.
Related term
object
Contrast with
class

interface   **1**   The connection and interaction among hardware, software, and the user. Hardware interfaces include plugs, sockets, wires, and electrical pulses traveling through them in a particular pattern. Hardware interfaces include electrical timing considerations such as Ethernet and Token Ring, network topologies, RS-232 transmission, and the IDE, ESDI, SCSI, ISA, EISA, and Micro Channel. Software or programming interfaces are the languages, codes, and messages that programs use to communicate with each other and to the hardware and the user. Software interfaces include applications running on specific operating systems, SMTP e-mail, and LU 6.2 communications protocols.

       2   In Java, an interface defines a set of methods to provide a required functionality. The interface provides a mechanism for classes to communicate in order to execute particular actions.

Related terms
application, class, Connection, Java, method, protocol

internationalization

The process of designing an application to work correctly in multiple locales.
Related terms
application, locale
Contrast with
localization

IP address

The unique 32-bit ID of a node on a TCP/IP network.
Related term
node

J2EE   *See* Java 2 Enterprise Edition (J2EE).

J2SE   *See* Java 2 Runtime Standard Edition (J2SE).

JAR   *See* Java archive (.jar) file.

Java   A programming language that is designed for writing client/server and networked applications, particularly for delivery on the web. Java can be used to write applets that animate a web page or create an interactive web site.
Related terms
applet, application, web page
Contrast with
JavaScript

Java 2 Enterprise Edition (J2EE)

A platform-independent environment that includes APIs, services, and transport protocols, and is used to develop and deploy web-based enterprise applications. Typically, this environment is used to develop highly scalable web-based applications. This environment builds on J2SE functionality and requires an accessible J2SE installation.

Related terms
application, application programming interface (API), enterprise, enterprise reporting, Java 2 Runtime Standard Edition (J2SE), protocol

Contrast with
Enterprise JavaBean (EJB), Java Development Kit (JDK)

Java 2 Runtime Standard Edition (J2SE)

A smaller-scale, platform-independent environment that provides supporting functionality to the capabilities of J2EE. The J2SE does not support Enterprise JavaBean or enterprise environment.

Related terms
enterprise, Enterprise JavaBean (EJB), Java 2 Enterprise Edition (J2EE)

Contrast with
Java Development Kit (JDK)

Java archive (.jar) file

A file format that is used to bundle Java applications.

Related terms
application, Java

Contrast with
web archive (.war) file

Java Database Connectivity (JDBC)

A standard protocol that Java uses to access database data sources in a platform-independent manner.

Related terms
data source, Java, protocol

Contrast with
data element, schema

Java Development Kit (JDK)

A Sun Microsystems software development kit that defines the Java API and is used to build Java programs. The kit contains software tools and other programs, examples, and documentation that enable software developers to create applications using the Java programming language.

Related terms
application, application programming interface (API), Java

Contrast with
Java 2 Enterprise Edition (J2EE), Java 2 Runtime Standard Edition (J2SE), JavaServer Page (JSP)

Java Naming and Directory Interface (JNDI)

A naming standard that provides clients with access to EJBs.

Related term
Enterprise JavaBean (EJB)

Java Virtual Machine (JVM)

The Java SDK interpreter that converts Java bytecode into machine language for execution in a specified software and hardware configuration.

Related terms
Java, SDK (Software Development Kit)

JavaBean A reusable, standards-based component that is written in Java that encapsulates the business logic of an application. A JavaBean can provide access to data or model the data itself.

Related terms
application, data, encapsulation, Java

Contrast with
Enterprise JavaBean (EJB), enterprise reporting

JavaScript

An interpreted, platform-independent language that is used to enhance web pages and provide additional functionality in web servers. For example, JavaScript can interact with the HTML of a web page to change an icon when the cursor moves across it.

Related terms
hypertext markup language (HTML), web page, web server

Contrast with
Java

JavaServer Page (JSP)

A standard Java extension that simplifies the creation and management of dynamic web pages. The code combines HTML and Java code in one document. The Java code uses tags that instruct the JSP container to generate a servlet.

Related terms
hypertext markup language (HTML), Java, servlet, tag, web page

JDBC *See* Java Database Connectivity (JDBC).

JDK *See* Java Development Kit (JDK).

JNDI *See* Java Naming and Directory Interface (JNDI).

join A SQL query operation that combines records from two tables and returns them in a result set that is based on the values in the join fields. Without additional qualification, join usually refers to one where field values are equal. For example, customer and order tables are joined on a common field such as customer ID. The result set contains combined customer and order records in which the customer IDs are equal.

Related terms
field, query, result set, SQL (Structured Query Language), table, value

Contrast with
inner join, join condition, outer join, SQL SELECT statement

join condition

A condition that specifies a match in the values of related fields in two tables. Typically, the values are equal. For example, if two tables have a field called customer ID, a join condition exists where the customer ID value in one table equals the customer ID value in the second table.

Related terms
field, join, table, value

joint data set

A data set that combines data from two data sets.

Related terms
data, data set

JSP   *See* JavaServer Page (JSP).

JVM   *See* Java Virtual Machine (JVM).

keyword   A reserved word that is recognized as part of a programming language.

label element

 A report item that displays a short piece of static text in a report.

Related terms
report, report item

Contrast with
data element, text element

layout   The designed appearance of a report. Designing the layout of a report entails placing report items on a page and arranging them in a way that helps the report user analyze the information easily. A report displays information in a tabular list, a series of paragraphs, a chart, or a series of subreports.

Related terms
chart, listing report, report, report item, subreport

layout editor

A window in a report designer in which a report developer arranges, formats, and sizes report elements.

Related terms
design, report

Contrast with
previewer, Property Editor, report editor, script editor

lazy load   The capability in a run-time environment to load a code segment to memory only if it is needed. By lazily loading a code segment, the run-time environment minimizes start-up time and conserves memory resources. For example, BIRT

Report Engine builds a registry at startup that contains the list of available plug-ins, then loads a plug-in only if the processing requires it.

Related terms
Business Intelligence and Reporting Tools (BIRT) Report Engine, plug-in

library

A collection of reusable and shareable report elements. A library can contain embedded images, styles, visual report items, JavaScript code, data sources, and data sets. A report developer uses a report designer to develop a library and to retrieve report elements from a library for use in a report design.

Related terms
Business Intelligence and Reporting Tools (BIRT) Report Designer, data set, data source, design, JavaScript, report element, report item, style

Contrast with
file types

library (.rptlibrary) file

In BIRT Report Designer, an XML file that contains reusable and shareable report elements. A report developer uses a report designer to create a library file directly or from a report design (.rptdesign) file.

Related terms
Business Intelligence and Reporting Tools (BIRT) Report Designer, design, extensible markup language (XML), report design (.rptdesign) file, report element

Contrast with
file types, report design (.rptdesign) file, report document (.rptdocument) file, report template (.rpttemplate) file

link   *See* hyperlink.

listener   *See* event listener.

list element

 A report item that iterates through the data rows in a data set. The list element contains and displays other report items in a variety of layouts.

Related terms
data, data row, data set, element, layout, report item,

Contrast with
grid element, table element

listing report

A report that provides a simple view of data. Figure G-12 shows a listing report.

Customer List		
Customer	Phone	Contact
ANG Resellers	(91) 745 6555	Alejandra Camino
AV Stores, Co.	(171) 555-1555	Rachel Ashworth
Alpha Cognac	61.77.6555	Annette Roulet

Figure G-12   Listing report

Related terms
data, report

local variable

A variable that is available only at the current level in an application. A local variable stays in memory in the scope of an executing procedure until the procedure terminates. When the procedure ends, the run-time system destroys the variable and returns the memory to the system.

Related terms
application, procedure, scope, variable

Contrast with
field variable, global variable

locale

A location and the language, date format, currency, sorting sequence, time format, and other such characteristics that are associated with that location. The location is not always identical to the country. There can be multiple languages and locales within one country. For example, China has two locales: Beijing and Hong Kong. Canada has two language-based locales: French and English.

Contrast with
localization

localization

The process of translating database content, printed documents, and software programs into another language. Report developers localize static text in a report so that the report displays text in another language that is appropriate to the locale configured on the user's machine.

Related terms
locale, report

Contrast with
internationalization

manifest

A text file in a Java archive (.jar) file that describes the contents of the archive.

Related term
Java archive (.jar) file

master page

A predefined layout that specifies a consistent appearance for all pages of a report. A master page typically includes standard headers and footers that display information such as page numbers, a date, or a copyright statement.

The master page can contain report elements in the header and footer areas only, as shown in Figure G-13.

The master page's header and footer content appears on every page of the report in paginated formats, as shown in Figure G-14.

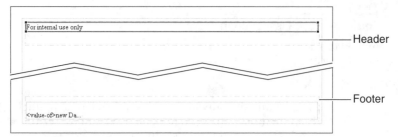

Figure G-13   Master page layout

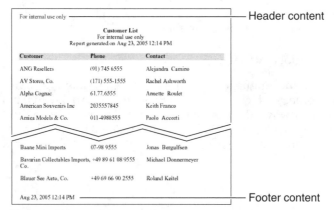

Figure G-14   Master page content

Related terms
Business Intelligence and Reporting Tools (BIRT), Business Intelligence and Reporting Tools (BIRT) Report Designer, footer, grid element, header, hypertext markup language (HTML), layout, previewer, report, template

member   A method or variable that is defined in a class and provides or uses information about the state of a single object.

Related terms
class, method, object, variable

Contrast with
global variable, instance variable, static variable

member variable

A declared variable within a class. A set of member variables in a class contains the data or state for every object of that class.

Related terms
class, data, declaration, object, variable

Contrast with
class variable, dynamic variable, field variable, global variable, instance variable, local variable, static variable

metadata Information about the structure of data that enables a program to process information. For example, a relational database stores metadata that describes the name, size, and data type of objects in a database, such as tables and columns.

Related terms
column, data, data type, table

method A routine that provides functionality to an object or a class.

Related terms
class, object

Contrast with
data, function

modal window

A window that retains focus until explicitly closed by the user. Typically, dialog boxes and message windows are modal. For example, an error message dialog box remains on the screen until the user responds.

Contrast with
modeless window

mode An operational state of a system. Mode implies that there are at least two possible states. Typically, there are many modes for both hardware and software.

modeless window

A window that solicits input but permits users to continue using the current application without closing the modeless window, for example, an Eclipse view.

Related terms
application, Eclipse view

Contrast with
modal window

multithreaded application

An application that handles multiple simultaneous users and sessions.

Related term
application

Navigator In BIRT Report Designer, an Eclipse view that shows all projects and reports within each project. Each project is a directory in the file system. Use Navigator to manage report files, for example, deleting files, renaming files, or moving files from one project to another. Figure G-15 shows Navigator.

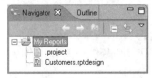

Figure G-15 Navigator

Related terms
Eclipse project, Eclipse view, report

node   A computer that is accessible on the internet.

Contrast with
domain name

null   A value that indicates that a variable or field contains no data.

Related terms
data, field, value, variable

numeric data type

A data type that is used for calculations that result in a value that is a number.
Report items that contain expressions or fields with a numeric data type display
numbers, based on the formats and locale settings that are specified by your
computer and the report design.

Related terms
data type, design, expression, field, format, locale, report, report item, value

numeric expression

A numeric constant, a simple numeric variable, a scalar reference to a numeric
array, a numeric-valued function reference, or a sequence of these items, that are
separated by numeric operators. For example:

```
row["price"] * row["quantity"]
```

Related terms
array, constant, function, operator, variable

Contrast with
Boolean expression

object   An instance of a particular class, including its characteristics, such as instance
variables and methods.

Related terms
class, instance variable, method, variable

object-oriented programming

A technique for writing applications using classes, not algorithms, as the
fundamental building blocks. The design methodology uses three main
concepts: encapsulation, inheritance, and polymorphism.

Related terms
application, class, encapsulation, inheritance, polymorphism

Contrast with
object

octal number

A number in base 8. An octal number uses only the digits 0 through 7. Each place represents a power of 8. By comparison, base 10 numbers use the digits 0 through 9. Each place represents a power of 10.

Contrast with
hexadecimal number

ODA

See open data access (ODA).

online help

Information that appears on the computer screen to help the user understand an application.

Related term
application

open data access (ODA)

A technology that enables accessing data from standard and custom data sources. ODA uses XML data structures and Java interfaces to handle communication between the data source and the application that needs the data. Using ODA to access data from a data source requires an ODA driver and typically also includes an associated tool for designing queries on the data source. ODA provides interfaces for creating data drivers to establish connections, access metadata, and execute queries to retrieve data. ODA also provides interfaces to integrate query builder tools within an application designer tool. In BIRT, ODA is implemented using plug-ins to the Eclipse Data Tools Project.

Related terms
application, Business Intelligence and Reporting Tools (BIRT), Connection, data, data source, driver, extensible markup language (XML), interface, Java, metadata, open data access (ODA) driver, plug-in, query

open data access (ODA) driver

An ODA driver communicates between an arbitrary data source and an application during report execution. An ODA driver establishes a connection with a data source, accesses metadata about the data, and executes queries on the data source. Each ODA driver consists of a configuration file and classes that implement the ODA run-time Java interfaces that conform to ODA. In BIRT, ODA drivers are implemented as an Eclipse plug-in to the Data Tools Platform project.

Related terms
application, BIRT technology, class, Connection, data, data source, driver, Eclipse, interface, Java, metadata, open data access (ODA), plug-in, query

open database connectivity (ODBC)

A standard protocol that is used by software products as one of the database management system (DBMS) interfaces to connect reports to databases that comply with this specification.

Related terms
database management system (DBMS), interface, protocol, report

Contrast with
Connection, data source, Java Database Connectivity (JDBC)

operator   A symbol or keyword that performs an operation on expressions.

Related terms
expression, keyword

outer join   1   A type of join that returns records from one table even when no matching values exist in the other table. The two kinds of outer join are the left outer join and the right outer join. The left outer join returns all records from the table on the left in the join operation, even when no matching values exist in the other table. The right outer join returns all records from the table on the right in the join operation. For example, if customers and orders tables are left outer joined on customer ID, the result set will contain all customer records, including records for customers who have no orders.

2   When creating a joint data set in BIRT, a type of join that returns rows from one data set even when no matching values exist in the other data set. The two kinds of outer joins are the left outer join and the right outer join. The left outer join returns all rows from the data set in the join operation, even when no matching values exist in the other table. The right outer join returns all rows from the data set on the right in the join operation. For example, if customers and orders data sets are left outer joined on customerID, the joint data set returns all customer rows, including rows for customers who have no orders.

Related terms
Business Intelligence and Reporting Tools (BIRT) technology, data set, join, query, result set, row, table, value

Contrast with
inner join

Outline   An Eclipse view that shows all report elements that comprise a report design, report library, or report template. Outline shows the report elements' containment hierarchy in a tree-structured diagram. Figure G-16 shows Outline.

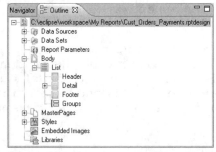

Figure G-16   Outline

Related terms
design, Eclipse view, hierarchy, library, report, report element, template

package   A set of functionally related Java classes that are organized in one directory.

Related terms
class, Java

Palette   An Eclipse view that shows the visual report elements for organizing and displaying data in a report. Figure G-17 shows Palette.

Figure G-17   Palette

Related terms
data, Eclipse view, report, report element

parameter   A report element that provides input to the execution of the report. Parameters provide control over report data selection, processing, and formatting.

Related terms
data, format, report, report element

Contrast with
cascading parameters, data set parameter, report parameter

parent class

See superclass.

password   An optional code that restricts user name access to a resource on a computer system.

pattern   A template or model for implementing a solution to a common problem in object-oriented programming or design. For example, the singleton design pattern restricts the instantiation of a class to only one object. The use of the singleton pattern prevents the proliferation of identical objects in a run-time environment and requires a programmer to manage access to the object in a multithreaded application.

Related terms
class, design, instantiation, multithreaded application, object, object-oriented programming

perspective

See Eclipse perspective.

platform   The software and hardware environment in which a program runs. Linux, MacOS, Microsoft Windows, Solaris OS, and UNIX are examples of software systems that run on hardware processors made by vendors such as AMD, Apple, Intel, IBM, Motorola, Sun, and Hewlett-Packard.

plug-in   1 An extension that is used by the Eclipse development environment. At run time, Eclipse scans its plug-in subdirectory to discover any extensions to the platform. Eclipse places the information about each extension in a registry, using lazy load to access the extension.

2 A software program that extends the capabilities of a web browser. For example, a plug-in gives you the ability to play audio samples or video movies.

Related terms
application, Eclipse, extension, lazy load
Contrast with
Eclipse Plug-in Development Environment (PDE)

plug-in fragment

A separately loaded plug-in that adds functionality to an existing plug-in, such as support for a new language in a localized application. The plug-in fragment manifest contains attributes that associate the fragment with the existing plug-in.

Related terms
application, localization, manifest, plug-in

polymorphism

The ability to provide different implementations with a common interface, simplifying the communication among objects. For example, defining a unique print method for each kind of document in a system supports printing any document by sending the instruction to print without concern for how that method is actually carried out for a given document.

Related terms
interface, method, object

portal A web page that serves as a starting point for accessing information and applications on the internet or an intranet. The basic function of a portal is to aggregate information from different sources.

Related terms
application, web page

Contrast with
portlet

portlet A window in a browser that provides a view of specific information that is available from a portal.

Related term
portal

previewer A design tool that supports displaying a report or data.

Related terms
data, design, report

Contrast with
layout editor, script editor, Standard Viewer

procedure A set of commands, input data, and statements that perform a specific set of operations. For example, methods are procedures.

Related terms
data, method, statement

process A computer program that has no user interface. For example, the process that runs a BIRT report is a process.

Related terms
Business Intelligence and Reporting Tools (BIRT), interface, report

project *See* Eclipse project.

Properties A grouped alphabetical list of all properties of visual report elements in a report design. Experienced report developers use this Eclipse view to modify any property of a report item. Figure G-18 shows Properties.

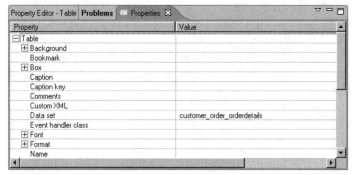

Figure G-18   Properties

Related terms
design, Eclipse view, property, report, report element, report item
Contrast with
Property Editor

property   A characteristic of a report item that controls its appearance and behavior. For example, a report developer can specify a font size for a label element.

Related terms
font, label element, report item, value
Contrast with
method

Property Editor

An Eclipse view that displays sets of key properties of visual report elements in a report design. The report developer uses Property Editor to modify the properties of report items. Figure G-19 shows Property Editor.

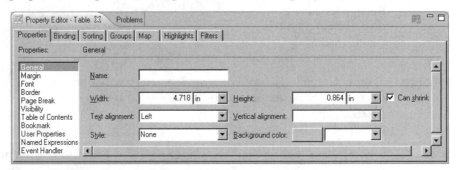

Figure G-19   Property Editor

Related terms
design, Eclipse view, property, report, report element, report item
Contrast with
Properties

protocol   A communication standard for the exchange of information. For example, in TCP/IP, the internet protocol (IP) is the syntax and order in which messages are received and sent.

Related term
syntax

publish   To copy files to a shared folder to make them available to report users and developers. Libraries and resource files are published to the resources folder. Templates are published to the templates folder.

Related terms
library, report executable file, resource file, template

query   A statement that specifies which data rows to retrieve from a data source. For example, a query that retrieves data from a database typically is a SQL SELECT statement.

Related terms
data row, data source, SQL SELECT statement

range   A continuous set of values of any data type. For example, 1–31 is a numeric range.

Related terms
data type, value

regular expression

A JavaScript mechanism that matches patterns in text. The regular expression syntax can validate text data, find simple and complex strings of text within larger blocks of text, and substitute new text for old text.

Related terms
data, expression, JavaScript, syntax

Contrast with
aggregate expression

rendering extension

A BIRT extension that produces a report in a specific format. For example, BIRT provides rendering extensions for HTML and PDF.

Related terms
Business Intelligence and Reporting Tools (BIRT), Business Intelligence and Reporting Tools (BIRT) extension, extension, hypertext markup language (HTML), report

report   A category of documents that presents formatted and structured content from a data sources, such as a database or text file.

Related terms
data source, format, structured content

report design (.rptdesign) file

An XML file that contains the complete description of a report. The report design file describes the structure and organization of the report, its constituent report items and their style attributes, its data sets, its data sources, and its Java and JavaScript event handler code. BIRT Report Designer creates the report design file and the BIRT Report Engine processes it.

Related terms
Business Intelligence and Reporting Tools (BIRT), Business Intelligence and Reporting Tools (BIRT) Report Designer, Business Intelligence and Reporting Tools (BIRT) Report Engine, data set, data source, design, event handler, extensible markup language (XML), Java, JavaScript, report, report item, style

Contrast with

file types, library (.rptlibrary) file, report document (.rptdocument) file, report template (.rpttemplate) file

report document (.rptdocument) file

A binary file that encapsulates the report item identifier and additional information, such as data rows, pagination information, and table of contents information.

Related terms

Business Intelligence and Reporting Tools (BIRT) Report Engine, data row, report item

Contrast with

file types, library (.rptlibrary) file, report design (.rptdesign) file, report template (.rpttemplate) file

report editor

In BIRT Report Designer, the main window where a report developer designs and previews a report. The report editor supports opening multiple report designs. For each report design, the report editor displays these five pages: layout editor, master page editor, previewer, script editor and XML source editor.

Related terms

Business Intelligence and Reporting Tools (BIRT) Report Designer, design, extensible markup language (XML), master page, layout editor, previewer, report, script editor

Contrast with

report design (.rptdesign) file

report element

A visual or non-visual component of a report design. A visual report element, such as a table or a label, is a report item. A non-visual report element, such as a report parameter or a data source is a logical component.

Related terms

data source, design, element, label element, report, report item, report parameter, table element

report executable file

A file that contains instructions for generating a report document.

Related terms

file types, report

report item

A report element that you add to a report design to display content in the report output. For example, a data element displays data from a data set when you run a report.

Related terms

data, data element, data set, design, report, report element, run

report item extension

A BIRT extension that implements a custom report item.

Related terms

Business Intelligence and Reporting Tools (BIRT), Business Intelligence and Reporting Tools (BIRT) extension, extension, report, report item

report library file

See library (.rptlibrary) file.

Report Object Model (ROM)

The set of XML report elements that BIRT technology uses to build a report design file. ROM defines report elements for both the visual and non-visual components of a report. The complete ROM specification is at:

```
http://www.eclipse.org/birt/ref/ROM
```

Related terms

Business Intelligence and Reporting Tools (BIRT) technology, design, element, extensible markup language (XML), report, report element

Contrast with

Report Object Model (ROM) element

Report Object Model definition file (rom.def)

The file that BIRT technology uses to generate and validate a report design. rom.def contains property definitions for the ROM elements. rom.def does not include definitions for report items that are defined by report item extensions, such as the chart element.

Related terms

Business Intelligence and Reporting Tools (BIRT) technology, chart element, design, property, report, report item, report item extension

Contrast with

Report Object Model (ROM), Report Object Model (ROM) element, Report Object Model (ROM) schema

Report Object Model (ROM) element

An XML element in rom.def that defines a report element.

Related terms

element, extensible markup language (XML), report element, Report Object Model definition file (rom.def)

Contrast with

report item, Report Object Model (ROM) schema

Report Object Model (ROM) schema

The XML schema that defines the rules for the structure of report design files. All BIRT report design files must conform to this schema. To validate a report design, open the file in a schema-aware XML viewer such as XML Spy. The ROM schema is at:

```
http://www.eclipse.org/birt/2005/design
```

Related terms
Business Intelligence and Reporting Tools (BIRT), design, extensible markup language (XML), report, Report Object Model (ROM), schema

Contrast with
Report Object Model definition file (rom.def)

report parameter

1 *See* parameter.

2 A report element that contains a value. Report parameters provide an opportunity for the user to type a value as input to the execution of the report.

Related terms
parameter, report, report element, value

Contrast with
cascading parameters, data set parameter

report template

See template.

report template (.rpttemplate) file

An XML file that contains a reusable design that a report developer can employ when developing a new report.

Related terms
design, extensible markup language (XML), file types, report, style, template

Contrast with
file types, library (.rptlibrary) file, report design (.rptdesign) file, report document (.rptdocument) file

report viewer servlet

A J2EE web application servlet that produces a report from a report design (.rptdesign) file or a report document (.rptdocument) file. When deployed to a J2EE application server, the report viewer servlet makes reports available for viewing over the web. The report viewer servlet is also the active component of the report previewer of BIRT Report Designer.

Related terms
application, Business Intelligence and Reporting Tools (BIRT) Report Designer, Java 2 Enterprise Edition (J2EE), previewer, report, report design (.rptdesign) file, report document (.rptdocument) file, servlet, web server

request   A message that an application sends to a server to specify an operation for the server to perform.

   Related term
   application
   Contrast with
   response

reserved word

   See keyword.

response   A message that a server sends to an application. The response message contains the results of a requested operation.
   Related term
   application
   Contrast with
   request

resource file

   A text file that contains the mapping from resource keys to string values for a particular locale. Resource files support producing a report with localized values for label and text elements.
   Related terms
   label element, locale, localization, resource key, text element, value

resource key

   A unique value that maps to a string in a resource file. For example, the resource key, greeting, can map to Hello, Bonjour, and Hola in the resource files for English, French, and Spanish, respectively.
   Related terms
   label element, locale, localization, resource file, text element, value

result set   Data rows from an external data source. For example, the data rows that are returned by a SQL SELECT statement performed on a relational database are a result set.
   Related terms
   data, data row, data source, SQL SELECT statement

Rich Client Platform (RCP)

   See Eclipse Rich Client Platform (RCP).

ROM   *See* Report Object Model (ROM).

row   **1** A record in a table.

   2 A horizontal sequence of cells in a grid element or table element.

   Related terms
   cell, grid element, table, table element

Contrast with
data row

RPTDESIGN

See report design (.rptdesign) file.

RPTDOCUMENT

See report document (.rptdocument) file.

RPTLIBRARY

See library (.rptlibrary) file.

RPTTEMPLATE

See report template (.rpttemplate) file.

run   To execute a program, utility, or other machine function.

schema   1   A database schema specifies the structure of database objects and the relationships between the data. The database objects are items, such as tables.

2   An XML schema defines the structure of an XML document. An XML schema consists of element declarations and type definitions that describe a model for the information that a well-formed XML document must contain. The XML schema provides a common vocabulary and grammar for XML documents that support exchanging data among applications.

Related terms
application, data, element, extensible markup language (XML), object, report, table, well-formed XML

scope   The parts of a program in which a symbol or object exists or is visible. Where the element is declared determines the scope of a program element. Scopes can be nested. A method introduces a new scope for its parameters and local variables. A class introduces a scope for its member variables, member functions, and nested classes. Code in a method in one scope has visibility to other symbols in that same scope and, with certain exceptions, to symbols in outer scopes.

Related terms
class, function, member, method, object, parameter, variable

script editor

In the report editor in BIRT Report Designer, the page where a report developer adds or modifies JavaScript for a report element.

Related terms
Business Intelligence and Reporting Tools (BIRT) Report Designer, JavaScript, report, report editor, report element

Contrast with
layout editor, previewer

scripting language

> *See* JavaScript and VBScript (Visual Basic Script Edition).

SDK (Software Development Kit)

> A collection of programming tools, utilities, compilers, debuggers, interpreters, and APIs that a developer uses to build an application to run on a specified technology platform. For example, the Java SDK allows developers to build an application that users can download across a network to run on any operating system. The Java Virtual Machine (JVM), the Java SDK interpreter, executes the application in the specified software and hardware configuration.
>
> **Related terms**
> application, application programming interface (API), Java, Java Virtual Machine (JVM), platform

section

> A horizontal band in a report design. A section structures and formats related report items. A section uses a grid element, list element, or table element to contain data values, text, and images.
>
> **Related terms**
> data, design, grid element, image, list element, report, report item, table element, value

select

> 1   To highlight one or more items, for example, in a report design. A user-driven operation then affects the selected items. Figure G-20 shows selected items.

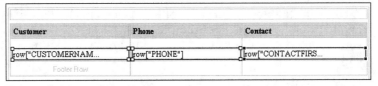

> **Figure G-20**   Selected items
>
> 2   To highlight a check box or a list item in a dialog box.
>
> **Related terms**
> design, report

SELECT

> *See* SQL SELECT statement.

series

> A sequence of related values. In a chart, for example, a series is a set of related points. Figure G-21 shows a bar chart that displays a series of quarterly sales revenue figures over four years.

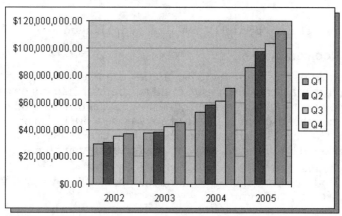

Figure G-21   Series in a chart

Related terms
chart, value

Contrast with
category

servlet   A small Java application that runs on a web server to extend the server's functionality.

Related terms
application, Java, web server

slot   A construct that represents a set of ROM elements that are contained within another ROM element. For example, the body slot of the report design element can contain one or more of any type of report item. Figure G-22 shows a body slot.

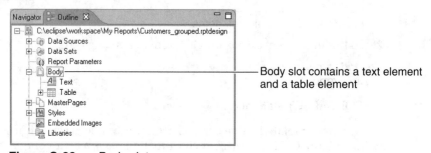

Figure G-22   Body slot

Related terms
design, element, report, report element, report item, Report Object Model (ROM) element

sort   To specify the order in which data is processed or displayed. For example, customer names can be sorted in alphabetical order.

Related term
data

Contrast with
sort key

sort key   A list of one or more column names or expressions. The order of the items in the sort key specifies the sort order of data rows. For example, a sort by State and Date is different from a sort by Date and State.

Related terms
column, data row, expression, sort

SQL (Structured Query Language)

A language that is used to access and process data in a relational database. For example, the following SQL query accesses a database's customers table and retrieves the customer name and credit limit values where the credit limit is less than or equal to 100000. The SQL query then sorts the values by customer name:

```
SELECT customers.customerName,
customers.creditLimit
FROM customers
WHERE customers.creditLimit >= 100000
ORDER BY customers.customerName
```

Related terms
data, query, sort, table, value

Contrast with
SQL SELECT statement

SQL SELECT statement

A statement in SQL (Structured Query Language) that provides instructions about which data to retrieve for a report.

Related terms
data, report, SQL (Structured Query Language), statement

Standard Viewer

A viewer that appears after the user runs a report. In the Standard Viewer, the user can perform basic viewing tasks, such as navigating the report, viewing parameter information, exporting data, and using a table of contents.

Related terms
data, parameter, report

Contrast with
previewer, report viewer servlet

state   *See* instance variable.

statement   A syntactically complete unit in a programming language that expresses one action, declaration, or definition.

static variable

A variable that is shared by all instances of a class and its descendant classes. In Java, a static variable is known as a class variable. The compiler specifies the memory allocation for a static variable. The program receives the memory allocation for a static variable as the program loads.

Related terms
class, class variable, descendant class, Java, variable

Contrast with
dynamic variable, field variable, global variable, instance variable, local variable, member variable

String data type

A data type that consists of a sequence of contiguous characters including letters, numerals, spaces, and punctuation marks.

Related terms
character, data type

Contrast with
string expression

string expression

An expression that evaluates to a series of contiguous characters. Elements of the expression can include a function that returns a string, a string constant, a string literal, a string operator, or a string variable.

Related terms
character, constant, expression, function, operator, variable

Contrast with
String data type

structured content

A formatted document that displays information from one or more data sources.

Related terms
data source, format

Contrast with
report

Structured Query Language (SQL)

See SQL (Structured Query Language).

style

A named set of formatting characteristics, such as font, color, alignment, and borders, that report designers apply to a report item to control its appearance.

Related terms
design, font, format, report, report item

Contrast with
cascading style sheet (CSS)

style sheet

> *See* cascading style sheet (CSS).

subclass The immediate descendant class.

> **Related terms**
> class, descendant class
>
> **Contrast with**
> superclass

subreport A report that appears inside another report. Typically, the subreport uses data values from the outer report.

> **Related terms**
> data, report, value

superclass

> The immediate ancestor class.
>
> **Related terms**
> ancestor class, class
>
> **Contrast with**
> descendant class, subclass

syntax The rules that govern the structure of a language.

tab The label above a page in a dialog box that contains multiple pages.

> **Contrast with**
> label element

table A named set of columns in a relational database.

> **Related term**
> column
>
> **Contrast with**
> table element

table element

 A report item that contains and displays data in a row and column format. The table element iterates through the data rows in a data set. Figure G-23 shows a table element.

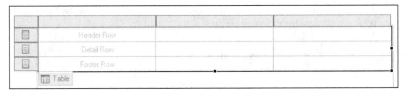

Figure G-23   Table element

Related terms
column, data, data row, data set, element, report item, row

Contrast with
grid element, list element, table

tag   An element in a markup language that identifies how to process a part of a document.

Related term
element

Contrast with
extensible markup language (XML)

template   In BIRT Report Designer, a predefined structure for a report design. A report developer uses a report template to maintain a consistent style across a set of report designs and for streamlining the report design process. A report template can describe a complete report or a component of a report. BIRT Report Designer also supports custom templates.

In Figure G-24, New Report displays the available templates and Preview displays a representation of the report layout for the selected My First Report, a customer-listing-report template.

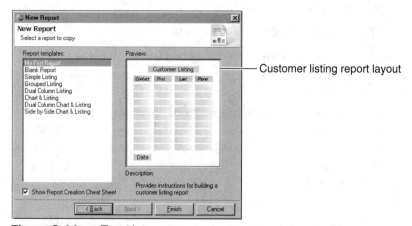

Figure G-24   Template

Related terms
Business Intelligence and Reporting Tools (BIRT), Business Intelligence and Reporting Tools (BIRT) Report Designer, design, layout, listing report, report, report design (.rptdesign) file

Contrast with
report template (.rpttemplate) file

text element

 A report item that displays user-specified text. The text can span multiple lines and can contain HTML formatting and dynamic values that are derived from data set fields or expressions.

Related terms
data set, expression, field, format, hypertext markup language (HTML), report item, value

Contrast with
data element, dynamic text element, label element

text file   *See* flat file.

theme   A set of related styles that are stored in a library (.rptlibrary) file. A theme provides a preferred appearance for the report items in a report design. A library file can store multiple themes. A report design can use styles from a single theme as well as styles defined in the report design itself.

Related terms
design, library (.rptlibrary) file, report, report item, style

Contrast with
cascading style sheet (CSS)

tick   A marker that occurs at regular intervals along the x- or y-axis of a chart. Typically, the value of each tick appears on the axis.

Related term
chart

Contrast with
tick interval

tick interval

The distance between ticks on an axis. Figure G-25 shows a tick interval in a chart.

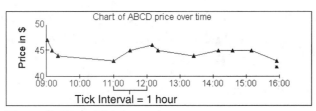

Figure G-25   Tick interval

Related terms
chart, tick

toolbar   A bar that contains various buttons that provide access to common tasks. Different toolbars are available for different kinds of tasks.

translator   *See* converter.

type   *See* data type.

Unicode   A living language standard that is managed by the Technical Committee of the Unicode Consortium. The current Unicode standard provides code points for more than 65,000 characters. Unicode encoding has no dependency on a platform or software program and therefore provides a basis for software internationalization.

Related terms
code point, character, internationalization

Uniform Resource Locator (URL)

A character string that identifies the location and type of a piece of information that is accessible over the web. http:// is the familiar indicator that an item is accessible over the web. The URL typically includes the domain name, type of organization, and a precise location within the directory structure where the item is located.

Related terms
character, domain name, hypertext transfer protocol (HTTP)
Contrast with
Universal Resource Identifier (URI)

universal hyperlink

See hyperlink.

Universal Resource Identifier (URI)

A set of names and addresses in the form of short strings that identify resources on the web. Resources are documents, images, downloadable files, and so on.
Contrast with
Uniform Resource Locator (URL)

URL   *See* Uniform Resource Locator (URL).

value   1   A quantity that is assigned to a constant, variable, parameter, or symbol.

2   A specific occurrence of an attribute. For example, blue is a possible value for the attribute color.

Related terms
constant, parameter, variable

variable   A named storage location for data that can be modified while a program runs. Each variable has a unique name that identifies it within its scope. Each variable is capable of containing a certain type of data.

Related terms
data, data type, scope
Contrast with
class variable, dynamic variable, field variable, global variable, instance variable, local variable, member variable, static variable

VBScript (Visual Basic Script Edition)

A Microsoft Windows scripting engine. VBScript is a subset of the Visual Basic language with some added functionality. Internet Explorer, Active Server Pages, and Windows Script Host support VBScript as a scripting language.

When used in Internet Explorer, VBScript processes code that is embedded in HTML. VBScript is similar in function to JavaScript. Stand-alone applications that were created using VBScript require Internet Explorer to run.

Related terms
Active Server Page (ASP), hypertext markup language (HTML), JavaScript

view
A predefined query that retrieves data from one or more tables in a relational database. Unlike a table, a view does not store data. Users can use views to select, delete, insert, and update data. The database uses the definition of the view to determine the appropriate action on the underlying tables. For example, a database handles a query on a view by combining the requested data from the underlying tables.

Related terms
data, query, table

Contrast with
Eclipse view

viewer
See previewer and Standard Viewer.

Visual Basic Script Edition

See VBScript (Visual Basic Script Edition).

web archive (.war) file

A file format that is used to bundle web applications.

Related terms
application, format

Contrast with
Java archive (.jar) file

web page
A page that contains tags that a web browser interprets and displays.

Related term
tag

web server

A computer or a program that provides web services on the internet. A web server accepts requests that are based on the hypertext transfer protocol (HTTP). A web server also executes server-side scripts, such as ASPs and JSPs.

Related terms
Active Server Page (ASP), hypertext transfer protocol (HTTP), JavaServer Page (JSP), request, web page

well-formed XML

An XML document that follows syntax rules that were established in the XML 1.0 recommendation. Well-formed means that a document must contain one or more elements and that the root element must contain all the other elements. Each element must nest inside any enclosing elements, following the syntax rules.

Related terms

element, extensible markup language (XML), syntax

World Wide Web Consortium (W3C)

An international, but unofficial, standards body that provides recommendations regarding web standards. The World Wide Web Consortium publishes several levels of documents, including notes, working drafts, proposed recommendations, and recommendations about web applications that are related to topics such as HTML and XML.

Related terms

application, extensible markup language (XML), hypertext markup language (HTML)

workbench

See Eclipse Workbench.

workspace

See Eclipse workspace.

XML (extensible markup language)

See extensible markup language (XML).

XML element

See element.

XML PATH language (XPath)

XPath is a subset of XSLT that supports addressing an element or elements within an XML document based on a path through the document hierarchy.

Related terms

element, extensible markup language (XML)

XML schema

See schema.

XPath

See XML PATH language (XPath).

Symbols

! formatting symbol 151
" (double quotation mark) character
  concatenation and 48
  filter conditions and 268
  format patterns and 143
  SQL statements and 88
  text file data sources and 74
" " as empty string 244
" " as literal space character 246
% (percent) character 234
% operator 164, 165
% wildcard character (SQL) 88
& formatting symbol 151
&& operator 254
+ operator 98, 246
, (comma) character 73, 246
. (period) character 250
/ (forward slash) character 249
; (semicolon) character 239
< formatting symbol 151
= operator 268
== operator 268, 272
> formatting symbol 151
? (question mark) character 250, 280
@ formatting symbol 151
_ wildcard character (SQL) 88
{} (curly braces) characters 91
| | operator 254, 272
… button
  chart titles and 430
  defined 572
  expression builder and 99
  externalized text and 547

hyperlink options and 498
legend text and 438
resource keys and 545
run-time connections and 78
sorting data and 182
text file connections and 76
XML files and 77
' (single quotation mark) character 74, 268

Numerics

3-D charts
  coloring areas in 420
  curve fitting and 453
  formatting 456
  rotating axes in 456
  selecting as type 374
  setting inset values for 422
  setting series depth in 455
  spacing series in 457
  transposing axes values and 411

A

absolute formatting 158
absolute paths 93
abstract base class 553
accessing
  BIRT RCP Report Designer 25
  BIRT Report Designer 11, 24
  chart builder 358
  data 22, 67, 73, 76
  Data Explorer 64
  data set fields 127
  databases 67, 77
  expression builder 99, 240

charts *(continued)*
- defined 560
- defining axis type for 407
- defining series type for 449
- displaying 350
- filtering data in 385
- filtering data rows for 263
- formatting areas in 416, 474
- formatting three-dimensional 456
- formatting values in 367, 387–389
- grouping data for 404–405
- hiding areas in 423, 430
- highlighting areas in 419
- highlighting values in 440, 509
- interactive features for 379, 497, 505–511
- linking to reports 510–511
- localizing 542, 546, 548
- missing labels in 446
- outlining areas in 419
- overview 349, 381, 415
- parts described 415
- previewing 356, 357, 412
- removing resource keys for 548
- resizing 357
- rotating 456
- selecting data sets for 353, 373, 384
- setting background colors for 417–418
- setting background images for 379, 418
- sorting data for 403
- specifying inset settings for 422
- specifying output formats for 365, 379
- specifying type 351, 365, 374
- viewing parameters for 385
- viewing sample data for 384, 413, 414
- with depth 374, 420, 448, 455

cheat sheet property 536
class hierarchy 561
class names 561
class variables 562
- *See also* instance variables; variables

classes
- aggregating data and 220
- defined 561
- formatting data and 148, 149
- selecting driver 69, 71

Classic Models sample database
- *See also* demo database
- building charts and 350

building listing reports and 32
- connecting to 318
- creating queries for 332
- specifying as data source 37
- specifying connection information for 36
–clean option 14, 80
client area inset settings 424
client sections (charts) 422, 424
CLOB fields 136, 138
CLOBs 134
closing values, plotting 379, 400
code
- editing 29, 558
- expressions as 239
- loading 585
- referencing columns and 96
- testing and debugging 23, 558
Code page. *See* script editor
code points 183, 562
Color By pick list 451
color palette (charts) 448, 451, 452
color picker (charts)
- category series and 452
- chart backgrounds and 417, 419
- plot areas and 426, 427
colors
- alternating row 163–165
- axis labels and 448
- axis lines and 444
- axis titles and 440
- background images and 491
- candlesticks 471
- cascading styles and 154
- chart areas and 416, 423, 425, 431
- chart backgrounds and 417–418
- chart legends and 433
- chart markers and 442
- chart outlines and 419
- chart shadows and 427
- chart titles and 431
- chart wall or floor and 420
- conditional formatting and 158, 162
- curve-fitting lines and 453, 454
- customizing 418
- data point labels and 473
- data series and 367, 450, 452
- dial regions and 466
- font properties and 147

D

hiding
    axis labels 447
    axis lines 444
    chart areas 423, 430
    chart legends 435
    chart series 449
    data point labels 473
    data points 509
    detail rows 187, 234
    dial labels 464
    leader lines 469
    marker labels 442
    report elements 175–177
    tick marks 445, 463
hierarchy 579
high values, plotting 379, 400
Highlight option 509
highlighting
    axes values 440
    chart areas 419, 423
    charts 509
    data 23, 215, 335
    data points 440, 443
Highlights page 159, 160, 163
horizontal alignment 165, 437, 492
horizontal spacing (charts) 427, 428
horizontal spacing (reports) 166, 170, 344
HTML (defined) 579
HTML elements 572
HTML formats 30, 31, 55, 136, 138, 143
HTML reports
    See also web pages
    adding lists to 134
    adding textual elements for 136, 138, 140, 143
    controlling pagination in 478–485
    creating master pages for 493
    customizing master pages and 485
    designing for 477
    displaying 478
    generating 30
    previewing 31, 42, 166
    resizing headers and footers for 488
    spacing defaults for 166
HTML tables 118, 167
HTML tags 51, 136, 139, 140, 141, 577
HTML text elements 117, 224
HTML value (content type) 139

HTML/Dynamic option 140, 143
HTTP (defined) 580
hyperlink expressions 500
Hyperlink Options dialog 498, 499, 500
Hyperlink property 500, 502
hyperlinks 497–502, 579
hypertext markup language pages. *See* web pages
hypertext markup language. *See* HTML
hypertext transfer protocol. *See* HTTP

I

i flag (expressions) 252
icons 129, 537
identifiers 238, 580
If expressions 160
if statements 255
if...else statements 142
Image Builder 132
image elements
    See also images
    adding 117, 129, 131
    creating column bindings for 109, 122, 132
    defined 580
Image file in BIRT resource folder option 130
image files
    deleting 130
    entering URIs for 131
    entering URLs for 131
    generating charts and 379
    managing 59
    moving 130
    opening 502
image formats 129, 379
images
    See also image elements
    adding as watermarks 490–492
    adding background 418, 490, 492
    adding to master pages 487
    adding to reports 129, 131
    adding to tables 122
    as static elements 118
    associating with data sets 132
    associating with templates 533, 536, 537
    changing 129
    charting data and 379

images *(continued)*
  defined 580
  displaying 117, 129, 175
  embedding 130, 131
  linking to 129, 130, 501, 502
  previewing 130
  retrieving remote 131
  sharing 519
Import CSS Style command 156
Import CSS Style dialog 157
Import Values button 291, 292
Import Values dialog 292
importing styles 153, 156–157
importing values 291, 292, 293
indexOf function 248
infinity symbol 244
information 53, 115, 133
  See also data
information systems 21
inheritance 580
inheriting styles 154
inline report elements 48, 166
inner groups 195, 196, 197
INNER JOIN clause 86
inner joins 100, 581
  See also joins
input
  adding messages for 175
  creating parameters for 278, 281
  prompting for 275, 277, 288, 298
input parameters 88, 283
input sources. *See* data sources
input streams 76
InputStream objects 76
Insert Column to the Left command 120
Insert Column to the Right command 120
Insert Grid dialog 333
Insert Group command 197
Insert menu 125
Insert Row Above command 119
Insert Row Below command 119
Insert Table dialog 40
inset settings
  axis labels 448
  axis titles 440
  chart areas 416, 421, 422, 424
  chart legends 436, 439
  chart titles 432

  curve-fitting labels 454
  data point labels 473
  dial labels 464
  marker labels 443
  plot areas 427
inset values 421
installation
  BIRT components 5
  BIRT RCP Report Designer 12–14
  BIRT Report Designer 9–11
  database drivers 69, 70
  Eclipse 24
  fonts 146
  JDK software 5, 6
  testing 11, 14
  troubleshooting 14–15
installation demo 5
installation packages 9
instance variables 581
  See also class variables; variables
instances. *See* objects
instantiation 581
INT type indicator 75
INTEGER data type 75
integers 147
  See also numbers
interactive chart features 379, 497, 505–511
interactive content 134
interactive images 379
interactive report viewer 31
  See also report viewer
interactive reports 497, 501
interactive viewing features 55, 497
Interactivity dialog 508
Interactivity Editor 508
interfaces 89, 582
  See also application programming
    interfaces; user interface elements
international users 56
internationalization 582
  See also locales
intersection options (charts) 408
Interval pick list 186, 189, 191, 192
Interval value 191
introductory information 124
invoice IDs 252
Invoke Font Editor icon 430
Invoke Script option 509

queries *(continued)*
  creating 85, 87, 102
  defined 597
  filtering data with 258, 262, 268, 277, 278
    examples for 259
  limiting data returned by 85
  matching text patterns and 267
  previewing result sets for 97
  retrieving data with 37, 81, 82, 85
  sorting data with 181
  validating 39, 97
Query section (Edit Data Set) 87
Query wizard 82, 90
question mark (?) character 250, 280
Quick Add section (Select Key) 545
quotation mark characters. *See* double
  quotation mark character; single quotation
  mark character

R

radio buttons
  adding values for 290–296
  formatting values for 288, 296, 297
  setting default values for 294, 296
  setting maximum number of values
    for 296
  sorting values for 294
  testing values in 309
randomly generated data 413, 414
range 597
range fill colors 442
range markers (charts) 440
range of values
  defined 597
  highlighting in charts 440
  searching 259, 266
  selecting grouping intervals for 186, 190
Range property 189, 191, 192
range test conditions 259, 266
rank function 222
ratio setting (charts) 467
RCP (defined) 571
  See also rich client platforms
RDBMS data sources 64
record-level elements (XML) 95
records 74, 257, 309
  See also rows
Reference Found dialog 66

referencing column bindings 111
RegExp objects 249, 251
  See also regular expressions
Regions button 465
Regions dialog 465
regression testing 558
regular expressions 249, 250, 251, 597
  See also expressions
relational databases 67
  See also databases
relational models 85
relational structures 85, 92
relative paths 93
release builds 7, 10, 12, 13
removing. *See* deleting
Rename command 65
renaming
  column bindings 111
  columns 96, 97, 351
  data sources 64, 65
  resource keys 550
rendering environments 55
rendering extensions 597
Repeat Header option 121, 479
repeated headings 200
replace function 245, 247
replacing
  multiple strings 245
  specific characters 249, 251
report descriptions 124
Report Design command 25
report design environments 23
  See also BIRT; Eclipse
report design files
  creating 29, 350
  defined 597
  editing 520
  opening 29
  overview 516
  saving 204
Report Design perspective 11, 25
report design perspective 10
report design views 26
report designer packages 4, 17
report designers 9
report designs
  See also page layouts
  accessing 29

unit spacing values 457
Units pick list 422
universal hyperlinks. *See* hyperlinks
Universal Resource Identifiers. *See* URIs
UNIX platforms 15
unpacking BIRT archives 5, 10
unusable data sets 67
updates 17
updating
   data formats 146
   designer packages 17
   list of values 291
   report designers 18
   report designs 520
   report libraries 528
upgrades 17
uppercase characters 151, 183
Uppercase format option 151
URI option 130
URIs 131, 502, 610
URL Redirect option 509
URL redirect option 510
URL Template property 72
URLs
   database connections and 67
   defined 610
   Eclipse Modeling Framework and 7
   Eclipse SDK software 6
   Graphics Editor Framework and 7
   image files and 131, 491
   installation demo and 5
   iText PDF library and 11, 12, 13
   JDBC connections and 69, 72
   JDK software and 5, 6
   ODA framework and 63
   program archives and 10, 12, 13
   redirecting from 509
   XML data sources and 77
   XML schemas and 77
   XML specification and 76
Use data set option 353
Use fixed base value option 191
Use identifier quoting option 89
user IDs 252
user interface elements 290, 296
user name parameters 78
User Name property 69, 78
user names 67, 69, 77

user-defined formulas 106
user-named styles 156
users
   changing at run time 77
   creating lists of values for 290–296, 297
   creating reports and 54, 56
   prompting 275, 277, 288, 298
   specifying filters 277, 278, 285

V

value axis 406, 409
value expressions 137, 269
value series
   See also data series
   building combination charts and 402
   changing 449
   coloring 367, 450
   creating multiple 391, 395, 398, 401, 403
   defined 382
   displaying options for 369
   formatting 448
   linking to 510
   setting chart type for 389, 393, 395, 400
   setting interactive features for 506, 507
Value Series section (Format Chart) 369
value series titles 461
VALUE-OF tag
   combining dynamic and static values
     and 141, 142
   formatting and 143, 148, 152
values
   See also data
   assigning to parameters 288, 289
   averaging 220, 221, 228
   calculating 128
   changing formats and 158
   combining from multiple fields 246
   combining with literal text 244
   comparing 259, 266
   computing number of unique 228
   concatenating 48, 98, 128, 246
   counting unique 221
   creating labels for 294
   creating pictures for 175
   data types as 238
   defined 610
   defining axis type and 407, 409